Cases in Marketing

Orientation, Analysis, and Problems

Fifth Edition

Thomas V. Greer

University of Maryland

Macmillan Publishing Company
NEW YORK
Collier Macmillan Canada
TORONTO
Maxwell Macmillan International
NEW YORK   OXFORD   SINGAPORE   SYDNEY

Macmillan Publishing Company

866 Third Avenue, New York, New York 10022

Collier Macmillan Canada, Inc.
1200 Eglinton Avenue, East
Suite 200
Don Mills, Ontario M3C 3N1

Library of Congress Cataloging-in-Publication Data

Greer, Thomas V.
   Cases in marketing : orientation, analysis, and problems / Thomas V. Greer.—5th ed.
      p.   cm.
   ISBN 0-02-347135-2
   1. Marketing—Case studies.   I. Title.
HF5415.G665   1991
658.8—dc20
                                                                    90-37398
                                                                    CIP

Printing: 1 2 3 4 5 6 7 8   Year: 1 2 3 4 5 6 7 8 9 0

Preface to the Fifth Edition

The fifth edition of this book, like its predecessors, is intended as an educational tool for the training of students of business administration. It is my hope that students and their instructors will find this edition both appealing and useful.

Eleven of the forty-eight cases in this edition are new, and seventeen retained from previous editions have been revised and updated. In selecting the cases, I have tried to meet the need of professors of business administration for a comprehensive and well-organized teaching aid. This edition continues to maintain a balance between large and small organizations. Eighteen cases focus on services, six of them on nonprofit organizations, whereas twenty-three cases deal with consumer goods and seven with industrial goods. Newer avenues for the application of marketing skills, such as professional sports, the arts, health care, philanthropy, and social marketing, are given prominent places in this new edition. In response to the social concern of many students, this edition includes several cases that can be used as springboards for discussions of the legal, social, and ethical environment of marketing. Two cases deal with companies owned by African Americans.

The cases are of varying levels of difficulty, and most of them can be used at more than one academic level. They vary in length from three to twenty-four pages, and the average length is about eight pages. This intermediate length provides ample content for student thought and analysis without the time demands of extremely long cases. However, many of the organizations are so well known that instructors can ask their students to read further about them in the library. Besides stimulating student analysis, these cases have been found to arouse vigorous discussion. The number of cases included is sufficient to allow most professors to use the book for several semesters without assigning a case more than once—if that is their policy.

Some cases lend themselves to chapters other than those in which they appear in this book. For example, "Huffy Bicycles" is placed in "Nature and Scope of Marketing," "Le Drugstore" in "Consumer Behavior," and "Tonka Toys" in "Advertising and Public Relations," but all three can also be used effectively in "International Marketing." "L.L. Bean" is placed in "Channels of Distribution" and Dr Pepper Company" in "Advertising and Public Relations," but both can also be used in "Products." "La-Z-Boy Chair Company" is included in "Products" but is also useful in "Channels of Distribution." "Neiman Marcus Co." is included in "Consumer Behavior" but can be effective in "Advertising and Public Relations." By giving some limited direction to the students, the professor can also use the four overview "Marketing Programs" cases at the end of the book for specialized purposes with specific chapters.

Considerable attention has been given to preparing the student for tackling cases effectively. The expository material at the beginning of the book should assist both the beginning case analyst and the student who has had previous case experience. This material includes a general discussion of the rationale of teaching and learning by cases and an explanation of a five step methodology for analyzing cases. A sample case is then presented, followed by an analysis by one of my *real* students and by my responses to that beginner's work. The student who reads these sections thoroughly before attempting the remainder of the cases will avoid many pitfalls. Some instructors may ask their students to study the cases differently or use a variety of approaches, depending on the type of case. Suggested discussion questions are provided separately, in the *Manual,* for the instructor's convenience.

An effort has been made to provide factual role models in the case content for the increasing number of women majoring in business. In addition, four professional women have contributed cases to this edition.

The case materials reflect the true diversity of both marketers and customers in society by including persons of differing socioeconomic status of both sexes and of several racial, cultural, and ethnic groups.

I happily acknowledge the cooperation of people in many organizations who made this compilation of cases possible. Also, I thank the adopters on the many campuses who have used the first, second, third, and fourth editions. A gratifying number of them have offered heplful advice.

For the preparation of cases, I extend special thanks to Richard Rosecky, "Power Tools, Inc." (A) and (B); Helena Poist, "Romano Olive Oil, Inc."; Patricia Stocker, "Denver Art Museum"; Robert Krapfel, "Universal Motors Parts Division"; Dee Wewer, "Head Sports Wear"; and Joanne G. Greer, "Volunteers in Health Care, Inc." and "Women's Exercise and Fitness Centers." Dr. Rosecky was a marketing executive with the subject company and is now on the faculty of Fordham University; Prof. Poist was director of marketing in her organization and is now on the faculty of the University of Maryland; Dr. Stocker was formerly with the Denver Art Museum and is now on the faculty of the University of Maryland; Dr. Krapfel was on the marketing staff of his organization and is now on the faculty of the University of Maryland; Dr. Wewer is vice-president of Head Sports wear, Inc.; and Dr. Joanne G. Greer is on the faculty of Loyola College of Maryland.

Thanks also go to Caroline Wroblewski for her help in countless administrative activities related to this edition.

Comments of users of this book are welcome.

T. V. G.

NOTE

These cases were prepared as a basis for class analysis and discussion rather than to illustrate either effective or inneffective handling of administrative situations.

Contents

1

Rationale and Methodology of the Case Method

AN INTRODUCTION TO THE CASE METHOD

You are about to use the case method in a marketing course. If you have not encountered this approach to learning before, you are probably wondering what it is and what it can do for you as a student.

The case method is a teaching device aimed at bridging the gap between classroom training and work organizations. The case presents to the student, in narrative and tabular form, a set of facts about a specific business situation. The student must sort out the relevant from the irrelevant, organize the facts into a clear exposition of the problem at hand, formulate possible solutions, choose and defend a particular solution, and design implementation for that solution.

Case development may take several forms, such as group discussion, recitation, written work at home, a timed written analysis in class, an individual or group oral report, a debate between teams, or role playing of a major incident in a case. Combinations of these forms are also used.

Many professors, government officials, and executives want to see students involved in the realistic problems faced by organizations. Some of these problems are in day-to-day operations, whereas others involve less frequent but highly important occurrences. In using the case technique, instructors are not attacking the place of theories and facts in the student's training. Rather they are combining these with practical busi-

1

ness problems or issues and developing a task integrating theory and practice, called a "case." Their purpose is to provide a more fruitful learning situation for you.

A well-organized lecture on several concepts concerned with, for example, product-line policy may seem clear and succinct, and students may think they see the ramifications and could apply these concepts as needed. Perhaps that is true. However, students who have to put themselves into the position of a manager, carefully determining managerial problems and thinking their way through them (all in relation to the composition of a product line), may (1) take the material on product-line policy more seriously, (2) see that the presented material does not stand majestically alone but is interrelated with other factors, and, most importantly, (3) learn something about the process of making a decision on behalf of an organization. That decision-making ability is highly useful to students in their own personal lives as consumers, but it is indispensable if they are to become—and remain—managers. The essence of the manager's work is making decisions.

Instruction by the case method is *participative*, and the main responsibility is on the student. In a sense, the case is raw material on which the student is asked to practice. Your benefit from the case method will be approximately proportional to the effort you put into your analysis of the case. Superficial treatment of the case will result in a superficial learning experience.

The use of the case method is not primarily to help you accumulate a store of knowledge or acquaint you with current business practices. These may come as side benefits. The primary purpose is to develop and sharpen your skills in working through a complex problem. The first stage of that invaluable process is learning to identify the problem or problems. Sometimes this is surprisingly elusive. If one lacks considerable experience with the work, one may discover to one's chagrin (and cost) that one is dealing with symptoms and side issues only. Other stages in the process may include screening and interpreting the facts, setting up alternative courses of action and calculating their relative costs and payoffs, making a specific recommendation and showing why it is the best alternative, and, finally, designing implementation.

Many students have remarked to the author that they are familiar with the case method because they have received instruction in business law through their study of court cases. Business cases are like law cases only in rare instances. In fact, they are different in both nature and purpose. A law case represents a decision that has already been made; it is history. It is important, even though the legal decision may seem illogical, because precedent is infinitely more important to law than to management. The law case is an official judgment and becomes an addition to the body of law. It is to be studied and heeded. Moreover, it was decided by an outsider, in fact, a third party outsider. A judge is imposing his judgment on the situation. In a business case, managers can disregard precedent unless that precedent has been blessed as organization policy. Even in that latter instance they normally have ample opportunity to overturn the policy by objectively showing that it does not suffice. Business managers seldom, if ever, use precedent to keep an issue from arising or to compel a certain solution to a problem. Even if they so desired, they could not do so, for the manifold factors of the business world change so rapidly that old solutions to uncertainties may furnish useful analogies but rarely definitive answers. In a sense, business cases are more like medical school cases, that is, patients to be studied by advanced trainees. The student makes an examination, collects and interprets data to produce a diagnosis, chooses among alternative treatments available, prescribes the specific treatment, and gives treatment.

Cases do not come in one standardized length or form. Some collections emphasize fairly lengthy cases of, for example, fifteen to thirty pages or more. Other collections emphasize short cases averaging one to three pages. This group averages nine pages. The intent of the cases presented in this collection is to provide you with a challenging amount of problem material without getting into the depth that you will probably encounter in some later courses. However, the more sophisticated student should bear in mind that some lengthy cases are not any more challenging intellectually than some cases of medium length. Whatever the length of a case or the average length in a collection, there is challenge to be found. Students with differing amounts of course background and business experience will see differing depths of material in the same case. Having a stronger background does not necessarily imply solving the case more quickly. A group of students in their second marketing course would probably carry the analysis of a given case far beyond what they did with the same case in their first course. Instructors in various settings may expect and demand different levels of quality from the students in analytical work. All instructors will expect the students to grow as they gain experience with the case method and to perform a better quality of analysis as they handle more cases.

The author has assembled a wide variety of cases in order to expose you to many kinds of problems. These cases are a shortcut in your development as a manager. It would take many years of varied work experience to meet the equivalent of the problems illustrated in the whole collection of cases. They are of varying degrees of intricacy, scope, and challenge. The cases are set in many different industries, but the abilities they will develop in the conscientious student are almost totally transferable from the given settings to any number of other settings. It is the skill of analytical problem solving that the cases seek to develop, rather than bits of knowledge about specific types of enterprises.

analyzing the cases will help you prepare for a career
cisions. Most persons will start their careers with little
make decisions. Within that limited authority a person must
reach the best decisions and be able to explain why those decisions
were reached. With experience you will develop the ability to make better
decisions. When you are promoted to a position with more authority,
you will have more problems about which to reach decisions. A large
proportion of your time will be spent on this function. This collection of
cases should assist in preparing you to do something constructive with
that first job. But more important, the experience of analyzing these cases
should assist you in handling more responsible positions in the business
world. The person with the analytical mind is going to move forward in
the organization.

TO THE STUDENT: A SUGGESTED
METHODOLOGY FOR YOUR WORK ON CASES

No single methodology for handling cases is ideal or holds a monopoly
on logic. Various persons experienced in cases can offer alternative approaches. If your instructor does not assign you a methodology, it is
suggested that you use the one presented as follows.

You may find the case method somewhat perplexing when you work
on your first case assignment. This happens because you may not have
built up a background of knowledge about marketing and you may not
have developed a logical framework of analysis for problem solving.

Your first effort should be to read the case assigned carefully enough
to remember many of the details presented in it. Most students find that
they need to read the materials several times. After reading the case with
great care it is important to identify the major problem(s) or question(s)
involved.

Step 1: The Problem(s) or Question(s)

Every case analysis requires the identification of the principal question or problem that requires an answer. Unfortunately, business problems
do not arrive labeled "problem." Therefore, you must learn to identify
the problem(s) raised. It is often appropriate to state the question in the
form of agreement or disagreement with the decision or recommendation
made by one of the persons in the case. Such a question might be, "Do
you agree with Belmont's proposed price change?" Or you might state
your question in the following form: "What should the price be?" On
occasion the main question needs to be broken down into subquestions,
such as the following: "What should the price be? Should someone have

the authority to adjust that price in dealing with customers and, if so, in what range? Should the price have a specified period of time during which it is in effect?"

It is imperative that you locate the basic problem(s) or question(s). For example, it is not meaningful to assert that low sales volume is the problem, since low sales volume is only symptomatic of an underlying problem such as poor supervision and control by sales managers, inadequate coordination of the several kinds of promotion, a poor compensation plan, or something else.

Step 2: The Facts

Some persons find it very helpful to visualize the system under consideration and to identify who is managing the various systems or subsystems. See if you find this to be of assistance. You may want to prepare a diagram depicting these relationships. Some students like to use a systems framework around the system under consideration, so that they can perceive the inputs and outputs of the system, the goals, the organization structure, the resources available, the set of products and/or services offered the market, the routine operations, the accomplishments, and the past and probable actions and responses of competitive and complementary systems.

It is vital that you sift and sort the facts of the case, even if there are a very large number of them. A time-consuming technique, but one that many persons find productive, is to rank-order the facts. List the most important fact first and the least important fact last. Between them fill in the various facts in descending order of importance for answering the question. Use your best judgment in building this list, but always ask yourself, "Just what do I need to know in order to answer the question?" Note that some facts may be irrelevant, but care should be taken in discarding any fact. Let your imagination play with the fact and see if it fits together with another seemingly irrelevant fact to make one highly relevant fact. When the facts have been completely arranged in order, you should review and revise your list once again on the basis of logic and your intuition.

A necessary categorization is to separate objective facts from particulars that are the opinions, assumptions, or premises of persons in the case. The latter are by no means unimportant, but they should be correctly labeled for future use and suitable weighting. Moreover, try to identify your own speculation and opinions that you may have formed, for they are not the facts of the case.

Remember the human factor in all of this. You must be alert to personal characteristics and personal relationships among the principals of the case. Given their life-style, sex, age, rank in the organization, job background, socioeconomic background, personality, and other factors, what would you expect them to do or say? What would surprise you or appear atypical? Not only must you look for these aspects but you must use them substantively and use them to help you judge the degree of objectivity in supposedly objective facts.

Enough facts have been presented in each case for you to develop intelligent solutions. However, if you feel it is imperative that you make an assumption in the absence of some extremely important fact, go ahead and make a reasonable assumption. Be sure to state that assumption clearly in your write-up. Exercise restraint in deciding whether to make an assumption. Because some instructors may not want you to make any assumption, clarify the policy in your class.

Additional information on some problems can be obtained from marketing textbooks and other reference materials in libraries. Some cases in this book include footnotes referring you to helpful readings. Carefully selected interviews are also a possibility. All of these may be worthwhile pursuits. However, you should be watchful for both conscious and unconscious biases. In interviews, you should remember that some of the information supplied you is probably indicative of the unique set of circumstances and experiences of the interviewee. It may be helpful background and provocative, but try to put it in perspective. Moreover, one must not postpone a decision until every conceivable information resource has been exhausted. Such behavior is both uneconomic and unreasonable. No manager has immediate access to every piece of data that may have a bearing on the problem. Time, cost, cost/benefit relationships, and lack of access to some data preclude such an extreme view.

Step 3: The Alternative Courses of Action

What can be done to take care of the problem? Stated in a more formal manner, what are the action alternatives, or alternative courses of action?

Often you will think of five or six alternative courses of action. However, you may need to dismiss some of these alternatives as unfeasible. For example, some courses may clearly violate the long-term objectives of the organization or some short-term goals of the operating period (such as a year or a quarter). These objectives and goals are sometimes stated but more often must be inferred. Capital constraints might rule out some alternatives and behavioral factors may also rule some out. If practicable, you should reduce the list of alternative courses of action to those three or four that need to receive the most careful, detailed consideration.

These remaining alternatives must be formally evaluated. You should list the advantages and disadvantages of each. Think in terms of the utility that each action alternative can deliver and the risk that it entails. This procedure requires great care, but if it is done well it puts you in good condition for Step 4.

Step 4: Your Decision and Reasoning

You should now select the action alternative that provides the best answer to the problem. In so doing, compare and contrast the sets of advantages and disadvantages developed in Step 3. Make your selection. Be sure that you articulate the main reasons for selecting one alternative over the others. For each rejected alternative, state why your chosen alternative is better. This not only clarifies your own thinking but also enables you to coherently ask other students during class discussion why they chose an alternative that you rejected and equips you to defend your choice. Your process of reaching a decision is a crucially important analytical ability–and you must do everything you can to make it a smoothly working ability. Articulating the process by trying to communicate it orally and in writing to other persons is excellent practice for developing and sharpening this vital managerial ability.

Step 5: Implementation of Your Decision

Your decision is not complete until you prepare at least gross operational plans for its implementation. Draw up a statement of (a) what must be done to carry out your decision; (b) what personnel must be assigned to do it; (c) when this act(s) should be carried out; and (d) about how much it will cost to do it. You are dealing with acts, existing or new personnel, a timetable, and a rough budget. Usually you cannot give highly detailed or precise answers to the questions of Step 5. However, gross estimates are infinitely better than no estimates at all, for they force you to bring to a logical conclusion a logical process of thinking.

2

A Sample Case Analysis and Critique

This chapter contains a case, "Cherry Tree Learning Materials Company," that is a highly useful introductory experience, although a little shorter than the average case in this collection. It is followed by an analysis that was written by a student for regular classroom work. This analysis is then critiqued by the author for your instruction.

It is suggested that you attempt to analyze the Cherry Tree Learning Materials Company case. Compare your work with the student work given and with the author's critique. This will give you a good preparation for your first case assignment.

CHERRY TREE LEARNING MATERIALS COMPANY—A SAMPLE CASE

Cherry Tree Learning Materials Company, founded in the middle 1950s, was a successful manufacturer of sixty different "special education" toys and games. *Special education* is the term generally used for the education of children with various physical, mental, or emotional disabilities. Sales had been growing by 7 to 8 percent annually for the past four years and in the latest year were about $4.8 million. Net profits after taxes the past year were about $179,000 and slightly less the year before that. Dividends totaling about $70,000 were paid out in each of those years.

The organization manufactured a line of toys and games designed to assist in the development of children with five types of problems, specifically dealing with motor skills, visual-motor skills, auditory skills, phonology skills, and structural and verbal syntax skills. For example, a product that had sold well and received much favorable comment from teachers and parents was the balance disc. About twenty-five inches in diameter, it was a rigid, round platform made of wood that could be locked in any preselected direction or left free for circular movement. The degree of tilt was scientifically determined and set at the factory. Safety treads on the surface discouraged slipping down or falling off. The child could stand, sit, or kneel on the surface. An edging protected the child's hand and fingers. This toy assisted in several ways, the most obvious of which was teaching equilibrium. It also helped the child learn body alignment, and coordinated mental and muscular activity, as well as developed the child's body image concept. The device also helped relate visual skills to body alignment and stato-kinetic functioning. This product was sold at $26.

Another example was sewing cards. These were cardboard rectangles with simple outline designs, such as a tree, a pear, or a house. The child was to use the thick, semisharp needles and colored yarn enclosed in the package. Several colors of yarn and eighteen designs were provided in the box of thirty-six cards. The objective was to develop eye-hand coordination, assist in learning colors, and furnish a vehicle for creative expression. This product was sold for $5.65 a box.

The executives of the company were interested in whether they could successfully offer their line of toys and games to children who had no difficulties. In other words, could they expand outside the "special education" market? This subject had been under extended discussion among all the executives.

One executive, Lawrence Teilman, stated that he opposed such a change of basic strategy because he thought Cherry Tree had done little to serve the special education market through *parents* of children who needed the products. He reasoned that, although schools might buy one or two units of an item for the classroom, promoting this item to parents for home use might result in the sale of eight or ten additional units per classroom of special education children. No one in the company perceived a problem of persuading teachers of the great usefulness of the products, and the executives believed that sales were limited primarily by school board budgets. Nevertheless, tax appropriations for special education were growing all over the United States. Their rate of growth was much faster than educational appropriations in total. Teilman believed that many teachers, if approached by a parent, would encourage the parent to buy additional materials for home use. The problem, in Teilman's opinion, was one of obtaining suitable mailing lists and sending catalogs with carefully worded cover letters directly into the homes of disabled children. However, he wondered if most educators would cooperate in compiling such lists. He also wondered if the U.S. Department of Education would release its extensive national mailing list for "Closer Look," a newsletter edited for the parents of disabled children. It was noted by several persons in Cherry Tree Company that most parents of disabled children ordinarily have rather small discretionary income because they incur extra costs with such children, especially medical costs.

The president of Cherry Tree, Terence Halsey, asked the sales department for a report on where orders had been coming from. About a week later the information came back that in the past year 86 percent of sales had been to schools and 14 percent to individuals. It was almost exactly the same the year before. A small percentage of the individuals might have been teachers in special education departments of schools or private tutors, but there was no way of finding out without inquiring.

Another executive, John Dearborn, noted approvingly that Teilman's proposal would not require any changes in the product line or any changes in promotion. Marketing to parents of normal children would, in Dearborn's opinion, require careful playing down of the fact that the products were originally designed for disabled children. However effective Cherry Tree's materials might be in facilitating learning, Dearborn believed that the typical parent of a normal child would feel some stigma in using them. Also, many of the skills taught by Cherry Tree materials were not difficult for a normal child to master without assistance, and the parent might conclude that the more expensive items in the product line were not worth the investment.

Clarence Stett agreed with Dearborn's objections. Nevertheless, he believed that a certain subset of the Cherry Tree product line had great potential for the market of normal children. Stett reasoned that some of these products were built around skills essential for pre-reading, reading, and writing, namely the visual-motor and visual-perceptual toys and games. The company's consulting psychologist, Elizabeth Freeman, reported that it appeared to her that there was near panic among conscientious middle-class parents lest their children not learn to read. Several executives said that their reading and observations supported Dr. Freeman completely. Stett believed that it would be necessary only to call these products to the attention of such parents. He believed that a mere knowledge of their existence would induce a sense of obligation to purchase them. If a new campaign were confined to these materials, a much smaller catalog could be used and advertising could focus on parents of four-to-seven-year-olds who could be reached through women's magazines.

George Higgins, another executive, thought that Stett's idea had potential but that advertising should focus on more specialized magazines such as *Parents* or the magazines of the Parent-Teacher Association. He said that subscribers to these periodicals probably were more committed to their role as parents than were nonsubscribers.

Roy Pasek, another executive, pointed out that, although expenditures for general education could be projected to stabilize or possibly decrease in the future because of the declining birthrate, expenditures for special education were increasing. He conjectured that parents of disabled children had now been politicized to the extent that they would demand public services for their children. Recent court decisions indicated that appropriate public special education programs would in time be the legal right of every child. Some estimates of involved children ran as high as 15 percent of the school population. Equipping of these new special education classrooms would be an attractive proposition for companies in the field. Pasek also said that thus far Cherry Tree had provided sturdy, good quality, conveniently assembled, but noninnovative teaching materials, many of which were available from other companies in a slightly different form or could even be built by the teacher. Pasek stated that perhaps Cherry Tree should cultivate its image as a specialist in educational toys and games for the disabled child and try to expand the product line with new items, of which as many as possible should be patentable.

Advise the executives of Cherry Tree Learning Materials Company.

A STUDENT ANALYSIS OF THE CHERRY TREE COMPANY CASE

Step 1: The Problem or Question

As I see it, the problem in this case is to find the best way to improve the market share of Cherry Tree Learning Materials Company, with particular emphasis on the possibility of expanding from a restricted market (handicapped children) to a much broader market (normal children). Probably the most pertinent question in this problem is, What market segment should Cherry Tree strive to obtain? Should the company keep the same market segment and try to achieve more sales there? (The present market is primarily schools.) Or should it attempt to make more sales to parents of these children? Should Cherry Tree bring out a new product line? Should it attempt to become a specialist in classroom equipment? And finally, should it attempt to market some or all of its products to normal children?

Step 2: The Facts

Cherry Tree Learning Materials Company is a successful manufacturer of sixty different special education toys and games. For the past four years, sales had been growing by 7 to 8 percent annually, with sales

EXHIBIT 1 Best-Selling Items in Cherry Tree's Product Line*

Item	Price	Skill Taught
Body puzzles	$ 3.00	body concept
Bead-sequencing kit	6.50	visual perceptual
Parquetry blocks	5.75	visual perceptual
Pegboards	10.50	fine motor; visual perceptual
Sponge balls	1.50	gross motor; body concept; visual perceptual
Storytelling posters (series of 10)	.75 each	prereading; concept development; language development
Balance disc	26.00	gross motor; body concept; etc.
Sorting box	11.00	fine motor; visual perceptual
Shape dominoes	1.75	fine motor; visual perceptual; procedural organization
Balance beam walking board	28.00	dynamic body balance; coordination; orthopedic correction
Stencil boards	5.75	visual motor; figure-ground discrimination
Sequential memory exercise cards	2.75	memory; visual-motor sequencing
Halves-and-wholes matching cards	1.75	visual discrimination
Dimensional puzzles, models 1 through 5	2.25 each	small muscle control; visual perception; spatial relations
Prewriting design cards	3.00	visual perception
Same-or-different cards, 4 sets	1.00 each	visual perception and discrimination
Color discovery cards	1.00	matching; memory
Comparison weighing scale	15.00	fine motor; visual perceptual; concept development
Coin rubber stamps	4.50	money value
Time teacher	4.25	clock reading
Sequencing picture cards, 4 sets	3.50 each	memory; concept development; prereading
Rhyming pictures	1.50	prereading; auditory discrimination
Talking letters	4.50	prereading; auditory discrimination
Sewing cards	5.65	visual perception; visual-motor coordination

* The items in the exhibit accounted for about 82 percent of sales.

last year approximately $4.8 million. Following are some facts and opinions, which I believe are important to this case, ranked in order of their importance.

Facts

1. In the past year, 86 percent of sales had been to schools, whereas only 14 percent had been to individuals.
2. Tax money given to schools for special education purposes has been increasing.
3. Keeping within the special education market would require very little change in products or promotion.
4. Expanding the market to normal children would require extensive changes, particularly in promotion.
5. Teachers were already convinced of the usefulness of Cherry Tree's products.
6. Many of the lower-priced toys were too simple for normal children to provide them any benefit.

Opinions

1. Teachers could convince parents of handicapped children of the usefulness of the toys.
2. Parents of handicapped children have small discretionary incomes because of high medical bills.
3. Parents will demand more money from government for their handicapped children.
4. Educators may not cooperate with Cherry Tree by releasing mailing lists of parents with handicapped children.
5. Normal children, and their parents, may feel uneasy using a product that they know was originally designed for a handicapped child.
6. Some executives believe that there would be a high demand for reading skills games and toys.
7. Expanded health services will soon become the right of every child.
8. Parents of normal children may feel that an expensive toy is not worth the investment.

Using these facts and opinions, together with the material presented in the case, I see six alternatives open to Cherry Tree. After listing these alternatives, I briefly explain them and then state the advantages and disadvantages of each.

Step 3: The Alternative Courses of Action

1. Keep the same market segment; i.e., sales primarily to schools and some sales to individuals. (Some of these individuals are perhaps teachers and private tutors.)

2. Attempt to market the ~~entire current~~ product line to parents of normal children.
3. Establish an additional product line, composed mainly of lower-priced items aimed at normal children, while retaining the present product line.
4. Place increased emphasis on marketing to *parents* of handicapped children.
5. Attempt to market only reading and prereading skills toys and games to parents of normal children. (These items are part of the company's current product line.)
6. Attempt to become a leading specialist in equipping special education classrooms while retaining the current market.

Alternatives 1 and 2 will be abandoned at this point, because neither would achieve Cherry Tree Learning Materials Company's objectives. The former should be abandoned because, although the company had been increasing its sales in this market, it has expressed a desire to expand, and the latter because all the executives seem to agree that an attempt to market the entire line to parents of normal children would result in failure. These collective judgments must be given great weight. This leaves us to consider alternatives 3, 4, 5, and 6.

Alternative 3
This choice would require a new product line, particularly of lower-priced items, which many parents could afford to buy.

Advantages of Alternative 3
1. There would be a better opportunity to sell to a large number of individuals, including parents of both normal and handicapped children.
2. There would be increased awareness of Cherry Tree's products because more consumers would own them.
3. With an expanded line of products, Cherry Tree could establish itself as a leader in the field of educational toys and games.

Disadvantages of Alternative 3
1. There are ever-present new product failures.
2. A very costly promotional program would be necessary to change the image of Cherry Tree so that parents of normal children would not be hesitant to buy products supposedly for "abnormal" children.
3. Loss of old customers because of this new image may occur.

Alternative 4
This action alternative, proposed by Lawrence Teilman, suggested emphasis on marketing products to parents of handicapped children to be used in addition to those provided at school.

Advantages of Alternative 4

1. It would require no changes in the products or promotion.
2. Teachers would convince parents of the usefulness of the products.
3. Cherry Tree's current product line included some low-priced toys that parents could almost certainly afford.

Disadvantages of Alternative 4

1. Without the cooperation of educators and government, it would be extremely difficult to contact these parents.
2. Even if contacted by the company, many of these parents may have such high medical and other expenses that they would not be interested in buying the products.

Alternative 5

This action alternative was suggested by Dr. Elizabeth Freeman, a consulting psychologist, and an executive, Clarence Stett. They believe that a large number of parents would seize the chance to help their children learn to read, especially middle-class parents. In fact, they believed that many parents would feel obligated to purchase reading skills toys and games.

Advantages of Alternative 5

1. There is an opportunity for a much larger market.
2. If the assumptions were correct, there would be an everpresent demand for these products.
3. About sixteen of the existing products in Exhibit 1 are applicable.

Disadvantages of Alternative 5

1. Parents of normal children may feel uneasy about having their children use a product associated with disabled children.
2. Cost of promotion to overcome this uneasiness must be incurred.
3. Some inexpensive toys and games would be too simple for normal children.
4. Parents may believe that the more expensive toys and games are not worth the money, because in time their normal children would master the skills involved anyway.

Alternative 6

This last action alternative, proposed by another executive, Roy Pasek, involved Cherry Tree's becoming a leading specialist in what Pasek saw as a booming field in the years to come. He believed that with increased special education budgets, the schools would be looking for companies to install specially equipped classrooms to handle the needs of these special students. He also believed that Cherry Tree, which already had a fine reputation in this field, would be a logical choice to take on this added responsibility. He believed that Cherry Tree should take the leadership of the industry, develop the needed products, patent as many of the new products as possible, and cultivate the image of a specialist and leader.

Advantages of Alternative 6
1. It is a fact that schools are receiving more funds for special education.
2. Cherry Tree could establish itself as a leader in the industry.
3. There should be a need for these special classrooms as teaching methods become more advanced.

Disadvantages of Alternative 6
1. There is the possibility of new product failures.
2. The factor of competition exists in a new branch of the industry with which Cherry Tree is not familiar.
3. Cost of promotional programs to cultivate this new image may be excessive.

Step 4: My Decision and Reasoning

I believe that alternative 6, Pasek's specialty and leadership concept, is the best action alternative in this case. I think it is superior to the new product line idea (alternative 3) for three reasons. First, it involves less risk to develop products for which there will almost certainly be a demand than to develop products in the hope of creating a demand. Second, it would be an easier project to promote an expansion of the company's image, one with even more responsibility, than to try to *change* the image from a producer of toys and games for disabled children only to a producer of such goods for *all* children. Finally, the opportunity to make a profit is greater because the company would be marketing a specialty good to organizations that have the necessary funds rather than a shopping or possibly even a convenience good to individuals who may not have the necessary purchasing power to afford it.

Pasek's action alternative is superior to alternative 4 (marketing to the parents of disabled children) for three reasons. First, obtaining adequate mailing lists is a prerequisite for this alternative course of action. Company executives have already expressed concern about the possibility of educators and government officials not releasing this information, or at least being reluctant to do so. Pasek's idea, on the other hand, would have the strong approval, if not all-out cooperation, of school officials, who I am sure would do everything in their power to obtain the latest, most modern equipment for their schools. A school's program is a reflection of the administrators in charge, and they are spending state and federal and local funds, not their own. The second reason again deals with monetary concerns. On the one hand, Cherry Tree would be trying to market to individuals with very limited incomes, and, on the other hand, Cherry Tree would be competing for contracts with state and local governments who, as we all know, never run out of money. Finally, whereas parents may not recognize the need for Cherry Tree's products, objective evidence seems to indicate that there are increased benefits and opportunities being offered to disabled children in public school systems and officials do recognize the need for special toys, games, and other equipment with which to teach "special children."

Alternative 5, proposed by Dr. Freeman and Clarence Stett, is a good idea and one that probably would succeed given the necessary effort. However, I feel that it is inferior to Pasek's idea for a number of reasons. First, I believe the fear that parents of normal children would feel uneasy about buying products that they associate with "abnormal" children is a very real one, a fear that promotional programs may not be able to overcome. The handling of motivational themes would be intricate. This would not be a problem with alternative 6, although the promotional programs would have to stress the idea of increased responsibility of the firm. Second, profit margins would be lower on the inexpensive home toys and games than on the institutional classroom equipment. Third, we come to a basic question again—who can better afford the products? As stated before, educational institutions using government funds have more purchasing power than individuals unless one is talking about very large numbers of individuals.

Step 5: Implementation of My Decision

Now that I have made my decision, I will attempt to implement it. To enable this plan to succeed, I believe Cherry Tree Learning Materials Company should do the following:

a. Expand its research and development department.
b. Slowly increase its promotional efforts.
c. Establish solid lines of communication with members of local and state school boards.
d. Continue its present successful operations.

I believe that the company should expand its research and development program immediately, possibly hiring one or two professionals if needed. I also believe that the company should hire as a consultant a school administrator with a good background in methods of teaching special education students, one who really knows what it is like to work directly with these children. This person would be invaluable in helping to determine the future needs of the teaching field.

The company should start slowly to increase its promotional programs, advertising in various education magazines, engaging in public-relations type activities, and perhaps sponsoring a project similar to Washington, D.C.'s, own Special Olympics for handicapped children. Slowly but surely the company should make itself known. Also, I would suggest sending a lobbyist to Washington, D.C., to try to encourage increased government support of special education in the school systems. I would set one year as this image-building goal.

During the implementation of this plan, I would expect Cherry Tree to carry on with its already successful operations. Therefore, it may be necessary to hire additional employees to handle tasks that might be overlooked in the effort to make the new plan successful. In other words, the company should not sacrifice those tasks that have been working in the past. With all efforts running smoothly, I would expect Cherry Tree to be able to take on its additional responsibility as specialist in equipping special educational classrooms in approximately one year.

I make no claims of being able to predict accurately the total cost of this program, but the following provides a breakdown of the types of costs and some "ball-park" estimates of such costs:

Costs of Program

Two new R&D people at $21,000 per year	$ 42,000	
One new consultant—part time	10,000	
One lobbyist	27,000	
Other additional labor cost	25,000	
Total employee cost		$104,000
R&D program	50,000	
Advertising and public-relations costs	100,000	
Total initial investment		150,000
Total (ball-park estimates)		$254,000

A COMMENTARY ON THE FOREGOING STUDENT'S ANALYSIS

The foregoing analysis of the Cherry Tree Learning Materials Company case was prepared by one of the author's students as part of regular course work and was the first case analysis this student had ever prepared. It is not at all bad. However, in the following paragraphs a number of observations are made that would strengthen the analysis and add perspective. The comments are not offered in order of importance and certainly are not all that could be said about the case and the student's analysis. One should note that the action alternatives in the Cherry Tree Company case are more readily visualized than in some of the later cases.

Among the several executives of the company only Terence Halsey, the president, is identified by position in the organizational structure. If one knew the positions of the other men, it would be helpful in judging their views and proposals for resolving the problem. Such views and proposals sometimes reflect the defense of a job, the seeking of influence or power, or other in-house political strategy. Regardless of internal company politics, one's outlook may be narrow and lack company perspective because one is well acquainted with only one specialty. The president of this organization is apparently remaining silent and listening to the ideas and arguments of his subordinates. In doing so he gains some freewheeling discussion and criticism of one manager's reasoning by another. However, after a decision has been made it will be somewhat harder in human-relations terms to bury the disagreements than if strong positions on the problem or issue had never been taken. It is a gamble taken by many top executives who believe the open forum does more good than harm. Some others believe in consensus or in limited discussion.

One does not know the rate of inflation or other change in prices and costs, but one should recognize that part of a sales growth curve may be the result of that inflation. Competitors probably experienced similar cost and price trends, but a company must not mislead itself about its real growth.

Cherry Tree Company did not know what fraction of its sales was going to schools and what fraction to individuals, an indication that there was little, if any, ongoing analysis in the marketing area of the firm. Such breakdowns of data are commonly known several times a year. Moreover, the company does not know how much of the 14 percent of sales that goes to individuals is really to parents. It is noted in the case that some of this segment may be educators (teachers or private tutors) ordering as individuals rather than through the schools. If 14 percent of sales is coming truly from parents when there has been no effort to cultivate such a market segment, it is quite encouraging to one contemplating the development of that segment. With small-scale sampling of the individual accounts, one could determine the real situation. The case does not make it clear whether these individuals who order are put on the mailing list for future company catalogs and, if so, for how long. The length of time that the account-holder's child needed the company's products would vary enormously, of course, according to type of disability, severity, and age of the child. Because such information is usually unavailable on the account, one might want to send the catalog until there had been no sales to that account for a designated number of periods.

One may be convinced that the status quo is not the best action alternative, but one should examine it and see what is encouraging and what is discouraging about it. One could infer that, given the status quo, Cherry Tree Company could live a rather comfortable life for a period of time and enjoy a rising demand fueled by tax appropriations and social awareness trends in government. Yet there are discouraging factors, such as the potential for market disruption by innovative competitors, potential entry of new competitors into an expanding market, and the apparent desire among the executives for the company to expand in a more directed and planned manner and more rapidly. One does not really know how long full development of the judicial and legislative trend toward social education will require. In addition, one should note the declining birthrate. This factor may be fully or partially offset for a period of years by the trend toward special education but eventually will be of importance to firms in the educational materials industry.

Although parents of mildly disabled children may be hesitant to admit that anything is wrong, it is a known fact that the parents who have above average education, income, and occupations will seek professional "special education" for their children before other parents will do so. In instances of mild disability, parental seeking of service may long precede the referral by the nursery school, kindergarten, or first grade teacher to these special services. Therefore, for mild disabilities among children about ages four to seven, the income argument in the case does not hold well. Parents of such special education children are likely to have as much if not more discretionary income than parents of normal children. After about age seven or eight, most children needing special education, regardless of the income of the homes they come from, have been referred by their teachers or parents. However, some of these children are not receiving the special services to which they have been referred. Of course, the definition of need for special attention and the measurement criteria by which children are classified vary from state to state and sometimes from school district to school district within a state. The trend is for the criteria to become more generous so that more children, even with marginal problems, are beginning to receive some professional assistance. In the United States, the trend is national in scope. States that are slow to change policies on such matters are prodded by federal grants that, as a prerequisite, may require adoption of better criteria.

The figure of 15 percent for the proportion of children ultimately involved in special education is not the average or a conservative estimate. Rather it is the highest estimate and so must be used with caution. A prudent manager would not normally use the top end of a range of estimates.

One must note that some teachers and parents regard extra teaching at home by the parents as more harmful than helpful. It may overtire the child, cut into his play time, raise his anxiety level, offset the novelty of the school and its teaching equipment, or pose the parent as a competitor of the teacher. In addition, some parents have no teaching skills, and some others have inadequate patience in a teaching situation. On the other hand, the Cherry Tree materials could be made available to the child in the home without formal teaching by a parent being involved.

If a national health insurance plan is adopted in the United States, parents of all disabled children or at least low-income parents of such children would find themselves with increased discretionary income. This result would depend, of course, on the specific benefit characteristics and income deduction features of such a national health insurance plan. Even if no such plan were instituted, rising public expenditures on special education might free some parents' income by absorbing all or part of the costs of testing, evaluation, periodic trained observation, and therapy that are now borne by the parents.

Most of the twenty-four items in Exhibit 1, which collectively comprise 82 percent of company sales, are low-priced relative to average family income in the United States. Fifteen of the twenty-four items are priced under $5. Only three are priced $15 or more. Also, if these items are specifically recommended by a pediatrician, other medical practitioner, psychologist, or physical therapist, one may be able to count them as medical expenses for purposes of income tax reporting.

The prices of the items in Exhibit 1 are low enough that one could logically consider whether rising demand would permit a general increase, thus increasing profits. This is unlikely, because the case states that the generic products of the company can be obtained from competitors. Apparently Cherry Tree has achieved only a limited degree of brand preference within generic categories. Increased prices do seem within the realm of possibility but only if all significant competitors also raise prices by similar amounts. Such behavior would have to avoid any conscious concerted action or consultation. If there were instances of company bidding for potentially large unit purchases by large school districts, the competitive bidding process might undo the general price rise.

One may wish to consider that, if Cherry Tree made even a small fraction of its sales to normal children, the parents of disabled children might gain more emotional utility from the brand name. It would serve to normalize and legitimize the consumption of Cherry Tree brand products in those parents' perceptions. This might result even if only three or four products for normal children were involved. For the market of normal children the manufacturer could emphasize such factors as sturdiness, safety, and general quality. However, the necessary advertising and creation of a new distribution channel for these few items might result in a net loss on them. In order to have a set of products for normal children that is large enough to interest retailers, Cherry Tree might have to spend a disproportionate share of its product development time and money in preparing more games and toys for normal children. The manufacturer might utilize direct-mail advertising to parents of normal children, but again a small number of products would be involved over which to spread the costs. Reaching people through direct mail can be costly per unit unless there is pre-existing motivation in the market. However, losses might be offset by gains made by sales to parents of disabled children. On the other hand, it is probable that special education teachers and supervisors would prefer to buy educational devices from a manufacturer known for excellence in educational matters rather than a manufacturer known for turning out toys and games per se. A point supporting the offering of products to normal children is that the company's salespeople might find it expeditious to call on supervisors of kindergartens and early elementary grades in conjunction with their calls on supervisors of special education, because such people frequently maintain their offices in the same school district headquarters building. Some existing products, such as pegboards and sorting boxes, might be suitable for normal children through this channel.

One interesting strategy would be to label the goods marketed for normal children as, for example, "Made by Kingston, a Division of Cherry Tree Learning Materials Company." The average price would be fairly low and attractive, because the most expensive items in the current line seem to be the ones that normal children are least likely to need. Parents of normal children might not recognize the brand name "Cherry Tree" anyway, and the alleged stigma probably would not be operative if the Cherry Tree label were not recognized. If the products offered to normal children were not redesigned and then failed to gain acceptance, there might be little cost in reclaiming them for the traditional market of the company. It might mean shipping, handling, and repackaging costs.

An interesting facet of the alleged stigma is that among some parents it would apply more to the disability of mental retardation than to other rather common disabilities, such as partial sight, difficulties of hearing and speech, muscular malfunctions, or hyperactivity. However, some parents of normal children do not distinguish among the disabilities. For some others the term *special education* connotes only mental retardation.

In contemplating the combination of the market composed of parents of the disabled, the company would want to consider the potential of the motivational theme "Used in N thousand special education classrooms." It would be accurate and would contain much emotional implication. If the company attempted to develop this market, it might consider offering "learning systems," sets or series of products aimed at specific disability patterns. A carefully written manual for parents' use of the products would be advisable. For example, a series shipped in three or four stages and aimed at assisting in visual-motor and visual-perception skills might include the following: sponge ball, bead-sequencing kit, pegboards, shape dominoes, parquetry blocks, storytelling posters, sorting box, stencil boards, sequential memory exercise cards, halves-and-wholes matching cards, dimensional puzzles, prewriting design cards, same-or-different cards, and sewing cards. These items total $78.65. Sold together with a manual, the price might be slightly cut, such as $73.50. The shipments might start with the simplest and work upward. Determining such a sequence might be difficult for many parents and impossible for others. Without such package deals, the unit purchase by individuals would almost always be smaller than unit purchases by schools. Order filling and handling lend themselves to economies of scale. The more stages a package deal has in it, the smaller are the economies of scale in order filling and handling.

Professional issues are involved in whether Cherry Tree can secure mailing lists of parents of handicapped children. It is unlikely that it will get much cooperation from any level of government or from schools, and it will get only limited amounts of cooperation from special education teachers. However, some parents would probably provide their names and addresses voluntarily if company salespeople could get blanks made available to them by their children's teachers. Some teachers would cooperate and some would not. Also salespeople could pass out literature and address blanks at organizational meetings of parents of the disabled, if this action was not in violation of the regulations of the place in which the meetings were held. Many clubs issue rosters of the membership free of charge. The officers of many voluntary organizations sell or rent the membership lists to list brokers in order to raise some funds or because they think the membership would like selected direct mail.

Because the company makes sixty products and only twenty-four are listed in Exhibit 1, the remaining thirty-six products must account for 18 percent of sales. This is an average of 0.5 percent of sales for each of these products. This situation may be justified, perhaps in light of having a complete teaching line, a desire to meet the needs of the rare case, and getting a school to order all or most of its needs from Cherry Tree instead of having to go to several competitors' catalogs. However, a firm should let the burden of proof rest with the low-volume products.

The possibility of copyrights and patents on future products gets one into areas of legal sophistication. Brand names and trademarks would be relatively easy for the company to protect, but patents for devices would be difficult to secure, would involve significant legal fees, would usually require several years to obtain, and probably could be designed around by competitors. Very few new toys and games even qualify for a patent. Manuals for products could be copyrighted, of course, without much problem. However, a competitor could paraphrase the manual and discuss the same learning principles and create a competitive manual without any copyright infringement. The copyright idea lends itself fairly well to the expansion of the company into children's books and magazines. Cherry Tree might find such items to have commercial potential especially for the partially sighted or for those with visual perceptual problems.

The case does not reveal if Cherry Tree has a new products department or other structure for developing products in an orderly and controlled manner. If the company remains a specialist in special education devices, it might wish to consider seeking research and development contracts from the federal government. Such contracts are sometimes the springboard for a product breakthrough or even product leadership in an industry.

Pasek's proposal in the case did not necessarily imply the student's interpretation of designing and offering complete classroom packages. It is not unreasonable to make that interpretation, but an equally plausible interpretation is that Cherry Tree should be a strong and innovative leader in the industry and seek a larger share of the market in the expanding and increasingly sophisticated field of special education materials.

The idea of classroom packages proposed by the student does not take cognizance of several difficulties. One is that the group of disabilities to be dealt with might vary enormously from classroom to classroom, with some children having multiple disabilities. The stages of development of the children in a classroom may be diverse. And some teachers would take offense at being handed a preplanned package instead of carefully selecting their materials piece by piece with specific reference to each current pupil. This prepackaged concept has worked well in marketing whole curriculums, such as elementary science for normal children, but the logistics seems formidable for any type of instruction as individualized as special education. The student did not sufficiently grasp this characteristic of the market. Even if the schools gave the teachers considerable discretion in working with the Cherry Tree Learning Materials Company representatives to put together the appropriate combination of products, the combination of pupils assigned to each teacher (and thus the combination of needs) would change from year to year. An interesting variant would be an attempt to market rather complete pools of educational equipment with varying numbers of units of some of the components. A pool would go to a certain school or subdistrict of a large school system and teachers would draw from it to meet their needs. Potential quantity price discounts might make it more attractive to school boards.

The student's implementation section, like many other attempts at showing implementation, is difficult to comment on. Some companies lobby in Washington, D.C., and in some of the state capitals. Much of the tax money spent on special education comes from the federal government. In addition, state monies usually subsidize school districts.

Cherry Tree may be too small to attempt a lobbying effort. Moreover, it would be supporting mainly a generic cause rather than its brand and would benefit from only a fraction of the total effect, if any. Some trade associations representing many companies of similar interests also lobby.

The indicated $50,000 expenditure on R&D programs may well be not just a one-time effort but one running for many years or indefinitely. The figure itself may be understated heavily. New salespeople may be necessary. Moreover, if output is to increase, a not unreasonable assumption, there may have to be additional investment in plant and equipment. The one-year estimate for the time required for advertising, public relations, and general image change is probably too short.

The amount of net profit after taxes in recent years can be related to the potential implementation costs. One may even consider the wisdom of reducing dividends in order to raise more cash for purposes of expansion without incurring further indebtedness or selling stock.

3

Nature and Scope of Marketing

HUFFY BICYCLES

Huffy Corporation, the largest manufacturer of bicycles in the United States, was established in 1928 as The Huffman Manufacturing Company. The name was changed in 1977, in part to reflect what many people had called it for years and also to make it agree with the brand name on the bicycles. The name change was received by the relevant publics without problem. Operating data are presented in Exhibit 1.

This company also had four other investments. First, there was a sporting goods division called Huffy Sports Company, which made basketball backboards, rims, nets, and other basketball accessories. This was an outgrowth of Huffy's long involvement in bicycle riding for recreation and better health. This division, the former Frabill Company of Milwaukee, Wisconsin, was acquired in 1977. The fishing and marine equipment portion of the Frabill product line was sold off in the early 1980s. An exercise equipment line was bought from a small California company, Pryamid Sports, Inc., in the early 1980s and added to the sporting goods division. However, after heavy losses, exercise equipment was eliminated in 1985.

Second, Gerico, Inc., was purchased in February 1983 and later renamed Gerry Baby Products. This wholly owned subsidiary in Denver

EXHIBIT 1 Huffy Corporation Financial and Operating Review

	Summary of Operations	1988	1987	1986
Net Sales		$335,713	$340,551	$294,698
	Operating profit (loss)	17,336	20,602	13,865
	Other deductions, net	(9,560)	(3,400)	(2,955)
	Earnings (loss) before			
	income taxes (benefit)	7,776	17,202	10,910
	Income taxes (benefit)	3,240	7,111	5,003
Net Earnings (Loss)		4,536	10,091	5,907
Earnings (Loss) per Common Share:	Primary	.54	1.22	.73
	Fully diluted	.54	1.17	.72
Other Financial Data	Common dividends declared	2,613	2,333	2,148
	Common dividends per share	.30	.29	.27
	Capital expenditures for plant and equipment	14,786	6,806	7,638
	Average common and common equivalent shares outstanding (in thousands):			
	Primary	8,427	8,294	8,049
	Fully diluted	8,917	8,943	8,741
Financial Position at Year End	Total assets	183,255	149,259	141,267
	Working capital	45,884	61,649	54,161
	Current ratio	1.8	2.2	2.1
	Net Investment in plant and equipment	41,360	27,895	27,495
	Long-term obligations	37,196	15,181	18,427
	Shareholders' equity	80,776	78,914	68,848
	Equity per common share	9.75	9.53	8.52
Additional Data[a]	Number of common shareholders	2,180	2,173	2,615
	Number of employees[b]	3,571	3,330	2,943

Notes: Dollar amounts in thousands, except per-share data.
   All share and per share data have been retroactively restated to reflect the three for two stock split effective July 1, 1988.
[a] 1978 thru 1984 data at June 30
[b] Full-time employees as of December 31, 1988

1985	1984	1983	1982	1981	1980	1979
$263,935	$269,482	$255,752	$195,288	$246,206	$221,644	$232,131
1,932	16,240	9,315	(4,230)	16,914	15,740	17,620
(2,333)	(1,551)	(3,187)	(5,483)	(2,837)	(4,118)	(2,951)
(401)	14,689	6,128	(9,713)	14,077	11,622	14,669
(646)	6,433	2,115	(5,938)	6,659	4,937	6,365
245	8,256	4,013	(3,775)	7,418	6,685	8,304
.03	.99	.49	(.66)	1.11	1.02	1.35
.03	.95	.49	(.66)	1.04	1.02	1.35
2,137	2,140	1,647	2,311	2,282	1,933	1,715
.27	.27	.22	.35	.37	.32	.29
5,356	5,605	2,824	6,012	7,378	11,831	13,336
8,063	8,061	8,060	6,404	6,383	6,206	6,045
8,063	8,756	8,751	7,101	7,079	6,668	6,045
129,264	136,603	138,812	108,618	132,606	112,241	105,232
50,034	58,110	55,741	42,683	49,419	47,656	38,084
2.2	2.6	2.3	2.7	2.2	2.8	2.1
26,679	26,869	26,545	36,983	38,409	35,903	29,051
19,529	28,253	29,284	30,703	31,941	34,974	23,771
64,678	66,573	60,615	44,020	50,970	43,714	39,354
8.07	8.31	7.61	6.91	8.05	7.19	6.49
3,019	3,467	2,821	3,221	2,930	2,848	2,356
3,073	2,749	2,928	1,924	3,137	2,457	2,987

made infant carriers, strollers, swings, bathtubs, and several other juvenile products. The former name, Gerico, unfortunately implied geriatric products. In 1985 Huffy bought Snugli, Inc., a maker of infant carriers, and added it to the Gerico subsidiary. In 1987 Huffy entered into a joint venture with Takata Corporation of Japan to make infant seats for cars, Takata supplying the production technology and Huffy the marketing. In January 1988 Huffy spent $11.8 million to acquire Memline Corporation, a maker of children's wooden furniture and gates under the brand name Nu-Line. This acquisition was to complement the Gerry line.

Third, YLC Enterprises, Inc., provided in-store assembly, warranty service, and general repair services for several types of products, including bicycles, physical fitness equipment, toys, furniture, gas grills, lawn mowers, and shopping carts, for 4,800 retailers operating 27,000 stores across the United States, most of them units of national and regional chains. About three-fourths of YLC's revenue came from bicycle assembly. This subsidiary relieved many retailers of service work they did not like and for which they did not want to be responsible. Most consumers were put off by the idea of assembling something themselves when the retailer was unable or unwilling to do it. Consumers also typically did not do the work right and often wound up with unsafe products. Operating in virtually all of the 200 largest geographical markets of the United States, YLC was the only national organization of its type. The sales growth of YLC had been remarkably high, but saturation of its market would come in time. YLC was founded in 1978 with Huffy as a 50 percent owner and K-Mart as the initial customer, but Huffy bought the other half in 1982. In the late 1980s YLC added the creation and maintenance of in-store displays for retailers.

Fourth, at the end of 1988 Huffy, using the $17 million Raleigh proceeds (see below) plus some other funds, acquired San Diego–based Washington Inventory Service (WIS) for $24.8 million. This company, with annual sales of just over $60 million, was meant to fit into a line of services offered retailers and to complement the assembly business. WIS provided all types of inventory services. The advantages to a retailer of using such a company were the following: (1) it received third party objectivity, resulting in independent counts; (2) regular workers were not taken off their jobs for inventory work; and (3) trained specialists and state-of-the-art data collection and processing equipment were used.

An automotive products division in Delphos, Ohio, that made gasoline cans, tire pumps, and several other automotive service products was operated for some years but sold in April 1982. In the early 1970s there was a lawn mower operation, but it did not succeed.

Until the late 1980s Huffy Corporation had not made a decision on whether to diversify in a serious manner and, if so, what strategy to use. However, the seriousness and strategy of its decision of the late 1980s was also questioned by some securities analysts, brokers, financial advisors, and journalists.

Until recently bicycles had accounted for the vast majority of the company's sales, in most years over 90 percent. That figure went down to 62 percent in 1987 and was now just over 50 percent. Sales of bicycles were mainly to large national and regional chains of department stores and sporting goods stores, some other mass retailers, and a few wholesalers. The heart of the distribution network was over 200 department store companies, some with many branches. In several recent years, one customer, K-Mart, accounted for 10 to 16 percent of all corporate sales. Some other highly significant customers were J. C. Penney Company, Inc., Montgomery Ward & Co., and F. W. Woolworth Co. Some large merchants offered Huffy-made bicycles with the Huffy name on them, whereas others preferred that their house brand be shown. In the late 1970s and in 1980, about 40 percent of the company's bicycles were sold under the private labels of major customers. This figure became 35 percent in 1981. In 1982 it became 24 percent and began to stabilize thereafter. The chains provided about 90 percent of all corporate sales until the beginning of the 1980s. The most recent figure was about 65 percent. Huffy was anxious to get this figure down to a little under 50 percent. In the 1982–1984 period, several large U.S. retail chains had switched much of their bicycle buying to foreign sources, the majority of which were Taiwanese. However, disappointed with quality, some of these chains switched a fraction of their purchases back to U.S. suppliers, including Huffy, as of 1985. It was a perplexing topic area for Huffy to consider for long-run policy.

Competitor Murray Ohio Manufacturing Company, now based in Brentwood, Tennessee, after a relocation, made the house brand carried by Sears, Roebuck & Co., its number one customer. A little over half of Murray Ohio's bicycle sales were as house brands. Murray was bought by a British company, Tompkins, PLC, in August 1988 for $228 million. Tompkins was a conglomerate making many products, including fluid controls, industrial fasteners, gauges, and the famous Smith and Wesson firearms. Murray Ohio was now the second-largest bicycle maker in the United States and had been number one until 1978. Seeing the trend lines of costs, prices, and imports, Murray began emphasizing lawn mowers, in which it found great success.

The other principal U.S. companies supplying the mass market were Murray Ohio, as noted, and AMF. Schwinn, the third-largest company, with about $215 million sales per year, carefully avoided the mass merchants. AMF was number four. Columbia (MTD) sold mainly to mass merchants but sold some units to specialty shops. Ross (Chain Bike Corporation), with annual sales of about $55 million, sold mainly to specialty shops but a few units to mass merchants.

There were slightly over 100 million bicycles in the United States in usable condition. A well-made, reasonably maintained bicycle had a life of twelve to twenty years, but children's bicycles were not maintained as well as adults' bicycles. At least half of the bicycles that were abandoned were not worn out. Instead, the reasons for abandonment were that the owner became bored with riding, wanted a different type or model of bicycle, or had outgrown the size of the product.

Nearly 100 million Americans rode a bicycle at least once in a while. Swimming was the number one type of recreational exercise, but bicycle riding was one of the four or five other important types of recreation vying for second rank. It was generally agreed that the popularity of bicycle riding at the beginning of the 1990s was slightly below the level of the late 1980s. Of the bicycles sold in the United States in a typical year, about 25 to 30 percent were sold to adults for their own use.

Unit sales of bicycles in the United States increased at an average annual rate of 7.7 percent from 1960 through 1978. The industry referred to the years 1972 through 1974 as the Bicycle Boom. About 13.9 million units were sold in 1972, 15.2 million in 1973, and 14.1 million in 1974. The peak year occurred thirteen years after the peak in the birthrate, but it was also influenced by widening interest in outdoor recreation and physical fitness. Throughout the 1970s, bicycle sales were helped a little by rapidly rising gasoline prices and frequent strikes by public transit workers, but the press drastically exaggerated the contribution of these two factors. Industry sales slowed in the late 1970s and early 1980s but still remained rather good. However, the year 1982, with only 6.7 million units sold, was the worst since 1965. Most of the industry had been unreasonably optimistic for some years. In 1983, 8.9 million units were sold; in 1984, 9.7 million units; in 1985, 11.0 million units; and in 1986, 11.4 million units. Industry sales of 12.4 million units in 1987 established a thirteen-year high. Sales in 1988 fell to 10 million units. Industry growth was expected to settle down to an annual rate of approximately 1 to 4 percent for several years. As of 1989 Huffy executives predicted a serious industry downturn every four to six years.

Huffy Corporation was quite expansionist and optimistic in the late 1970s. The organization enlarged its main bicycle factory in Celina, Ohio, in 1978. Construction of a large bicycle plant in Ponca City, Oklahoma, which cost $16 million, was started in 1979; and its first bicycle came off the assembly line in 1980. The company believed it was the most modern bicycle production facility in the world, and it was enlarged in 1982. Huffy closed its Azusa, California, bicycle plant in October 1982 and shifted that production to its facility in Ponca City. When the Oklahoma plant was planned, there was no intention to close the California plant. Demand did not justify keeping the Azusa factory open, however. Then in April 1983 the company closed its Ponca City plant and centralized all bicycle production in the Celina, Ohio, facility. Forecasting of demand had been incorrect to an alarming degree.

The company redesigned production operations in Celina and installed a great amount of new equipment. Workers were retrained, motivated, and given a sense of participation in decision making and management. Morale and productivity soared, even beyond expectations. Production rose in the plant even as the labor force was reduced by 25 percent and quality of product was raised. Unit product costs declined to the point that the company could compete cost-wise with Asian manufacturers. The Celina plant enjoyed the lowest number of man-hours per bicycle manufactured in the world but was not the lowest overall cost producer in the world.

Huffy's share of the combined imports and domestic production of bicycles (in units) was about 25 percent in the latest year, compared to about 20 percent for Murray Ohio. Huffy Corporation's share of domestically produced units was about 39 percent and had been that for several years. The corresponding Huffy figures for 1974 and 1980 were 23 percent and 35 percent, respectively. Because, on the average, the bicycles sold in specialty shops commanded a much higher price and Huffy did not have much distribution through such shops, Huffy's share of the market in terms of dollars was around 18 percent, much lower than its share calculated on units of product. Huffy's top-of-the-line Huffy brand bicycle sold for just over $200, whereas the prestigious brands started at about that price.

Bicycle specialty shops sold about 25 percent of all bicycles in the United States as of the mid-1980s, down from 46 percent in 1968. However, this one-fourth share in units amounted to a 40 percent share in dollars because, on average, a bicycle in a specialty shop sold for about 60 percent more than a bicycle sold in a large national or regional chain store. Some of the many prestige brands usually found in specialty shops were Schwinn, Puch, Gitane, Fuji, and Motobecane.

Adult consumers were more important to specialty shops than to mass retailers. There were several reasons: (1) higher prices, (2) greater brand prestige, (3) greater retailer prestige in the local community, (4) claimed and perceived higher quality of products, (5) claimed and perceived higher quality of information before the sale, and (6) claimed and perceived higher quality of service after the sale. People were hesitant to pay specialty-shop prices for a child's bicycle, especially because the child would outgrow it rather quickly.

Huffy had had a significant problem with the image of its bicycles. The company clearly was designing products chiefly for children. Its products were perceived by the great majority of people as toys. Most adults who did not see them as toys, nevertheless, saw them as too inexpensive and aimed at unknowledgeable or klutzy consumers or both. It was embarrassing to most adults to be seen on a Huffy. Schwinn spokespersons were openly, publicly contemptuous of Huffy. Even among children there was a problem. On the "sissiness" scale, Huffy ranked rather high. The older the consumer, the more at a disadvantage Huffy was. Bicycle specialty shops did not want to stock Huffy brand products mainly because of these reasons. A secondary reason was that such shops were fearful, with very good reason, that some regional or national chain stores would undercut the prices of Huffies that the locally owned specialty shops would try to charge.

To combat these problems, Huffy did quite a number of things. It worked on product design so as to offer a greater assortment of bicycles, including several types of bicycles that might satisfy the swings of fashion. The company saw the potential for the BMX (bicycle motocross) style of product rather early and began to make it successfully. This product was a motorcycle-styled bicycle with wide, knobby tires. The main appeal was to teenagers, but there was some appeal to young adults. Huffy also brought out sidewalk bicycles for children and Huffy Scat tricycles for young children. Contests were held in conjunction with Cap'n Crunch's Peanut Butter Cereal, a Quaker Oats Company product, the prizes being Huffy brand bicycles. The company also formed a professional racing team, and it heavily publicized all racing team victories. Advertising became more dynamic and interesting.

However, two other actions had loomed larger in the company's overall strategy to alter its image. First, Huffy acquired an exclusive, long-term license to manufacture and distribute Raleigh brand bicycles in the United States from T I Raleigh Industries, Ltd., of England, a prestigious maker of bicycles for over a century. Also included was the right to use the Raleigh name on exercise equipment. This brand, which had about 3 percent of the American market, had been made in Taiwan and Japan for Raleigh under contract for several years. Huffy planned to continue using this source for some of its Raleigh supply, but it also leased manufacturing buildings in Kent, Washington, for production. These facilities were leased until 1988, subject to six consecutive options to renew for additional terms of three years each at a rent to be determined. Raleigh sold at retail for about $245 to $1,400. Raleigh was the second-largest brand, after Schwinn, sold in the specialty shop segment of the U.S. market. Despite the Oriental sourcing in recent years, the Raleigh name still carried a very special mystique, that of a high-quality European bicycle ridden by a knowledgeable, sophisticated person through the leafy English countryside. The visual image was remarkably strong. Huffy Corporation established its Raleigh effort as a wholly owned subsidiary, Raleigh Cycle Company of America, to try to separate this line as much as possible psychologically from the Huffy line. Some Raleigh dealers refused to handle Raleigh after Huffy began to have responsibility for its production and marketing. As one such dealer put it to a customer, "The quality of Raleigh is now just as good as the Huffy you see in the big chain toy store down the street. It's just a painted-over Huffy." Credibility was a problem for Huffy Corporation.

The second major part of the corporate strategy had been to gain some presence in the 1984 Olympics, emphasize the results indefinitely, and then aim for later Olympic Games also. The U.S. Cycling Federation selected Huffy Corporation and its Raleigh subsidiary to produce bicycles at Huffy's Technical Development Center in Dayton, Ohio, to be used by the U.S. National Cycling Team in worldwide competition, including the Olympics. These bicycles were designed by people with extensive scientific and engineering talent and were hand-built. Every bicycle was tailored to the individual characteristics of the rider as well. These products were put to the competitive test rather early on in their development at the 1984 Summer Olympics. Americans had not won an Olympic bicycling medal since 1912, but this time they won nine of them, five of the nine on Huffy-made Raleigh bicycles. Included were the gold medal earned by Connie Carpenter for the women's road race and a gold earned by Stephen Hegg for the individual pursuit race. Hegg's bicycle received considerable news media coverage because of its unusual appearance. Called the "High Tech Bike" and the "Funny Bike," it had a 24-inch front wheel, a 27-inch solid disc rear wheel, and aerodynamic sprint style handlebars. Silver medals were won by Norman Vail in the sprint race and the U.S. team in the 4,000-meter pursuit race. A bronze medal was taken by the 100-kilometer road race team. Of the twenty-three Americans participating in the Olympics, thirteen rode bicycles made by Huffy technical development personnel.

It was clear from the beginning that things were not going to be easy for Huffy's Raleigh subsidiary. In 1988 this division was sold at an after-tax loss of $2.9 million to Derby International Corporation of Luxembourg, after showing large operating losses most years and devouring inordinately high shares of the top management's time. The only bright factor was that this event freed up some capital for use in other operations.

Dumping

Most of the U.S. bicycle industry believed that there was some "dumping" of bicycles in the U.S. market in violation of U.S. laws and a loose set of understandings more or less agreed on in an international treaty. Much of the industry and certainly Huffy believed that Taiwan was the chief culprit. The Bicycle Manufacturers Association, a trade group and often the spokesperson for the U.S. industry, filed antidumping charges with the International Trade Commission against Taiwan and several other countries. There was very little chance of winning the legal dispute, however.

The U.S. tariff on foreign-made bicycles ranged from 5.5 to 11 percent and had been stable for many years. The sizes usually bought for children paid a tariff of 11 percent; and those usually bought by adults and older teenagers, 5.5 percent. The tariff on bicycle parts was from 6 to 10 percent depending on type of part. The Bicycle Manufacturers Association had long claimed that the average bicycle tariff in the world was 24 percent and that no country had lower bicycle tariffs than the United States. In 1985 the association reduced the claimed figure of 24 percent to 20 percent but reiterated that U.S. producers had to pay their workers extraordinarily high wages and fringe benefits and needed the protection of a higher tariff. The U.S. bicycle manufacturers, including Huffy, imported selected components. For example, a large fraction of the multispeed hubs came from Great Britain, West Germany, and Japan. Many of the tires came from India, South Korea, and Taiwan; and many of the coaster brakes from Mexico, Japan, and West Germany; and derailleur systems, from France.

The word "dumping" had to do with the sale of foreign-made goods at questionably low prices. There had never been a really clear meeting of the minds on what constituted dumping. Moreover, even when a definition could be temporarily adopted for the sake of argument, the relevant economic data were difficult to gather and extraordinarily difficult to verify. Dumping was usually thought of as the pricing policy whereby a company sold a product abroad for a figure either below its cost or for less than it charged in its home country. There was no general meeting of the minds on how to handle fixed versus variable costs or what a reasonable profit was. There was also no general agreement on what role was played in "cost" by subsidies that the government of a country might make to a producer in that country.

The uncertainty was given some structure by a major international treaty, the General Agreement on Tariffs and Trade (GATT), signed in 1947 by many countries, including the United States. Many other countries signed later, and the number of signatories was now 97. This treaty was administered by a permanent secretariat in Geneva, Switzerland. In prohibiting the dumping, Article Six of the GATT contained the following language:

> For purposes of this article, a product is to be considered as being introduced into the commerce of an importing country at less than its normal value, if the price of the product exported from one country to another (a) is less than the comparable price, in the ordinary course of trade, for the like product destined for consumption in the exporting country or, (b) in the absence of such domestic price, it is less than either (i) the highest comparable price

for the like product for export to any third country in the ordinary course of trade, or (ii) the cost of production of the product in the country of origin plus a reasonable addition for selling cost and profit.

However, the preceding failed to take into account the level of the effects of imports on the companies in the importing country. Less-developed countries were able to write into the treaty agreement a clause that limited the right to prohibit importation of low-priced goods implied in the preceding definitional language. This resulted in the following further language of the treaty:

If as a result of unforseen developments and of the effect of the obligations incurred by either party to this agreement, any product is imported into the territory of one of the parties in such increased quantities and under such conditions as to (a) cause or threaten serious injury to domestic producers or to the establishment of domestic production in that territory of like or directly competitive products, or (b) cause serious disruption of traditional patterns of trade in that product or directly competitive products, the injured party shall have the right, in respect of such products, and to the extent and for such time as may be necessary to prevent or remedy such injury, to suspend the obligation in whole or in part.

The treaty and a subsequent code of interpretation of Article Six authorized any member nation to adopt antidumping duties against an offending nation. For example, if the illicit price in nation X was determined to be $10 per unit of product too low, a tariff or additional tariff could be imposed by nation X for $10 per unit of relevant product against the imports from the offending nation. The number of allegations and formal complaints was rising in some countries, including the United States. Most did not result in any action. These complaints were handled by the International Trade Administration, part of the Commerce Department, and the International Trade Commission. In the United States, a complainant had to prove both price discrimination and significant injury to the domestic industry. Minor injury or injury to the complainant only was not sufficient.

Imported bicycles became quite important in the United States in the 1950s and temporarily peaked in 1972 at 37 percent of the U.S. market. U.S. tariffs on bicycles were reduced in 1968. The import percentage fell for several years and bottomed out at 17 percent in 1979. (See Exhibit 2.) It turned up in 1980 with a 23 percent share. Huffy believed that the upturn in 1980 came about because many U.S. mass merchants expected a domestic shortage of bicycles in 1980 that did not materialize. In 1981 and 1982 imports took 23 percent, and in 1983, 30 percent. In 1984 and 1985 the share surged to 42 percent and 49 percent, respectively.

EXHIBIT 2 Share of the U.S. Market Held by Imported Bicycles in Selected Years

	Percentage of Units
1960	31
1965	18
1968	21
1969	28
1970	28
1971	26
1972	37
1973	34
1974	28
1975	23
1976	21
1977	20
1978	20
1979	17
1980	23
1981	23
1982	23
1983	30
1984	42
1985	49
1986	57
1987	58
1988	55
1989	50

EXHIBIT 3 Bicycles Sold through Mass Merchants as a Percentage of All Bicycles Imported from the Source Nation

Source Nation (in order of number of bicycles sold in U.S.)	Percentage of Units
Taiwan	23
Japan	15
South Korea	100
Poland	100
France	0
Britain	0

Industry analysts had developed some data about imports. (See Exhibit 3.) This exhibit showed, for example, that about 17 percent of the bicycles entering the United States from Japan were sold through large merchants, the remainder going through shops that specialized in bicycles. The corresponding figure for the largest supplier, Taiwan, had been declining for several years. It was 60 percent in 1980. This was explained by both rising quality of Taiwanese bicycles and carefully planned marketing attempts by Taiwan to place the goods in bicycle specialty shops in the United States.

Advise Huffy Corporation.

LONDON FOG

London Fog was an extraordinarily well-known brand name. In fact, the brand name was far better known than the company, whose official name was Londontown Corporation. Located in a suburb of Baltimore, this organization was founded in 1922 and was the oldest as well as the largest rainwear maker in the United States. Its sales exceeded $165 million per year and were growing.

The United States rainwear industry lost about seventy-five manufacturers between the late 1960s and the middle 1980s through merger and bankruptcy. About twenty firms remained, several of which were in some difficulty.

The extent to which the London Fog brand name was familiar to American consumers was quite impressive. In standard, unaided tests among properly constituted samples of men, more than 90 percent said, "London Fog" after the interviewer said, "Raincoat." The corresponding figure for women was less but still impressively high. Thus, the brand awareness, recognition, and recall were among the highest ever achieved by an American manufacturer.

Londontown Corporation made men's and women's raincoats and rainproof outerwear. It had about 60 percent of the men's raincoat market and about one-third of the women's raincoat market in the United States. The company added men's and women's other outerwear to its product line only in the late 1970s. Among the types of outerwear were quilted jackets in several lengths and weights and light-weight windbreakers and golf jackets. These were marketed as a collection under the trade name "Outdoors Unlimited by London Fog." It was hoped that use of the word "unlimited" would call to the consumer's attention that the garments were for warmth as well as protection from the rain. Company advertising headlined the collection as "rugged and ready jackets and coats for women and men." In 1983 and 1984, Londontown introduced the London Towne label. According to company executives, this was done to add some new and different channels of distribution. In 1985 the organization added another collection of men's and women's outerwear and gave it the brand name "Winning Edge by London Fog."

Moreover, Londontown Corporation licensed several other companies to manufacture rain hats, umbrellas, shoes, and other products using the name London Fog. Some of the firms paying to use this famous brand name were Gold Star Hat Corporation, Bowen Shoe Company, Fashion Rite, Miller Brothers Industries, and Schertz Umbrellas, Inc.

The advertising of London Fog typically utilized a line drawing modeled on the Big Ben tower of the Houses of Parliament in London. Often the advertisements also used a statement that had become strongly associated with the brand: "London Fog lets you laugh at the weather." Both print and electronic media were used heavily. Among the minor types of advertising were multicolor leaflets for retailers to stuff inside regular monthly bills to their customers. Some consumers thought of London Fog as a British organization. Britain enjoyed a reputation as a source of fine clothing for men.

A much larger organization, Interco, Inc., acquired a majority interest in Londontown Corporation on February 25, 1976. Interco was a conglomerate that manufactured apparel, footwear, and furniture and owned several retailing firms. The headquarters office was in St. Louis. Realizing "the importance of the entrepreneurial spirit in its executives," one of Interco's stated corporate policies was to acquire a company only if the management wished to continue on an active basis.

The Apparel Manufacturing Group in Interco consisted of eleven apparel companies operating fifty-one manufacturing plants and twelve major distribution centers across the United States. In March 1984, Interco acquired Abe Schrader Corporation, which made women's dresses, suits, coats, sportswear, and ensembles in the medium- to medium-high price ranges. The sales of the Apparel Manufacturing Group in fiscal 1985 were $943,077,000. See Exhibit 1 for other years. London Fog was by far the best-known brand name in the entire Apparel Manufacturing Group.

Among the clothing brands Interco owned were Don Robbie, Devon, Clipper Mist, College-Town, Queen Casuals, John Alexander, Stuffed Shirt, Stuffed Jeans, Pant-her, Smith & Jones, LeTigre, Petite Concept, Rejoice, Cowden, It's Pure Gould, T. A. Whitney, Tour de France, Big Yank, Donegal, Cherokee, and Campus. Interco also manufactured large amounts of clothing for the house brands of several retail chains. Among Interco's footwear brands were Florsheim, Winthrop, Rand, Worthmore, Hy-Test, Grizzlies, Thayer McNeil, Miller Taylor, Avenue, Crawdads, Personality, Miss Wonderful, J. G. Hook, diVina, Phillips, and Thompson, Boland & Lee. The major furniture brands owned by Interco were Ethan Allen, Broyhill, Kling, Knob Creek, and Restocrat. The conglom-

EXHIBIT 1 Sales of Interco and Its Apparel Group by Year, 1977–1985 (in thousands)

	Interco	Apparel Group
1985	$2,625,746	$943,077
1984	2,678,886	880,122
1983	2,566,606	877,341
1982	2,673,769	899,161
1981	2,368,456	850,970
1980	2,024,307	818,380
1979	1,851,458	731,259
1978	1,666,657	640,487
1977	1,566,432	576,019

orate entered the furniture business in the calendar year 1980. Ethan Allen, Inc., was purchased February 1, 1980, and Broyhill Furniture Industries, Inc., December 1, 1980. The products of these two large furniture makers were almost all upper-middle-priced and were very well-known. Through these two acquisitions just ten months apart, Interco became the largest furniture manufacturer in the world.

The Interco retailers included, among other, Golde's, a department store with ten branches in and near St. Louis, and Idaho Department Stores, a chain of seventy-seven junior department stores in Texas and the Northwest. Other operations included thirty large home improvement centers in the Midwest called Central Hardware, eighty-eight men's specialty shops in the Midwest and South called Fine's or Fine's United, seventy-two discount department stores in the Southeast under the name Sky City Discount, and a national chain of Florsheim shoe shops. The company opened thirty-nine new Florsheim shops in 1985 alone. Interco also operated stores under the names of Benchley, Carithers, Jeans Galore, Keith O'Brien, Standard Sportswear, United Shirt, and Thornton's. In addition, Interco owned Senack, Inc., which operated a large national chain of leased shoe departments in many independent department stores and large apparel stores. The heavy emphasis in the Retail Group was on clothing and shoes. In 1984, Interco sold most of P. N. Hirsch & Company, a chain of 385 junior department stores in the Northwest and Southwest, and consolidated the retained units into the Idaho Department Stores operation. Interco also sold Albert's, a chain of sixty-three women's specialty shops, in late 1984 and Eagle Family Discount Stores, a chain of 210 self-service stores, in early 1985. All three components were sold because of their poor earnings. There was concern in Interco and within the Retail Group about performance, priorities, and emphasis just as there was concern in the four divisions or groups of the conglomerate about the importance of each to Interco.

The Apparel Manufacturing Group provided 35.9 percent of Interco's sales. Londontown Corporation provided over one-sixth of the apparel sales and between 6 and 7 percent of Interco's total sales. The conglomerate had annual sales of $2,625,000,000 and about 48,000 employees. The corresponding figures four years earlier were $2,368,000,000 and about 56,000 employees. (See Exhibits 2 and 3.)

Londontown was no longer independent. As with any subsidiary of a conglomerate, fundamental changes in the company and its product line and capital investments were subject to review by the management at the Interco headquarters. However, Londontown was rewarded with much more quasi-independence than a typical subsidiary of a typical conglomerate.

The president of Londontown at the time of the acquisition, Jonathan P. Myers, was appointed to be one of the six vice-presidents of Interco. Four of them, including Myers, were appointed to the Interco Board of Directors. Myers, his father, his wife, his sister, and his brother-in-law together had owned about 42 percent of the Londontown corporate stock and thus became sizable stockholders of the conglomerate. The market value of their shares on the stock exchange more than doubled when the acquisition was concluded. Jonathan's elderly father, Israel Myers, had begun working for London Fog in 1923 at the age of sixteen. He was largely responsible for the later growth of the company until he chose to go into retirement as his son and son-in-law gradually assumed active management roles.

Londontown Corporation had a history of considerable innovation. Israel Myers detected a rising consumer interest in lightweight rainwear in the early 1940s. His first such sale was to the U.S. Army, which awarded him a contract for 10,000 raincoats. Because rubber was scarce, the company made coats of synthetic rubber on a sheet of cotton. Soon after World War II, as supplies became plentiful again, Londontown began making private label rainwear for J. C. Penney and Sears, Roebuck & Co. In 1951, London Fog experimented with a new synthetic fabric, Dacron polyester, made by a process developed by Du Pont. London Fog was one of the first manufacturers to buy the revolutionary new cloth, which

EXHIBIT 2 Sales by Group as a Percentage of Interco's Total Sales, by Fiscal Year, 1977–1985

	1985	1984	1983	1982	1981	1980	1979	1978	1977
Apparel	35.9	32.9	34.2	33.6	35.9	40.4	39.5	38.4	36.8
Footwear	22.1	21.1	21.3	22.0	23.6	27.4	29.0	30.3	31.4
Furniture	21.2	20.1	17.8	19.3	13.2	1.0	0	0	0
General Retailing	20.8	25.9	26.7	25.1	27.3	31.2	31.5	31.3	31.8

EXHIBIT 3 Operating Earnings to Sales as a Percentage, by Interco Group, by Fiscal Year, 1977–1985

	1985	1984	1983	1982	1981	1980	1979	1978	1977
Apparel	8.8	11.4	10.8	11.7	12.9	12.9	13.1	13.5	13.5
Footwear	9.4	10.3	10.5	13.4	15.0	11.8	11.4	8.8	9.9
Furniture	9.7	11.0	6.3	10.7	12.8	15.0	–	–	–
General									
Retailing	3.2	4.2	3.3	3.4	4.2	6.5	7.0	7.3	6.5

repelled water, did not wrinkle, and had good visual appeal. The source was Wamsutta Mills, which had been licensed by Du Pont to manufacture the new fabric. However, the first Dacron melted during the sewing process. Du Pont, Wamsutta, and London Fog worked together to develop a lubricant that solved the problem, and by 1953 satisfactory London Fog Dacron rainwear was in production. In early 1954, Saks-Fifth Avenue stores, in a major promotion paid for by Londontown, were the first to introduce the revolutionary new raincoats. This retailer had thirty days of exclusive rights to sell the product. This introduction gave the new product a high-fashion and status stamp. The sales growth thereafter was quite rapid. That status of the new product was ironic. Israel Myers was very fond of recalling that in earlier years the manufacturing of raincoats was the lowest-status portion of the entire apparel industry.

There was a noteworthy difference in the risks involved in manufacturing raincoats for women as opposed to those for men. Men demanded the same raincoats not just year after year but decade after decade. Although women's rainwear did not exhibit the extremes of design or rapid change of the women's dress industry, it did change appreciably. London Fog did not give adequate attention to those changes prior to 1970. In 1969 the company suffered high losses by not responding to the women's fashion cycle. London Fog became acutely conscious of the need to forecast women's fashion, to observe the slow changes in men's fashion, and to remain alert to the possibility that men's fashion might begin to change more rapidly than in the past. Major rainwear manufacturers might have the ability to influence the men's fashion cycle to change more quickly. Most business observers considered London Fog to be a trendsetter for women's raincoats.

The company had many competitors, but all of them were much smaller. For women, two of the largest were Forecaster of Boston and Misty Harbor. Two well-established imports form Britain, Burberry's and Aquascutum of London, England, were peripheral competitors in that their price lines were from 40 to 90 percent higher than London Fog's, whose price lines were considered in the medium- to upper-medium range and topped out at about $200. Some other important imports were Induyco and Cortefiel from Spain, and Diane Von Furstenberg and Calvin Klein from Hong Kong. For men's rainwear a major competitor was Gleneagles, Inc., also located in Baltimore. It was a division of Hart Schaffner & Marx but was only a fraction of the size of London Fog.

The number and sizes of competitors in the future were in doubt even though the number of domestic producers had declined markedly. The fundamental facts were that the production of raincoats was extremely simple and low-skilled, such production required relatively low capital investment and unsophisticated equipment (i.e., it was labor-intensive), and the United States was moving toward fewer restrictions on international trade.

London Fog used a selective distribution policy in selling goods to retailers. The company had traditionally placed a suggested retail price on each garment and had carefully avoided selling to discounters. Virtually all stores charged the full list price on London Fog products. In 1977 and 1978 the Federal Trade Commission accused the manufacturer of price-fixing, that is, dictating to the retail accounts the prices to charge ultimate consumers. This ability of manufacturers to practice resale-price maintenance had been legally rescinded by Congress as of early 1976. London Fog signed a consent order, not admitting any wrongdoing but promising not to dictate the prices that retailers could charge in the future.

At the time of the case, Mark H. Lieberman, previously the marketing vice-president, had succeeded to the office of president of Londontown Corporation. Jonathan Myers, now age forty-seven, became chairperson of Londontown's Board of Directors but was no longer an Interco vice-president or a member of the Interco Board of Directors. Lieberman was appointed to the Operating Board of Interco but not its Board of Directors. The conglomerate's Operating Board had twenty-four members, twenty of whom were what Interco called "the principal officers of Interco's major operating companies." The other four persons were Interco's chairperson of the Board of Directors, president, executive vice-president, and senior vice-president. The executives of the conglomerate referred to this body, which met monthly, as "the heart of our business." Londontown Corporation also had an Operating Board, consisting of its management team plus four Interco senior corporate officers, which met quarterly.

Suddenly in mid-1988 a hostile and determined takeover attempt was made against Interco by Steven and Mitchell Rales, well-known Washington, D.C., financiers. It became necessary for Interco's management to sell off many of the assets of the company in order to defeat the takeover attempt. Sales volume was approximately cut in half in doing so.

One of the most important divestments was Londontown Corporation, sold at the beginning of 1989 for $178 million to Eldersburg Acquisition

Corporation, consisting of several senior management officials of the subsidiary. Burlington Coat Factory Warehouse Corporation also tried to buy Londontown and offered $190 million. This company, a New Jersey-based retailer emphasizing price appeal, was one of the country's largest outerwear retailers and one of the largest sellers of London Fog rainwear. However, Londontown had never been willing to sell to Burlington. That company's stocks had always had to come from third parties who had overbought London Fog products. This was a point of considerable annoyance to Burlington. The higher offer was turned down by Interco. The reason presented for the rejection of the higher offer was that Eldersburg Acquisition could provide cash immediately but Burlington would most likely require several weeks. Interco had a demonstrable need for cash immediately, although the interest expense to borrow the difference between the two offers for a short while would have been small compared to that difference. However, it was getting hard for Interco to borrow significant sums.

The senior managers involved who suddenly became the new owners were the president, Mark Lieberman, and four vice-presidents. They were Edward Frey, executive vice-president for operations, Douglas Hilman, executive vice-president for marketing, Zachary Goldman, vice-president for administration, and Stanley Rubin, senior corporate vice-president for styling and merchandising. The firm was now independent again and they had to make plans. Parental control would be gone but so would the parent's capital and connections for product design, marketing, and materials procurement.

Advise Londontown Corporation.

H. G. PARKS SAUSAGE

Founded in 1951, H. G. Parks, Inc., was a well-known manufacturer of pork sausage. It was established by Henry G. Parks, Sr., when he was thirty-five years old, and it grew to become, at one time, the seventh largest minority-owned firm and the second largest publicly held minority-owned firm in the United States. This second fact means, of course, that the Parks stock was publicly traded on the open market. From the beginning there was another large investor besides Parks. However, that man, William L. Adams, was a silent partner. Adams was a prominent black business executive in Baltimore and a member of the city council. H. G. Parks, Sr., also served on the city council from 1963 to 1969.

The Parks enterprise was sold in 1977 for $5.5 million to Norin Corporation of Miami, Florida, a conglomerate with annual sales of about $650 million. Besides the principal owners, Parks and Adams, there were about 900 other stockholders. The price received by each stockholder was more than twice the price of the stock on the open market. H. G. Parks, Sr., stayed on as a consultant, but not as an employee of Norin, under a seven-year contract. According to some people in the corporation and in the community, a great sense of loss was felt by the Parks employees and many members of the community. The company had been successful and respected and carried symbolic value.

Although H. G. Parks, Inc., had sales of $15 million and a net profit of almost $1 million in the year before the sale, it did not prosper under Norin's ownership. Although there were allegations of poor management decisions and insufficient management involvement and interest, the underlying causes were not clear. However, it was clear that H. G. Parks, Inc., was severely affected by the high inflation rates of the 1970s. For example, the prices of the raw materials went up 100 percent, and annual insurance premiums went up by $70,000. Sales began to decrease. A severe cash flow problem developed.

In August 1980, Norin sold the Parks organization to Canadian Pacific Enterprises, a manufacturing subsidiary of Canadian Pacific Railroad. Shortly thereafter, H. G. Parks, Inc., was transferred to the jurisdiction of another Canadian Pacific Railroad subsidiary, Canellus, Inc., based in Syracuse, New York. After a short delay, Canellus put Parks up for sale and gave H. G. Parks, Sr., and the company employees a forty-five-day first right of refusal to buy the business. The founder of the firm, then aged sixty-four, declined to buy it back or to become a major investor in it. He said, "My day is past."

During the next few weeks nine persons pooled savings and borrowed money in order to purchase the Parks corporation. A short extension of the forty-five-day period was necessary. Leading the investment group was sixty-year-old Raymond V. Haysbert, president of H. G. Parks, Inc., since 1975. A former college professor of business administration, Haysbert joined Parks, Inc., in 1952, when the organization employed only six people. Haysbert put in his personal savings of $100,000, took out a second mortgage on his house, and borrowed $22,000 on his Visa, MasterCard, and American Express credit cards.

Although the investors together had a large amount of funds, they did not have enough to meet the asking price of $4.6 million. At that point they approached the Baltimore City Council and its subsidiary board of finance and requested assistance.

Specifically, the nine investors asked that $2.5 million of low-interest, industrial development bonds be issued to help them finance the purchase. Such bonds were a popular but controversial device for local or state government or both to subsidize the building of such projects as stadiums, industrial parks, docks, and factories. A state, county, or city issued bonds either for itself or on behalf of selected private projects.

These securities were for the purpose of economic development of local areas and the creation of the accompanying jobs.

Issuance of such bonds specifically to benefit private enterprises was authorized in the 1960s. Their usefulness depended on the fundamental point that the federal income tax does not apply to securities issued by state and local governments as part of the traditional division of powers between the national government and the state governments. These bonds were attractive to individual buyers because the interest the bonds paid was exempt from federal income tax. The bonds were economical to the issuer because they carried an interest rate that was below prevailing market rates for other loans. Most tax experts and many business executives, politicians, and consumer activists contended that this device was undesirable and had been abused and that all private enterprise should utilize the usual money markets for funds.

After a lengthy debate on the desirability and propriety of issuing such bonds for the benefit of the nine investors at Parks, Inc., the City Council voted thirteen to two to do so. A major issue was the criticism that H. G. Parks, Sr., would be back in a position of considerable economic power at Parks, Inc., using local government financial aid after he had sold that same company at a substantial gain and kept that gain. All this was, of course, legal. Victorine Q. Adams, wife of William L. Adams, was a member of the City Council but abstained on this vote. Such bonds had already been voted earlier for several other companies by the City Council.

The city issued $2 million in bonds for Parks, Inc., at low interest rates and sold $600,000 worth to Commercial Credit Corporation and $1.4 million to Equitable Trust Company, at which time the $2 million was paid to Canellus on behalf of the nine investors. Now the company was theirs, but, of course, they were responsible for repayment of the bonds and the accompanying interest over a long time period.

Haysbert, the largest investor, was named president and chief executive officer of H. G. Parks, Inc., and his son was appointed the personnel manager. The manufacturing vice-president, G. T. Day, and the vice-president-comptroller, A. S. Choksi, were also major investors. Choksi was a naturalized American citizen originally from India. H. G. Parks, Sr., made a token investment in the company and was appointed chairperson of the Board of Directors and given a lifetime contract as a consultant to the company. Haysbert was a well-known community leader, articulate and witty, and president of HUB (Help United Baltimore), an organization of about 600 black business and professional people. He served on the board of directors of several corporations and numerous nonprofit organizations.

The Parks firm was well-known in its trade territory, partially because of its advertising. Just before the purchase by Norin, Parks, Inc., was spending $1 million per year on advertising, but Norin required this figure to be cut substantially. Parks, Inc., did not spend a greater share of its sales on advertising than was common in the industry, but its advertising tended to be noticed. The company popularized a statement, "More Parks sausage, Mom, please!" This statement was widely used in the company's advertisements, both print and electronic. This expression was usually accompanied by a photograph of a young child, usually a boy. Many different children of all races were used. The child was always cute and appealing and spoke the sentence enthusiastically. The sentence sought to integrate auditorily or visually or both the words "Parks" and "pork." On the front of the company's plant, a bold sign in red proclaimed, "The House of More Parks Sausages, Mom, Please!" Interestingly, for several years the company used the expression "More Parks sausage, Mom!" without the word "please." Parks, Inc., received thousands of letters from consumers saying the children in the advertisements were brats for not saying "please." When this word was added, the company received thousands of letters of approval from consumers. Moreover, the company made intensive use of the two following expressions: "Famous flavor found only in Parks. Famous flavor!"; and "Nothing pleases people like Parks." Both were sometimes sung to a simple tune in advertisements appearing in the electronic media. Both of these statements relied on a principle in communication design: emphasis on the sound of one letter, F or P in these instances, stated fairly rapidly and with an interesting meter. Most familiar English language sounds, if deliberately repeated several times with a small planned sequence of variations, are noticeable and memorable. The statements were more effective in electronic media than in print media. Often two of the three statements were used in the same advertising, separated by some space on the page or by a few seconds of time.

In addition, the Parks organization had recently begun to advertise its sausages as an excellent ingredient to add to the stuffing served with roast turkey. Such messages were directed toward the Thanksgiving and Christmas holiday periods. The use of sausage to give stuffing a different flavor was the resumption of an old American and British tradition but presented as a new idea in cooking.

The sausage industry was highly competitive. Competitors included all the large national meat-packing companies, such as Oscar Meyer, Hormel, Armour, Wilson, Swift, Jimmy Dean, and Bob Evans plus many regional operations, most notably Mash's, Briggs, Fischer's, Green Hill, Hillshire, Esskay, Gwaltney, and Smithfield. Formerly owned by LTV, Inc., a large Dallas-based conglomerate, Briggs had recently been sold to Mash's but was to operate with its own production and marketing. Mash's management planned for Briggs to provide in-house competition for Mash's existing products. Formerly a subsidiary of ITT (International Telephone and Telegraph), another conglomerate, Gwaltney had recently been sold to Smithfield Foods, Inc. Also, Esskay, a Baltimore independent that had been experiencing difficulties with labor and production costs and was losing money, was sold to Smithfield Foods. Like Briggs, Gwaltney was to operate with its own production and marketing, and Smithfield's management was planning to encourage competition between Gwaltney and the existing Smithfield business. On the other hand, Smithfield had planned to operate the Esskay facility in Baltimore as a physical distribution center with no production there. Under enormous pressure from militant labor unions and many community leaders, the company agreed to have some production in Baltimore. Processing of some cured pork products, including sliced bacon and ham, was thus moved to the Esskay facility. Smithfield's corporate headquarters was in the suburbs of Washington, D.C., but the plant bearing its name and the Gwaltney plant were about 185 miles south in Smithfield, Virginia. Founded in 1936, Smithfield was by far the largest meat company in the East with about $1 billion in annual sales. This aggressive organization also had recently bought Patrick Cudahy, Inc., a century-old firm in Wisconsin.

Another competitor entered the East Coast in 1986, but its products could not be offered for sale until 1987 because of lengthy curing of the meats. Fiorucci Foods, Inc. (U.S.A.), a wholly owned subsidiary of 100-year-old Salumificio Cesare Fiorucci, S.p.A. of Rome, built an ultramodern plant in the suburbs of Richmond, Virginia. One of the largest makers of cured meats in Europe, it was known for spicy and other strong-flavored products. If successful along the East Coast, Fiorucci Foods would seriously consider going national.

All these national companies and most of the regional companies had broader meat product lines than did H. G. Parks, Inc. However, Parks, Inc., had been adding some new meat products. Its line already included very spicy, spicy, and mild products. Port sausage, available in both rolled form and links, dominated the line, but there was also a pork scrapple and an all-beef sausage. The all-beef sausage was developed specifically to meet a need expressed by two important institutional customers, the Department of Corrections in both New York City and the District of Columbia. Moslem inmates could not eat the pork sausage that Parks, Inc., was already supplying these two organizations. Bacon and brown-and-serve sausage were added in 1982 and 1983. The latter product was not only convenient to the consumer but also had the majority of the fat removed. Another health-related step was to reduce slightly the salt content of the entire product line. In recent years, U.S. per capita consumption of pork and beef had declined slightly, mainly because of serious concern about cholesterol content and high calories. Corn dogs were added later. The prices of most Parks products were slightly above those of most of its competitors.

Besides new products, Parks, Inc., was pursuing food service contracts. This type of agreement called for the supplying of large quantities of food to lodging places, restaurant chains, and institutional accounts. The corporation already had contracts with the Eastern region of Pizza Huts, the Philadelphia public school system, some military installations through the U.S. Defense Department, the Northeastern New England part of the Howard Johnson hotel and restaurant chain, and, as noted, the correctional operations of New York City and the District of Columbia. Expansion opportunities with Howard Johnson had looked promising. However, Howard Johnson had just been divided and sold. A relatively unknown but highly successful company, Prime Motor Inns, based in Fairfield, New Jersey, was the new owner of the hotel operation, which had 500 locations, and 199 of the freestanding restaurants. Marriott Corporation was the new owner of the remaining 350 freestanding restaurants. Several years earlier, Parks, Inc., had had a sizeable contract to supply Marriott Corporation but had given it up after finding it could not earn a profit and still meet the prices which that company was willing to pay.

Parks, Inc., had given considerable attention to 8-A-type sales contracts, but was not heavily dependent on them. Such agreements derived from provisions in federal (and some state) laws that allocate a certain percentage of the government procurement budget or a certain sum of money to be used exclusively to buy goods and services from the minority-owned sector of the economy. This was often termed the "set-aside" rule. A minority-owned business might, of course, face stiff competition for such contracts from other minority-owned firms. The federal government was planning to modify its policy so that larger minority-owned companies would enjoy such benefits for a limited time period only. The political process of making such a change, if at all, would require several years. More important, a 1989 interpretation of the set-aside principle by the U.S. Supreme Court cast serious doubt on the legality of most set-aside policies and required elaborate tests consisting of statistical economic studies to substantiate such public procurement policies.

The output of the company was distributed through most of the Northeast from northern Virginia to Massachusetts. The 52,000 square foot plant and offices were in the Camden Industrial Park in Baltimore. The distribution area extended approximately 440 miles north, 175 miles west, and 80 miles south of Baltimore. Physical distribution centers were operated in West Haven, Connecticut; Somerset, New Jersey; New York City; and Philadelphia, as well as Baltimore. The company's brand sold at a satisfactory rate in the Baltimore metropolitan area, which had a population of about 2.5 million, but no better than many out-of-town competitors. This area provided about 4 percent of company sales. On the other hand, metropolitan New York City, with about 12 million population, accounted for 55 percent of company sales. Parks, Inc., entered Richmond, Virginia, in 1982 but did not succeed there.

There were about 240 employees, about 80 percent of whom were members of minorities. Of the total, 110 were production and maintenance workers. This category of employees was unionized and was paid relatively high wages and fringe benefits. The union had recently won a substantial increase in compensation, with the increments spread over a period of several years. For this reason, plus the fact that quite a few local manufacturing companies were slowly reducing their work forces, it appeared that there would be labor peace for several years.

Sales for 1980 were about $16 million, thus exceeding the 1977 level, but the company sustained a loss of $400,000. Sales for 1981 reached about $17 million, but the financial results were borderline, and the plant was operating at only 65 percent of production capacity. In 1983 the company made a net profit of almost $1 million. In 1984 sales reached $20 million, and the company was again profitable. Sales rose to $25.5 million in 1985, fell to $23 million in 1986, rose to $28.2 million in 1987, but fell to $21 million in 1989.

In 1987 Sara Lee Corporation, a Chicago-based diversified food manufacturer, one of whose products was Hillshire brand sausage, bought 45 percent of the Parks stock. Thereafter some of the Parks products were contracted out to a Sara Lee facility in Baltimore for production. The Parks factory concentrated on the items it could make most efficiently. Many industry observers believed that it was only a matter of time until Sara Lee or another very large organization would try to buy all of Parks.

The state and city had plans to construct a large sports facility on the land occupied by the Parks factory and adjacent businesses. Therefore, in 1989 Parks broke ground in Baltimore for a modern new factory of 114,000 square feet.

Although the firm was successful, there was considerable concern about future directions of Parks.

Advise H. G. Parks, Inc.

4

Consumer Behavior

NEIMAN MARCUS CO.

Neiman Marcus Co., one of the most famous retailers in the world, was reviewing its basic marketing strategy. It was perceived by the public to handle high-quality merchandise and to be unusually service conscious. However, Neiman Marcus Co. had experienced a sudden, unexpected change of ownership in recent years. With the rather difficult transition period over, a new long-run strategy was now possible, in fact probably necessary.

This company was established in 1907 in Dallas by Herbert Marcus, along with his sister and brother-in-law, Carrie Marcus Neiman and Al Neiman. Being only marginally active in the company when he and his wife divorced, Al Neiman gave up his fraction of the ownership. "Aunt Carrie," an extraordinarily talented buyer, became one of the legendary characters of American business history.

From its original and only location Neiman Marcus Co. grew to comprise twenty-three stores in nineteen cities. With company growth central to its focus, it now planned specifically to open branches in suburban Denver, downtown Minneapolis, suburban Cleveland, and Paramus, New Jersey (in that order) in the very near future; and generally, to open eight to ten additional stores by 1995. Exhibit 1 shows the branches, size,

EXHIBIT 1 Selected Data on Neiman Marcus

Neiman Marcus

	Revenues	Operating Earnings (Loss)
1989	$1,111,956,000	$57,754,000
1988	$ 926,196,000	$55,941,000

Stores

Locations	Year Operations Began	Gro Sto Sq. F
Dallas (Downtown)	1907	311,
Dallas (NorthPark)	1965	218,
Houston (Galleria)	1969	200,
Bal Harbour, Florida	1971	97,
Atlanta	1972	148,
St. Louis	1974	131,
Northbrook, Illinois	1976	145,
Fort Worth	1977	124,
Washington, D.C.	1977	132,
Newport Beach, California	1978	135,
Beverly Hills, California	1979	179,
Dallas (Prestonwood)	1979	128,

Locations	Year Operations Began	Gross Store Sq F
Westchester, New York	1980	136,
Las Vegas	1981	99,
Oakbrook, Illinois	1981	112,
San Diego	1981	106,
Fort Lauderdale	1982	81,
San Francisco	1982	178,
Houston (Town & Country)	1983	150,
Chicago (Michigan Avenue)	1983	187,
Boston	1984	109,
Palo Alto, California	1985	120,
Total		3,230,

BERGDORF GOODMAN

1989	$170,993,000	$23,206,000
1988	$148,336,000	$17,862,000

Locations	Year Operations Began	Gross Store Sq F
New York City	1901	250,

and year when each of these operations would begin. Moreover, Neiman Marcus Co. was engaged in an aggressive national program of refurbishing and upgrading selling space. Over the three latest years more than one-third of the square footage of its stores had been so treated. Much of the remaining two-thirds would be refurbished and upgraded in the future, but neither had details been decided nor schedules set. In recent months the refurbishing activities had been expedited in many branches.

Although some members of the family remained active company employees until the late 1980s, the Marcus family members sold Neiman Marcus Co. in 1969 to Carter Hawley Hale Stores, Inc. This Los Angeles-based retail conglomerate owned (1) Emporium Capwell department stores in northern California, (2) Broadway department stores in southern California, Arizona, New Mexico, Colorado, and Nevada, (3) Weinstock's department stores in northern California, Nevada, and Utah, (4) Thalhimer's department stores in Virginia, North Carolina, South Carolina, and Tennessee, (5) Bergdorf-Goodman department store in New York City, and (6) Contempo Casuals, a chain of 192 apparel shops located chiefly in the West and targeted to women aged seventeen to twenty-five. The reason given by the Neiman Marcus Co. owners for the sale was to have access to capital for the purpose of expanding their company, which at that time operated only two stores in Dallas and one in Houston. The company's reputation, assisted by its widely circulated Christmas catalog, extended far beyond Texas. The new owner immediately began expanding nationwide, opening at least one new store a year throughout the 1970s and one to three stores each year during the early 1980s.

However, Carter Hawley Hale found itself the target of a determined takeover attempt by The Limited, a Columbus-based major retail chain composed primarily of women's apparel shops. General Cinema served as the white knight in the rescue. That highly successful company operated nearly 1,400 movie theaters, was an independent bottler of Dr. Pepper, 7-Up, and Pepsi-Cola products in several regions of the country, and held an 18 percent stake in Cadbury Schweppes, the large British-based international maker of soft drinks and confectionery. As it restructured in 1987, Carter Hawley Hale swapped Neiman Marcus Co. and two other properties for the shares held by General Cinema. General Cinema set up Neiman Marcus Co. as a publicly traded company called Neiman Marcus Group, Inc., and listed it on the New York Stock Exchange, at the same time owning 59 percent of the new organization. The remaining 41 percent was bought by about 17,000 other investors. According to the terms of its agreement with Carter Hawley Hale, General Cinema could not buy additional shares piecemeal until January 1993. It could make an offer for the entire company, but if its offer were not accepted by 50 percent of the other shareholders, it could not buy any shares.

In the restructuring this new company was also given the famous one-location Bergdorf Goodman in New York City and Contempo Casuals. With perhaps the preeminent retail location in the world at Fifth Avenue and 58th Street, Bergdorf Goodman was one of the most elegant and expensive stores in the world. In the newly created company Bergdorf Goodman accounted initially for about 11 percent and Contempo for about 13 percent of the sales. Both Neiman's and Bergdorf's were quite profitable, but Contempo Casuals was unprofitable. Operations headquarters for the Neiman Marcus stores was left in Dallas; and for Contempo Casuals in Los Angeles. Operations headquarters for Bergdorf Goodman remained in New York, of course. Neiman Marcus stores employed about 10,000 people, of whom almost three-fourths were full-time. This full-time percentage at Neiman's was higher than the corresponding figure for department stores as an industry.

In earlier years Bergdorf Goodman operated a branch in a high-income area near White Plains, a suburb just north of New York City. This branch did not do well at all. Carter Hawley Hale let it be converted to a Neiman Marcus operation and it succeeded quickly. Looking back on this event, executives realized that while Neiman Marcus' special expertise lay with affluent suburbanites, Bergdorf seemed adept in understanding affluent New York City people. Although Neiman did well with high-income city people in Dallas and Houston, strong ties were established there before either of these two cities had become very large.

In late 1988 Neiman Marcus Group purchased Horchow Mail Order, Inc., a Dallas-based company handling expensive merchandise, for $119 million. Horchow had an annual volume of $115 million, principally in hard goods such as occasional furniture, dinnerware, and jewelry but also some apparel and linens. Its 100 skilled buyers and its mailing lists were major resources. Neiman Marcus Group operated Horchow's the first year at a loss but hoped that the Horchow and Neiman Marcus catalog operations could be mutually supportive in the long run. The two were run in an integrated manner. Neiman Marcus built a new distribution center at Las Colinas, near Dallas, to serve the catalog activities of Neiman Marcus and Horchow.

Carter Hawley Hale had pumped large amounts of money into expansion of Neiman Marcus but not a great amount into maintenance or improvement of existing branches. Public relations and publicity had also been downplayed. Carter's leadership was perceived in the industry as solid and dependable but unexciting and unimaginative. Observers universally agreed that Neiman Marcus had not lost its reputation for high quality goods and service. Still, its previous image as a leader, innovator, and trend setter had suffered considerably under Carter's ownership, and it was no longer the favorite of the news media. Trendy, glitzy Bloomingdale's had taken on many of the characteristics of Neiman's during that time period, to the great dismay of many Neiman Marcus executives and customers and some of the Marcus family members. It had been particularly galling in that Neiman Marcus from its very first day had been an expensive, glamorous, and service-minded store while Bloomingdale's had been a dull, budget-minded, middle-class to lower-middle-class store until it upgraded in the 1960s. Many other industry analysts noted that, as part of the large, complex Carter Hawley Hale organization, Neiman Marcus remained very nice but had lost most of its entrepreneurial vim and vigor and was a bureaucratic cog in the machine.

The opportunity to regain lost ground and even more was now here. It was particularly interesting to Neiman Marcus at this time that Federated Department Stores, Inc., the parent of Bloomingdale's, Burdine's, Sanger-Harris, Lazarus, Rich's, and many other retailing holdings, had gone bankrupt in the Campeau financial difficulties. This event imposed financial constraints on Bloomingdale's for quite some time to come, possibly a new owner, or even both, with all the uncertainties and reorganization that that implied for Bloomingdale's. In fact, Campeau searched unsuccessfully for a buyer for Bloomingdale's several months prior to the bankruptcy. Therefore, the long-run strategies of the Neiman Marcus stores, the dominant part of Neiman Marcus Group, were being rethought. The very wealthy board chairman of General Cinema was a highly conservative, even austere man who hated publicity. He was known chiefly as a highly generous philanthropist. Yet he had no plans to let his personality interfere with Neiman's tentative objective of cosmopolitan, glamorous leadership in the world of retailing. Neiman Marcus executives wanted their stores to be the ones that people always found most exciting and worth talking about.

Both Neiman Marcus and Bergdorf Goodman described themselves as large specialty stores rather than department stores. This was because they did not handle as many types of merchandise as a traditional department store and because some executives thought that the term implied more exclusivity (i.e., less mass appeal). Two things were wrong with this reasoning. First, almost all traditional department stores had cut back on variety and, second, the term "specialty store" was traditionally used by writers and government officials to describe an operation with a narrow merchandise offering, such as a jewelry, book, or shoe shop, regardless of its pricing policy or image. Both the general public and the customers clearly thought of Neiman Marcus and Bergdorf Goodman as department stores and referred to them by that term. Neiman Marcus also spoke of itself as a "network," not a "chain" of stores.

Besides being quite accomplished at advertising, Neiman Marcus had always handled other forms of promotion well. One of its extraordinary promotional occurrences was the 1984 film "The Store." This was a two-hour documentary made by a distinguished producer-director, Frederick Wiseman, for public television under a grant from the Corporation for

Public Broadcasting. As part of a fifteen part series on American institutions, Wiseman selected Neiman Marcus to represent retailing after making films on other major institutional types such as hospitals and high schools. It explored many aspects of Neiman Marcus operations. This film, presented again and again for educational purposes on public television, had considerable entertainment quality. As the film gently drew one's attention to the status climbing of some of the customers depicted, it put Neiman Marcus in a good light. After finishing the film Wiseman remarked that he had chosen that company because it did its work so well.

Some additional non-advertising promotion will be helpful in comprehending Neiman Marcus. In one example of Neiman's creativity, most of the members of the Dallas Symphony Orchestra were brought in to serenade customers having tea. However, Neiman's was best known in the industry for originating the so-called "Fortnightly" in the 1950s. This was an integrated celebration: a selected country, with emphasis, of course, on regular merchandise from that country and other goods brought in from that country for the event, plus entertainment and decorations derived from that country's heritage, artists and artisans, and various media events. For example, the downtown Dallas store once had the British ambassador to the United States wait on customers for a time period during British Fortnightly. Later the Fortnightly evolved into a longer period, usually a month. Neiman's was flattered but chagrined when Bloomingdale's also adopted the ethnic or geographical showcase concept.

Several noteworthy examples from the catalog will also be helpful. His-and-hers submarines once received great amounts of free publicity, as did his-and-hers airplanes, elephants, and ostriches. Another merchandising success receiving worldwide coverage was his-and-hers kittens of a new breed, entitled California Spangled, developed just for Neiman Marcus. This required selected breeding through eleven generations to produce a type unlike the thirty recognized feline breeds. Spots are rare in the domesticated cat. This type had spots duplicating the shape of those of leopards in nature, rather than the perfect polka dot spots of the Mau or the crescent-shaped spots of the Ocicat, two existing breeds. Moreover, the California Spangled was offered in one's choice of colors: silver, bronze, gold, red, blue, black, or charcoal. The price was $2,800 per pair. According to Neiman Marcus: "All the genetic magic that produces the lush spotted coats of the world's big cats has been duplicated for the small, perfect bodies of these leopards for your living room." The new breed did not yet have the endorsement of the Cat Fanciers Association, the final authority in the cat world, but this fact did not bother the retailer.

Although Neiman Marcus had a tradition of splashy and sometimes grandiose sales promotion, it also had a tradition in its five Texas stores of quiet, personalized service and warm relationships with customers that often lasted four or five decades. One Neiman practice remembered fondly by several thousand elderly women in the Southwest was the store's careful allocation of extremely scarce nylon stockings to its loyal customers by name during the time of World War II and the years following it. Also noteworthy, the company was willing to open a Texas store after normal hours for wealthy customers who were time-pressed or needed privacy. This resulted in millions of extra dollars in sales and much good will, often with people in powerful, influential positions. Most sales personnel in those four stores were so closely in tune with their customers that they could telephone important people at home on unlisted numbers, describe something new that was just right for the customer, and make a sale of thousands of dollars without the customer having seen the merchandise. The trust of the customers in the four old-line stores was without equal among large retailers. The old-line salespeople were also respected for their willingness to advise customers against very expensive apparel that looked bad on them. This sort of sales behavior was becoming quite rare in the United States.

Stanley Marcus, son of one of the founders and chairman of the company from 1950 to 1977, cautioned in the mid-1970s and several times in the 1980s that bigness for Neiman Marcus could well be damaging to everything for which it had stood. He stated that there was an inverse relationship between a company's quality standards and the number of branches it maintains. Marcus was also critical of widely held ownership, saying that it produces a lack of both the understanding of consumer behavior and the motivation to provide quality and service. Stanley Marcus was an articulate, popular speaker and consultant who was widely respected and influential in U.S. business.

Advise the Neiman Marcus stores.

GARZA'S BOWLING CENTERS

Marian and Henry Garza, owner-managers of Garza's Bowling Centers, were concerned about the image of bowling per se, the image of bowling in their community, and the image of their company. They were also specifically concerned about the mix of people that came to their two places of business, which they had bought four years earlier. The Garzas had been making a modest profit that allowed them a good standard of living, but they wanted to improve earnings and raise the value of their investment.

The Garzas immediately moved to their community after purchasing the business. They had been reared in this Southwestern U.S. state and lived in three of its cities but never in this community. Both had had experience as managers but not in the bowling industry. The Garzas were gregarious and liked people. Besides bowling, they enjoyed softball, baseball, volleyball, boxing, and wrestling.

Bowling

The recreation known as bowling apparently evolved from the game of skittles, which was based on the older game of bowls. These older activities were brought to the United States by the English and Dutch settlers in the seventeenth century. Because both were played outdoors several of the colonial settlements along the U.S. east coast contained bowling greens in parks from their earliest days. There was a small amount of evidence that the ancient Egyptians played a form of the game and may have originated it.

Clearly bowling was one of the two largest participation sports in the world. The global data were imprecise, but it was estimated that slightly over 100 million persons in 80 countries played the game as of the early 1990s. Only soccer was of comparable size and geographical dispersion. Just as with soccer, the number of participants was not proportionally spread. Sixty-seven million, two-thirds of the world's bowlers, were in the United States as of the early 1990s. This figure, constituting about 26 percent of the population, included all Americans who bowled at least once a year. Although the national data were imprecise, it appeared that approximately half of these 67 million bowled frequently but not necessarily in leagues. Included in the half were the approximately 17 million who were enrolled in leagues. Participation dropped nationally in the late 1970s and through the mid-1980s as people became quite concerned with health-related activities such as aerobics, cycling, jogging, running, and swimming. A modest national growth trend in casual, non-league bowling began in 1986, but the industry was worried about the strength of the trend, its length, and how widespread it was in its demographics.

The clothing worn by many bowlers began to change on the national scene in the late 1980s. Newcomers to the game tended to perceive the traditional bowling shoes as unacceptably ugly. To build on this viewpoint and encourage it several shoe manufacturers brought out functional styles resembling jogging sneakers and soft-soled boat shoes. Curiously enough, how a person looked from the rear seemed to be more important in bowling than in most other types of recreation. Many newcomers rejected as low class the traditional shirts with company sponsor logos on the back furnished to league players. Good quality casual shirts, blouses, pants, and skirts became the thing to wear to bowl. Bowling bags became available that looked like airline carry-on luggage. Nike spent an undisclosed but significant amount advertising that one should look nice while bowling and, of course, use that company's products. Referring to him as the "Roll Model" in their advertising, Nike hired the well-known professional bowler Marshall Holman to demonstrate and promote its goods. What all of these trends amounted to was that in a crowd one could not easily identify a person who was on the way to the bowling center. The same things were happening in the Garza's community but with a considerable lag behind the nation at large.

Besides having active detractors, the game was clearly associated in the public mind with blue-collar, beer-guzzling, pot-belly types and brash personalities. The character Fred Flintstone was indelibly linked in the public mind with bowling and many people drew on that character to describe others who enjoyed bowling. "The Honeymooners" characters Ralph Kramden and Ed Norton had also been part of the image for many years. In addition, some theorists believed that the basic format of bowling was primarily for the release of anger and aggression in the participants. For example, the bowler might pretend that the head pin was a boss.

Many enthusiasts for bowling had pressed the Olympic Games authorities to include bowling, because they enjoyed this recreation and they wanted the recognition for themselves and the activity. Much of the leadership and funding in this drive came from Brunswick Corporation, of Skokie, Illinois, a major manufacturer of bowling equipment, other leisure products, and defense and aerospace products. Opponents emphasized the prevalence of smoking and drinking by bowlers and that such behavior ran counter to athletic values and ideals. They pointed not only to the image of bowling per se but to the fact that average or even below-average bowlers could sometimes bowl a perfect 300 game. Opponents asserted that this could not happen in the other Olympic activities. Bowling was depicted as a recreation, not a sport. Proponents argued that opponents were being elitist and that critics were confusing health-related fitness with performance-related fitness. Proponents also noted that extremely serious bowlers regularly use a weight-lifting program. After lengthy dialogue, bowling was made an exhibition sport in the 1988 Olympics in Seoul, South Korea. However, this status was temporary and was well below the status of demonstration. Bowling participants could not march in the ceremonies or live in Olympic housing. The 1992 Olympics in Spain did not schedule bowling even as an exhibition.

Garza's Operations

The two centers belonging to the Garzas were on opposite sides of town in a metropolitan area of about 150,000 population. One was about one and a fourth miles east of downtown and the other about two and a fourth miles west of downtown. Both were in free standing buildings in respectable, safe commercial neighborhoods. About thirteen years old, the structures were built by the previous owner, Harry Webb, who retired at the time of sale. He called them Harry's Bowling Alleys. Both Webb and the present owners had maintained the buildings well. They were structurally sound and clean.

Each center had a small, well-lighted parking lot. There was also some well-lighted curbside parking. The number of curbside spaces legally useable increased greatly after 6:30 P.M. when certain parking regulations were no longer in force. Automobile ownership in the community was extraordinarily high. Although both centers were located on bus routes, virtually all customers came in their automobiles.

The Garzas really wanted to understand bowling in the overall context of consumer behavior. Like many others in the industry, the Garzas preferred to change and upgrade the general image of bowling, which they had personally enjoyed since childhood. They often felt both professionally and personally embarrassed by things people said and implied about bowling. Of course, they were vitally interested also from an economic point of view, because they believed that their centers could not be disassociated from the image of the game. As soon as they bought the business they started calling it Garza's Bowling Centers, because the majority of the people working in the industry believed that the term "alley" was apt to convey an undesirable idea. They started calling the ball "gutter" the ball "channel." Many of the regular customers ridiculed the word changes.

The new owners redecorated the interiors of the two buildings in a restrained, low-key style, installed carpeting, planted some ornamental evergreen shrubbery alongside the buildings, and repaved the parking lots. In the past few weeks they had done more minor refurbishing in order to keep the places neat and attractive. They kept the original wood floors of the lanes, although high-quality synthetics were available and would last longer than wood. It was widely believed in the industry that such synthetics tended to raise scores slightly. They provided balls, of course, but many customers brought their own.

Some bowling centers in other, larger cities were now installing a television monitor, attached to a computer, above each lane. Customers could watch television as they bowled or use the set to post their scores. Secretaries of bowling leagues under such an arrangement do not have to calculate averages and standings, because the computer does it for them and prints out the results for the next league session. Bowling center management can make announcements on the monitors or offer congratulations for high scores or special events such as birthdays. Marian and Henry Garza did not think well of such equipment and considered it extremely costly and subject to breakdown. They had no plans to buy it. In addition, they had heard an enthusiastic bowler in another community say the following after a computer and monitors had been installed: "I miss scoring. I was the team captain and the scorekeeper, and for a long time I felt a real void." They had heard similar statements from several other people.

There was only one competitor in town, Royal Bowling Center, located on the near north side about one and a half miles from downtown. Owned by James Fondren for many years, it was well established and appeared to be doing all right. The Garzas and Fondren occasionally saw each other at civic affairs and Chamber of Commerce meetings but barely knew each other. No bowling center chains had ever operated in this community.

Marian and Henry Garza kept in close touch with everything about their organization. They noticed from the beginning that there was a difference in the composition of customers, or "customer mix" as they termed it, between the two locations. The east-side center tended to draw a noisier crowd, predominantly male and apparently working class, whereas the west-side branch tended to draw middle-class people. Later, as they got to know people and also observed and measured more closely, they concluded that in the east-side center about 75 percent of the customers were male, compared to about 55 percent in the other. The west side customers were apparently predominantly middle class. The owners realized, of course, that the west side population was predominantly middle class and the east side population predominantly working class, whereas the population on the north and south sides was rather mixed. Nearly all of the poor also lived on the east side. As in nearly all communities the middle-class population here had higher incomes on average than the working class. As far as the Garzas knew there had never been any violence in the buildings or parking lots since they had bought the business. The owners had recently read a published report on U.S. recreation habits from a highly respected marketing research firm that concluded, among other things, that telecasts of bowling drew relatively small audiences and that the people in those audiences tended to have below-average income and education and be above average in age. They realized that these data were about television, not active participation in bowling, but they were disturbed anyway.

The Garzas' two establishments had similar capacity, but the organization had always done a little more sales volume in the east-side establishment. About 60 percent of volume in the eastern branch came through league play, compared to about 35 percent in the western branch. Both figures were stable, not showing any trend for about three years. Both centers had rather light traffic during the day except on Saturdays, although prices were about 25 percent lower during the day Monday through Friday.

The prices charged for a game were the same in the two locations and duplicated those of the competitor. Game prices had gone up through the years approximately in line with inflation.

Prices in the two Garza establishments for identical refreshments were the same, but a few months earlier the owners had changed the list of foods and beverages available in the west-side branch. Quiches, deluxe hamburgers and hotdogs, espresso, Perrier water, and fruit juices were introduced in the west-side branch and these were instant successes. A license to serve alcoholic beverages was impossible in this community. The general reputation of food in U.S. bowling centers was poor. The Garzas did not allow smoking in the food area or in the active playing area. It was permitted in a lobby-type area behind the lanes.

Advise Garza's Bowling Centers.

LE DRUGSTORE

The idea of the now well-known business Le Drugstore was unconventional at the time of its founding, 1958, and remains so today. The corporate, legally proper name was Publicis, S.A., and this name appeared on some objects in the store, such as the napkins and ashtrays. But the usual operating name and the one by which customers knew the firm was Le Drugstore. It was owned by the second largest advertising agency in France.

On a business trip to New York in the mid-1950s, Paris advertising executive Marcel Bleustein-Blanchet caught a head cold during a spell of unpleasant weather. To complicate matters, he ran out of tissues at two in the morning. Bleustein-Blanchet knew that one could not buy tissues in Paris at that hour at any price and assumed that New York City would be the same. Nevertheless, he looked. To his delight he found that not just one but many New York City drug stores were open, and he bought the tissues he needed.

This little episode caused Bleustein-Blanchet a great deal of thought on his trip home and afterward. What would happen if someone were hungry and wanted a meal in Paris at that time of the night? French eating places and shops were notoriously rigid in their hours of operation and they stayed open relatively few hours. Yet, very probably most French consumers had never recognized this characteristic, for they had grown up with it and expected nothing different. Bleustein-Blanchet began to seriously consider setting up a business in Paris where one could buy a meal and tissues for one's cold and a great many other items, even late at night.

No equivalent of the American drugstore existed in the French economy and society, regardless of the question of operating hours. Bleustein-Blanchet's investment needed a name to describe this type of business, but nothing in the French language appeared to be suitable. Thus he selected the English-language word *drugstore* and Gallicized it to "le drugstore."

Location was judged to be a critical factor. Bleustein-Blanchet bought the old Astoria Hotel, an elegant building on the celebrated Avenue des Champs Elysées near the Arc de Triomphe, and placed Le Drugstore there. It was a choice that was bound to capture people's attention. If they did not see it, at least they would probably hear about it. Moreover, this location was on one of the most beautiful and famous streets in the world and was reasonably convénient for a large number of persons. This site was near many other shops, several specialized museums, embassies, office buildings, and some apartment houses, but it was well to the northwest of the real center of downtown. In fact, it was considered to be at the edge of downtown. However, it was fairly close to the Bois de Boulogne, a large beautiful park, and several high-income, close-in residential neighborhoods composed mainly of townhouses and apartment houses. Le Drugstore was not the sort of place one would probably go downtown specifically to visit, unlike the major department stores or fashionable boutiques, and other specialty shops in the center of the city. Yet, perhaps in time it would come to attract passersby on the Champs Elysées and people who lived nearby. Le Drugstore opened its doors in 1958.

The store offered not only time convenience to those who lived or worked nearby but merchandise-mix convenience and innovation as well. Le Drugstore was set up to include several departments, which many persons connected with the firm preferred to call shops or boutiques. It included a soda fountain, which was both an American-style soda shop and American-style medium-priced restaurant; a pharmacy; a department for sundries; a tobacco shop; perfume boutique; record shop; toy shop; luggage shop; and a clothing shop. To top off the variety, the founder included two small movie theaters in Le Drugstore. Copper fixtures from an old luxury cruise ship were used to carry out a nautical decorative theme. Publicis, S.A. spent more than U.S. $1 million in readying the old hotel structure for this highly unconventional package of goods and services.

Besides many French dishes, Le Drugstore served an American-style breakfast and, of course, American snack foods such as hamburgers. Eggs and toast were available for the tourist, visiting business person, or French consumer satiated with croissants. Even the unthinkable catsup was available for the hamburger. What is more, breakfast was available from 8:30 A.M. until 2 A.M., and dinner service began at 5 P.M. Both schedules were unique in France and perceived as barbarian by virtually all French people. The typical French breakfast was a hot beverage plus croissants or rolls with butter and sometimes jam or jelly. The French dinner time was normally no earlier than 7:30 P.M. and more commonly about 8:30 P.M.

Commercial success came quickly to Le Drugstore. It was considered chic for some time, but instead of dying as a fad usually does, it was accepted by enough people to make it a viable business.

Nevertheless, most Francophiles, especially of the American variety, were noisily critical of Le Drugstore, calling it a gross, ugly intrusion of the American culture into the French culture. Countless French also were angered by this new institution. The many French language purists were outraged. Concern about the name *Le Drugstore* was greater than concern about the breaks with tradition in products, product mix, and hours of operation. Some Parisian merchants and restaurateurs resented the competition and the unusual and aggressive style in which it was offered.

Most native English-speakers found it difficult to comprehend the anger of the French-language purists, especially when linguistic experts estimated that only about 40 percent of contemporary English word stock came from Old English. In fact, most English language experts maintained that the migration of words from one living language to another was a natural process. Many added that it made a language more fun and more interesting.

After a short while it was realized that the underlying cause was apparently a large, long build-up of concern and resentment about word transplants from many other languages, most notably English, and about a century of decline in the international use of French as the world language of diplomacy and business. English had pushed ahead of French on a global basis, but French had a strong command of second place. Moreover, English was the most popular choice of foreign languages among students in French schools.

Most cultures of the world have no organization that attempts to govern the language, monitor its use in publications, rule on the appropriateness of words, or prepare the official dictionary, but both France and Spain do. In France it is called the French Academy. However, a much more militant group, called the Office of the French Vocabulary, had organized in 1957 with about 3,500 distinguished members. This new organization noted disdainfully that it had taken the French Academy twenty-four years to critically review the words beginning with the letters *A* through *C* in the latest round of work. The Office of the French Vocabulary launched a major crusade to purge the French language of expressions such as weekend, businessman, parking, hardware, software, and drugstore. Some broad-minded French noted that the language was derived from Latin and had a strong component of Greek and a noteworthy amount of German. General Charles de Gaulle was elected president of France in 1958 on the general theme of returning France to *gloire* (glory). He instituted many changes and actively led an increasing hostility to the United States and Britain and rejection of their cultures. Nevertheless, Publicis, S.A. persevered in its operations, weathered the public relations storm, and kept its trade name as well as its mode of operating.

In 1965 Le Drugstore was bold enough to add a branch two miles southeast of the original. Bleustein-Blanchet bought the Royal Café at

the corner of Boulevard Saint Germain and Rue de Rennes, one of the busiest intersections on the Left Bank. This was at the heart of the literary district of the city, St. Germain des Pres, in the neighborhood so loved by many English-language writers and at the edge of the university district. Le Drugstore number two was given approximately the same mix of departments as the parent location, except that a car rental service was installed and a large book department was placed in the basement. The cinema seated 300 and the soda fountain 200. This new branch became quite popular rather quickly. Also in that year, 1965, President Charles De Gaulle was re-elected, principally on a platform of hostility to almost everything Anglo-American and a revival of French glory.

The language debate never completely ceased, but it diminished somewhat through the late 1960s. However, in 1970 President Georges Pompidou appointed fifteen committees to identify popular foreign words and think of possible French-language replacements. In 1973 he denounced the influence of Anglo-Americanism. Pompidou appointed three large committees of prominent people to again investigate the problem and prescribe how to rid the language of foreign influences. The president and many French scholars and intellectuals took the position that their language was the foundation of their civilization and that their civilization was the highest ever achieved on earth. Some 350 foreign terms, mostly from the English language, were immediately and officially banned from use in the conduct of French government affairs, even without waiting for the predictable reports from the committees. The motivation was not just long years of anger and frustration but the increased threat of more English-language incursions because of the entry in 1973 of Britain and Ireland into the European Economic Community, which France, one of the EEC founders, had previously opposed.

Publicis, S.A. was ready for expansion again by 1970. The management selected a busy location slightly over one mile east of the first location and closer to the heart of downtown than the original location. This branch number three was on Avenue Matignon at Le Rond Point, a major circle formed by the Avenue des Champs Elysées, Avenue Franklin Roosevelt, Avenue Matignon, and other streets. It was one and six-tenths miles northwest of branch number two. This third branch also included a sidewalk café, a cinema with 350 seats, and a restaurant with 312 seats. The decor emphasized wood, marble, stainless steel, and leather. Within a short time this new branch was successful. Moreover, Publicis, S.A. negotiated a part ownership in Pub Renault, a semi-British-style operation on the Champs Elysées about midway between Le Drugstore branches numbers one and three.

A disastrous fire destroyed the original Le Drugstore in 1972. Over 1100 customers and employees were evacuated successfully in just over six minutes. Many regular customers expressed great disappointment and emotional support for the company. The management rebuilt but this time stressed a modernistic design and used a decorating scheme of "railway car chic." The new store included all the old features. The restaurant was enlarged to seat 300 and the two cinemas enlarged to seat 500 and 280. A bar and a terrace facing the Champs Elysées were added to the sidewalk café. The re-opened Le Drugstore number one was an instant success.

In 1981 Le Drugstore finally reached the very busy heart of the downtown area. The company opened branch number four at 6 Boulevard des Capucines extremely close to the Paris opera house about one and a fourth miles east of the Avenue Matignon branch. Departmentation was similar to branches one and three.

Le Drugstore number one had a sales volume of about U.S. $16 million in the most recent fiscal year, and the three other locations had combined sales of about U.S. $23 million. Employment at the four totaled about 750. Approximately one million Parisians lived within one and a half miles of one of the four Le Drugstore locations.

As in several nations of the world, the capital city of France is the undisputed leader in more than government. Paris dominates France in the fine arts, performing arts, communications, finance, manufacturing, and distribution. It is the hub of transportation for the country. As of the latest census, there were 2,317,227 persons within the city limits of Paris. The suburbs contained another 6,232,671 persons, for a metropolitan area total of 8,549,898. Population density in the city was very high, and population density in the suburban areas was higher than in the United States. The population of France was 52,599,430. Neither the Paris metropolitan area nor the nation was showing any significant population growth.

Advise Le Drugstore.

ROMANO OLIVE OIL, INC.

Founded in the early 1900s in Baltimore, Romano had been importing only the finest quality olive oil from the Mediterranean countries for more than seven decades. Much of the olive oil came directly from groves and processing plants of the parent organization, a growers' cooperative in Spain. Under the policies of the parent organization, the rest of the olive oil had to be purchased through the cooperative. The Spanish cooperative utilized Romano as its marketing organization in the United States. Although the parent wanted to sell as much gallonage as possible through Romano, the American subsidiary's management, almost all U.S. citizens, strongly preferred a healthier "bottom line" (net profit) than what they were achieving. These two goals were somewhat in con-

The Romano case was prepared by Helena Poist.

flict, apparently because of the price the parent company was charging the American subsidiary for the olive oil. This price was above that that could be obtained on the open, free market. Romano accounted for about 10 percent of all olive oil imports into the United States. Since almost all olive oil consumed in the United States was imported, Romano also accounted for about 10 percent of U.S. olive oil sales and was by far the largest marketer of the product.

Olive Oil

In its wild state the olive plant is a low, thorny bush, but in its domesticated form it is a tree that can reach thirty feet in height. Native to the Middle East, the olive plant prefers a semidry, mild climate. Because of the fruit and the rich oil obtained from the fruit, the olive became a staple of the diet in the Middle East and spread to all the countries of the Mediterranean Basin in the early years of civilization. Later the olive was brought to California and a few areas of Latin America. Olives and, to a great extent, olive oil became very important exports of Italy, Greece, Spain, and Portugal. California olives were generally sold as canned fruit and were seldom made into oil.

Olive oil was versatile and had been used in various cultures and eras for a variety of purposes besides food preparation. For example, ancient Greeks used olive oil as a body liniment, muscle toner, and relaxant, and for medicinal purposes. The Egyptians mixed it with special herbs and spices to make a perfumed body ointment and cosmetic base. In biblical times olive oil was used in lamps and for religious rituals and blessings. In such times it was used even as a weapon, such as in pouring boiling oil over a fortress wall.

In modern times, however, the primary use of olive oil has been in food preparation. Olive oil has a unique flavor, and it was generally agreed that it surpassed the various vegetable oils in quality. Of particular value was virgin olive oil, which came from the first extraction of the olives. Such a product involved a "cold press" process, which meant that no hot water or chemical solvents were added to obtain the oil.

Romano's Operations

The oil arrived in drums and tanks in Baltimore harbor, where it was inspected for quality by United States Customs, the Food and Drug Administration, and company technicians. At the Romano plant, also in Baltimore, there was continuous quality control by the company laboratory until the product was shipped out to customers. The oil was stored in thirty-two large, 30,000-gallon, glass-lined, temperature-controlled tanks. The bottling and canning facilities of the plant could process all of the company's retail sizes, that is, two ounces, eight ounces, sixteen ounces, and thirty-two ounces (one quart), as well as the bulk-size institutional and industrial containers. Romano wanted retail distribution of the gallon-size containers but had not been able to convince retailers.

Romano produced a line of olive oil products to suit the various consumer needs. This line consisted of the following: Romano 100 percent Virgin Olive Oil, Romanza 100 percent Olive Oil, Laco Pure Olive Oil, and Avallo 10 and 20 percent Blended Oil. Romanza combined the special flavors of select olive oils and was slightly lower in price than virgin olive oil. Laco had the taste of pure olive oil but was much inferior in quality to virgin and used primarily for the institutional trade. Avallo was a special blend of the less expensive soya cooking oil with a mild taste of pure oil in 10 percent and 20 percent quantities. The Romano brand was the primary line in retail sizes, whereas the other brands were sold primarily to food service establishments in the gallon and larger sizes only.

The Spanish parent company sold only the finest grades of olive oil, even though olive oil came in many different grades. At the same time, the average consumer was unable to distinguish among these different grades. Similarly, the prices of the higher grades of olive oil were far above those of the lower grades. Therefore, it was difficult for Romano, Inc., to market a superior product while its competitors marketed an inferior product.

Currently Romano had national distribution, but not in all major supermarket chains and not in all container sizes. The leading seller was the eight-ounce package followed by the sixteen-ounce and the quart container. Romano had no retail distribution of the gallon size. The main product competition consisted of other imported olive oils, oils that were blended (olive oil and soybean), and the domestic vegetable oils such as Wesson and Mazola. These competitors tended to sell oil in quart and gallon size containers.

Romano had a network of nineteen warehouses throughout the country from which the company served customers in all fifty states. One hundred food brokers represented Romano in their respective marketing areas. Four regional managers and a national sales manager worked closely with these people and the headquarters marketing team to provide the best quality and service possible for all retail and wholesale customers.

Major firms importing olive oil obtained their supplies in several different ways. These included the following:

1. Importing prepackaged oil bearing the exporter's name.
2. Importing prepackaged oil bearing the brand name designed and controlled by the importer.
3. Importing in 128-ounce (one gallon) cans and repacking into retail containers bearing the importer's brand.
4. Importing bulk oil and repacking into retail containers bearing the importer's brand.

Because of the ease of entering the industry, there were a great many regional competitors. They were entrenched in local markets and usually enjoyed lower retail prices than firms that sold nationally. These lower prices were mainly the result of higher freight costs incurred by national competitors to reship the goods. More than 100 different olive oil brands were marketed in the metropolitan New York City market. Romano chose to import in bulk in order to ensure quality and to control shipments to customers. Although this method of importing was the cheapest, freight differentials resulted in the local and regional competitors having lower prices regardless of the form in which they imported the olive oil.

Because it was both pure and imported, Romano brand olive oil had the disadvantage in the market place of selling at a premium price. As indicated previously, Romano competed with several vegetable oils, such as Wesson, which came from much larger companies who had large advertising budgets behind them. Besides being lower in price, such oils made claims of other advantages that might or might not be deterrents to Romano. The first consisted of health-related selling points, that is, polyunsaturated fats and low cholesterol. The second was taste appeal, that is, low flavor level.

As to health-related selling points, the consumer was presented with data on fat, cholesterol, and saturated and polyunsaturated fat. The corn oil companies heavily advertised and publicized these data in selling the benefits of corn oil. Whereas the cholesterol content of both corn oil and olive oil was zero, olive oil had a higher percentage of the nonsaturated and saturated fats than did corn oil. Corn oil had the advantage of being higher in the polyunsaturated fats. In restricted diets and diets designed to regulate cholesterol, physicians tended to recommend a restriction of the saturated and nonsaturated fats and an increase of the polyunsaturated fats. How much of a factor this had been in terms of influencing the sale of olive oil was not known, but it had to be faced as a possible deterrent to sales. Perhaps because of the heavy use and sales appeal of corn oil and other vegetable oils, many consumers had not acquired a taste for olive oil. In fact, the younger generation had grown up in an era of news, publicity, and advertising of corn oil. It might be possible, however, to counteract this negative factor.

Total olive oil industry sales in the United States had been declining for several years. Two of the reasons were the ethnic connotation of the product and the high and increasing prices of olive oil to the consumer. As Romano's management saw it, the real challenge, in terms of growth, was to expose the nonethnic consumer to the benefits of olive oil.

Romano's strategy of exposing the nonethnic consumer was in line with its current consumer profile. Although its consumers could not be precisely defined in terms of demographics, the majority of them were ethnic. The nonethnic users were primarily (1) women in their early twenties who were inexperienced cooks and followed recipes to the letter and (2) middle-aged women who were gourmet cooks. Most of Romano's sales were in the smaller containers, whereas many competitors sold primarily the gallon sizes. This led the company to believe that a good many of its consumers were nonethnic users, and that this would ensure Romano an edge in this market if the benefits of olive oil were known by the public.

Olive oil was primarily a commodity, as many people viewed it. Many ethnic consumers bought whatever olive oil was lowest in price, regardless of quality. Also, because of the high price of olive oil, some of these consumers were also moving toward the olive oil and soybean blends. On the other hand, nonethnic consumers tended to buy only the best olive oil and shop for a brand. A company objective was for consumers to buy Romano olive oil and to pay the premium price for it.

Olive oil was almost exclusively a consumer product. Specific data on the end use were currently unavailable. However, trade estimates suggested that upwards of 85 percent of all olive oil was sold at retail for home consumption. Commercial and institutional users accounted for the remaining 15 percent or less. Trade sources indicated that commercial users consisted only of high-priced hotels and restaurants specializing in European cuisine, which bought olive oil for the sake of authenticity. However, because the price of olive oil was higher than substitute oils, the current use of olive oil was minimal. Generally, olive oil was not used by other sectors of the hotel and restaurant trade. The manufacturing sector did not use olive oil to any appreciable extent because substitute oils were just as good and cost less. The exceptions were small manufacturers of European-style cuisine and gourmet foods. However, the quantity of olive oil used by such firms was insignificant.

Importers believed that the relatively high price of olive oil was the prime reason that consumption was not greater. In their view, this was an almost insoluble problem. The relative price of olive oil was slowly dropping, but the likelihood of the price of olive oil approaching the price of other oils was remote. The price of olive oil was expected to remain at least an order of magnitude greater than that of the vegetable oils. In 1971, the price of olive oil was twice the average price of similar oils, but by 1975 it was three times the price of other oils. The price of olive oil reached a peak of 3.35 times the average of other oils in 1976. After that time the relative price of olive oil declined to about 3.0 and leveled off.

Olive oil was not heavily or widely promoted. The limited promotional monies and activities were aimed at ethnic markets. This was especially true in areas with large numbers of Italians and Puerto Ricans, such as San Francisco, New York City, Miami, Houston, and several New England cities. Actual national expenditures for advertising and sales promotion of olive oil were not available. However, estimates indicated that these figures were insignificant compared to the promotional and advertising expenditures on cooking and salad oils in general.

All importers of olive oil sponsored trade promotions. Various forms were used, but the most common was the conventional "off-invoice." This meant that the retailer received the promotional money off the regular price. In return for $1 or possibly $2 per case (on a $40 per case value), the retailer provided some or all of the following: in-store displays; reduced retail price; and mention in the retailer's local flier (handbill).

Most of the olive oil industry trade promotions were staged with small retailers in ethnic areas. The major retail chains avoided these trade promotions because the per-case cost was prohibitive. Such a chain's initial outlay was high, but the anticipated sales volume was relatively modest compared to the high turnover items competing for the large retailer's attention. Olive oil trade deals seldom warranted even advertising space in the local newspapers because of the low volume and other items competing for the valuable space.

Research Studies

In order to better understand the consumer, Romano conducted a small but carefully done survey of 250 people in the Baltimore area. The majority of respondents had not used any olive oil within the past year. In rank order the main reasons given by the respondents were the following:

1. Cost too much
2. Never thought of it
3. Too greasy
4. Dislike Flavor
5. No reason
6. Not good for health

Those who used olive oil offered two main reasons for doing so. The first was that recipes called for it and the second was the flavor. The differences between light and heavy users of olive oil appeared to be the following:

1. Light users used olive oil when recipes called for it. (They tended to buy two-and four-ounce packages.)
2. Medium users used olive oil because of flavor and preference as well as the fact that recipes called for it. (They tended to buy eight- and sixteen-ounce packages.)

EXHIBIT 1 Romano, Inc., Selling Expenses, Most Recent Year

	Amount
Salaries and wages	$150,112
Fringe benefits	24,225
Supplies	3,842
Telephone	20,505
Advertising	45,404
Contract services	7,500
Travel and entertainment	90,001
Dues and subscriptions	1,230
Warehouse breakage	4,538
Brokerage commissions	301,446
Unsalable merchandise	6,154
External samples	18,125
Taxes, licenses, and permits	9,545
Insurance	13,494
Depreciation	8,209
Miscellaneous expenses	537
	$704,867

3. Heavy users used olive oil because they preferred the taste. They also believed that it was more healthful than other oils. Recipes emerged as only a minor factor for heavy users. (They tended to buy quarts and gallon-size packages.)

Several interesting things had been fairly well established in previous studies in the industry and were rather widely known in the industry. Different ethnic groups bought varying types of olive oil. Preference for olive oil appeared to differ among ethnic groups in the following ways:

1. People of Italian descent preferred a lighter olive oil typical of that supplied by Spanish and Italian exporters.
2. People of Greek and Portuguese descent preferred a heavier oil. In addition, they bought oil to which they were most accustomed. The Greeks bought Greek oil and the Portuguese bought Portuguese oil.
3. First-generation Americans of Mediterranean descent had a latent preference for olive oil. They would prefer to use olive oil whenever they required oil because they preferred its distinct flavor and believed in its health-giving properties. But, because of high prices they restricted their use of olive oil to salads and other purposes where its taste was critical. Where taste was not important they used

EXHIBIT 2 Romano, Inc., Profit and Loss Statement, End of Most Recent Year

		Amount
Gallons sold		1,207,069
Gross sales		$11,022,150
Less: freight	$443,413	
promotional allowances	381,447	
discounts allowed	159,130	
storage and handling	93,242	
Net sales		$ 9,944,918
Cost of sales		7,448,892
Gross contribution		$ 2,496,026
Manufacturing overhead		288,182
Net contribution		$ 2,207,844
Selling expenses	$704,867	
Administrative expenses	325,350	
Net operating income		$ 1,177,627
Other income		42,147
Other deductions		331,168
Net profit before taxes		$ 888,606
Estimated income taxes		455,158
Net profit		$ 433,448

a cheaper vegetable oil. The implication was that lower prices could induce users to use more olive oil and for all cooking purposes.

4. Upon arrival in the United States most immigrants did not have much discretionary income. As a result, they used cheaper oils. Over time, they became more affluent and switched back to the more costly but preferred oils. The implication was that increasing incomes of new immigrants might result in increased demand for olive oil.

5. High prices and inflation had switched some ethnic users away from olive oil, either partially or completely. Over time, some came to like and prefer these substitute oils. The implication was that some users may have been irrevocably converted to other oils.

Two demographic variables also appeared to influence the use of olive oil. These were the following:

1. The greatest use of olive oil occurred among affluent families. Use declined sharply among families with an annual income of less than $20,000.

2. Most of the users of olive oil resided in large metropolitan areas.

In evaluating the nonethnic market, olive oil and salad oils were directly or nearly directly substitutable. That is, one might be substituted for another without significantly affecting the taste, texture, and smell of the oil or any product made from it. However, for some purposes only a specific oil could be used. The degree to which an oil had a uniquely desirable property determined, at least in part, the price that users were prepared to pay for it.

Advise Romano Olive Oil, Inc.

BOY SCOUTS OF AMERICA

The Boy Scouts of America was one of the most well-known and respected social service organizations in the United States. Although it was successful by ordinary and prevailing standards, it had several problems that needed careful analysis and thought.

History and Background

This organization was the largest national group in the 102-nation Boy Scout World Conference. Around the world there were slightly over 10 million members. The movement started in 1907 in Britain with an experimental camp for twenty-two boys conducted by then inspector general of cavalry in the British Army, Lieutenant General Sir Robert Stephenson Smyth Baden-Powell, First Baron Baden-Powell of Gilwell, who was better known in Britain as a hero of the South African (Boer) War of 1899-1902. A few months later he published his famous book *Scouting for Boys*. Although Baden-Powell merely wanted to furnish advice to existing youth organizations and did not intend to start a separate organization, it was soon obvious that a separate movement had begun. The Boy Scouts movement quickly spread, first to Chile; then to Canada, Australia, and New Zealand; and in 1910 to the United States, the result, in part, of some missionary work conducted by Canadians. In the same year, the movement spread to Sweden, Norway, France, Mexico, and Argentina. Baden-Powell, who was designated Chief Scout of the World, lived until 1941.

Baden-Powell's experimental camp, held on Brownsea Island in Poole Harbour, Dorsetshire, allowed him to try out some of the ideas he had accumulated in a long career of largely outdoor activities, much of it spent in India, Afghanistan, and Africa. It emphasized hiking, sailing, canoeing, camping, mapping and map reading, signaling, knotting, and first aid. Just as important to the founder, the participating boy had to promise that on his honor he would do his best to do his duty to God and country, to help other people at all times, and to obey the Scout law, which was a simple code of chivalrous behavior easily comprehended by the child. All this training was to complement, not substitute for, the boy's formal education. Baden-Powell thought that boys should organize themselves into small groups of about six or seven. Their training should progress in steps with periodic recognition of accomplishments. Designation of ranks and award of badges would constitute the recognition.

As Scouting spread internationally, the basic pattern was retained: an outdoors orientation, programmed learning rewarded by the granting of rank and badges, and doing a daily good turn. Minor adaptations were made for national traditions and cultures, and different uniforms were designed for different age groups. However, there was a universal theme in the Scouting literature: "To develop desirable qualities of character, citizenship, and personal fitness." Scouts were expected to be trustworthy, loyal, helpful, friendly, courteous, kind, obedient, cheerful, thrifty, brave, clean, and reverent.

A permanent secretariat, the Boy Scout World Bureau, was established in Ottawa, Canada, to gather and disseminate information, help members with problems, and unify the international movement. The U.S. Scouting movement annually donated about $500,000 to the World Bureau. A world meeting for professionals and adult volunteers was held periodically, two recent locations of which were Copenhagen, Denmark, and Dearborn, Michigan. Scouts held a world jamboree every four years, two recent locations of which were Lillehammer, Norway, and a park in the province of Alberta, Canada.

Baden-Powell intended Scouting for boys of ages eleven to fifteen, but it was soon apparent that there was a social need and viable demand for service to boys both younger and older. In 1916, Baden-Powell introduced the Wolf Cubs, based on ideas in Rudyard Kipling's famous novels. This organization was to serve boys of ages eight to ten and to prepare them to become Scouts at age eleven. The Wolf Cubs spread quickly across Europe but did not reach the United States until 1930, where the organization was termed the Cub Scouts. The United States version of the Wolf Cubs had much more parental participation than the European version.

Organization Structure and Policies

The basic unit of the Cub Scouts was called a den and was guided by a person called a den leader, who was sometimes assisted by a Boy Scout called the den chief. At the beginning of the 1980s the title "den mother" was abandoned, and the title "den leader" established as men were permitted to take on these duties for the first time. Ten-year-old boys, although members of Cub Scouts, held separate meetings if there were enough of them. They were termed Webelos, an acronym for "We'll be loyal Scouts." The Webelos unit had to be led by a man. A pack was made up of several dens. Each den normally met once a week except in the summer. Once a month the pack met under the direction of the cubmaster. Both men and women could be cubmasters, but men outnumbered women by a ratio of six to one. A member started at the Bobcat rank and could work upward to the Wolf rank and then the Bear rank. A Webelo could earn the Arrow of Light Award. The den leaders and Webelos leader were accountable to the Pack Committee, a group of adult volunteers responsible for the welfare of the pack. The activities of the Cub Scouts were centered in the immediate neighborhood, and most were conducted in the houses of the adult leaders. Nearly all boys lived within walking distance of the meetings. Occasionally, some community service was performed, such as gathering items for Goodwill Industries or collecting waste paper. Meetings often consisted of work on crafts and study of American Indian lore, religious symbols, and patriotic and historical themes. Each meeting, lasting about forty minutes to an hour, contained several minutes of recreation; and some trips were made to museums, historical locations, and other places of interest.

Cub Scouts had always worn uniforms of dark blue and gold. In response to vigorous criticism about rigidity, waste, and the fact that families do not have unlimited income, Scouting finally made one small concession in 1983. The pack henceforth could elect to have the boys in its Webelos den wear either the traditional blue and gold or the Boy Scout khaki uniform with insignia, neckerchief, and cap that would identify them as Webelos Scouts. The individual, however, had no choice.

A new program, or division, of Scouting was launched in 1982, specifically as a remedy for the disappointing and falling membership size of the Cub Scouts. This program was named Tiger Cubs and was designed for seven-year-old boys. According to national headquarters, "It introduces families to the values of Scouting one year earlier than had been possible previously. It provides a natural flow into Cub Scouting when these boys become eight years of age." In its first year it enrolled 84,050, and this figure climbed to 123,643 in 1983 and 145,310 in 1984.

The names of the total organization and of the intermediate age group of eleven to thirteen were the same—Boy Scouts. The exact range of years that was to be included in this intermediate group had always been subject to disagreement. The Boy Scouts included a good many fourteen-year-olds who were in the eight grade in school, for the Explorer Scouts did not want boys until they were at least in the ninth grade. Boy Scouts were organized into patrols and troops, the former consisting of usually five to eight boys who elected a patrol leader from among their membership. Most patrols adopted names, often humorous, such as the Tweety Birds, and designed flags for themselves. Two or more patrols made up a troop, which was headed by an adult termed the scoutmaster. The various patrol leaders in the troop constituted the Patrol Leaders Council, which planned the activities for the entire troop. They elected a senior boy leader who presided at the planning meetings. The scoutmaster was accountable to the Troop Committee, a group of adults responsible for the troop's welfare. The scouts all wore khaki uniforms, but the neckerchief color and design were chosen locally.

The Boy Scout started as a Tenderfoot. After passing a specified number of tests, mostly concerned with his ability to take care of himself outdoors, he gained the rank of Second Class Scout. After mastering specified camping and hiking skills, he advanced to First Class Scout. Promotions were not related directly to age or passage of time but to passing tests, demonstrations, and completing tasks. Advancement to the rank of Star Scout and then Life Scout depended on service to Scouting and superior proficiency demonstrated through the earning of badges. The highest rank was Eagle Scout, which required the earning of eleven specified badges in outdoors, fitness, and service subjects plus thirteen badges in fields of the boy's own choice. Examples of these were dog care, woodworking, oceanography, gardening, journalism, consumer buying, traffic safety, and hog production. Over 115 different modules leading to badges were available. The Eagle Scout rank was further divided in that one could earn an Eagle Palm in the ascending order of bronze, gold, or silver, for every five additional merit badges beyond the twenty-four required. Very few boys progressed as far as the Eagle Scout rank.

The Explorer Scouts were set up many years ago for boys who were in high school. The precise time varied from area to area, but in the early 1970s girls were permitted to join the Explorers. This change raised concern among the Girl Scouts, Campfire Girls, and some other girls' groups. The number of female members of the Explorers' division was a sensitive topic and usually not announced. Significant participation by girls in the Explorer Scouts seemed to depend on the principal activity of the post. It was noticed that, if the vocational focus was paramedical, there tended to be good participation by girls. For example, a post that was sponsored by a community rescue squad that let the girl and boy Explorers ride in the ambulances with them was quite popular and was considered successful.

Organizational units were usually called "posts," but a few specializing as Sea Scouts called their units "ships." Although an adult supervised activities, the unit was largely self-governing. There were no ranks within the group, but there were various merit badges to be won. Explorers wore green field uniforms or blazer dress uniforms, depending on the occasion, whereas Sea Explorers wore navy blue or white sailor suits.

Explorer activities included experiences in citizenship, community service, outdoor activities, social events, and learning about vocations. There were two types of posts, general interest and special interest. The general interest post spent its time primarily in outdoor activities, such as camping, hiking, and water sports. The special interest post spent its time on one particular subject area, usually a vocational area, so as to give Explorers an opportunity to investigate future careers. Examples were law, law enforcement, medicine and health services, veterinary medicine, aviation, and engineering. This program derived from a pilot test conducted in 1976 under a grant from the U.S. Department of Education. Programming for some occupations was subsidized by grants. The American Bar Association funded the programs in law, the Law Enforcement and Assistance Administration funded the program in law enforcement, the American Medical Association funded the programs in medicine and health services, and the Aircraft Owners and Pilots Association funded the program in aviation. The Air Force provided no funds but furnished time, talent, and general assistance for the aviation efforts. Area or regional conferences were sometimes held on specific vocations or issues, an example of which was an ecology conference for Explorers at Slippery Rock College. Each year several sports, normally sailing, surfing, and target skills, were played all the way to a national championship. There was also a competition in public speaking extending to the national level.

There was considerable dissatisfaction about the Explorers' segment of Scouting. In 1984 the Scouting movement reorganized and restructured the Explorer operation after running a pilot program in selected councils in 1983. A program called Varsity Scouts was set up strictly for boys of ages fourteen to eighteen, which amounted to reestablishment of pre-1970s operations. The Explorers' division as constituted since the early 1970s was retained and recognized as a valuable program. Moreover, the scope of the Explorer program was expanded to age twenty and assigned the title Career Awareness Exploring. Scouting headquarters revealed in 1985 that 43 percent of Explorers in 1984 were female. Although the age span for Explorers had been increased from fifteen through seventeen to fifteen through twenty, there was little realistic hope of attracting many members of age eighteen through twenty.

Cub Scout packs, Boy Scout troops, and Explorer Scout posts belonged to districts, which in turn, belonged to "local" councils. There were 413 councils in the United States and Puerto Rico, examples of which were Indianhead Council, St. Paul, Minnesota; Long's Peak Council, Greeley, Colorado; Theodore Roosevelt Council, Phoenix, Arizona; and West Michigan Shores Council, Grand Rapids, Michigan. For several years there had been a trend toward a consolidation of smaller local councils, and about 110 had been eliminated as separate entities. For example, Montclair Council Number 346, Orange Mountain Council Number 337, and Newark Council Number 349 became Essex Council Number 336 with offices in Newark, New Jersey. Several local councils made up an area, and several areas made up a region. There were six regions in the United States. For example, the East Central Region comprised Ohio, Indiana, Michigan, West Virginia, most of Wisconsin and Illinois, and parts of Kentucky; and it was divided into six areas and seventy-eight local councils.

All the local councils belonged to the national organization, and they elected the National Council, which governed the Boy Scout movement and appointed the chief scout executive. Management was in the hands of this executive and about 3,850 paid, full-time professional and professional-technical employees, about 580 of whom were in the national headquarters office in Irving, Texas, a suburb of Dallas. Formerly in North Brunswick, New Jersey, the headquarters was moved in 1979. The remaining professional and professional-technical employees were in regional, area, and local council offices. For example, sixty-six professional staff members were in the office of the New York metropolitan councils whereas the corresponding figures were fifty-six in Chicago, thirty-two in Pittsburgh, and thirty-four in Washington, D.C. There were also a good many other employees, such as office clerks and warehouse workers. The chief scout executive administered an annual national budget of more than $100 million, which did not include council, district, and unit budgets. The aggregate of the council annual budgets was over $200 million. Unit budgets varied greatly but would normally not be above a few thousand dollars or below $250. The new national headquarters building suffered damage of $1.5 million from a fire caused by arson in 1980, but it was all covered by insurance.

There was some low-key feeling on the part of many professionals at the local council level that the national office was perhaps oriented too much toward change. On the other hand, some observers and some of the people in the national headquarters thought that the local councils were somewhat resistant to change.

The full-time professional and professional-technical employees in national and regional offices prepared programs, program aids, and training materials; offered courses of instruction for adult volunteers; planned and controlled production and sales of uniforms and equipment; and generally assisted local councils in their work. National headquarters published *Boy's Life*, a magazine for boys; *Exploring*, a magazine for Explorer Scouts and their adult leaders; *Scouting*, a magazine of program aids for adult leaders; and *Cub Scout Handbook, Boy Scout Handbook, Explorer Scout Handbook*; and miscellaneous instruction books and pamphlets. All in all, there were about 2,000 separate publications. The Magazine Publications Division consistently earned a large net profit. (See Exhibit 1.)

Like many other nonprofit organizations, Boy Scouts of America did not practice full public disclosure of information on its finances and number of members. It was rather loathe to release data, especially in detail, in a timely manner and in a consistent way so as to permit objective, thorough analysis of comparable blocks, segments, and series of data. Statements of officials and publications were often vague. This manner of handling data was completely legal for nonprofit organizations but

EXHIBIT 1 Financial Results from Two Activities in Recent Years, Boy Scouts of America

Year	Magazine Publishing Revenue	Magazine Publishing Profit	Supply Operations Revenue	Supply Operations Profit
1978	$10,614,000	$ 742,050	$36,253,000	$ 3,959,000
1979	10,629,000	933,000	38,726,000	3,770,000
1980	10,768,000	930,000	41,489,000	2,774,000
1981	10,596,000	832,000	52,897,000	4,523,000
1982	11,413,000	647,000	51,417,000	6,215,000
1983	13,144,000	1,892,000	54,074,000	7,251,000
1984	Not available	934,000	51,813,000	5,921,000
1985	Not available	486,000	61,995,000	8,496,000
1986	13,611,000	1,336,000	61,862,000	9,547,000
1987	14,558,000	2,866,000	67,720,000	9,926,000
1988	15,082,000	2,137,000	74,971,000	10,946,000

would have been inappropriate for business organizations with publicly traded shares of stock. It was not at all clear to what extent the historical problem with data was attributable to carelessness, inadequate management expertise, evasiveness, lack of time, or perhaps the nature of the organization. Of course, regular financial audits by outside accountants confirmed that there was no dishonesty with funds.

National headquarters also included the Supply Division, which specialized in equipment and uniforms. It maintained a network of five physical distribution centers around the nation. The product line included almost 6,000 items; for example, there were eight types of pocket knives and five types of wallets. The most widely needed products were stocked in approximately 3,000 department stores and sporting goods and apparel shops that had entered into distribution contracts with Boy Scouts of America. The more uncommon items could be ordered from the physical distribution centers. The supply division shipped more than 200,000 orders a year to these retailers, to the 600 Scout camps, and to the local councils.

In 1979 the Scouts had a world-famous designer, Oscar de la Renta, create a new uniform, and the supply division promoted it as "the sharp new look." The uniform cost a boy a minimum of $38 for one pair of long trousers, one long-sleeved shirt, a belt, a cap, a neckerchief, and a metal neckerchief slide for a Cub Scout and a minimum of $41 for a similar outfit for a Boy Scout or Explorer. A boy also needed a short-sleeved shirt, short pants, and high-top socks for use in late spring or early fall. This outfit cost $24 for a Cub Scout and $29 for a Boy

Scout or an Explorer. A sales tax was added in some jurisdictions. The national organziation continuously emphasized to its subordinate organizations that boys had to wear uniforms, and adult volunteers had an ethical obligation to wear uniforms. The usual advertising theme for this was, "You owe it to your Scout team to set the proper uniform example." Leaders were strongly urged to conduct formal inspections of the boys for proper and complete uniforms. The wearing of medals and ribbons on the uniform was encouraged by the hierarchy. Many accessories were available, such as raincoats, warm jackets, vests, swim trunks, shoes, ties, and a variety of special headgear and shirts, all bearing Scouting insignia. The Supply Division consistently earned a large net profit. (See Exhibit 1.)

Financial support for Scouting came from the United Way (or its equivalent in some communities); direct donations; interest earnings on endowments; profits from sale of equipment, uniforms, and publications; membership fees; and, at the unit level, profits from unit sale of such fund-raising merchandise as candy, light bulbs, or seeds. The national organization's Local Council Finance Division published a manual entitled *Developing Prospects to Finance the Local Council* and furnished advice to local Scout workers on how to raise money and manage their finances. Typically, the United Way supplied 30 percent to 35 percent of council budgets. The annual national membership fee consisted of $2.00 for Cubs and Boy Scouts and $3.50 for Explorers and adult leaders. Each of these figures represented a $1.00 increase put into effect September 15, 1975. Packs, troops, and posts added varying amounts to the national fee for their local use, so that a member usually paid about four or five times the national fee. The national fee and usually the local fee were prorated for boys who joined after the beginning of the Scout year. The activities year in most units ran from early fall to early summer. Boarding camps were available for a charge in many locations, the most famous and prestigious of which was the Philmont Scout ranch in New Mexico.

Scout units regularly raised extra money by selling various kinds of merchandise. A common example was the arrangement with Hershey, which would charge the Scout unit $22.50 for a case of forty-eight bars of Hershey's milk chocolate with almonds, Krackel, or Reese's Peanut Butter Cups in the $.75 size. The sales revenue would be $36.00, and the gross profit was $13.50. Because there was no expense, the net profit was also $13.50. At the same time, either as individuals or a unit, the Scouts earned ten "gift points" per case sold, which were redeemable in merchandise. For example, thirty points were required for a football; forty, for an Everready flashlight; 270, for a Hot Foot sleeping bag; and 420, for a Coleman camp stove. Unsold candy could not be returned.

Some Issues and Problem Areas

During its history, the U.S. Scouting movement had been of enormous proportions. Cumulatively, approximately 61 million American males had been members of the Scouts at some time during the years when they were between ages eight and seventeen. Because the movement began only in 1910 and membership was relatively low in the formative period, almost one half of American males of age eight or above living in the early 1990s had been Scouts at some time.

Nevertheless, size of membership in the Cubs, Boy Scouts, and Explorers was a problem. The situation was even worse, however, for analysis of the data showed that the fraction of the youth market being reached at any given time was low. Exhibit 2 presents Scout membership for recent years broken down into Cubs, Boy Scouts, and Explorers; the United States male population in each age category for the nearest date; and the percentage share of the market. One experienced, knowledgeable Scouting official made this comment on the problem: "To many pack and troop leaders who already have all the boys they can handle, there is simply no personal satisfaction in an expanding membership for Scouting." He pointed out, however, that in the view of high-level volunteers and Scouting professionals, "a steady intake of new boys is what Scouting needs, above all else, to stay alive and healthy."[1]

It was also a source of great concern that so many boys dropped out of the organization. Some boys were active for a few weeks or months and then stopped participating or dropped their membership. Exhibit 3 shows the year-end membership as a percentage of all who were active at some point during the year for the sixteen-year period 1965-1980 and selected earlier years. Cub Scouts are separated out in this exhibit, but the data for Boy Scouts and Explorer Scouts were inextricably mixed.

Although they do not constitute a random sample, a few critical excerpts from people's comments on Scouting might be noted. Two boys whose sister had enjoyed Girl Scouts and whose parents, both of whom worked, were supportive and willing to have them join, said, "Scouting is irrelevant." A dependable but dissident scoutmaster stated, "It's sort of paramilitary." One parent said, "I don't like the gun ads in the magazine," whereas another said, "The higher-ups tell you too much about what you don't need to know but not enough about what you do need to know." One adult volunteer complained, "Parents don't really understand the problems of the leaders or even appreciate our hard work," whereas another adult volunteer, a Cub Scout leader, stated, "I think a good many parents send us their little boys just to be baby-sat."

---

[1] Robert W. Peterson, "Scouting's 'Middle Man': The Commissioner," *Scouting*, 65:6, (November-December 1977), pp. 8–10.

EXHIBIT 2 Scouting's Share of the Market in Recent Years

	U.S. Population	Scouting Membership	Share of Market
	July 1, 1989	Dec. 31, 1988	
Age 7	1,908,000	313,703	16.4%
Age 8–10	5,503,000	1,835,642	33.4
Age 11–13	5,145,000	969,685	18.8
Age 14–17	6,908,000	57,009	.8
Age 15–20	21,605,000	1,056,962	4.9
Unduplicated potential	35,865,000	4,233,001	11.8%
	July 1, 1986	Dec. 31, 1985	
Age 7	1,729,000[a]	169,051	9.8%
Age 8–10	4,951,000[a]	1,499,259	30.3
Age 11–13	4,944,000[a]	1,014,456	20.5
Age 14–17	7,455,000[a]	48,430	.6
Age 15–20	22,206,000	1,023,812	4.6
Unduplicated potential	35,571,000	3,755,008	10.6%
	July 1, 1985	Dec. 31, 1984	
Age 7	1,658,000[a]	145,310	8.8%
Age 8–10	4,929,000[a]	1,492,890	30.3
Age 11–13	5,024,000[a]	1,040,828	20.7
Age 14–17	7,527,000[a]	36,949	.5
Age 15–20	22,442,000[b]	940,918	4.2
Unduplicated potential	35,973,000	3,656,895	10.2%
	July 1, 1981	Dec. 31, 1980	
Ages 8–10	5,176,000[a]	1,696,552	32.8%
Ages 11–13	5,347,000[a]	1,065,004	19.9
Ages 14–17	15,764,000[b]	447,469	2.8
	26,287,000	3,209,025	12.2%
	July 1, 1980	Dec. 31, 1979	
Ages 8–10	5,379,000[a]	1,711,237	31.8%
Ages 11–13	5,320,000[a]	1,446,057	7.0
Ages 14–17	15,219,000[b]		
	25,918,000	3,157,294	12.2%
	July 1, 1979	Dec. 31, 1978	
Ages 8–10	5,447,000[a]	1,787,791	32.8%
Ages 11-13	5,391,000[a]	1,515,478	7.0
Ages 14–17	16,276,000[b]		
	27,114,000	3,303,269	12.2%

EXHIBIT 2 *(Continued)*

	U.S. Population	Scouting Membership	Share of Market
	July 1, 1978	Dec. 31, 1977	
Ages 8–10	5,336,000[a]	1,843,033	34.5%
Ages 11-13	5,588,000[a]	1,622,854	7.3
Ages 14–17	16,651,000[b]		
	27,575,000	3,465,887	12.6%
	July 1, 1977	Dec. 31, 1976	
Ages 8–10	5,311,000[a]	1,873,898	35.3%
Ages 11–13	5,833,000[a]	1,338,959	23.0
Ages 14–17	16,773,000[b]	386,914	2.3
	27,917,000	3,599,771	12.9%
	July 1, 1976	Dec. 31, 1975	
Ages 8–10	5,384,000[a]	1,966,570	37.1%
Ages 11–13	6,057,000[a]	1,502,495	24.8
Ages 14–17	16,879,000[b]	433,500	2.6
	28,320,000	3,932,565	13.9%
	July 1, 1975	Dec. 31, 1974	
Ages 8–10	5,583,000[a]	2,178,315	39.0%
Ages 11–13	6,208,000[a]	1,678,003	27.0
Ages 14–17	16,922,000[b]	471,336	2.8
	28,713,000	4,327,654	15.1%
	July 1, 1974	Dec. 31, 1973	
Ages 8–10	5,829,000[a]	2,447,607	42.0%
Ages 11–13	6,308,000[a]	1,907,180	30.2
Ages 14–17	16,881,000[b]	488,324[c]	2.9
	29,018,000	4,843,111	16.7%
	July 1, 1973	Dec. 31, 1972	
Ages 8–10	6,054,000[a]	2,486,706	41.1%
Ages 11–13	6,350,000[a]	1,954,697	30.8
Ages 14–17	16,747,000[b]	459,283	2.7
	29,151,000	4,900,686	16.8%
	July 1, 1972	Dec. 31, 1971	
Ages 8–10	6,204,000[a]	2,476,564	39.9%
Ages 11–13	6,365,000[a]	1,932,413	30.4
Ages 14–17	16,556,000[b]	396,542	2.4
	29,125,000	4,805,519	16.5%
	July 1, 1971	Dec. 31, 1970	
Ages 8–10	6,308,000[a]	2,438,009	38.6%
Ages 11–13	6,346,000[a]	1,915,457	30.2
Ages 14–17	16,281,000[b]	329,192	2.0
	28,935,000	4,682,658	16.2%

EXHIBIT 2 *(Concluded)*

	U.S. Population	Scouting Membership	Share of Market
	July 1, 1970	Dec. 31, 1969	
Ages 8–10	6,346,000[a]	2,380,336	37.5%
Ages 11–13	6,355,000[a]	1,909,299	30.0
Ages 14–17	8,101,000[a]	302,349	3.7
	20,802,000	4,591,984	22.1%

[a] Male only.
[b] Male and female.
[c] According to Scouts headquarters, this figure included "over 100,000 girls." This is the only time that data, even approximated, had been released on female members before 1985.

EXHIBIT 3 "End of Year" Membership Compared to "During Year" Membership of Scouts, 1965–1980, and Selected Earlier Years

December 31	Boy Scouts and Explorers	Cub Scouts	Combined
1980	72.8%	62.2%	66.7%
1979	71.2	62.9	66.4
1978	70.4	64.0	66.8
1977	73.6	67.3	70.1
1976	69.3	64.9	66.9
1975	69.4	64.0	66.6
1974	68.4	62.0	65.1
1973	71.8	65.1	68.2
1972	73.8	66.1	69.6
1971	74.1	66.2	69.8
1970	72.6	66.5	69.3
1969	71.1	66.1	68.4
1968	72.8	67.8	70.2
1967	73.0	68.4	70.6
1966	72.5	68.2	70.3
1965	72.8	68.1	70.4
1960	72.2	67.5	69.8
1955	70.6	71.9	71.2
1950	70.1	65.6	68.2
1945	69.4	68.1	69.0
1940	71.2	68.2	70.6
1935	71.5	69.5	71.4

The ups and downs but long-term decline in membership of Explorer Scouts was especially troubling. Exhibit 4 presents the types of organizations that sponsored Explorer Scout units at the end of 1980 and in four earlier years dating back to 1965. The units sponsored by schools and PTAs as a percentage of all units declined by a very small amount, but the corresponding decline among religious institutions was sizable. The fraction sponsored by civic and community organizations rose sharply, however. Many different civic and community organizations cooperated; but the largest, in terms of number of Explorer units sponsored, were, in order, business firms, Lions Clubs, American Legion and Women's Auxiliary, fire departments, professional and scientific societies, police departments, Kiwanis Clubs, Rotary Clubs, settlement houses, Veterans of Foreign Wars and Women's Auxiliary, Knights of Columbus, Junior Chambers of Commerce, and Elks.

A severe drop in the number of Explorer posts sponsored by religious bodies occurred between December 31, 1965, and December 31, 1980. On the earlier date, such institutions sponsored 11,908 Explorer posts, which represented 51.8 percent of such posts. On December 31, 1980, fifteen years later, religious bodies sponsored 6,854 Explorer posts, which represented 30.5 percent of such posts. Moreover, these posts contained only 16.8 percent of Explorer Scout membership, down from 23.8 percent at the end of 1976. See Exhibit 4.

Within the category of religious sponsors, an interesting change occurred. At the end of 1965, the Church of Latter-Day Saints (Mormons) sponsored 2,788 Explorer Scout posts, or 23.4 percent of all such posts. Mormons were the first in sponsorship among religious bodies, the Methodist Church was second with 2,370 posts (19.9 percent of all posts), the Roman Catholic Church was third with 1,560 posts (13.1 percent of all posts), the Presbyterian Church was fourth with 1,214 posts (10.2 percent of all posts), and the Baptist Church (all branches) was fifth with 1,110 posts (9.3 percent of all posts). At the end of 1980, however, the Mormon Church sponsored 4,257 Explorer posts with 34, 977 members, which accounted for 62.1 percent of all Explorer posts and 46.6 percent of Explorer members in the religious sponsorship category. As of December 31, 1980, the Methodist Church sponsored only 557 posts numbering 9,078 members; the Roman Catholic Church, 559 posts numbering 9,964 members; the Presbyterian Church, 299 posts numbering 4,589 members; and the Baptist Church (all branches), 320 posts numbering 4,268 members. It should be noted that the Knights of Columbus, an organization that the Scouts records classified as civic and community, was a Roman Catholic laymen's organization but not related to any one Catholic parish. The Knights of Columbus sponsored 47 Explorer posts with 652 members at December 31, 1980. Among churches in the United States, the largest in total membership was the

EXHIBIT 4 Sponsorship of Scout Units by Type of Organization, Five Selected Years

Sponsors of Units	Cub Scouts Percent of		Boy Scouts Percent of		Explorers Percent of		Total Percent of	
	Units	Members	Units	Members	Units	Members	Units	Member
Religious Bodies								
December 31, 1980	43.4	40.6	57.8	56.8	30.5	16.8	47.1	42.7
December 31, 1976	41.8	38.9	54.1	55.3	35.2	23.8	46.1	43.4
December 31, 1972	42.1	NA	53.1	NA	38.6	NA	46.4	NA
December 31, 1970	41.6	NA	53.9	NA	44.2	NA	47.6	NA
December 31, 1965	43.0	NA	55.7	NA	51.8	NA	50.3	NA
Civic and Community Organizations								
December 31, 1980	24.9	25.4	28.9	29.0	55.6	58.3	31.9	31.2
December 31, 1976	25.8	24.9	31.5	29.8	55.1	60.7	33.0	30.6
December 31, 1972	25.7	NA	31.1	NA	52.7	NA	32.6	NA
December 31, 1970	25.3	NA	30.6	NA	47.3	NA	31.0	NA
December 31, 1965	22.3	NA	28.8	NA	37.5	NA	27.7	NA
Schools and PTAs								
December 31, 1980	31.7	34.0	13.3	14.2	13.9	24.9	21.0	26.1
December 31, 1976	32.4	36.2	14.4	14.9	9.8	15.5	20.9	26.1
December 31, 1972	32.3	NA	15.8	NA	8.7	NA	21.0	NA
December 31, 1970	33.1	NA	15.5	NA	8.5	NA	21.4	NA
December 31, 1965	34.7	NA	15.5	NA	10.7	NA	22.0	NA

Roman Catholic, followed by the Baptist (all branches), and then the Methodist.

Separate records of Scouting membership by race and ethnic background were not maintained. However, it was clear that blacks and Hispanics had never participated very heavily in the Scout movement, especially in the inner cities. Therefore, in 1965, the National Council subsidized several local councils in special projects to reach some blacks and Hispanics. Included were Chicago, Cleveland, Newark, Philadelphia, Los Angeles, Baltimore, Washington, St. Louis, Cincinnati, and Detroit. Practically all program materials became available in Spanish although some were previously available. There was an additional small outreach effort centered in Bluefield, West Virginia, and Springfield, Missouri, for disadvantaged rural youths. Responses in the inner cities were moderately encouraging. A second effort, launched in 1969, again produced moderately encouraging results. It had been extremely difficult to find adult volunteers in the inner cities to work with Scouts. Turnover of such workers was several times as high as in suburbs and small towns. One Scouting professional summarized it this way in a newspaper interview: "The trouble is, people don't stay around. If they're interested in helping kids, they're also interested in bettering themselves. And if they succeed, they move."[2] David Barrie, the head of the Cadet Corps, a friendly rival of the Boy Scouts in New York City, summarized the Scouts this way: "The virtues are impeccable, but the needs of children in the ghetto are different."[3] Participation by minorities in suburban areas was reasonably good and remained so. Data from the Bureau of the Census, summarized in Exhibit 5, showed that on July 1, 1976, 14.1 percent of all boys in the United States in the age groups eight through seventeen were black and that this figure was forecast to rise to 15.1 percent by mid-1982 because of a higher birthrate among blacks than in the population at large.

There were currently two important legal disputes, and a third dispute had been settled without litigation. A woman in Connecticut was suing because she wanted to be a scoutmaster, but females were not allowed. The rationale for the defense was that boys need men as role models. A man in California who was a self-avowed homosexual was suing to gain registration as a Scout leader. Scouting defended by arguing it was a private organization and as such had the right to set standards for its recognition of adult volunteer workers. The Scouting movement was particularly sensitive on the homosexual issue because of major scandals in Louisiana and Maryland a short time before in which several male adult volunteers who were not self-avowed homosexuals had allegedly

---

[2] Barry Newman, "Boy Power," *The Wall Street Journal*, February 9, 1974, pp. 1, 19.

[3] Ibid.

EXHIBIT 5 Black Boys as Percentage of All Boys, By Scout Age Group, United States, 1976 and 1982

July 1	Cub Scout Age		Boy Scout Age		Explorer Age		Total	
	Black Boys	All Boys	Black Boys	All Boys	Black Boys	All Boys	Black Boys	All Boy
1976	778,000	5,384,000	856,000	6,057,000	1,186,000	8,597,000	2,820,000	20,038,0
	14.5%		14.1%		13.8%		14.1%	
1982	761,000	4,906,000	813,000	5,460,000	1,110,000	7,467,000	2,684,000	17,833,0
	15.5%		14.9%		14.9%		15.1%	

92

EXHIBIT 6 Merit Badges, Most Frequently and Least Frequently Awarded, in Rank Order, Five Recent Years Combined and Sixty-Three Years Combined

Most Frequently Awarded, in Rank Order

Five Recent Years Combined	Sixty-three Years Combined
1. Swimming	1. Swimming
2. First aid	2. First aid
3. Cooking	3. Cooking
4. Camping	4. Firemanship
5. Lifesaving	5. Camping
6. Conservation of natural resources	6. Home repairs
7. Canoeing	7. Lifesaving
8. Nature	8. Safety
9. Home repairs	9. Public health
10. Safety	10. Pioneering
11. Citizenship in nation	11. Personal fitness
12. Citizenship in community	12. Nature
13. Fishing	13. Canoeing
14. Rowing	14. Citizenship in home
15. Hiking	15. Citizenship in community
16. Pioneering	16. Scholarship
17. Reading	17. Reptile study
18. Basketry	18. Citizenship in nation
19. Firemanship	19. Athletics
20. Personal fitness	20. Hiking
21. Music	21. Wood carving
22. Leather work	22. Rowing
23. Citizenship in home	23. Woodwork
24. Rifle and shotgun	24. Music
25. Archery	25. Fishing

Least Frequently Awarded, in Rank Order

Five Recent Years Combined	Sixty-three Years Combined
1. Small grains	1. Metallurgy
2. Cotton farming	2. Engineering
3. Fruit and nut growing	3. Radio
4. Forage crops	4. Landscape architecture
5. Sheep farming	5. Railroading
6. Farm records	6. Theater
7. Beekeeping	7. Fruit and nut growing
8. Pigeon raising	8. Small grains
9. Textiles	9. Cotton farming
10. Farm management	10. American business

sexually abused a large number of young boys. Despite defending both legal actions vigorously, Scouting lost both disputes at the trial level but was appealing these decisions to higher judicial levels.

In the third dispute, just settled without litigation, the membership of a fifteen-year-old boy in West Virginia, Paul Trout, was in process of cancellation because he was an atheist. He had been a Scout for seven years. This six-month-long dispute did not become a lawsuit, but it attracted extensive international attention. Letters to Scout headquarters ran in favor of permitting atheists to participate. The National Executive Board of the Scouts voted to change policy so that Trout could remain in the organization. The board reaffirmed the Scout oath, which requires duty to God. At the same time it decided to remove the definition of God as a Supreme Being from all Scouting materials. A formal resolution was adopted: "While not intending to define what constitutes belief in God, the Boy Scouts of America is proud to reaffirm the Scout Oath and its declaration of duty to God." Some observers considered the statement to be classic double-talk. The parents of Trout stated that they had not planned to sue and that they respected the right of the Boy Scouts to be a religious organization. However, they believed that the Scouts organization had not been aboveboard and open about such matters.

Charter renewal was a perennial problem, virtually every adult volunteer perceiving it as a terrible chore. The rate of noncooperation was rather high, as much as 15 percent in a few large cities. In addition, a great many units were late in complying. According to professional Scout executives, most adult leaders at the grass-roots level were action-oriented people who disliked and often had a low regard for paper work of any type. Many volunteers saw paper work as an interference with getting the real job done. Charter renewal amounted to filling in extensive forms and collecting money once a year. These forms had to do with continuing the sponsorship agreement between the civic, religious, or educational organization and the area council of the Boy Scouts of America, listing all members and adult volunteers and their addresses and what position they would hold in the organization, reporting whether the adult leaders needed further training, and collecting and transmitting all required fees plus optional fees for magazine subscriptions. Recently, the whole process of rechartering had been renamed the "annual service plan" in an attempt to persuade adult volunteers that it had the purpose of helping units.

Advise the Boy Scouts of America.

5

Marketing Research

WATERSIDE SAVINGS AND LOAN ASSOCIATION

A large, out-of-state savings and loan (S&L) association acquired a smaller Florida S&L association. This long-established, federally chartered Florida company had not failed and, in fact, was now in average financial condition, but earlier it had been in marginal condition. The entire S&L industry in the United States, including Florida, had been somewhat depressed for several years, and many organizations had suffered severe losses. Some had gone out of business, and many had merged with stronger organizations. An organization about twice as large as Waterside and whose trade territory overlapped the northern half of Waterside's trade territory had failed a few months before and had been taken over by the federal government for the protection of depositors and disposition of assets.

The S&L industry in the United States was composed of about 3,400 institutions and many thousands of branches of those institutions. Aggregate assets of the industry were over $900 billion. Traditionally, S&L organizations were in only the home mortgage business; and they could not offer checking accounts, consumer loans, commercial loans, or trust services. S&L organizations could legally pay a higher interest rate on savings than commercial banks and enjoyed some special income tax breaks. The rationale from a public policy viewpoint was that S&Ls provided a special and highly desirable service, the financing of housing, and thus deserved special treatment. However, such institutions were highly vulnerable to interest rate risk, something quite dangerous to their survival. They borrowed, that is, took in deposits, on the short term but lent for long periods of years. Thus, if interest rates rose significantly, the S&L institutions had to pay more while at the same time being saddled with assets that were bringing in interest income at the older, lower rates of interest. This fact of life, as interest rates rose through the years, was proving devastating to the industry. Through a series of changes in U.S. law and regulations culminating in extensive deregulation and change in the form of the Garn-St. German bill of 1982, these institutions began to resemble commercial banks. It became lawful for S&Ls to offer checking accounts, consumer and commercial loans, and trust services. This statute also permitted S&L institutions and commercial banks to pay whatever rate was necessary to attract deposits. S&Ls continued to enjoy the special privileges of lenient capital requirements and the ability to get cheap money from Federal Home Loan banks, which borrowed it by using the U.S. Treasury's credit rating. ARMs (adjustable rate mortgages) were also developed.

The acquired Florida company had no distinctive reputation. Rather, it was considered a dependable, middle-of-the-road "thrift." This term in financial circles had long been used to help distinguish S & Ls from the commercial banks. By industry standards, Waterside was considered just barely a medium-sized institution. The acquired organization operated five branches in several small cities adjacent to each other. In fact, these small cities were almost one continuous large city, and many real estate experts believed the towns would constitute a continuous developed strip within fifteen years. Waterside's organizational headquarters, formerly in the original branch, number one, had been moved to the newest and largest branch, number five, two and a half years earlier when that branch opened. At the time of the case, there were no plans for new branches although it was widely assumed within the organization that eventually new branches would be needed. Branch number one was the northernmost in the network of locations, and the other four branches were scattered to the south over a range of about eighteen miles. Branch number five was about halfway between the northernmost and southernmost branches.

All the branches observed the same days and hours of operations. All branch lobbies were closed on Saturdays and Sundays. However, drive-up windows were open in all branches on Saturday mornings to 12:00 P.M. ATMs (automatic teller machines) could be used at all hours on all days of the week.

The new parent did not assign its own name to the Florida subsidiary but instead gave it the name Waterside Savings and Loan. The reasoning was primarily that the acquirer's name would not carry much, if any, meaning to most present and potential customers. The new parent did not judge the old name of the Florida organization to have great market worth and, in fact, considered it rather innocuous. Therefore, a new name was thought up and adopted.

In Waterside's trade territory there were several competitors. There were five commercial banks, each with three to eight branches, and four other S&L associations each with three to six branches. There was a sizeable credit union serving the employees of a major company and two very small credit unions.

Two years after the change of ownership, the director of marketing for Waterside, Ivan Lassiter, launched a research study. An experienced middle-aged banker, he had worked for Waterside for several years before the takeover. He was transferred to the marketing position at the time of the takeover. Lassiter handled advertising and public relations work for Waterside.

Lassiter designed the questionnaire reproduced as Exhibit 1. This survey form was neatly stacked at every teller's window in all branches for people to fill in. Lassiter instructed the tellers to keep the stack of forms in clear view of the customers, and his careful observations indicated that this instruction was carried out. Because of lack of time and considerable pressure of other duties, the tellers could not invite all customers to fill in the form. The marketing director understood this point, and in order to have consistent research procedures, he instructed *all* tellers not to invite customers specifically to participate in the project. If people took forms, they were asked politely but firmly to fill them in before they left the teller's window and then to hand them back to the teller. People were not permitted to take the forms away with them. The study got under way on July 8.

The number of customers who filled in the form as a percentage of customers who visited the bank intrigued Lassiter. He established the number of transactions conducted during one recent week at branch number two, a location that the bank officers consider to be average. Then, based on previous research conducted by the bank that showed the average customer's visit took care of 1.1 transactions, Lassiter estimated the number of customers. He compared the number of customers to the number who filled in the form. He was disappointed to find a participation figure of about 8 percent.

Waterside had 27,510 accounts. About 3,400 people had multiple accounts. There were approximately 23,900 unduplicated names on the customer lists of the organization.

Lassiter began to wonder if perhaps there should be a set of weights used in interpreting the survey data collected. Should the views of a

Dear Customer,

As a customer, you are very important to us here at Waterside Savings. Please help us to serve you better by answering this short questionnaire concerning our hours and branch locations.

Thank you for banking at Waterside Savings!

1. How frequently do you come to the bank to do business?
   _____ More often than once a week
   _____ Once a week
   _____ Once every two weeks
   _____ Once a month
   _____ Once a quarter

2. Would you prefer to:
   _____ Come in the lobby to do business
   _____ Use the walk-up
   _____ Use the drive-up
   _____ Use the ATM

3. Do you:
   _____ Conduct business at one particular branch
   _____ Use whichever branch is convenient

4. If you conduct business at one particular branch, which one is it?

   _____

5. Is the branch where you bank:
   _____ Close to your home
   _____ Close to your office
   _____ Close to shopping
   _____ Other

6. Do you bank:
   _____ In the early morning (8:00 A.M. – 10:00 A.M.)
   _____ At lunchtime (11:00 A.M. – 2:00 P.M.)
   _____ In the late afternoon (3:00 P.M. – 5:00 P.M.)
   _____ In the early evening (5:00 P.M. – 7:00 P.M.)

7. Do you most frequently bank on:
   _____ Monday
   _____ Tuesday
   _____ Wednesday
   _____ Thursday
   _____ Friday
   _____ Saturday

8. Would you like to be able to bank in the branch lobby:
    _____ On Saturday mornings from 9:00 A.M. – 12:00 P.M.
    _____ On Saturday afternoon from 12:00 P.M. – 3:00 P.M.

9. Are our hours and locations convenient for you?
    _____ YES   _____ NO

10. If "No," what would be the most convenient for you?

_____

_____

customer who maintained two accounts with the bank be accorded twice as much weight as those of a customer who maintained one account? Alternatively, if the average month-end balance in customer number one's account was three times as high as that of customer number two, should the views of customer one be assigned more weight? Lassiter's administrative assistant, Charles Rivera, noted that alternatively perhaps customers who came to the bank most often should be accorded more weight. Rivera had been with Waterside since finishing college about two years earlier.

Exhibit 2 displays the data collected for question 1 divided by branch. Exhibit 3 displays the data collected for question 9 cross-tabulated to the answers for question 5. Exhibit 4 displays the data collected for question 9 cross-tabulated to the answers to question 1.

Lassiter had instructed the tellers to urge the respondents to be thorough in filling in the questionnaire. Nevertheless, there were thirty incomplete forms, which he discarded. The marketing director noticed with great interest that two people had written on their questionnaires that they usually banked by mail and two others had written sentences

EXHIBIT 2 Answers to Question 1 by Branch

	Branch					
	1	2	3	4	5	Total
More often than once a week	21	33	43	47	29	173
Once a week	40	61	82	86	62	331
Once every two weeks	49	72	100	103	74	398
Once a month	103	153	206	208	169	839
Once a quarter	41	61	81	41	67	291
	254	380	512	485	401	2032

**EXHIBIT 3 Answers to Question 9
Cross-tabulated to Answers to Question 5**

	Yes	No	Total
Close to your home	674	188	862
Close to your office	641	229	870
Close to shopping	145	58	203
Other	50	47	97
	1510	522	2032

whose essential message was that they appreciated the bank's showing enough concern about the consumer to make such an inquiry. One teller voluntarily reported to Lassiter that, although not certain, she thought she noticed the same elderly woman fill in the form near the beginning of the project and again about two weeks later. The teller did not question the customer about this possibility.

The marketing director stated that he was especially looking forward to the analysis of the data from this project in that he had a benchmark for question number nine. Two and a half years earlier, his predecessor, Miles Swenson, no longer with Waterside, had asked that single question in a skeletal study. Swenson conducted that study in the headquarters, branch number five. In that simple project every customer had had a chance to fill in a card-size form containing that single question and hand it back to the teller. During that study, lasting exactly three weeks, 451 people had participated. Of these 451 people, 321 had said yes, and 130 had said no in answer to the question. Those who had participated constituted about 8 percent of those who had visited the branch during that time period. Charles Rivera added that he thought it would be useful to establish a second benchmark. He explained that he meant a determination of what the customers of First Federal Savings and Loan, the leading competitor, thought of that competitor on the same set of questions Waterside was asking.

At the end of three full weeks, Lassiter was wondering if the collection of data should stop, for it seemed that they had in hand a great number of completed questionnaires, 2,032 to be exact. He was eager to analyze the information and interpret it in a report to Clarence Lazini, the president and chairperson of the board of Waterside Savings and Loan. Lazini had indicated earlier that he was not completely familiar with such research methods but was pleased to see the work being done and would try to be reasonably receptive to its results as he guided the organization.

Advise Waterside Savings and Loan Association.

EXHIBIT 4 Answers to Question 9 Cross-tabulated to Answers to Question 1

	Branch 1		Branch 2		Branch 3		Branch 4		Branch 5		Total	
	Yes	No	Yes	No	Yes	No	Yes	No	Yes	No	Yes	No
More often than once a week	18	3	29	4	40	3	26	3	42	5	155	18
Once a week	33	7	54	7	72	10	53	9	73	13	285	46
Once every two weeks	39	10	61	11	85	15	62	12	85	18	332	66
Once a month	69	34	106	47	143	63	118	51	145	63	581	258
Once a quarter	21	20	32	29	42	39	38	29	24	17	157	134
	180	74	282	98	382	130	297	104	369	116	1510	522

VOLUNTEERS IN HEALTH CARE, INC.

Volunteers in Health Care, Inc. (VHC) was a nonprofit corporation that was organized in 1968 to provide medical, psychological, and dental care for the medically indigent and other selected low-income populations in the northern suburbs of an Eastern city. The founders, a group of medical doctors who were predominantly psychiatrists, were still active in the group, although younger colleagues had assumed almost all of the management.

The original group of physicians augmented their ranks with their own former students, younger colleagues, and professional friends. There had never been a problem with recruitment of volunteer medical professionals, and the medical director had to decline additional volunteers in certain specialty areas. For example, there was consistently an excess of volunteers in pediatrics. A CPA, a former member of the board of directors, performed the annual financial audit free of charge. There had never been a volunteer lawyer, however, in spite of efforts to recruit one. In addition, no one with formal training in business management had ever been involved in VHC. The value of services donated in the most recent year, based on the county health department wage schedule, is displayed in Exhibit 1.

The founders had multiple interests in the organization, including the following:

1. Indignation about the plight of elderly persons and children who "fell through the cracks" of the health care system. Such persons either had too much income to qualify for welfare or did not apply for it. But because they or their parents were unemployed or marginally employed, they lacked private health insurance or were insured only intermittently. Preventive health care, such as checkups, and monitoring of chronic illnesses, such as high blood pressure, was particularly lacking. Hospital care was less of a problem because hospitals built with federal or state funds could not turn indigents away. A major regional children's hospital, although a private foundation, also accepted all indigent patients.

2. A research interest in psychosomatic disorders and a related need to stay active in general medical work, although they earned their living as psychiatrists.

3. A desire to demonstrate to their psychiatric colleagues the effectiveness of "talk" therapy with lower-class persons, who in the United States usually were given tranquilizers when stressed or depressed. VHC's founders were particularly influenced in this research interest by the writings of psychiatrists who had worked in the British national health service, such as Donald Winnicott.

This case was prepared by Joanne G. Greer, Ph.D. of Loyola College, Baltimore.

EXHIBIT 1 Estimated Value of Donated Services

Number of Volunteers	Staff	Hours	Rate	County Pay Rate
14	Physicians	1,306	$23.02	$30,064.12
22	Board members[a]	781	23.02	17,978.62
12	Psychologists	1,145	15.99	18,308.55
20	Nurses	779	9.69	7,548.51
5	Lab Technicians	159	8.84	1,405.56
4	Medical students	24	8.84	212.16
2	Dieticians	61	10.63	648.43
12	Clinic assistants	411	6.05	2,486.55
2	Registrars	51	6.05	308.55
7	Office	209	7.72	1,613.48
1	Auditor	80	23.02	1,841.60
101		5,006		$82,416.13
	FICA			5,266.39
	State Unemployment			1,648.32
	Workmen's Compensation			346.14
	Total			$89,676.98

[a] Board member compensation is the same for all board members, physician, non-physician, professional, or client, according to county policy.

VHC provided services at six sites, visiting a different site each evening from 7:30 to 10:30 P.M. The sites were located in county-subsidized housing units which were reserved for the elderly and a few totally disabled persons. Paid county employees furnished other services to these buildings, such as security guards, maintenance, and minimal recreational programs. Most residents lived on small private incomes plus social security incomes from retirement or from total disability ratings, and had too much income to qualify for the state's Medicaid program but too little income to afford private doctors' fees. Transportation to physicians was a severe problem even to residents who had funds to pay the doctors' charges, because public transportation was poor and they were fearful of being injured while entering and leaving buses and crossing busy streets.

The space for the medical clinics at each site was donated by the county, although it was not exclusively dedicated to VHC. Examining rooms were often utilized by other personnel, such as county social workers, outside of clinic hours, and the only space reserved for VHC was a large closet at each site to hold basic equipment such as centrifuges and equipment for specimen collection. Patients made appointments by telephoning VHC's one-room office, until recently located in a converted former county school building, which had been subdivided for use by various volunteer groups. Each evening a volunteer registrar picked up the files of patients expected at the clinic, set up the examining rooms, and arranged folding chairs at the waiting area. He or she greeted the patients, supervised their flow through the clinic, and recorded the services rendered. Payments were accepted on a voluntary system, and the usual total receipts for an evening were less than $10, with individual payments as low as fifty cents. Many paid nothing, although recently a sign had been posted stating, "VHC is staffed entirely by volunteers. Contributions gratefully accepted."

In reality, VHC had four paid staff: a nurse, a social worker, a secretary, and a lower-level manager who was promoted from secretarial work. The nurse took calls from patients, made appointments, and made decisions during the day about patient emergencies. For example, she might consult by telephone with a patient's doctor at his or her regular employment, or direct a patient to go to the hospital emergency room for a medical crisis. The social worker assisted new patients in contacting various sources of volunteer or tax-subsidized services in the county. Patients requiring medical services not available through VHC were assisted by the social worker to find local sources of help. For example, a patient requiring oral surgery for receding gums was put in touch with the clinic of a local dental school, and a nutritionist was found to assist several diabetic patients with menu planning on a fixed income.

The supply of clerical help was more than adequate, as spouses of the physicians and their friends sometimes volunteered for typing and filing for a few hours a day. It was particularly easy to get office volunteers ever since the county had recently moved VHC to an attractive suite in a new senior citizens day-care center. VHC had had only one daytime professional volunteer, a retired social worker, who made home visits and school visits to coordinate care for children receiving psychotherapy from VHC evening volunteers. She also took initial case histories of psychotherapy patients, which were presented to volunteer therapists at their weekly group meeting so they could each choose the type of patient they preferred working with. She had recently resigned, and psychotherapists now received only a name and telephone number for each referral.

Psychotherapists also had to "hustle" office space in the county buildings to see their patients, because there wasn't sufficient auditory privacy to conduct psychotherapy in the physician's examining rooms during evening clinics, even when the rooms were free. Nevertheless, there was no lack of psychotherapists because of an important career benefit they received by volunteering. Several distinguished senior professors of psychiatry provided the volunteers with free case supervision, a form of tutorial teaching, for each of their clinic cases. Ordinarily, such supervision cost $75 to $105 an hour, and theraptists regarded supervision by a well-known educator as a prestigious form of continuing education.

VHC's sources of income and types of expenditures for the past year are displayed in Exhibits 2 and 3. The main sources of income were grants from United Way, the county health department, and an "adolescent parent" grant program. The services to adolescent mothers and their infants had been eliminated from the state and federal plans for the coming fiscal year, so no further funds would be available from that source. The previous week United Way had notified the chairman of the VHC board of directors that no further United Way funds would be available until VHC performed an evaluation and hired a professional manager. United Way also objected to the research interest the physicians had in the patients, in spite of the fact that any patient included in a research study signed an informed consent form. The fees received from Medicare, Medicaid, and the county health department grant would not be sufficient even to maintain current operations, much less recruit a manager. Some of the patients had private health insurance, but the largest company refused to consider VHC for direct payment because VHC did not have a fixed fee schedule for services, but simply accepted whatever

EXHIBIT 2 Volunteers in Health Care, Inc. Statement of Revenues and Expenditures and Changes in Fund Balance

Most Recent Fiscal Year Ended June 30	
Revenues	
United Way	$50,962.00
County Health Dept.	17,385.00
CETA	1,041.01
Medical Fees	15,409.00
Donations	550.00
Interest	211.49
Miscellaneous	144.34
Total Revenues	$82,148.26
Expenditures	
Program	
Clinic	62.558.51
CETA	5,914.77
Adolescent Parent Education	6,282.93
Total Program	$74,756.21
General & administrative	14,932.28
Total Expenditures	$89,688.49
Excess of revenues (deficiency) over expenditures	(7,540.23)

EXHIBIT 3 Volunteers in Health Care, Inc. Analysis of Functional Expenditures Most Recent Fiscal Year Ended June 30

	Program			General & Administrative	Total
	Clinic	CETA	Total		
Salaries & registrar fees	$51,062.97	$775.25	$51,838.22	$13,653.00	$65,491.22
Payroll taxes	4,257.86	51.55	4,309.41	1,169.92	5,479.33
Employee benefits	1,102.03	–	1,102.03	310.84	1,412.87
Total personnel costs	$56,422.86	$826.80	$57,249.66	$15,133.76	$72,383.42
Interest	–	–	–	5.59	5.59
Transportation	4,171.82	–	4,171.82	77.95	4,249.77
Contributions	–	–	–	–	400.00
Depreciation	424.50	–	424.50	92.32	516.82
Insurance	2,567.00	–	2,567.00	87.00	2,654.00
Laboratory fees	3,288.20	–	3,288.20	–	3,288.20
Office supplies and extensions	1,302.60	–	1,302.60	367.40	1,670.00
Repairs & maintenance	650.26	–	650.26	159.50	809.76
Medical supplies	1,471.40	–	1,471.40	–	1,471.40
Telephone	427.65	–	427.65	646.41	1,074.26
Miscellaneous	296.13	–	296.13	1,036.58	1,332.71
	$71,022.42	$826.80	$71,849.22	$17,606.71	$89,455.93

the patient was willing to pay. Consequently, the patients collected the insurance reimbursements and usually pocketed them, making a token donation to VHC. One patient was known to have collected $500 from an insurance company in reimbursement for psychotherapy visits, had donated $50 to VHC, and then used the remainder to take a vacation.

Two letters to the insurance company to negotiate a contract for direct payment to VHC had received short, stereotyped responses of refusal, signed by a correspondence clerk.

In a special meeting to discuss strategy, board members were offended by United Way's demand for an evaluation. Claire Washburn, the board president and wife of a former volunteer, commented, "Our program is sterling, and it breaks my heart to think they would question our integrity." Dr. Vincent Jones, one of the original founders, questioned whether the United Way's funds were worth the effort and wanted to pursue more vigorously obtaining direct reimbursement status with private insurors. VHC was currently receiving a grant from the county health department because VHC could care for the medically indigent more cheaply than county clinics, and Dr. Jones thought the county would give more business if pressed. He also thought there was a possibility of taking over the county operation completely, under a "capitation rate" payment arrangement. The county clinics had high costs, were poorly run, and had just received a large amount of negative coverage in the news media.

Because the county clinics primarily delivered care to medically indigent children, assuming responsibility for these patients would enable VHC to use the volunteer pediatricians it was currently turning away for lack of work.

Under the capitation rate mode of payment, the responsible payor, in this case the county, negotiates a per head annual payment with a health care provider, usually a clinic. The health care provider is responsible for service even if the provider incurs a loss. On the other hand, the provider receives the payment for all covered persons, even those who use no services that year. Medicaid experiments with capitation rate had been quite successful in that equal-quality care for patients with lower annual costs had resulted. Under capitation rate reimbursement, there is no financial incentive for the provider to provide unnecessary services, or to "ping-pong" the patient from doctor to doctor.

Another option was posed by a new board member, Reverend Father Anthony Carlucci. A priest-psychologist, he often referred pastoral counselors in training to VHC as volunteers so that they could work under VHC's fine psychotherapy supervisors. Carlucci proposed trying to put together an ecumenical coalition of affluent local churches to assume part of VHC's costs.

Claire Washburn, the board president, was wary of the risks involved in giving up the United Way money, but Barry Water, a community activist board member, noted that, if VHC dropped out of United Way, it would have total freedom in its own fund-raising activities. He emphasized that United Way closely monitored all fund-raising plans of member agencies, discouraged highly aggressive efforts of those agencies, discouraged their approaching charitable foundations, and prohibited any fund-raising efforts at all during the time period, usually three months, when United Way itself was attempting to raise money. Water went on to note that the local children's hospital had successfully given up its connection with United Way.

The board president pointed out that some response had to be made to United Way's request for an evaluation of the VHC program, but she, for one, had no idea how to go about it, particularly in light of United Way's expressed dislike for research in the clinics.

Advise Volunteers in Health Care, Inc.

STEPIK AND NEWCOMB MARKETING RESEARCH AGENCY

Stepik and Newcomb was a successful marketing research agency operating in several cities, including a large city in the Eastern United States. It enjoyed a reputation for integrity and quality service. As was true of most marketing research companies, most of this firm's experience with the consumer had been with the middle and upper-middle classes. It appeared that proper servicing of a major new client, Harvest World Corporation, might require some changes in the firm's orientation. Harvest World was a regional retail chain with stores in New York, Connecticut, Massachusetts, Rhode Island, New Jersey, Pennsylvania, and Maryland. It characterized its stores as discount houses. They were all located in small cities and in middle-class suburbs of large cities. Harvest World operated two suburban stores in this metropolitan area.

This client was interested in setting up inner-city stores but not necessarily downtown stores. It was interested in string-street locations that often occur from two to four miles from downtown shopping districts but not far enough out to compete with suburban planned shopping centers.

Stepik and Newcomb was quite aware of its lack of experience in analyzing low-income consumers.[1] It was also vaguely aware of a problem that one writer described in the following manner:

[1] David A. Schwartz, "Coping with Field Problems of Large Surveys Among the Urban Poor," *Public Opinion Quarterly*, 34 (Summer 1970), pp. 267–272; and Herschel Shosteck, "Survey Research in the Inner City," in Fred C. Allvine, Ed., *Combined Proceedings of the 1971 Conferences* (Chicago: American Marketing Association, 1971), pp. 640–643.

The marketing executive who relies on information derived from his [or her] own life experiences is usually handicapped when faced with the problems of marketing to low-income groups, because their life-style is quite different from his [or her] middle-class one[2].

One of Harvest World's research questions was to establish the current company image. Another was to determine an appropriate merchandise mix for the new stores. The company dealt in few soft goods but many hard lines. It stressed furniture, rugs, carpeting, major appliances, small appliances, lamps, phonographs, radios, television sets, records, clocks, watches, jewelry, typewriters, bibelots, table flatware, plastic dishes, and toys. It also had ready-made curtains, furniture slip-covers, tablecloths, and place mats. Another question dealt with appropriate pricing policies, and yet another was concerned with appropriate advertising themes and effective media to reach the prospective inner-city customers.

Stepik and Newcomb began by thoroughly studying the data for the city in question from the latest census of population and of housing. Second the agency conducted traffic counts of pedestrians, cars, and buses at many different possible locations and analyzed the store affinity advantages, if any, for Harvest World at the various locations.

Next, in order to study the client's image, the agency designed a semantic differential instrument based on the work of Osgood and his colleagues.[3] The researchers used a seven-interval scale and bipolar adjectival pairs, as given in Exhibit 1. For the purpose of cross-classification, questions were asked on the following: occupation, place of employment, income, age, size of household, and places where credit had been established.

On the basis of a pilot study of thirty-seven addresses, in which there was an unusually high incidence of no one at home or no adult at home, the agency decided that it would need to start with a larger than average sample. This was decided despite the fact that the client was willing to pay for a call-back, or second visit, to the households in question. Being conservative, the agency feared that even on the second visit a sizable fraction of the sample still would not be at home. The pilot study

---

[2]Kelvin A. Wall, "Marketing to Low-Income Neighborhoods: A Systems Approach," *University of Washington Business Review* (Autumn 1969), pp. 18–26. Reprinted in William Lazer and Eugene Kelley, *Social Marketing: Perspectives and Viewpoints* (Homewood, Ill.: Richard D. Irwin, Inc., 1973), pp. 453–461. Also see Bradley Greenberg and Brenda Dervin, "Mass Communication Among the Urban Poor," *Public Opinion Quarterly*, 34 (Spring 1970), pp. 232–234.

[3]See Charles E. Osgood, G. J. Suci, and P. H. Tannenbaum, *The Measurement of Meaning* (Urbana: University of Illinois Press, 1957). Also see William A. Mindak, "Fitting the Semantic Differential to the Marketing Problem," *Journal of Marketing*, 25 (April 1961), pp. 28–33; and Robert F. Kelly and Ronald Stephenson, "The Semantic Differential: An Information Source for Designing Retail Patronage Appeals," *Journal of Marketing*, 31 October 1967), pp. 43–47.

EXHIBIT 1 The Semantic Differential Instrument Used by Stepik and Newcomb

Mean		7 Extremely	6 Very	5 Slightly	4 Both, Neither, or No Opinion	3 Slightly	2 Very	1 Extremely	
4.1	Happy	:	:	:	:	:	:	:	Sad
4.9	Inexpensive	:	:	:	:	:	:	:	Expensive
3.9	Neat	:	:	:	:	:	:	:	Unkempt
4.0	Dependable	:	:	:	:	:	:	:	Undependable
3.9	Fair	:	:	:	:	:	:	:	Unfair
4.0	Truthful	:	:	:	:	:	:	:	Deceptive
4.1	Spacious	:	:	:	:	:	:	:	Crowded
4.0	Public-minded	:	:	:	:	:	:	:	Self-serving
4.3	Modern company	:	:	:	:	:	:	:	Old-fashioned compan
—	Distinctive atmosphere	:	:	:	:	:	:	:	Ordinary atmospher
—	Relaxing	:	:	:	:	:	:	:	Not relaxing
—	Strong	:	:	:	:	:	:	:	Weak
—	Friendly	:	:	:	:	:	:	:	Stern

also indicated that the length of the personal interview would have to be limited, for many became impatient or bored before it was over, and two terminated the interview before the interviewer was finished. For this reason, the final four pairs of adjectives were deleted from the semantic differential instrument, leaving nine pairs.

Stepik and Newcomb generated a proper geographical cluster sample and sent experienced field interviewers out to conduct the interviews. Some problems arose with the agency's local interviewer staff, which was composed of people who worked on an on-call basis. They held no full-time jobs. Stepik and Newcomb had on-call arrangements with seven undergraduate men and seven undergraduate women at local universities and seven housewives aged thirty-seven to fifty-six. All were white. The agency had given intensive interviewer training to all when they were first hired. For this project the agency chose to use the more mature women. To start with, one woman reported that she was sick and another refused to participate in this project. Later two other women dropped out. This put a heavy work load on the remaining three women, but they completed the interviews only four days behind schedule. One consolation in this turn of events was that the fewer the interviewers, the greater was the consistency among the interviews conducted.

The marketing research agency's usual experience had been that about 64 percent of the intended household sample was obtained on the first visit and another 15 percent was obtained on the second attempt. In the Harvest World project the agency found 50 percent at home on the first visit and 13 percent at home on the second attempt. No substitutions were allowed. The refusal rate was in line with the agency's general experience. The mean ratings on the semantic differential instrument are given in the left-hand column of Exhibit 1.

Advise Stepik and Newcomb as to the remainder of the research project.

6

Products and Product Strategy

LA-Z-BOY CHAIR COMPANY

La-Z-Boy Chair Company perceived itself as the most widely recognized name in motion furniture. Although it made several other furniture products, it was best known for its upholstered reclining chairs. Exhibits 1 through 3 show the firm's recent financial statements.

This organization was traceable back to the mid-1930s in southeastern Michigan, when Edward M. Knabusch and his younger cousin Edwin J. Shoemaker formed a partnership with the intention of manufacturing specialty furniture, including a reclining wooden chair that they had invented. They envisioned it for lawn and porch use. They took this chair to a furniture retailer in nearby Toledo, Ohio. "Clever idea," the store manager told them, "but folks will want something more comfortable. If you can make an upholstered chair that reclines, you'll have something you can sell."

A self-taught artisan, Knabusch took this as a challenge. He developed a chair and in 1928 opened a roadside business, a combination workshop and retail store, called Floral City Furniture Company, on the highway between Detroit and Toledo. A good showperson, Knabusch put the place of business on the map by staging tent shows, a miniature circus for children, and other colorful events.

A modern manufacturing plant and headquarters offices were built in 1941 in nearby Monroe, Michigan, for the organization. It incorporated on May 1, 1941, and renamed itself La-Z-Boy Chair Company. The new

EXHIBIT 1 La-Z-Boy Chair Company, Consolidated Statement of Income and Retained Earnings (Dollar amounts in thousands, except per share data)

Year Ended	April 19, 1989 (52 weeks)	April 30, 1988 (53 weeks)	April 25, 1987 (52 weeks)
Net sales	$553,187	$486,793	$419,991
Cost of sales	397,776	352,069	289,779
Gross profit	155,411	134,724	130,212
Selling, general and administrative	106,937	91,354	85,469
Income from operations	48,474	43,370	44,743
Interest expense	7,567	4,008	1,877
Other income (Includes interest income of $1.9 million in 1989, $1.2 million in 1988, $1.3 million in 1987)	3,067	2,662	2,081
Income before income taxes	43,974	42,024	44,947
Provision for income taxes			
Federal — current	21,051	17,931	19,558
— deferred	(7,112)	(4,832)	(1,175)
State	2,569	2,444	1,900
Total tax expense	16,508	15,543	20,283
Net income for the year	27,466	26,481	24,664
Retained earnings at beginning of year	161,629	142,485	124,951
Less: Cash dividends ($.46 per share in 1989, $.40 in 1988 and $.39 in 1987)	8,232	7,337	7,130
Retained earnings at end of year	$180,863	$161,629	$142,485
Weighted average shares (thousands)	17,886	18,285	18,401
Net income per share	$1.54	$1.45	$1.34

plant was then converted to war goods production for almost four years. Afterward the company resumed making the reclining chair and gradually began to offer several models of the basic product.

Corporate growth in the 1960s and 1970s was centered around the launching in 1961 of the Reclina-Rocker chair, which was introduced to

EXHIBIT 2 La-Z-Boy Chair Company, Consolidated Balance Sheet (Dollar amounts in thousands)

		April 29, 1989	April 30, 1988
Assets	**Current Assets**		
	Cash and cash equivalents	**$ 18,159**	$ 13,207
	Receivables, less allowances of $6,153 in 1989 and $4,976 in 1988 for doubtful accounts.............	**143,141**	130,584
	Inventories.........................	**65,641**	66,822
	Other current assets	**8,881**	8,825
	Total Current Assets............	**235,822**	219,438
	Property, plant and equipment, net...............................	**79,845**	84,160
	Goodwill, less accumulated amortization of $1,112 in 1989 and $220 in 1988	**25,563**	26,257
	Other long-term assets	**7,777**	6,737
	Total Assets....................	**$349,007**	$336,592
Liabilities and Shareholders' Equity	**Current Liabilities**		
	Short-term debt.....................	**$ 2,924**	$ 10,744
	Current portion of long-term debt..	**6,679**	7,039
	Accounts payable...................	**21,800**	16,815
	Payrolls and other compensation...	**20,103**	16,046
	Other accrued liabilities.............	**15,346**	13,098
	Estimated income taxes	**8,227**	1,764
	Deferred income taxes.............	**1,796**	6,868
	Total Current Liabilities.........	**76,875**	72,374
	Long-term debt	**70,641**	76,215
	Deferred income taxes.............	**7,198**	9,238
	Shareholders' equity Common shares, $1.00 par value—40,000,000 authorized; 18,640,740 issued..............	**18,641**	18,641
	Capital in excess of par value....	**6,075**	6,493
	Retained earnings	**180,863**	161,629
	Currency translation adjustments ..	**665**	320
		206,244	187,083
	Less: Treasury shares, at cost (826,773 in 1989 and 616,937 in 1988)	**11,951**	8,318
	Total Shareholders' Equity	**194,293**	178,765
	Total Liabilities and Shareholders' Equity	**$349,007**	$336,592

EXHIBIT 3 La-Z-Boy Chair Company, Consolidated Statement of Changes in Shareholders' Equity

	Common Shares	Capital in Excess of Par Value	Retained Earnings	Currency Translation Adjustments	Less: Treasury Shares	Total
Balance at April 26, 1986	$18,641	$5,783	$124,951	$(659)	$ 1,744	$146,972
Purchase of treasury shares					17	(17)
Currency translation adjustments				210		210
Exercise of stock options		271			(374)	645
Dividends paid			(7,130)			(7,130)
Net income			24,664			24,664
Balance at April 25, 1987	18,641	6,054	142,485	(449)	1,387	165,344
Purchase of treasury shares					7,557	(7,557)
Currency translation adjustments				769		769
Exercise of stock options		439			(626)	1,065
Dividends paid			(7,337)			(7,337)
Net income			26,481			26,481
Balance at April 30, 1988	18,641	6,493	161,629	320	8,318	178,765
Purchase of treasury shares					5,420	(5,420)
Currency translation adjustments				345		345
Exercise of stock options		(418)			(1,787)	1,369
Dividends paid			(8,232)			(8,232)
Net income			27,466			27,466
Balance at April 29, 1989	$18,641	$6,075	$180,863	$ 665	$11,951	$194,293

succeed the company's original upholstered reclining chair. According to company executives, "Our business has been built around a singularly successful product, the world-famous and widely imitated Reclina-Rocker." This product was a breakthrough in technology and comfort. It incorporated various features that previously had not been combined in one chair. It was built to rock and recline and had a movable footrest, which could be raised from its normal vertical position at the lower front of the chair to the desired horizontal position by use of a hand lever on the side of the chair. Much later, a swivel base was designed and offered as a customer option.

Subsequent to that introduction, the company vastly expanded its upholstered residential furniture line. After considerable research and development work, the organization in 1970 brought out the Sofette, a two-seat reclining unit in which each seat operated independently of the other. In 1973, La-Z-Boy introduced La-Z-Rocker, a line of swivel rockers that flexed their backs based on the weight of the individual. A line of sleep sofas called La-Z-Sleeper was brought out in 1977; and a line of ottomans to accompany the La-Z-Rockers in 1978. In late 1979 the company introduced the Reclina-Way reclining chair to replace the former Wall-Recliner chair. Placed only a few inches from the wall, the smooth glide action of this product required only gentle shoulder motion to put it into operation. A helpful device was patented and put into use in 1981. This innovation, called the Swivel-Stop, locked La-Z-Rocker swivel rocker chairs in position when not in use. This device maintained a stable position when one sat down or got up. Also, according to company executives, "People had one objection to all swivel rocker chairs: they invariably faced the wrong direction. With Swivel-Stop the chair stays facing the direction you want when it is unoccupied."

An interesting piece of work was perfected in 1981, a new handle-footrest mechanism for Contract Division chairs. It was more simple and durable than the previous device. Because of the lower profile of this new mechanism, the company began experimenting with a high leg recliner for the residential market. This mechanism permitted the design of a chair that had a lighter look and higher style. In late 1982 the company brought out a line of stationary sofas called La-Z-Sofa.

A line of reclining chairs with high legs of exposed wood was introduced in 1983 and called the La-Z-Lounger. The La-Z-Boy residential products, on the whole, had always been casual-looking. For houses with both a living room and a family room, La-Z-Boy was more likely to be considered for purchase for the latter. The introduction of chairs with exposed wooden legs was an attempt to attract people with more formal tastes. In 1983 the company made an appeal to the person who preferred elegance and tradition by launching its Presidential Collection. This line combined reclining features with eighteenth-century styling. Skirted bottoms were replaced with exposed wooden legs in a choice of Queen

Anne or Chippendale styles. Also in that year the company brought out Reclina-Rest, a new line of reclining chairs. This stationary, multiposition recliner offered a footrest and reclining action that operated independently of each other, so that the number of combinations of positions expanded greatly. The La-Z-Sleeper was replaced in early 1984 by a new line of sleep sofas called Signature II, which offered a new exclusive mechanism and optional quilted innerspring mattress. In late 1984 the company introduced Eurostyled models in the Signature II sleep sofa line together with coordinated Reclina-Rocker chairs and La-Z-Sofa stationary sofas. Eurostyles reflected a movement in the fashion centers of Europe toward understatement and relaxed contours. La-Z-Boy's interpretation of this trend incorporated softly plumped saddlebag arms, double-pillowed seat backs that were adjustable for individual comfort, and shirred front rails. These changes not only produced attractive, interesting furniture, but they were also an overt attempt to appeal to trend-conscious consumers. The company's traditional emphasis had been strongly on comfort.

The company introduced a line of modular units in 1985 that featured the Reclina-Way mechanism and named them Motion-Modulars. This set of products was not only an expansion but also a rational response to the strong U.S. trend toward smaller houses and the mixed trend toward smaller living rooms or family rooms or both. Motion-Modulars could be arranged in many configurations, creating, for example, a straight or curved sofa, a love seat and a chair with an ottoman, a corner grouping, or even a sleep sofa in two sizes. Units could be bought individually or together, of course. Adding a unit later exposed the consumer to the risk of a tiny change in the color or texture of fabric. La-Z-Boy did not manufacture its own fabrics. Even if it had done so and concentrated on consistency, absolutely perfect uniformity in textures and especially in colors was impossible. What interior decorators and furniture salespersons often recommended in this case was for a consumer to add another piece of upholstered furniture in an obviously different but carefully coordinated color. In fact, most consumers did not want all the upholstered furniture in a room to match, thinking it looked rather dull.

In 1989 the company introduced the Twincliner sofa, the end units of which reclined separately. In the same year the company introduced a newly engineered recliner mechanism for its Reclina-Way recliners, which made these products easier to operate and allowed them to be placed only five inches from a wall or other object. Also introduced was a sleep sofa containing a three-inch longer bed. The company also greatly expanded the number of its chairs and sofas on which leather upholstery was available.

Much earlier, La-Z-Boy had made an interesting diversification of the product line. In 1971 it entered the office-seating market by designing and offering an item unique in its field, a high-backed executive recliner. Several other chairs for office use were designed and added to this initial offering. For many years thereafter the company operated as though it had two suborganizations, the Residential Division and the Contract Division. However, this arrangement was not formalized until 1984, at which time each division was given its own vice-president. In 1982 the company expanded into desks and office furniture components, specifically, credenzas, bookshelves, and tables. They were offered in traditional, modern, and contemporary styling and in sizes and qualities suitable for what the company described as "executive, middle management, and secretarial requirements." However, La-Z-Boy was the distributor of these casegoods, not the manufacturer. The company acquired and modernized a 153,500 square foot manufacturing plant in Leland, Mississippi, in 1985 and dedicated it to the making of contract-market products. This was the smallest of the organization's fourteen manufacturing facilities. Pilot production of desks and other casegoods began in 1985, and the company became self-sufficient in these goods by 1986. Compared to the purchased casegoods previously offered, La-Z-Boy now felt that it could offer better construction, styling, features, and finish. For example, the new in-house production of desks offered central locking systems, improved slide mechanisms for heavily loaded drawers, and hand-rubbed desktops for greater beauty and wear resistance. The total U.S. demand for non-residential furniture was about half as large as that for residential furniture.

The company went into health-care seating for hospitals, clinics, and nursing homes in 1973. Although the potential demand of the health-care industry did not match that of office furniture, it was large and showed some signs of growing. La-Z-Boy reclining chairs were used in patient rooms, where they presented a comfortable alternative to the bed for people who were well enough to get up and down. They were also used in some specialized treatment situations such as hemodialysis and in many kinds of treatment for the very old and feeble. In 1987 the company launched a reclining chair on casters with an articulating arm tray table and a concealed footrest. Cheerful fabrics and vinyl coverings were available and emphasized in health-care seating.

In the middle and late 1980s La-Z-Boy introduced electrically powered Lectra-Lift chairs that featured mechanisms designed by the company to provide extra stability to people who needed assistance in standing or sitting. A luxurious variation on this concept, the Lectra-Lounger power recliner, was brought out for the top-of-the-line customer. Most demand for these products came from health-care institutions. By 1989 the company was well along in developing a new type of mobile chair for homes and institutions that eliminated side wheels, included a stowable meal tray, and was equipped for intravenous treatment.

The Contract Division acquired the rights in 1981 to make the Back-Jack floor rest from Concept Engineering, Inc., of Lincoln, Nebraska, and introduced it at once. Shaped like the number 7 lying on its open side, this item was an upholstered, lightweight, and portable leisure seating meant mainly for the beach, pool, or camping. Unlike the rest of the company's product line, it was distributed through sporting goods stores, home improvement centers, and mail-order catalogs and even in some redemption catalogs for trading stamps. La-Z-Boy abandoned this product at the end of 1983.

The lodging industry was selected by the Contract Division in 1984 as another area for sales development efforts. In gratifyingly short time, the division sold several large orders for chairs and sleep sofas to well-known hotel and motel chains.

The majority of sales growth in the company had been internally generated, but there had been several acquisitions. In 1979 La-Z-Boy purchased the net assets of Deluxe Upholstering, Ltd., from the Molson Companies, Ltd., which included a 124,300 square foot manufacturing plant in Waterloo, Ontario. This firm had previously manufactured La-Z-Boy products for fifty years under a licensing agreement. In 1985 La-Z-Boy relocated its Waterloo manufacturing plant to an existing facility of 209,820 square feet in the same city. The Waterloo plant was expanded in 1989 to its present size of 257,340 square feet.

Departing radically from previous practice in expanding the present line, La-Z-Boy made two acquisitions in 1986. The first was Burris Industries, Inc., of Lincolnton, North Carolina, which was established in 1936 and had 1985 sales of $10.6 million. Employing 260 people, Burris emphasized the upper end of the motion-chair market, which La-Z-Boy had not specifically cultivated, and was showing a net operating loss. Burris chairs had more sophisticated looks than La-Z-Boy and were sold mainly in high-priced furniture and department stores. Joining the Burris line of chairs were several with the Scandinavian look, including exposed areas of solid oak, and several with upholstered Eurostyle designs with soft contours and luxuriously padded seats, backs, and arms. Burris also continued to make modular incliner groups of seating units. Several Burris products that were in the medium range rather than the upper end were deleted by the new owners. La-Z-Boy appointed some of its own experienced employees to the top positions at Burris but directed that subsidiary to operate in its own name and to handle its own sales effort.

The second 1986 acquisition was RoseJohnson, Inc., a manufacturer of commercial furniture in Grand Rapids, Michigan. The firm, formed in 1983 through the consolidation of Rose Manufacturing Company and Johnson Furniture Company, made furniture for offices and the hospital industry. RoseJohnson employed 275 people and had annual sales of $20 million at the time of acquisition. Top management was retained. RoseJohnson's products were competitively priced and targeted mainly to the middle-quality range. The new subsidiary's products included "open plan" systems and casegoods, one line of which was for upper-level managers and the other for middle-level managers and support personnel. RoseJohnson also made some casegoods for hotels and dormitories.

Another acquisition was made in September 1986, which fell in fiscal 1987. La-Z-Boy bought Hammary Furniture, Inc., of Lenoir, North Carolina, a maker of residential occasional tables, cabinets, chests, and upholstered furniture whose annual sales were about $22 million. The physical assets were comprised of a manufacturing facility and warehouse in Lenoir and another manufacturing facility in Granite Falls, North Carolina. For the new parent Hammary almost immediately launched a new line of tables called "La-Z-Boy CompaTables," which were specifically finished to match La-Z-Boy furniture, and sold them exclusively through La-Z-Boy Showcase Shoppes.

The wave of expansion and diversification continued in January 1988 with acquisition of Kincaid Furniture Company of Hudson, North Carolina, for $53 million. Employing 1,400 and doing a yearly sales volume of about $75 million just before its change of ownership, Kincaid made solid wood dining room and bedroom furniture. Previous acquisitions were made almost entirely from current earnings, but $50 million of the Kincaid cost was borrowed from banks. The 1988 La-Z-Boy sales figures include $20.6 million representing three months of sales by Kincaid. Excluding Kincaid, 1988 sales rose 11 percent over 1987.

With the Kincaid acquisition La-Z-Boy had broadened its furniture line to cover nearly all aspects of a house and had become both the largest manufacturer of upholstered furniture, with seven and a half percent of the market, and the largest manufacturer of solid wood bedroom and dining room furniture in the United States. As of 1989 residential furniture constituted 92 percent of the company's sales. Of this 92 percent portion, 80 percent was upholstered and 20 percent was bedroom and dining room furniture, tables, cabinets, and other casegoods. Because of the increased complexity in the company, La-Z-Boy reorganized itself into seven operating divisions: La-Z-Boy Residential; La-Z-Boy Contract; Burris; Hammary; Kincaid; La-Z-Boy Canada; and RoseJohnson.

Data on some competitors were imprecise, but it appeared reasonably clear that La-Z-Boy was the eighth largest among thirty manufacturers of residential furniture in the United States and definitely the largest of fifteen makers of reclining chairs. It employed about 7,700 people. Its reclining rocker and other motion chairs as of 1989 enjoyed 27 percent of the market for such chairs, and the competitor with the second-largest market share sold about half as much of this product type. The reclining rocker still provided a little over half of the company's sales in 1989, compared to about 70 percent in 1986.

The strong sales growth trend of early years ended in 1975 and an actual decrease occurred, but there was a rebound in 1976 and again in

1977. Sales growth in 1978, 1979, and 1980 was no greater than the rate of inflation in the economy. In 1981 there was a decline of 1.6 percent, which of course represented an extremely large decline when adjusted for the inflation of that year. In 1981 and 1982 there was great self-examination in the corporation, and in 1982 there was the largest number of new style introductions in the organization's history. In 1982 the momentum resumed, and there was again noteworthy growth in 1983, 1984, and 1985. The year 1984 saw a surge of 29 percent; and 1985, a rise of 8 percent in sales. In 1986 sales rose 21 percent, in 1987 23 percent, in 1988 16 percent, and in 1989 14 percent. The 1988 sales were affected to a very small degree by an eighteen-week strike at the Canadian plant. Exhibit 1 presents La-Z-Boy's operating statements for the period 1987 through 1989.

Patents were highly important in the growth and development of the La-Z-Boy Chair Company, especially on its reclining-chair and rocking-chair mechanisms, and to its present competitive position. As of the late 1980s the corporation had fifty patents, most of which involved residential products. The original reclining mechanism patent, so crucial to the success of the company from 1961 forward, expired in 1978. According to R.G. Micka, vice-president of La-Z-Boy, "Patents are guarded carefully and are very important to the conduct of business in the nation's furniture trade." Competitors arose but did not copy the La-Z-Boy reclining chair mechanism, and instead developed their own. According to Micka, "Tooling up for production on this mechanism is cost-prohibitive for most manufacturers if La-Z-Boy specifications and tolerances are to be met." The corporate executives believed that La-Z-Boy was now so well-established in the industry that the loss of any single or small group of patents would not significantly affect the business.

Most products were made on the receipt of an order from the retailer or business user. A few popular models were made for stock and held in warehouses for immediate shipment. Company sales were considerably lower in the summer than in the remainder of the year, but the scheduling of production, when possible, was planned to maintain a uniform level of manufacturing activity throughout the year.

The company operated manufacturing plants in Redlands, California; Neosho, Missouri; Dayton, Tennessee; Siloam Springs, Arkansas; Leland, Mississippi; Newton, Mississippi; Tremonton, Utah; Lincolnton, North Carolina; Lenoir, North Carolina; Hudson, North Carolina; Monroe, Michigan; Grand Rapids, Michigan; and Waterloo, Ontario. It had a parts warehouse and distribution center in Prairie, Mississippi. The company had two facilities in Florence, South Carolina, a manufacturing plant and a fabric-processing center. The one dealing in fabrics was small and employed only a few people, but it received and redistributed all fabrics to all the company's manufacturing plants. The headquarters people calculated fabric requirements of each plant based on furniture production schedules, and the fabric processing center then shipped the appropriate amounts of the appropriate fabrics. Each plant made only a few items in the product line. The Monroe headquarters plus the facilities in Redlands, Dayton, Siloam Springs, Waterloo, Lincolnton, Grand Rapids, Lenoir, and Hudson were owned. The Neosho, Florence, Newton, and Tremonton plants as well as the automated Fabric Processing Center were financed by issuance of industrial revenue bonds and were occupied under long-term leases. The Leland plant was under long-term lease between the Board of Supervisors of Washington County, Mississippi, and La-Z-Boy. The company received small amounts of royalty income from the sale and licensing of its trademarks, trade names, and patents to foreign manufacturers in Norway, Italy, West Germany, South Africa, New Zealand, and Australia.

The principal raw materials used by La-Z-Boy in the manufacture of its furniture were hardwoods for solid wood dining room and bedroom furniture, casegoods, occasional tables, and for the frame components of seating units; plywood and chipwood for internal parts; steel for the mechanisms; cotton, wool, synthetic, and vinyl fabrics, and leather and polyurethane foam for cushioning. In 1989 the company voluntarily stopped using foam containing chlorofluorocarbons. This change did not add to materials costs in production. The steel and wood products were purchased from several sources, usually located in the vicinity of the particular plant having the need; whereas covering materials and polyurethane were purchased from a sizeable number of sources on a centralized basis. La-Z-Boy fabricated the majority of the parts in its products, largely because parts of suitable quality made to its exact specifications were not obtainable from outside suppliers at prices La-Z-Boy considered reasonable.

Fabrics were highly important in the residential furniture business. There was extensive testing of fabric samples for strength, abrasion, fading, and general wear. The fabric-buying function was housed in the Monroe headquarters. Fabric buyers' recommendations, based on both functional and aesthetic considerations, were presented to the Fabric Review Committee and then to corporate management for final approval. Because of its large buying power, La-Z-Boy was able to obtain a few fabrics on an exclusive basis.

A new testing laboratory went into operation in 1985. It was twice as large as the facility it replaced and was equipped better. Not only were fabrics tested, but padding, springs, finishes, frames, glues, reinforcements, and mechanisms also were tested.

Research and development (R&D) typically amounted to about 0.7 percent of sales. An activity carried out principally at corporate headquarters, R&D was a combination of pure engineering and the application of artistic design and comfort to engineering concepts. R&D effort began converting to CAD (computer-aided-design) in

1983 and was almost completely changed over by 1990. This allowed almost instant recombinations of variables and minute alterations to product proposals. The computer display screen was more versatile than the printed or hand-drawn diagram. Plant engineering departments in the various company facilities scattered across North America were on-line, which made possible the exchange of design data instantaneously in electronic form and the printing of full-size product drawings in a few minutes at any location. Electronics also were being applied effectively to the cutting of fabric so as to minimize wastage.

The Residential Division maintained year-round showrooms in six cities for dealers and participated in several furniture shows/markets annually. It had ninety-four sales representatives, all paid on a commission basis. The company shipped its residential products to approximately 9,000 locations, but the number of retail stores carrying some or all of the line was an unknown but larger figure. This was because some shipping destinations served several branches of one retailer. The largest retailer account was Montgomery Ward, which had over 300 branches.

The company also distributed through Showcase Shoppes, the number of which grew from 230 in 1986 to 300 in 1989. Such a business was a locally owned merchant who had agreed through contract to handle only La-Z-Boy products and use the name Showcase Shoppe. This permitted a consumer to see most of the range of La-Z-Boy residential furniture displayed to advantage in coordinated room settings. The manufacturer set the standards for the store location, size, design, layout, presentation, signage, customer service, and staffing of each store. They averaged 6,900 square feet in size. Showcase Shoppes accounted for 35 percent of the sales of La-Z-Boy's Residential Division in 1988. Nearly all such stores were in metropolitan areas. In rural areas and small cities, La-Z-Boy dominated the motion furniture business, but in metropolitan markets the company was only one of several strong and several marginal contenders. The Showcase Shoppes began in 1975, and by now only a small number were added each year. As the Showcase network grew, the number of shipping destinations for the Residential Division declined. This decline was about 33 percent between 1975 and 1985, but for the fourteen year period 1975 to 1989 the decline was about 20 percent. La-Z-Boy dropped a few accounts on its own initiative. Of course, La-Z-Boy knew that the total number of furniture stores in the United States also declined from about 23,000 in 1980 to about 16,000 in 1990.

The La-Z-Boy Gallery program began in 1987. It was an arrangement whereby independent furniture retailers, mainly in medium-size communities, dedicated a consolidated floor area to only La-Z-Boy products. Each cooperating store had to use the full room display method and allocate enough space for at least eight rooms of La-Z-Boy furniture. The average size of dedicated selling space was 3,800 square feet. The number of stores in this program increased from thirty-seven in 1987 to seventy in 1988 and ninety-four in 1989, and more were planned by La-Z-Boy for the early 1990s.

The Contract Division maintained its own sales force. The contract line was handled through 1,300 office furnishings stores, a few mail-order catalog companies, and a substantial number of contract dealers. A contract dealer normally handled only sizeable specialized customer orders. La-Z-Boy was eager to establish a relationship with more contract dealers. Almost two-thirds of contract furniture orders were placed by interior designers, architects, and Contract Division dealers. The Contract Division maintained permanent showrooms in Chicago, Atlanta, and Dallas and set up numerous temporary exhibits at shows that specialized by industry.

Advise La-Z-Boy Chair Company.

McDONALD'S CORPORATION

McDonald's Corporation was one of the best-known companies in the United States and Canada and constituted a success story seldom equaled. Systemwide sales were over $18 billion and had shown an average 13 percent growth rate over the past ten years. Total assets and stockholders' equity were rising rapidly. No dividends were paid until the twenty-second year of the organization's life, all the profits being plowed back into fast expansion of the system.

Restaurants operated by McDonald's itself furnished about 22 percent of systemwide sales; whereas franchised restaurants accounted for about 65 percent of sales. Most franchisors operated from 15 percent to 20 percent of their outlets, but McDonald's operated 25 percent of its outlets. This figure was down from 1978, when McDonald's operated 27 percent of its outlets. In comparison, Burger King operated 15 percent of the restaurants bearing its name. It was relatively easy for McDonald's to get competent franchisees, because the average net profit per franchised location after all types of expenses and fees was $120,000 per year.

The approximately 700 restaurants operated by several affiliates in foreign countries, chiefly Japan and Taiwan, were responsible for about 9 percent of the sales. An affiliate was a company in which McDonald's held equity but only 50 percent or less. McDonald's owned exactly 50 percent of the Japanese affiliate.

The combined sales of foreign affiliates, foreign franchises, and company-owned units abroad amounted to about 30 percent of company sales, but these sales were increasing faster than domestic sales. The corresponding percentage in 1985 was only about 20 percent. Twenty of

McDonald's twenty-two largest volume restaurants were abroad. There were McDonald's restaurants in fifty-one countries.

McDonald's held about a 20 percent share of the U.S. market for fast foods in total but about 45 percent of the burger market, and it was much larger than its competitors. In terms of sales, it was more than twice as large as Kentucky Fried Chicken and Burger King; three times as large as Wendy's; more than four times as large as Hardee's, Pizza Hut, and Church's Fried Chicken; and more than five times as large as Dairy Queen.

McDonald's selected each location and constructed the store's internal facilities. McDonald's formerly had a policy that each building had to be freestanding, but this proved too inflexible. The company preferred to own each building, but many highly desirable locations could not be bought. With ownership of 60 percent of the buildings it occupied, McDonald's was the largest holder of commercial real estate in the United States. This policy tied up enormous amounts of capital, but the company thought it gained in the long run from the property's appreciation of value and the certainty of occupancy. Besides, it had no shortage of capital for expansion. There was a greater shortage of sites into which to expand.

A franchisee who operated an establishment paid McDonald's a large initial franchising fee, half in cash and half to be paid later, and a security deposit, plus an annual franchise fee of 3.5 percent of sales and an annual building rental of 8.5 percent of sales. These figures were slightly lower in franchise contracts signed prior to 1987. The franchise lasted for twenty years and included intensive training at the company's Hamburger University in Elk Grove Village, Illinois; management counseling; assistance with operations, advertising, and public relations; financial advice; materials for employee training; and the financial benefits of volume purchasing. However, McDonald's was not in the business of supplying the franchisees. Instead, it negotiated supply contracts with outside companies.

Growth, Development, and Policies

The company was founded in 1955 by Ray Kroc, who sold malted-milk machines. His curiosity was piqued in 1954, when he received an order for eight units from one hamburger restaurant, for that meant someone had found it necessary to make very large numbers of malts simultaneously. That establishment was McDonald's in San Bernardino, California, an eight-year-old firm owned and operated by Maurice "Mac" and Richard McDonald. The two brothers had developed the concept of the assembly-line hamburger and accompanying french fries. They had pioneered in the use of a standardized beef patty, with a standardized sauce, and an infrared lamp to keep the cooked potatoes crisp. In front of the restaurant was a large sign displaying two golden arches. The prices were quite low. Kroc was extremely impressed with what he saw: good value for the money, speedy service, elimination of wastefulness, cleanliness, the absence of anything to be stolen, and standardization. The McDonald brothers had franchised six other establishments in California to use their name and their complete set of procedures, but they were cautious and conservative about expanding further and wanted very much to avoid the traveling that inevitably would go with expanded operations. Kroc talked with them for three days while they assembled hamburgers. Finally, they worked out a contract whereby Kroc would have the exclusive right to sell the McDonald's name and complete package of procedures to franchisees and would get a percentage of sales made by franchisees. Six years later, in 1960, Kroc completely bought out the McDonald brothers' interests for $2.7 million.

Ray Kroc believed strongly in the concept of systems. He frequently instructed people, especially franchisees, that there was a science to making and serving a hamburger. He described his operating philosophy with two acronyms, QSC/TLC, which meant "Quality, Service, Cleanliness/Tender Loving Care." He emphasized that the company gave a person a chance to get into business for himself or herself without taking the entire risk alone. But that person had to agree to follow a proved way of conducting the business. Although Kroc saw the extreme importance of systems in creating and running an organization, he believed that systems should be no more complex than necessary. He frequently called attention to a favorite rule of thumb called KISS for short, which translated "Keep it simple, stupid."

The system included physical standardization. Kroc believed that the public would react positively to a standardization that featured not only places that turned out the same food but that were extremely clean inside and outside and were staffed by courteous people. Most of the industry of which McDonald's was part had a reputation for slovenly conditions and unconcerned, often surly employees in those early years. Another point emphasized to franchisees, managers, and employees was the need to maintain scrupulously clean restrooms.

McDonald's believed strongly in monitoring the work of franchisees and its own restaurant managers. Standardization and enforcement of policies could not really be accomplished without management audits. Accordingly, twice a year, internal consultants conducted a highly detailed inspection lasting about three days and rendered a written report with grades and comments on management practices. Among the categories critiqued were the food and beverages, cleanliness, neatness, speed of service, courtesy, and friendliness. In addition, internal consultants frequently visited the restaurants on a random basis for brief, informal inspections. Poor showings on these inspections, although they were informal, would lead to intense scrutiny. McDonald's clearly had some of the tightest control procedures in the food industry.

The company emphasized suburban locations, thus tapping the great U.S. population movements of the late 1950s and 1960s. Most existing fast-food firms chose to remain in the cities and ignored the suburbs. In the 1970s, McDonald's expanded into the cities and into some small towns.

The Product Line

Although it was realized that the "product" was far more than the food, the heart of McDonald's product was the food itself. The company was devoted to simple, bland foods that would have a rather broad, repetitive appeal and would be easy to make. The hamburger sandwich fitted these criteria, but as food traditions go, it was a relative newcomer. Hamburger meat originated in medieval Eastern Europe as raw beef shredded by a dull knife. Baltic region traders brought it to Hamburg, where it is still eaten both cooked and raw. German immigrants later brought it encased in bread to the United States. It is claimed that the hamburger was introduced by these immigrants in the Cincinnati area and also in St. Louis. There is good documentation that the first large-scale public offering of the hamburger was at the St. Louis World's Fair of 1904. New Haven, Connecticut, however, claims that a restaurant called Louis Lunch was the first to popularize this German dish.

There was always great concern for appropriate product characteristics and an appropriate product mix. Kroc determined that the company's first hamburger patty had to measure 1.6 ounces and go in a bun 3.5 inches in diameter. He decreed that the bun must contain extra sugar so that it would brown faster and that the sandwich must contain exactly one-fourth of an ounce of onion. In 1963 the company introduced its double burger and double cheeseburger. Although it believed passionately in standardization, McDonald's was always interested in new product development and in the improvement of the product line. Despite the fact that it had people engaged in research, McDonald's was quite receptive to product ideas arising from its franchisees. One of the great breakthroughs came from franchisee Lou Groen, who operated a restaurant in a Roman Catholic neighborhood in Cincinnati. On Fridays his sales dropped by about half. In 1961 he began experimenting with a breaded fish filet sandwich and his Friday sales increased. In 1963 this product became an official part of the McDonald's menu and soon thereafter was named the Filet-o-Fish. This was the first expansion beyond burgers, french fries, and beverages. Franchisee Jim Delligatti of Pittsburgh saw that he was losing some trade to a nearby competitor who offered an oversized hamburger. Accordingly, he put two all-beef patties, special sauce, lettuce, cheese, pickles, and onions on a sesame seed bun. The company adopted it in 1968, called it the Big Mac, and it became the best-selling item in the product line.

Something more radical was developed in 1972 by franchisee Herbert Peterson in Santa Barbara, California, who saw that his restaurants might be more profitable if they opened at 7 A.M. rather than 10 A.M. Peterson had always enjoyed eggs Benedict and thought that the masses would like something similar if he could simplify it and adapt it to the company's price structure and operating system. After six months of experimentation he introduced his Fast-Break Breakfast, a sandwich of Canadian bacon, cheese, and an egg on an English muffin. Along with earlier openings, this product was introduced in most McDonald's restaurants in the United States in 1976 under the name Egg McMuffin. This product added over 10 percent to sales the first year. Soon thereafter the breakfast menu in the chain was expanded by adding fruit juices; Danish pastries; English muffins; hash brown potatoes; a platter of sausage and hot cakes; and a platter of sausage, scrambled eggs, and hash brown potatoes. Most units of the chain adopted the 7 A.M. opening except on Sundays, when the opening was usually set at 8 A.M. Breakfast was served until 10:30 on weekdays and 11:00 on weekends in nearly all branches. By 1989 breakfast was providing 21 percent of McDonald's sales in the United States.

On average, McDonald's kept about twenty proposed products in various stages of research and development. Most would not even reach the test-marketing phase. Besides risk of failure of a product, there was the grave concern that a new product that sold well might really accomplish nothing for the company but shift demand from an established product.

The company developed the Quarter Pounder in 1972 to replace the double hamburger. This new product caused McDonald's great public relations difficulties, for an official investigation by the U.S. Department of Agriculture showed that in no instance did the meat used exceed three ounces in weight. A belated advertising campaign by McDonald's emphasized the point that the patty used in the Quarter Pounder weighed a quarter of a pound *before* cooking.

In 1975 the company successfully added McDonaldland cookies, a bland, vanilla-flavored product made of flour, sugar, shortening, corn syrup, salt, leavening, lecithin, and artificial flavoring in the shape of fantasy characters from the company advertising and sales promotion. It was sold in two-ounce (fifty-six grams) portions packed in pasteboard boxes. Very much like the traditional "animal crackers," these were a hit, especially with children. The cookies were manufactured by the Keebler Company, already well-known to children through its famous elves. Hot cherry and apple pies cooked in an individual serving size followed in all locations. Pumpkin and blueberry pies were offered seasonally in selected locations starting in the mid-1980s. The cherry pie was withdrawn in most locations later. Ice cream sundaes and cones were introduced in many locations as a test market and later adopted. Hot tea was added in most locations in 1977 and iced tea shortly thereafter. "Chocolaty chip" cookies were added in the mid-1980s.

Exhaustive product development research on chicken began in 1971. The cooking of chicken, even merely frying it, offered many options to be evaluated carefully. For example, Kentucky Fried Chicken restaurants in the United States offered a choice of soft or extremely crispy chicken. In 1980 two major chicken products entered test markets. One was the McChicken sandwich, composed of a boneless chicken patty of combined dark and light meat, shredded lettuce, and a dressing that resembled mayonnaise, all on a bun. The other was Chicken McNuggets, bite-size lumps of boneless chicken served with a choice of three sauces or dips. The basic idea for Chicken McNuggets resulted from an elevator conversation between Fred Turner, the company chairperson, and Rene Arend, the head chef in the organization's laboratory kitchens. At the time Arend was experimenting with recipes for the proposed Onion McNuggets, but Turner suggested experimentation with chicken as well. After a long, careful test-marketing effort, the decision went against the chicken sandwich, but the McNuggets were added to the product line. In 1986 Wendy's added to its line a similar product called Crispy Chicken Nuggets. In the late 1980s McDonald's tested two versions of a chicken sandwich, one of them spicy, and then brought back the McChicken sandwich. The rising concern of much of the public about the cholesterol level of beef was influential here. Moreover, this addition of chicken was far simpler than addition of fried chicken parts, which had been considered by the top management.

The company began testing the McFeast in 1978. This product was an extra large burger topped with tomato slices and lettuce. It finally evolved into the McDLT, a regular size cheeseburger with lettuce and tomato slices that was introduced in 1985. In that year, small-scale test marketing began on bacon, egg, and cheese biscuits, sausage biscuits, and sausage and egg biscuits. The biscuit products were added to the regular product line by the late 1980s.

The company's first experience with fresh lettuce and tomatoes, connected with the McDLT, inevitably encouraged it to experiment with salads. Test marketing of salads was begun in late 1984, and by 1986 this testing had spread to numerous cities. Instead of a salad bar, the proposed products were individually made and prepackaged salads in three varieties, one of them containing shrimp. McDonald's management emphasized the convenience of the products, whereas competitors pointed out the inflexibility of choice for the consumer and lack of freshness. Mc-Donald's, however, received some advantages from prepackaged salads instead of a salad bar. The company avoided four undesirable results: (1) the messiness inevitably associated with a salad bar and the area adjacent to it; (2) the labor to keep the bar stocked and clean and to clean the floor area immediately around it; (3) the loss of portion control; and (4) the loss of valuable space that could be used for tables. The company also gained the advantage that customers in the drive-throughs could order a prepackaged salad, whereas they could not select from a salad bar. McDonald's also gained from the fact that a customer who was in the restaurant for breakfast could buy a prepackaged salad to have at the workplace for lunch, although very few customers seemed to have thought of this point. McDonald's hinted at the sanitation advantage of a prewrapped individual salad in place of an open salad bar, but it was too sensitive a point to promote straightforwardly. Ironically, McDonald's had a problem on its hands and received much bad publicity in 1986, when six persons in Maryland became quite ill from shrimp salads assembled in an allegedly unhygienic manner by McDonald's employees. Despite this incident in Maryland, the company was very happy with the test marketing of the salads.

Management analysts concluded that, unlike the addition of most other items in the past, the sale of salads rarely cannibalized the sale of other products. In fact, not only did many people add a salad to their order, but many people came to McDonald's only because they could now get both a non-beef protein and a green salad. McDonald's understood that sometimes entire groups of people had had to bypass McDonald's because one person in the group could not, or would not, eat the previous menu items. This was known in the trade as the "veto factor." The salads added about seven percent to sales and were adopted in 1987. In that same year Hardee's added three salads, including one that contained seafood, to its line.

Several products were tried in the late 1980s. Pizza was test marketed in a few locations, starting in 1987. Because of different ingredients and cooking time, it would be a major change if adopted later. McDonald's planned to use the biscuit ovens for the pizza after the breakfast trade was over, if it added this product. Company staff people were divided in their preferences for a small, individual pizza or a large size. Unlike the major pizza chains McDonald's used frozen dough for the product. Both as a seasonal promotion and short test market in December 1989 and January 1990 McDonald's offered eggnog milk shakes, peppermint sundaes, and orange sauce for the chicken nuggets. A product called the Cheddar Melt began a test market in late 1989. It consisted of a bun made of both rye and wheat flour, described as a "light rye" bun, one-fourth pound of ground beef, grilled onions, and a small amount of melted cheddar cheese. Hardee's had been doing considerable volume in various melts. Moreover, McDonald's set up an experimental restaurant in a Sears department store and also licensed the term "McKids" to Sears for labels on certain children's clothing. In addition, work in the company's product laboratories continued on a pasta salad, a taco salad, chili, and chicken-noodle soup. The company was also considering adding yogurt and sherbet to the menu.

For markets abroad, McDonald's made a few additions to the standard menu. For example, it added soup in Japan, chicken croquettes and apple sauce in Holland, fried chicken in Australia, spaghetti in the Philippines, wine in France, and beer in West Germany. A few substitutions were used, such as mustard and mayonnaise in place of catsup in Holland, except when catsup was requested, and spinach leaves instead of lettuce in the Soviet Union, where lettuce was virtually unknown. Market research conducted by various fast-food corporations indicated that most foreign customers wanted the standard American menus with only a few additions if they were going to an American-owned eating place. If they wanted non-American food they would go to a non-American restaurant. McDonald's had much more business abroad than any other American restaurant organization. A few other modifications were adopted by the company in a few countries, such as restroom attendants in a few places whom one had to tip and more dining room employees in a few places where most customers refused to bus their own trays to a waste disposal can. In many countries customers lingered far longer than McDonald's had intended, because there was a cultural tradition of spending a long time relaxing before, during, and after eating. Even stopping by for a soda was often an extended event.

Interestingly enough, when one McDonald's branch in California applied to local authorities for a beer license in 1984, there was an avalanche of complaints, and the application was withdrawn. This test action had been watched closely by the entire chain and, in fact, the entire fast-food industry.

McDonald's had been ultraconservative and cautious in accepting new product ideas. The company used a long lead time and finished off the development process with extensive test marketing. Nevertheless, it had had some failures: the roast beef sandwich, the pineapple burger, the Triple Ripple ice-cream cone, and the chopped beef sandwich. While still in test markets, the McRib sandwich was judged a failure. It was made of "restructured beef," which was less desirable cuts of beef reformed into attractive shapes to look like steaks. Many people in the company were emotionally attached to the McRib and found its failure depressing. About the same time, Burger King also failed with a steak sandwich. McDonald's widely test-marketed fried onion cubes in 1979 but decided against them. In the fast-food restaurant industry as a whole, a clear majority of the new products introduced had failed. McDonald's had always done much better than the average.

The company was anxious to ensure that the cooking process be systematic to keep its products consistent. Cybernetic deep fryers continuously adjusted to the moisture in potatoes so that all servings would have the same degree of brownness, and lights on the grills alerted the attendant to flip the patties. In 1984 ten seconds of cooking time was added to the cooking of a burger. Size of potatoes, the Burbank russet type, was controlled carefully in purchasing contracts. Because potatoes could not be controlled in advance, special scoops were designed to apportion the cooked potatoes correctly.

Besides preparing the foods according to company policy, McDonald's was vitally interested that the food also be in good condition when served. Therefore, the chain had a policy of throwing away unserved burger patties after ten minutes, french fries after seven minutes, and coffee after thirty minutes. Such losses were minimized through careful planning and control, of course, and in some branches by holding so little in reserve that the customer usually had to wait, despite the policies about immediate service. Norms for such food and beverage losses were built into the budgeting process, and franchisees and managers were fully advised about these expectations.

The styrofoam packages around the food and beverages had evoked many vigorous complaints from environmentalists but served to insulate the products better than those of competitors. In the late 1980s McDonald's finally yielded on the use of chloroflourocarbons, which helped to destroy the earth's ozone layer, in making the packaging plastics. However, the replacement ingredient, pentane, was alleged to cause smog and eye irritation. Moreover, all packaging materials made of styrofoam had serious problems of biodegradability. In the late 1980s McDonald's began a test arrangement with a New England firm to attempt to recycle the plastic materials from several hundred of its restaurants into nonpackaging materials. The economics and technology of the test were not going to be clear for several years. The critics wanted paper packaging, which most of McDonald's competitors used.

Major competitors of McDonald's were giving increasing attention to their own product development and improvement of their own present product lines. Whereas McDonald's was an independent organization, Burger King had been purchased by Pillsbury, a large conglomerate, several years earlier. Kentucky Fried Chicken had been purchased by Pepsico, another large conglomerate, in 1986. Pepsico also owned Pizza Huts and Taco Bell. Although much smaller than McDonald's, the Burger King, Kentucky Fried Chicken, and Pizza Hut chains had access to their parents' considerable capital, product development laboratories, and expertise, and a tradition of commitment to new product development.

Pillsbury was bought by Grand Metropolitan, a British conglomerate, in 1989. Through aggressive advertising and on-premises sales promotion, Burger King was well on its way toward making the King character as well-known as Ronald McDonald. Wendy's, a competitive hamburger chain founded in Ohio in 1969 and not affiliated with any parent or conglomerate, now employed forty-two people in its new product development operation.

Besides the matters already mentioned, there was concern about demographic trends, the taste of the company's food, and criticism of the nutritional characteristics of the company's product line. Demographic trends were extremely unsettling. It was clear that the company's trade was primarily with children, teenagers, and adults under age thirty-five. Customers thirty-five years of age or over contributed only about 23 percent of sales, although they constituted about 43 percent of the U.S. population. Children age fifteen or under accounted for 20 percent of sales, whereas persons age sixteen to thirty-four accounted for 57 percent. This fact was acceptable as an application of the principle of aiming at a target market. However, the U.S. birthrate had declined dramatically, and the population was aging. Wendy's was aiming at the over twenty-five market and was faring well. It featured a stylish decor, and its customers were not expected to clear off their tables. Wendy's was also doing well abroad. Wendy's offered beer and/or wine in many of its foreign branches.

After Ray Kroc went into semiretirement and ownership of McDonald's' corporate stock became slightly more diffused, the new board chairperson, forty-six-year-old Fred L. Turner, who had started out as a McDonald's cook, encouraged some physical changes. There were several objectives, one of which was to attract more middle-aged and older adults. McDonald's worked quickly to moderate the garish exterior look of the restaurants, which were often in multicolored candy stripes. Other factors to be dealt with were the feelings of upper-middle-class people who found McDonald's visually jarring at best and unacceptably offensive at worst, occasional ethnic feelings, and occasional zoning regulations. A neat brown brick exterior of no particular architectural style was the usual result. Moreover, many golden arches signs were greatly reduced in size and some were merely attached to one wall of the building. Drive-through service bays were added in over 1,000 units, chiefly in the warmer regions of the United States, a throwback to the early years of some competitors. This proved highly popular. In the branches having drive-throughs slightly over half the sales volume came from the drive-through customers. New uniforms for employees were designed and made available in a variety of colors to suit the decor. A few California and Maryland units of the chain experimented with having a hostess, attired at night in an attractive long gown, and substituting candlelight for the usual lighting. Such tests were deemed failures. In a second cycle of architectural changes, McDonald's authorized fifteen new exterior and interior designs: English Tudor, Country French, New England, Western, Spanish, Old English, Dutch Colonial, Tahitian, Caribbean, French Quarter, Alpine, Midwesterner, Williamsburg, Cambridge, and Gas-light.

In addition, the company began to broaden what was acceptable as a location. It started to seek sites in educational institutions, airports, zoos, military bases, and elsewhere. It even opened a branch in a children's hospital. In a unique arrangement, a McDonald's in College Park, Maryland, near the University of Maryland began to offer regular free McShuttle bus service to and from several places on the campus. The same branch was the first in the chain to offer home delivery, but this service failed. Burger King was test-marketing the use of mobile restaurants built on oversized vans. McDonald's had been successful with a number of mall restaurants, but it began an interesting experimental restaurant in a suburban Minneapolis mall in which there was no seating area and no burgers were on the menu. The earliest McDonald's also had no seating.

Although many people were virtually oblivious to the taste of the food they were eating and many were unable or unwilling to give the time it took to savor the taste, there was a modest trend toward increasing American interest in cooking. Gourmet authors and food commentators drew large audiences in person and through the media. Craig Claiborne and Julia Child both found McDonald's french fries good, but James Beard concluded, "The whole thing is aimed at the six-year-old palate." Gael Greene noted that the cheese tasted like glue and added, "I love the malts—thick, sweet and ice cold. They're better than if they were real."[1]

Social criticism of the nutritional characteristics of food served by McDonald's and other fast-food organizations had been growing for several years.[2] These products were termed "junk food." McDonald's was frequently the focus of criticism, not because it was the worst but because it was the largest. Among the most vocal were black critics who charged that McDonald's expansion into the inner city enticed the poor with low-nutrition food. As a matter of fact, McDonald's had a month-long advertising campaign in the early 1970s on the theme that each person should eat other foods in addition to what the company offered. A detailed research project done by Consumers Union and published in

---

[1] "The Burger That Conquered the Country," *Time*, September 17, 1973, p. 85; and "Love in the Kitchen: The Outcome? Cuisine, Now Chow," *Time*, December 19, 1977, pp. 54–61.

[2] The social criticism of McDonald's early years and up to 1976 can be found in the highly opinionated book by Max Boas and Steve Chain, *Big Mac: The Unauthorized Story of McDonald's* (New York: E.P. Dutton & Co., Inc., 1976).

its *Consumer Reports* showed that Big Macs contained more salt per ounce than the burgers served by McDonald's major competitors but that McDonald's shakes and french fries contained less salt per ounce than the average for the fast-food industry.[3] Of course, a customer could request french fries without salt. In late 1984, McDonald's began a test market of unsalted burgers and pancakes in the Chicago metropolitan area. Nearly all the company's product line was unquestionably high in fats, sugar, and salt as well as calories. The real nutritional problem was not just McDonald's food but the severely unbalanced and overcaloric diet of a substantial fraction of the U.S. population, which included many millions of McDonald's regular customers. In partial answer to the critics, McDonald's published a small booklet, "McDonald's Food . . . The Facts," which contained information about the ingredients and nutritional characteristics of the food. It was available in the branches and from the company's Nutrition Information Center in Oak Brook, Illinois. Most McDonald's branches began displaying nutritional information posters in 1990.

McDonald's management issued a written statement: "McDonald's menu will continue to evolve to remain responsive to customer preferences, and our commitment to high-quality ingredients will remain unchanged." In addition, Michael Quinlan, who had worked his way up through operations and then become senior executive for operations, became company president and chief executive officer. In an organization in which only half the officers held university degrees, he was a real oddity in that he held an M.B.A.

Advise McDonald's Corporation.

GIBSON GREETINGS, INC. (A)

Gibson Greetings, Inc., was the oldest and third-largest producer of greeting cards in the United States. It was successful and had been growing rapidly in recent years but now faced some challenging problems and some opportunities to develop further certain of its successful strategies.

Composition of the Industry

The greeting card industry in the United States was comprised of three large companies and many small companies. The number of small firms varied from time to time but averaged around 500. Hallmark Cards, Inc., based in Kansas City, Missouri, held approximately a 40 percent share of the card market whereas American Greetings Corporation, based in Cleveland, Ohio, held about 30 percent, and Gibson Greetings, Inc.,

[3] "Fast Food Chains," *Consumer Reports* (September 1979), pp. 508–513.

based in Cincinnati, held about 10 percent. Norcross was once prominent and a challenger for third place but had gone bankrupt.

Established in 1910, Hallmark was clearly the leader, but its market share had slowly fallen from well over 50 percent in the 1960s. Both American Greetings Corporation, established in 1906, and Gibson Greetings were highly aggressive and increasing their share of the annual national market for cards of about $4 billion. Gibson had doubled its share of the market during a six-year period of the early and middle 1980s. Growth in market share slowed after that point.

All three organizations made wrapping supplies and paper party goods as well as cards. Hallmark's total sales were about five times as high as Gibson's; and American Greetings Corporation's sales, about three times as high as Gibson's. Hallmark had about 18,000 employees, and American Greetings, about 21,800. Exhibit 1 presents Gibson's recent operating statements and balance sheets.

The whole card industry was characterized by intense competition, but it was a growth industry. Consumption of cards grew rapidly from the mid-1960s into the 1970s, then approximately stabilized over a short period, and then began to rise rapidly again. The no-growth period coincided with widespread sluggishness in the economy and some increases in the use of long-distance telephone calls. The long-distance people were seemingly influential in saying, "Reach out and touch someone." Over the period 1965–1986, greeting card industry sales rose an average of about eight and a half percent per annum.

Although Gibson and American Greetings Corporation were rather specialized, Hallmark was already diversified and becoming more so. In 1984 the industry leader acquired Binney & Smith, Inc., makers of Crayola crayons, a product whose brand name was virtually synonymous with crayons. Hallmark also had ownership interests in real estate, textbook publishing, and broadcasting. Earlier, of course, it had added new products such as paper goods for parties, candles, mugs, and albums. Greeting cards provided about half of Hallmark's sales volume, down from nine-tenths in the 1960s. About 200 of Hallmark's employees worked in the company's new Technical and Innovation Center opened in 1983; and 700, in research and creativity. The select 200 were working on new ways to design and print cards. At any given time, Hallmark had an average of 32,000 different card designs in its entire line. Only about 10 percent of the designs lasted for more than a year, but the company's general-use card with purple pansies had been in production since 1941. Although the Hall family still held 70 percent of the shares and employees held the rest, Hallmark was slowly transferring much of the significant authority to professional executives who were not emotionally attached to the greeting card industry. Both Hallmark and American Greetings had export sales, but they were not large in the total sales mix. Gibson had only trivial foreign sales, about one percent of its total.

EXHIBIT 1 Gibson Greetings, Inc. Operating Statement and Balance Sheet

			Years Ended December 31,				
	1988	1987	1986	1985	1984	1983	1982

Summary Income Statement Data (dollars in thousands except per share amounts)

	1988	1987	1986	1985	1984	1983	1982
Revenues:							
Net sales	**$402,230**	$358,027	$321,769	$328,782	$300,385	$240,574	$197,075
Royalty income	**2,117**	1,556	1,437	1,130	1,133	963	627
Total revenues	**404,347**	359,583	323,206	329,912	301,518	241,537	197,702
Cost of products sold	**190,246**	172,781	156,183	159,004	143,704	112,311	95,262
Selling, distribution, and administrative expenses	**151,938**	137,916	121,215	111,848	98,894	79,360	68,736
Interest expense, net	**5,432**	5,437	5,610	7,493	6,426	7,950	14,420
Income before income taxes and extraordinary items	**56,731**	43,449	40,198	5,567	52,494	41,916	19,284
Income taxes	**21,706**	19,349	17,575	22,900	24,147	19,524	5,268
Income before extraordinary items	**35,025**	24,100	22,623	28,667	28,347	22,392	14,016
Extraordinary items	**—**	—	—	2,797	—	—	—
Net income	**$ 35,025**	$ 24,100	$22,623	$ 31,464	$ 28,347	$ 22,392	$ 14,016
Income per share before extraordinary items (1)	**$ 2.25**	$ 1.53	$ 1.43	$ 1.81	$ 1.79	$ 1.44	$ .97
Net income per share (1)	**$ 2.25**	$ 1.53	$ 1.43	$ 1.99	$ 1.79	$ 1.44	$ .97
Dividends per share (1)	**$ .29**	$ .25	$ .25	$ .24	$ .19	$ .26	$ —

EXHIBIT 1 *(Continued)*

				Years Ended December 31,			
	1988	1987	1986	1985	1984	1983	1982
Summary Balance Sheet Data (dollars in thousands)							
Working capital	**$160,283**	$136,896	$123,234	$117,524	$103,204	$ 63,269	$ 31,790
Plant and equipment, net	**57,797**	53,436	58,674	50,054	38,492	17,127	7,505
Note receivable from related party	—	—	—	—	30,954	30,954	30,954
Goodwill	—	—	—	—	—	—	—
Total assets	**326,368**	288,946	274,956	261,371	243,263	182,130	148,233
Short-term debt (2)	**61,402**	51,388	46,753	52,000	29,500	23,674	46,476
Long-term debt	**18,6377**	23,329	28,017	32,700	35,200	—	9,167
Subordinated note payable to related party	—	—	—	—	30,778	30,778	30,778
Excess of fair value of companies acquired over cost, net	**4,330**	5,780	7,230	8,680	10,130	11,580	13,030
Stockholders' equity	**186,105**	153,858	138,004	118,871	91,012	65,344	15,016

(1) All information relating to the number of shares of common stock outstanding and data presented on a per share basis has been adjusted to reflect a 7-for-1 common stock split effected in April 1983 and a 3-for-2 common stock split effected in March 1985.
(2) Includes the current portion of long-term debt, which consisted of $2,692 in 1988, $2,688 in 1987, $2,683 in 1986, $2,000 in 1985 and 1984, $14,621 in 1983, $2,000 in 1982, and $682 in each of the years 1981, 1980, and 1979.

The small card company portion of the industry was quite healthy and could not be taken lightly. Although the average life of small companies was short, any one of them might become another Gibson quickly. On the whole, this part of the industry was inventive and daring, especially in designing products and finding market niches. Among the most noteworthy small competitors were Papercraft Corporation, CPS Inc., California Dreamers, Roserich Designs Ltd., Sunrise Publications, Paper Moon Graphics, Avanti, Inc., Current, Inc., Maine Line, Broom Designs, Inc., Sun Cards, L'Image Graphics, and Blue Mountain Arts. Paper Moon Graphics, a Chicago organization, was distinguished for quirky humor and striking drawings. Avanti, a Detroit company, was known for contemporary color photography. Founded in 1950 and based in Colorado Springs, Current, Inc. sold its cards only by the box (including mixed use assortments) and only by mail and offered low prices and good value. Maine Line, of Rockport, Maine, emphasized cards that appealed principally to women.

One of the most creative small manufacturers was Blue Mountain Arts, founded in Boulder, Colorado, in 1971. It was known for its distinctive cards featuring rambling poetry and pastel watercolor designs. Highly successful, Blue Mountain had sales of slightly over $20 million and normally about 300 card designs in its line. Relations between Blue Mountain and the 20,000 retailers that carried its products were unusually cordial. In the industry Blue Mountain was best known for suing Hallmark, alleging that the latter had copied its cards and had repeatedly pressured retailers to drop the Blue Mountain brand. The Blue Mountain cards and the Personal Touch line from Hallmark were strikingly similar, with the same pastel colors, images, border, and the uneven cut on the card's right side that characterized Blue Mountain. The federal court ruled in favor of Blue Mountain, and Hallmark's appeals to higher level courts were unsuccessful. Hallmark signed a consent decree. It had to refrain from the alleged tactics, including "infringing Blue Mountain's trade dress," or artistic style, and pay an undisclosed but large amount of damages to the small company. These damages were rumored in the industry to be about $50 million. Blue Mountain became a hero among small firms. The practical effect of this court decision was virtually to ensure that there would be a large number of healthy small companies in the industry.

Ethnic cards were becoming an important part of the industry in the United States. Broom, established in Detroit in 1971, Sun, established in Washington, D.C., in 1982, and L'Image, established in Los Angeles in 1983, made cards that showed only black people. Retailers in Detroit, Washington, D.C., and Los Angeles in particular were enthusiastic about these three firms. Gibson launched its own black product line in the mid-1980s, including cards celebrating the birthday of Martin Luther King,

Jr. Moreover, Gibson purchased from the King estate the exclusive right to reproduce King's portrait and his famous "I have a dream" speech on greeting cards. A few small firms had offered Spanish language cards in the United States for about a decade. Gibson followed suit in the mid-1980s, naming the specialized line "Success."

The best-known small company was Recycled Paper Products, Inc., of Chicago. Founded in 1971 by two men just finishing college and enthusiastic about conservation issues, this organization was originally intended only to influence large card makers to switch to recycled paper stock. The founders anticipated going out of business when that occurred, satisfied that they would have done their bit for conservation. Instead, the company had been quite successful and grown rather large, and the founders had added on cards made from regular paper so that printing could be clearer and colors true. It now ranked fourth in the industry with over $60 million annual sales and was still growing faster than the industry.

Gibson's Assets, Policies, and Practices

The Gibson organization was founded by Robert H. Gibson in 1850 as a small manufacturer of greeting cards. It was incorporated in 1885 in Ohio under the name Gibson Art Company. The name was changed to Gibson Greeting Cards, Inc., in 1960, and the common stock was listed on the New York Stock Exchange from 1962 to 1964. C.I.T. Financial Corporation purchased all of Gibson in 1964 and set it up as a wholly owned subsidiary with the name Gibson Greeting Cards, Inc. RCA Corporation acquired C.I.T. in 1980. In January 1982, RCA sold the Gibson organization to investors William E. Simon and Raymond G. Chambers and several members of the operating management of Gibson. Together Simon and Chambers bought about 65 percent of the common stock; and the several managers, about 23 percent. The remainder was bought by the general public.

Both Simon and Chambers were investment bankers, and the two were chairperson of the board and president, respectively, of Wesray Corporation, a private investment banking firm. Simon was formerly deputy secretary of the U.S. Treasury in 1973, the first administrator of the Federal Energy Office between 1973 and 1974, secretary of the Treasury from 1974 to 1977, chairperson of President Reagan's Productivity Committee, a member of President Reagan's Economic Policy Advisory Council, and a director of several major corporations, including Xerox, United Technologies, Dart and Kraft, Halliburton Company, Power Corporation of Canada, and Citicorp and Citibank. He was active in many national charities and was also president of the U.S. Olympic Committee. Chambers was a well-known investor and banker. Both Simon and Chambers were directors, but not officers, of Gibson.

The board chairman was Thomas M. Cooney, who was previously the president and chief executive officer of Gibson and before that the executive vice-president of Fairmont Foods Company. The president and chief executive officer was Benjamin Sottile, a marketing specialist who was previously president of Revlon's Group 1 Beauty Group and before that the corporate senior vice-president at Warner Communications. There were several vice-presidents. One of them was Donald R. Taub, vice-president in the office of the president. Earlier in his career he was president of Rust Craft Greeting Cards, Inc., a wholly owned subsidiary of American Greetings Corporation but formerly an independent manufacturer. Until recently there had been a vice-president, Webster Schott, who was previously vice-president and creative director of American Greetings Corporation and before that job was vice-president, executive editor, and publisher of Hallmark Cards, Inc. There was very high turnover of vice-presidents in the Gibson organization during the 1980s. Organization structure at headquarters was also uncommon.

In 1984 and early 1985 there was considerable negotiation between Gibson and Walt Disney Productions. An agreement for Disney to acquire Gibson was reached, but this plan was canceled in February 1985 at a time when Disney itself was in a state of flux and new principal stockholders were taking over there.

Gibson employed about 3,200 people on a full-time basis and about 4,700 on a part-time basis as of early 1989, compared to about 2,500 and 1,600, respectively, in 1985. In addition, it hired full-time temporary workers, typically about 500 to 800, because the work load of the organization was influenced by seasonality. Need grew in the summer and peaked in September. This variation in need was in both manufacturing and warehousing workers. The seasonality of sales is shown in Exhibit 2.

Gibson designed and manufactured greeting cards, gift-wrapping paper, paper party goods, gift-wrapping accessories, and several specialty products such as calendars, stationery, plaques, candles, and related gift items. The paper party goods included tablecloths, cups, plates, and napkins in various sizes. The gift-wrapping accessories included tissue paper, kraft paper, tags, ribbons, bows, and assorted decorative trim items. The company bought a few specialty items, such as tins and ceramic mugs, which it could not make. In late 1989 Gibson acquired New Peck Corporation, of Bloomington, Indiana, a privately held maker of Christmas tags, holiday decorations, and bulletin board aids. New Peck was assigned to the Cleo operations and served to expand the product offerings of Cleo. Greeting cards provided about 50 percent of Gibson's sales; gift wrap, about 41 percent; and other items, about 9 percent. At American Greetings Corporation, cards provided 64 percent of sales, and that percentage was rather steady. Gibson enjoyed a larger share of the market for wrapping paper than for greeting cards and was number three in the wrapping paper industry, but company sales of cards were growing faster

EXHIBIT 2 Gibson Greetings, Inc., Quarterly Sales as a Percentage of Annual Sales

Year	Quarter 1 Jan. 1–Mar. 31	Quarter 2 Apr. 1–June 30	Quarter 3 July 1–Sept. 30	Quarter 4 Oct. 1–Dec. 31
Most recent	14.4	14.3	31.6	39.7
Two years ago	13.4	14.0	30.6	42.0
Three years ago	14.3	13.0	31.2	41.5
Four years ago	11.2	14.0	35.5	39.3

than those of wrapping paper. Moreover, retail and wholesale prices were rising faster for cards than for paper. It was now common for the industry to offer many cards at retail for $2.00 or more, and cards under $.75 were becoming rare. Mean price in the industry was about $1.30.

There were several ways of segmenting the greeting card product line, but the most common, traditional way was to divide between "everyday" and seasonal cards. The everyday cards accounted for about 52 percent of Gibson's card sales; and the seasonal cards, for about 48 percent. These percentages at Gibson had been steady for about five years. The corresponding figures for American Greetings Corporation were 58 and 42 percent. For the industry as a whole, everyday cards and seasonal cards were tied at 50 percent each, but the share for everyday cards was slowly increasing. Everyday cards were divided into conventional and studio, that is, humorous cards. Studio cards were sometimes called "contemporary." The seasonal cards were devoted to holiday or festive periods, which included, in declining order of Gibson's sales, Christmas, Valentine's Day, Mother's Day, Easter, Father's Day, graduation, and Thanksgiving. In the industry at large, however, Easter was a little better than Mother's Day. Christmas cards, which once accounted for well over half of the industry's seasonal sales, now accounted for one-half, and the share was decreasing, although extremely slowly. Hallmark and American Greetings offered 3,200 and 2,500 Christmas card designs, respectively. Halloween was considered by some industry people a good target for expansion. Many managers in the industry distinguished between conventional and contemporary seasonal cards. Some new festive events were being identified through marketing research and cards created to honor them. One successful example, especially popular with teenagers, conveyed congratulations on getting a driver's license. Another honored the completion of a successful diet. Because of changing family relationships, demographics, and life-styles, some cards had been introduced recently that said, "To Mom and her husband" or "To Dad and his wife."

There was less artistic freedom in creating the Mother's Day products than in most of the other seasonals. Most Mother's Day cards used floral themes and decorations. Males bought the majority of cards for that occasion, and males associated flowers with femininity. There were very few contemporary cards for Mother's Day and virtually none with goofy drawings and wisecracking messages. The marketing research had established that the demand for such cards was tiny and that very few consumers felt comfortable joking about their mother, although feelings about Father's Day were more varied. Hallmark alone made 1,000 different cards for Mother's Day.

Gibson maintained a full-time staff of artists, art directors, writers, and creative planners who designed the majority of the company's products. It also purchased the services of Helen Steiner Rice, called the "poet laureate of inspirational verse" by *The New York Times*. Writing exclusively for Gibson cards, she prepared warm, traditional verse that some people described as "syrupy." Although they sold well, these cards were seldom selected by any shopper under the age of 25. In the late 1980s Gibson began a major effort to get more out of its Steiner literary properties by launching a line of cards, called Sunshine and Rainbows, containing very short excerpts from Steiner's inspirational writing, surrounded by contemporary art work. These were aimed at young adults. Gibson also kept its traditional Steiner line.

All of the big three of the greeting card industry had been slow and conservative about designing cards that might be perceived as risque or overly suggestive, although several small firms were prospering with such products. In the late 1980s Hallmark launched a new product line entitled "Shoebox Greetings—A tiny little division of Hallmark" that was mostly suggestive. For this line Hallmark claimed "Not a fuddy-duddy card in the bunch." Gibson and American Greetings made the same move but more quietly and decorously. Such designs were always part of a humorous theme.

Design of Gibson's everyday cards began approximately 18 months in advance. Finished designs of seasonal cards started into production about 15 months before the holiday. The majority of the designs for Gibson's everyday cards were replaced every 15 months, but birthday and get-well cards were replaced every 12 months; and sympathy, wedding, and baby congratulations, every 18 months. The life of a gift-wrap design was longer, occasionally exceeding two years.

All three leading companies introduced their first audio cards in late 1983, after several small manufacturers pioneered them principally through novelty and gift shops. The technology consisted of a chip and a miniaturized battery and speaker embedded in the card. Only a few designs were attempted. Gibson offered a card that played Christmas carols, and American Greetings offered a card with a printed message "Keep a song in your heart and me on your mind" and the music from the song "Let Me Call You Sweetheart." Hallmark offered a card showing two fat bears dancing, one with a rose clenched flamenco style in its teeth, to the lilting strains of "I'm in the Mood for Love." Initial retail price was about $7 for all three companies, but some designs that came out a little later sold for about $5. A small percentage of units produced did not work, and a few played even though the card was closed. Some people reported being startled by sudden bursts of spirited music. The price plus undependability and the tinny quality of the music produced less than encouraging results. In 1985 Gibson brought out a few audio cards that also flashed multi-colored lights. These very expensive cards with audio and lighting features were continued but sold poorly. There was the perpetual hope in the industry that expensive cards could replace inexpensive gifts, such as handkerchiefs or small boxes of candy, in consumers' buying habits.

Many people in the United States greeting card industry referred to it as the "social expression" business, and many retailers spoke of their "personal expression" department. These were apt terms as applied to U.S. culture. Americans bought more cards per capita than did Europeans. The latter preferred cards that were decorated but had no message, a product hard to sell to Americans. The few Americans who bought them were well-educated, articulate, sophisticated, and cosmopolitan. Gibson launched such a line of cards in the late 1980s. Such cards had sold rather well in the extremely specialized segment of shops located in art galleries and museums, where they normally included reproductions of paintings or selections from famous paintings. Gibson launched a line of cards in the late 1980s that had attractive decoration but no wording. Europeans were more formal and under most circumstances expected to write in the appropriate message themselves. Most of them found cards made for the United States lacking in taste. Most Americans admired sentiment but were too emotionally inhibited to express it in their own words and handwriting, whereas most Europeans were more restrained in what they wanted to say but had very little trouble writing it down. Most Europeans perceived appropriate greeting cards as just another type of stationery, yet there was a small but detectable change going on among younger Europeans. Another point was that Americans thought of themselves as too busy to write a letter, even a short note on a small card, but actually were not any busier than most Europeans. Some U.S.-made cards or adaptations of U.S. cards made abroad by American firms or both had been doing rather well in Great Britain for quite a few years. In the United States, women sent the great majority of cards. The highest frequency of use occurred among middle-aged women of middle income.

Gibson's gift-wrapping paper was sold under several brand names, but Cleo brand accounted for most, and the great majority of that volume was for Christmas. In fact, it was the largest-selling brand of Christmas wrapping paper in the world. Cleo's production capacity was increased by one-fourth in 1984. Cleo brand also included several accessories such as ribbons, bows, and gift boxes. Cleo Wrap Division was the innovator of reversible wrapping paper, paper with a different pattern printed on each side. Some slow, uneven upgrading of Cleo brand products was occurring. There were several producers of gift wrap that did not produce greeting cards. Cleo brand wraps retailed at prices well below Gibson's other wraps and were distributed mainly to mass merchandisers, variety store chains, discount department stores, supermarket chains, and drugstore chains.

Traditionally, gift-wrapping paper suffered serious shelf wear while in the store. It soiled quickly, sometimes faded, and was occasionally torn. Recent progress in printing made the paper less likely to fade, and improved plastic film provided a stronger, more dependable cover. The three leading companies stayed about equal on this topic of product development.

Gibson also marketed some cards under the Cleo brand. Cleo's card line emphasized packaged juvenile valentine cards and was the leading producer of such cards in the nation, but Cleo also produced a few boxed Christmas cards. Some of the cards as well as some of the wraps featured the long popular Fuzzy Friends characters created by Gibson and the newer but successful Classroom Classics, which were actually created by children.

Gibson gave considerable emphasis to the use of the proprietary characters in card design. It had purchased licenses to use the following: Garfield; the Super Powers (Superman, Batman, and Wonder Woman); Sesame Street (Big Bird, Cookie Monster, Kermit, Miss Piggy, Bert, and Ernie); Loony Tunes (Bugs Bunny, Elmer Fudd, Porky Pig, Tweety Bird, Sylvester, Pepe LePew, Yosemite Sam, and Road Runner); the Hummel figurine characters; Cracker Jack; and Hershey's. Licenses were usually for one to four years, subject to certain renewal options, and most were exclusive. Gibson continued to add to its portfolio of characters. In 1984, it bought the rights to use My Little Pony and Charmkins from Hasbro-Bradley, Inc., the largest toy maker in the United States. In 1986 Gibson bought the rights to use Pound Puppies from Tonka Toys. Barbie and Designing Women were added in 1987 and 1988, respectively.

Garfield the cat, a character developed by the cartoonist Jim Davis that drew about 70 million newspaper readers a day, was the single most popular character and was not licensed to any competitor of Gibson. Each Garfield card was designed and edited by Davis. Gibson sold an average of about 40 million greeting cards per year that used Garfield themes. In 1986 Gibson began to make a limited number of designs of pop-up cards using the Garfield character. Pop-ups were more difficult to manufacture than regular cards.

In a major coup the exclusive right to the Disney characters (Donald Duck, Mickey Mouse, Pluto, Goofy, and others) was acquired in 1985. Previously, Hallmark had enjoyed these rights. According to short-term plans, such properties were to be used only in the Gibson and Buzza brands. As a result of this licensing arrangement, Gibson received the exclusive right to operate card shops at both Walt Disney World in Florida and the Disneyland theme parks. Hallmark had the Peanuts characters, Heathcliff, and Jim Henson's Muppets, but American Greetings did not rely much on proprietary characters. Gibson had the strongest collection of proprietary characters in the industry.

Among appealing animal ideas, an underexploited theme was the koala, an Australian marsupial that most North Americans thought of as a cuddly little bear. QANTAS, an Australian airline, frequently showed this animal in its advertising. Gibson created Kirby Koala, and it immediately proved to be the most successful character the company had ever created. Some three million cards per year were being sold, and the koala theme extended to wrapping paper, party supplies, and gummed trim. Gibson began licensing other manufacturers to use Kirby Koala on infant wear, puzzles, stuffed toys, and ceramics. The company also started licensing the Gibson mouse, created by Jean O'Brien exclusively for Gibson.

Archival American Greetings, Inc., had scored a rousing success in recent years with its Strawberry Shortcake. Introduced in 1980, it was a little doll-like character with a pink bonnet and was surrounded by a sprinkling of polka dots and strawberries. Young girls liked it very much, and American Greetings licensed this character for use on countless items, earning tens of millions of dollars from it. In late 1982, Hallmark belatedly tried to match Strawberry Shortcake with its introduction of Shirt Tales. This was a group of tiny animals all living in a hollow tree wearing T-shirts with their shirttails hanging out and going about performing good deeds. Commercial results were not impressive.

Advise Gibson Greetings, Inc.

POWER TOOLS, INC. (A)

Power Tools, Inc., was a large and diversified manufacturer of power tools and labor-saving devices for home and industry. Founded in the early 1900s, the firm's headquarters was in the Middle Atlantic states. It was included in the *Fortune 500* list of large U.S. corporations and produced and marketed its products on a worldwide basis.

During the early years of its existence, the company was primarily a manufacturer of a variety of machines and equipment. For example, at one time it manufactured industrial scales. As time passed, however, the firm expanded into the production of universal electric motors. This led to the placement of a chuck onto the spindle of an electric motor; this was the earliest electric drill. It was large and cumbersome but offered the user the ability to drill holes without being tied to the traditional fixed-in-place drill press.

During the 1930s and extending into the 1940s the firm grew to specialize in the manufacture of electrically driven portable power tools. The firm grew and prospered. It developed a variety of electrically driven tools, such as various sizes of drills, percussion hammers, and a variety of grinders. During the late 1940s and early 1950s the firm entered the "do it yourself" market. It was able to develop the previously unexplored

This case was prepared by Richard Rosecky, Ph.D., who is on the staff of the company being considered.

homeowner's market. This propelled the firm into a period of tremendous growth. In addition to the industrial markets, the firm increased in size by selling tools to the homeowner. This provided the firm with very large economies of scale. The price of the typical one-fourth-inch drill dropped from the $50 or $60 range to the $10 range. In the process, the firm doubled its sales about every ten years.

The Industrial/Construction Division

During its early years, the primary focus of Power Tools, Inc., was on the industrial user. As mentioned, the company provided grinders, drills, and a variety of other expensive engineered products. The company considered itself to be a pioneer in the growth of the industrial markets. It sold its products exclusively through the traditional "mill supply" houses. This emphasis on the industrial nature of the business was continued in the Industrial/Construction Division even as the phenomenal growth in the Consumer Products Division occurred.

During the 1950s, however, there was considerable growth in construction products offered by the Industrial/Construction Division. Circular saws, finishing sanders, routers, and a variety of other new products were developed in parallel with the Consumer Products Division. Thus, the Industrial/Construction Division was able to take advantage of the economies of scale being produced in the factories of the Consumer Products Division. Specifically, the construction type of product continued to be sold through a distribution channel intermediary now called "Industrial Distributors" that also included a new variety of business that served construction contractors directly. These new distributors were unlike the traditional mill supply houses in that they were considerably smaller and catered to a construction contractor rather than to the traditional plant engineer or plant maintenance manager.

The growth of the construction products portion of the Industrial/Construction Division propelled the division to impressive new heights. The company viewed its traditional industrial products as slow growth areas. The traditional products were now characterized by very cyclical and low growth rates. The construction products were viewed differently; their rate of sale growth was twice the rate of growth of similar industrial products.

The Development of New Products

The growth of the Consumer Products Division was visible to the public, which drove the price of the company's common stock to new highs. What was not as visible, although it was quite profitable, was the growth of new products in the Industrial/Construction Division. A variety of improvements upon existing products was made in addition to the introduction of completely new products, often at a considerable profit. The circular saw was developed specifically for the Consumer Products Division, but it could be improved on and added to so as to make it a high-quality construction device.

In addition, the division prided itself on being a broad line manufacturer. It offered a variety of alternative tools in terms of size, quality, and performance. The division offered utility-duty products, heavy-duty products, and super-duty products. As an example, the division offered one-fourth inch, three-eighths inch, five-sixteenths inch, half-inch, one-inch, and larger sizes of drills. It offered end-handle drills, pistol-grip drills, right-angle drills, all insulated drills, and others.

The concept of driving a screw with a drill evolved as part of the development of the drill line. This led to the development of the electrically driven power screwdriver, which was essentially a drill with a chuck that was designed to hold a screw and then drive it into the material. This product development was quickly found to be popular, and soon the other major manufacturers of power tools were eager to enter the market. The product exhibited all the attributes of the life-cycle curve. Only recently had the annual rate of growth begun to taper, and, in fact, the sales of this product by Power Tools, Inc., recently started a rapid decline.

Electric Screwdrivers Today

The total United States demand for electric screwdrivers was approaching $17 million per year. Because it viewed itself as the pioneer in the electric screwdriver business, Power Tools, Inc., was perplexed and annoyed by its present situation in that business. Several salient facts that had been gathered and are presented as Exhibit 1 seemed to portend danger to the company's valued and profitable line of electric screwdrivers. These products were manufactured in the company's oldest plant, which was located in the East.

The Influx of Domestic Competition

The concept of the electric screwdriver flowered in the late 1960s and was further developed throughout the 1970s. The fundamental economic strength of this product concept was the labor-saving aspect. Parallel to the labor-saving aspect were the many useful refinements and variations of the basic product. Depth-sensitive models, models with adjustable clutches, models with reversing features, and other variations were developed to serve specific market segments. However, no sooner had Power Tools, Inc., developed a new advance than a competitor would copy the idea and enter the market. This was possible because any manufacturer of a drill could convert it to a screwdriver by modifying the front

EXHIBIT 1 Pertinent Data on Electric Screwdrivers

	1970/71	1974	Latest Year
Total U.S. market			
$ (millions)	$ 6.1	$ 10.4	$ 16.6
Units (000)	87.5	146.7	188.0
U.S. power tool market			
as a percentage of U.S.			
total tool market ($)	13%	17%	20%
Company share of electric			
screwdrivers market ($)	32%	24%	13%
Makita share of electric			
screwdrivers market ($)	NA	NA	8%

end of the drill to accomodate the screwdriver attachments. Soon Power Tools, Inc., noticed that it had many competitors in the sale of electric screwdrivers.

This pattern of events led to a corresponding decline in the firm's market share. In the early years this organization had dominated the market, holding about a two-thirds share. As time had passed, its share had slipped gradually to 24 percent in 1974 and an estimated 13 percent currently. In a recent general sales slump, the electric screwdriver market declined as badly as, or worse than, other sectors of the power tool business. Sales of the product then increased but did not recover to quite the preslump level.

The Influx of Foreign Competition

During the late 1970s the firm was intensely bothered by the aggressive new efforts of Japanese manufacturers in the screwdriver market. The introduction of the Makita brand of power tools was especially noteworthy. This line of power tools was offered for sale in the United States at prices that were well below the general price level. Power Tools, Inc., viewed the quality of the Makita power tools as being commensurate with their price.

In recent years the Makita Company added insult to injury by announcing its intention to commence manufacturing at a West Coast facility that it proposed to finance in the United States. The total bond offering was made for $60 million and the plant was built. This new facility was soon to come on line. Power Tools, Inc., estimated that a majority of the new Makita plant's output would be electric screwdrivers that would compete directly with the company's own screwdrivers.

Advise Power Tools, Inc.

McILHENNY COMPANY – PRODUCERS OF TABASCO BRAND PRODUCTS

McIlhenny Company, located on Avery Island in the Louisiana coastal marshes about seven miles south of the town of New Iberia, manufactured two products. One was very old and extremely well-known around the world and the other was a much later addition. The first was Tabasco Brand Pepper Sauce, introduced in 1868, and the other was Tabasco Brand Bloody Mary Mix, introduced more than 100 years later in 1972.

The key ingredient in the two products was the red pepper, known more technically as the *capsicum frutescens*. Ranging from three to four feet in height, this plant is a genus of the *Solanaceae* (night-shade) family. Its pungent flavored fruit is known as *tabasco pepper,* a varietal name. Cayenne pepper is a distinct variety not to be confused with *tabasco pepper*. Some species of this plant are bushy in appearance and are cultivated in tropical and subtropical regions. It is native only to the Western Hemisphere. Under its Central American and Mexican name, chili, the fruit was widely used in various sauces and to some extent as a flavoring in pickled foods.

The McIlhenny Company took great interest and pride in *capsicum*. The Indians of Central America and southern Mexico domesticated this plant around 2500 B.C. and used it widely as a seasoning for their diet of corn, squash, tomatoes, fish, and game. A friend of the founder of the present company brought back some of the seeds from Mexico following the Mexican-American War of 1848. By the late 1850s Edmund McIlhenny was growing *capsicum* plants in his vegetable garden on Avery Island. The company and the family worked for the next 140 years on improving the *capsicum* plant. Family members constantly involved themselves in selecting seed peppers for each new crop, and no outside pepper contaminated the strain in all those years. Botanists recognized the present plant as a distinct variety.

Until recently all the peppers used in the company's production had been grown on Avery Island, and 40 percent of the peppers were still grown there. With the advent of federal and state unemployment compensation, food stamps, and many other welfare benefits, agricultural labor became increasingly difficult to obtain. Beginning in the early 1970s pepper crops brought to maturity could not be harvested because of a lack of agricultural labor.

The company started raising peppers in Mexico, Guatemala, Honduras, Colombia, and Venezuela. The seeds for all foreign-grown peppers were supplied by McIlhenny Company, and no peppers were ever purchased on the open market. Some of the foreign peppers were propagated by contract under supervision of McIlhenny field people. In some instances the company leased land and raised the crop itself. The foreign-grown peppers were shipped to Avery Island for curing and aging as soon as their condition permitted transportation.

After the picked peppers were ground up they were steeped in their own juices in large white oak reusable casks that were similar to whiskey barrels. A wooden cover with tiny holes drilled through it was placed on top of each cask. Next, a thick layer of salt from the company's Avery Island salt mine was spread over the cover. This salt seal allowed the actual vapors of fermentation to escape and at the same time prevented fresh air from ever entering the barrel. This mash had to be aged for three warm seasons of fermentation and strengthening. These seasons might be three summers or two summers and a warm spring. The company president personally inspected every single barrel for both smell and taste before releasing it for mixing with 100 grain vinegar and salt. Approximately 30 percent mash was combined with 60 percent vinegar and 10 percent salt and the resulting mixture was stirred constantly for about a month. Then the remaining pieces of pepper seeds and skins were screened out of the sauce. The seeds and skins, called "chaff" after drying, were sold to unaffiliated organizations that steamed them to obtain oil of capsaicin, the stinging material in Ben-Gay balm, "red hot" candies, and other products.

Tabasco brand pepper sauce was also made abroad. The first foreign production was in London, which was soon followed by production in Montreal. Mexico City, Caracas, and Madrid production operations were added later. However, the pepper mash used in these foreign operations was made on Avery Island and shipped abroad. All in all, approximately 55 million bottles were sold in 125 countries annually. Some foreign production was under licensing agreements and some was under partnership agreements. However, in every case it was required that samples of the finished sauce be submitted periodically to Avery Island for examination and approval. Foreign sales accounted for about 40 percent of total sales and the percentage was rising.

McIlhenny Company distributed Tabasco Sauce and its newer product, Tabasco Brand Bloody Mary Mix, in the U.S. civilian market through food brokers. The personal selling effort was under the supervision of regional sales managers who were directed by a national sales manager. Military food brokers were used for the military segment of demand. The regular two-fluid-ounce container of Tabasco pepper sauce was supplemented by the development of a twelve-fluid-ounce size for restaurant chefs and a 128-fluid-ounce size for food manufacturers.

The company president, Walter Stauffer McIlhenny, thought that the company would aim toward further product diversification. He explained his thoughts in the following manner:

We are constantly considering the addition of new products and have reviewed hundreds of suggestions. Obviously our prime purpose in adding a new product is to increase our profit. An important second consideration is that your account with your broker becomes more important with two or more items bringing greater revenues into his office. Accordingly the manufacturer is then in a position to command more effort from the brokers' retail force and their management team as well.

The advertising medium used for the pepper sauce was magazines, both consumer-type publications and those directed to restaurants and distributors. Among those selected in the latter category were *Food Service Marketing, Restaurant Business,* and *Institutions/Volume Feeding Management.* For the Bloody Mary mix the choice was basically the same, although a small amount of newspaper advertising was also placed. For both products consumer magazines were emphasized. For sales purposes the planning unit was one dozen. The advertising allocation for pepper sauce was 40 cents per dozen, a figure that had not varied for the past twenty years. Of course, as physical sales volumes had grown so had the total advertising budget.

The name Tabasco and the familiar diamond-shaped label were protected by a U.S. Patent Office trademark registration at an early date. Nevertheless, much litigation was required to combat firms that attempted copies or near copies of the famous name and marks. McIlhenny Company succeeded in confirming its exclusive rights to the name, the diamond label, and the color pattern of the packaging.

The "Bloody Mary" was one of the two or three most popular alcoholic mixed drinks in the United States. Apparently an American creation and still strongly identified with the United States abroad, it surfaced in the mid-1930s. The Bloody Mary was popular in its own right but also acquired a reputation within a few years as an antidote to hangovers. In the United States well over half of all vodka, the top selling distilled spirit, went into this type of beverage. Recipes for Bloody Marys varied, of course, as to stirring or shaking, serving with ice cubes or strained, ratios of ingredients, and the use of additives such as a sprig of mint or a wedge of lime. What is more, product spin-offs had developed, including the Bloody Maria, made with tequila instead of vodka; the Danish Mary, made with aquavit instead of vodka; the Bull Shot, in which beef bouillon replaced tomato juice; and the Bloody Bull Shot, half tomato juice and half beef bouillon. However, virtually everyone included Tabasco Sauce and Worcestershire sauce with the spirits and juice or bouillon. Some people were purists and refused to use prepared mixes, but their numbers were apparently decreasing.

Over a period of years, Tabasco Brand Bloody Mary Mix achieved nationwide but somewhat spotty distribution. First a six-fluid-ounce can with an easy-open flip top was introduced, and later a twelve-fluid-ounce version in the same sort of can was brought out. Still later a thirty-fluid-ounce clear glass bottle with a screw-type lid was introduced. The most common price at retail for the first product was two for 69 cents, whereas for the second and third products the most common figures were 59 cents and $1.29, respectively. The ingredients were listed on the containers in the following order: concentrated tomato juice, water, fresh frozen concentrated lime juice, Worcestershire sauce, salt, and Tabasco pepper sauce.

McIlhenny Company had never experienced a product failure, but it had dropped two items many years before. In the early 1900s the firm operated a successful oyster-canning plant. However, when the pressures of the Mississippi River at New Orleans began to pose a continuing threat to the city and the U.S. Army Corps of Engineers permanently diverted some of the water into the Atchafalaya Basin, the nearby oyster beds became muddy and could not survive. In addition, for a good many years McIlhenny packed green Tabasco peppers in vinegar under the label Island Pride peppers-in-vinegar. However, rising sales of the pepper sauce, which required ripened peppers, forced withdrawal of this item from the market.

Besides the pepper sauce and Bloody Mary mix, the McIlhenny family had other business interests. They owned but leased the island salt mine to International Salt Company of Clarks Summit, Pennsylvania, which produced Sterling brand salt. Exxon Company produced oil on, and adjacent to, the island. Moreover, the family of Edward A. McIlhenny operated Jungle Gardens, a 200-acre area that was devoted to natural vegetation, botanical exhibits, and Bird City, a noted refuge. McIlhenny Company, of course, continued to be owned by the descendants of Edmund McIlhenny and his wife Mary Eliza Avery McIlhenny, whose grandfather had first acquired the property.

Further Background on the McIlhenny Organization and Avery Island

McIlhenny Company was started in 1868 by Edmund McIlhenny, a former New Orleans banker and grandfather of the present head of the enterprise, Walter S. McIlhenny. However, Edmund's father-in-law, Judge Daniel Dudley Avery of Baton Rouge, had acquired the island on which the business was located many years earlier. And Avery's father-in-law, John Craig Marsh, had acquired partial ownership in 1818. At the time of the case younger men of the family had also entered the management, so six generations of the extended family had been involved in the island's economic activities. Known earlier by the names of E. McIlhenny and E. McIlhenny Sons, the organization was renamed McIlhenny Company in 1907.

Geologists do not consider Avery Island, once called Petite Anse (little handle), a real island. Yet it appears to be one, set as it is among a great expanse of marshes, swamps, and bayous about six miles from Vermillion Bay. Rising 152 feet above sea level, this island is really a column of solid salt about ten miles deep over which there is a cap of rich soil. Part of the island is covered with subtropical forest.

Indians produced salt on the island in early times. In the late 1700s John Hayes rediscovered the long-abandoned brine springs and began producing salt. Because of a rise in demand occasioned by the need for salt in making munitions for the War of 1812, the salt works were expanded. However, after that war foreign competitors nearly put the salt operation out of business and the island's economy turned to the growing of sugar cane. Demand for salt again surged at the opening of the Civil War in 1861. John Marsh Avery, son of Daniel Dudley Avery, then re-established the island's salt industry, which quickly became the principal salt supplier to the Confederacy. In expanding the salt works Avery made the first discovery of rock salt on the North American continent. Admiral David Farragut of the Union Navy shelled the facility in 1862 in an unsuccessful attempt to halt company operations. In April 1863 a Union land force under General Banks attacked and destroyed the company's facilities. The family had to flee to San Antonio, Texas, for safety and to live with relatives. They could not return for over three years, during which time their rich plantation land and crops suffered from neglect.

The hardy pepper plants survived the years of neglect. With the salt business in ruins and food supplies monotonous in the post-Civil War period, gourmet Edmund McIlhenny had both the time and the inclination to experiment with recipes. He began experimenting with various ways of making a piquant yet pleasing pepper sauce. He refined the basic methods for making the sauce, which was to crush the peppers, thus making a mash, then straining the mash, and adding salt and vinegar. The resulting aromatic mixture was then put into wooden barrels to age, so that the flavors and fragrances could steep and intermingle. McIlhenny let friends taste the concoction and found that they liked it. In 1868 he processed enough sauce for 350 bottles and sent the entire output as free samples to a selected group of wholesalers. In 1869 he received his first order for the sauce, which was assigned a wholesale price of $1 per bottle. Always highly conscious of spices and condiments, Europeans also accepted the new product. Like many other companies of the coastal South, McIlhenny was international in its outlook and opened an office in London in 1872.

Edmund McIlhenny died in 1890 and was succeeded by his son John Avery McIlhenny. Some members of the family were interested in the island's salt deposit. A firm called Chouteau and Price sank a shaft 90 feet deep in 1867 but abandoned operations in 1870. The American Salt

Company and the family agreed on a lease in 1880 and the lessee began producing large quantities of salt, using the early shaft.

Transportation of the salt had always been a severe problem and promised to be so for the new product. Three alternatives were tried and all failed: a causeway running north toward New Iberia; an embankment and tramway to Bayou Petite Anse; and a canal to Vermillion Bay. In 1883 railway service from New Orleans to the West was inaugurated and in 1886 a branch was opened from New Iberia south to the island, thus solving the problem. By this time the New Iberia Salt Company had taken over the salt operations. In 1898 the family organized its own Avery Rock Salt Mining Company, which sank a new shaft, still in use, to a depth of 518 feet. The mining operation was put in the hands of Sidney Bradford, an engineer married to Edmund's daughter Marigold.

During the 1890s Avery Island became established as an important wildlife refuge. Edmund's second son, Edward (Ned) Avery McIlhenny, became a naturalist who made several scientific expeditions to the Arctic. Edward McIlhenny became alarmed that the snowy egret, a beautiful white heron native to the Louisiana swamps, was rapidly declining in number and faced extinction. This bird had been slaughtered by hunters who wanted a few special plumes for use in women's hats. After a long search Ned found egret chicks, which he took back to Avery Island and successfully raised. Counting on a trait found in some birds he released them in the late fall for their natural migration south across the Gulf of Mexico. In the spring, six of the birds returned to him to form the nucleus of the island's large bird colony called Bird City. Thereafter the company continued to show extraordinary interest in ecology and conservation.

In 1906 John McIlhenny was appointed a U.S. Civil Service commissioner and turned the firm over to his brother Ned, who served as president of the company for the next forty years. Ned wrote several books and many magazine articles on the topics of egrets, alligators, wild turkeys, and folk music. He personally banded 189,289 birds in order to accumulate data to study their migratory routes. Despite Ned's other interests, sales of Tabasco Sauce continued to rise during his long administration. He worked well with his brother Rufus, who took on some of the management burden in the later years.

Rufus died in 1940, at which time the company called in Walter Stauffer McIlhenny, the son of John McIlhenny and nephew of Ned, to participate in the management. However, World War II intervened and Walter McIlhenny, a Marine Corps reserve officer, went on active duty. Ned suffered a stroke and Walter succeeded him in 1949. Walter's interest in the corps continued and he rose in the Reserve to the rank of Brigadier General. He modernized the Tabasco production line with up-to-date filing and labeling equipment but retained the picturesque, atmospheric buildings. He selected a new advertising agency, hired the company's first national sales managers, and expanded company interests abroad.

Humble Oil brought in an oil well at the edge of the island in 1942, and in a few years there was an extensive field. Although oil was a severe potential threat to the island's ecology, the problem was solved in a variety of ways, such as by burying the pipelines, bypassing certain trees, and filling and sodding over pits.

APPENDIX TO McILHENNY COMPANY

Principal Competitors of Tabasco Brand Bloody Mary Mix

There were several noteworthy competitors of McIlhenny's new Bloody Mary mix. All of them were nonalcoholic, as was the McIlhenny entry. Selected information about the competitive products follows:

1. Holland House Bloody Mary Cocktail Mix, made by Holland House Brands Company, Ridgefield, New Jersey, a division of National Distillers. This organization had a line of drink mixes, which included Manhattan, Screwdriver, Side Car, Tom Collins, Whiskey Sour, Daiquiri, Pink Squirrel, and eighteen others, including a low-calorie version of the popular Whiskey Sour. A few of these products, including the Bloody Mary, were available in both liquid and instant dry mixes. However, the Screwdriver, Pink Squirrel, Love Bird, Grasshopper, Wallbanger, Tequila Sunrise, and Vodka (White) Sour were only available in an instant dry mix.

This brand of Bloody Mary mix was offered in three variations. The first was Regular, which was designed and promoted to be a traditional Bloody Mary, whereas the second was Extra Tangy, "the traditional Bloody Mary with extra zesty flavor." The third was Smooth N' Spicy, "a unique flavor system consistent with contemporary taste preferences; a welcome change of pace from the traditional." These three mixes were promoted on the label as "skillful blends of choice ingredients backed by experience that dates back to 1887." The traditional version from Holland House included tomato juice from tomato juice concentrate, lemon juice concentrate, natural flavors, salt, citric acid, monosodium glutamate, calcium carrageenan, hydrolyzed vegetable protein, iso-ascorbic acid, spice extractives, and less than 0.1 percent each of sodium benzoate and sodium metabisulfite as preservatives. This brand was offered at a prevailing retail price of $1.09 in a twenty-four-fluid-ounce clear bottle with a screw-type lid. It was also offered in a six-fluid-ounce can at a prevailing price of 35 cents. Both the regular and extra tangy versions were available in such cans.

At first the can had a solid top, but it was replaced by the easy-open flip top in 1978. Holland House Smooth N' Spicy was also available in a thirty-two-fluid-ounce (one quart) clear glass bottle with a screw-type lid at a prevailing price of $1.30.

2. Snap-E-Tom, made by Heublein, Inc., Hartford, Connecticut. Heublein made several other mixes, such as the Hereford's Cows series. Snap-E-Tom had the following ingredients: water, tomato paste, green chilies, salt, onion, and citric acid. It was available as a single pack and a three-pack. The can had a solid top and contained six fluid ounces. The prevailing retail prices were 27 cents and 79 cents, respectively. Because Heublein had just introduced a bottled whiskey sour that contained the alcohol, many industry observers were watching to see if later there would be a bottled Bloody Mary that contained the vodka.

3. Libby's Bloody Mary Mix, made by Libby, McNeill, & Libby, Chicago. This product had the following ingredients: water, tomato paste, cider and distilled vinegar, salt, spices, dextrose, hydrolyzed vegetable protein, citric acid, onion powder, jalapeno peppers, soy sauce solids and dextrans, flavorings, sugar, monosodium glutamate, garlic powder, caramel color, and hydrogenated vegetable oils. It was offered only in a five-and-a-half-fluid-ounce can with an easy-open flip top, which was shipped and displayed as a six-pack. The prevailing price at retail was $1.25 per six-pack. Some retailers were willing to sell an individual can removed from the six-pack at a prevailing price of 21 cents.

4. Schweppes Bloody Mary Mixer, made by Schweppes U.S.A., Ltd., Stamford, Connecticut. This product had the following ingredients: concentrated tomato juice, water, Worcestershire sauce, lemon juice, vinegar, sucrose, citric acid, salt, red pepper, celery salt, black pepper, carrageenan. It was available in a twenty-five-fluid-ounce clear glass bottle with a screw-type lid at a prevailing price of 95 cents. This product was also offered in a four-fluid-ounce clear glass bottle in a three-pack at a prevailing retail price of $1.05. Some retailers were willing to break the three-pack and sell an individual bottle at 35 cents.

5. Mr and Mrs "T" Bloody Mary Mix, made by Mr. and Mrs. T. Products, a division of Taylor Food Products, Inc., El Segundo, California. This product had the following ingredients: water, tomato paste, concentrated tomato juice, vinegar, salt, sugar, invert sugar, dried onion, concentrated lemon juice, Worcestershire sauce, artificial flavor, spices, potassium sorbate and sodium benzoate as preservatives, and dry garlic. It was available as a single pack and consisted of a six-fluid-ounce can with an easy-open flip-type top. The prevailing price at retail was two for 65 cents. This brand was available also in a

twenty-four-fluid-ounce size in a clear glass bottle with a screw-type lid at a prevailing price of 99 cents.

6. Heinz Bloody Mary Mix, made by H.J. Heinz Company, Pittsburgh, Pennsylvania. This product had the following ingredients: tomatoes, water, vinegar, corn sweetener, salt, concentrated lemon juice, hydrolyzed vegetable protein (with disodium inosinate, disodium guanylate), potassium sorbate as a preservative, molasses, spices, natural flavoring, anchovies, and onion powder. It was available in a thirty-two-fluid-ounce clear glass bottle with a screw-type lid. The prevailing price was $1.55.

7. Angostura Bloody Merry-Maker, made by A-W Brands, Inc., Carteret, New Jersey, a subsidiary of Iroquois Brands, Ltd., under license from Angostura, International, Ltd., Toronto, Canada. This product had the following ingredients: Worcestershire sauce, Angostura aromatic bitters, red pepper sauce, salt, celery flavoring, natural lemon flavor, and 0.1 percent sodium benzoate as a preservative. It was available only in an eight-fluid-ounce clear glass bottle with a screw-type lid at a prevailing retail price of $1.59. This product was added in small amounts, usually three to five dashes, to vodka and plain tomato juice.

8. V-8 Spicy Hot Vegetable Juice Cocktail, made by Campbell's Soup Company, Camden, New Jersey. This product was being promoted both as an appetizer and as a mixer for alcoholic drinks. The ingredients were water, tomato concentrate, concentrated juices of carrots, celery, beets, parsley, lettuce, watercress, and spinach, with salt, ascorbic acid (vitamin C), natural flavoring, and citric acid. It was available only in a six-fluid-ounce can with an easy-open flip top, and these cans were in a six-pack. The prevailing retail price was $1.09 per six-pack. Some retailers were willing to sell an individual can at a prevailing price of 19 cents.

9. Steero Bloody Mary Cocktail Mix, made by American Kitchen Products Company, Jersey City, New Jersey. This product had the following ingredients: tomato juice, water, lemon juice, Worcestershire sauce, salt, sugar, and spices. It was offered in an eight-fluid-ounce can with a solid top at a prevailing retail of 39 cents. This company had just introduced a closely related product, Bullshot Cocktail Mix, which contained the following ingredients: water, tomato paste, monosodium glutamate, lemon juice, salt, citric acid, sugar, beef extract, caramel color, natural and artificial flavorings, spices, and Worcestershire sauce. This product was offered in an eight-fluid-ounce can with a solid top at a prevailing retail price of 43 cents.

In addition, three other brands should be acknowledged. Master's Mix Bloody Mary Mix, made by several companies under licenses from Professional Mixers, Inc., a Sacramento, California, firm, was available in a 25.6-fluid-ounce clear glass bottle with a screw-type lid. There was variation, but the prevailing retail price was about $1.39.

Schweppe's U.S.A., Ltd., was beginning to distribute Rose's Bloody Mary Mix under license from L. Rose and Company, Ltd. Both Schweppes and Rose were British organizations. Policies on package sizes and preferred prices were not completely settled yet. It appeared certain that Rose's would be in a twenty-four-fluid-ounce clear glass bottle with a screw-type lid and the retail price would be relatively high. Promotion as a prestige product was likely.

Sacramento Tomato Plus Vegetable Cocktail, made by Borden, Inc., New York City, had recently moved from western to national distribution. It was made of the following ingredients: water, tomato paste, salt, dried chili pepper, ground celery seed, dehydrated onion, powdered onion, ascorbic acid (vitamin C), natural flavorings, and spices. Although this product was now being promoted as a self-contained beverage, observers considered it probable that the product would later be promoted as a mixer for vodka, gin, and aquavit. It was offered in a five-and-a-half-fluid-ounce can, and these were in a six-pack. The prevailing retail price was 99 cents. Some retailers were willing to sell an individual can removed from the pack at a prevailing retail price of 17 cents. This product was also available in a forty-six-fluid-ounce can with a solid top at a prevailing retail price of 81 cents.

Advise the McIlhenny Company.

7

Channels of Distribution

L.L. BEAN, INC.

L.L. Bean, Inc. was reviewing its long-run strategies, giving special attention to channels of distribution. One of the legendary companies in American business, it was founded by Leon Leonwood Bean in 1912 in Freeport, Maine, a coastal town twenty miles northeast of Portland with a population of about 6,000. As L.L. Bean became highly successful, so also did it become a household word in most of the United States and, to a great extent, in Canada.

An orphan with a eighth-grade education, Bean was born in 1872 and reared in the hills of Western Maine. The company began when Bean, borrowing $400 to get started, began selling through mail order a rubber-bottomed hunting boot of his own design. While still employed at his brother's haberdashery shop in Freeport, Bean managed to spend as much time as possible hunting and fishing. He tired of having cold, wet feet while hunting. In his search for protection and comfort. Bean found that all-rubber boots kept his feet dry but were uncomfortable and clumsy; all-leather boots, on the other hand, provided good support but were heavy and wet. Experimenting in his brother's basement, Bean thought of putting some rubber overshoe bottoms on lightweight leather uppers, whereupon he had the town cobbler stitch the two materials together. Then he asked several of his friends to test the product. Their reaction was highly positive.

After obtaining a mailing list of the people who had already purchased a Maine hunting license, Bean then prepared a brochure, and started production of the boot using his brother's basement. Since most people were quite skeptical of mail ordering, he offered a guarantee to the buyer. Ninety of the first 100 sold were returned for a full refund, because the uppers and bottoms would not stay sewn together. The rubber was not strong enough to hold the stitched-on leather tops. Bean refunded the money, redesigned the product, borrowed more money, and tried again with more direct mail advertisements. From then on, it was success after success. The product, named the Maine Hunting Shoe, had cowhide uppers that did not stiffen and rubber bottoms with crepe innersoles. The bottoms normally wore out with extensive use but could be replaced readily by the factory. The company provided a rebuilding service for these boots, which had been known to last for fifty years. The boot could not be patented and so there were now hundreds of other similar brands, nearly all of which were inferior in quality. By the late 1980s Bean was still making about 270,000 pairs of the Maine Hunting Shoe annually. If customers were dissatisfied with the durability of this product they could get a free replacement regardless of the age of their unit.

Early on the founder wrote a policy statement that he called the Golden Rule of L.L. Bean: "Sell good merchandise at a reasonable profit, treat your customers like human beings, and they'll always come back for more." Expanding on this thought, the company set forth the following;

Practical and functional products—all represent a solid value and deliver a fair return for the money.

An unconditional guarantee. We do not want you to have anything from L.L. Bean that is not satisfactory. Return anything you buy from us at any time if it proves otherwise.

Bean created a retail salesroom in his factory in 1945 and provided it with a night bell for the convenience of fishermen and hunters traveling through Freeport late at night. In 1951 he expanded this store and opened it twenty-four hours a day, 365 days a year.

The company founder added several types of hunting and fishing apparel in the late teens; in the 1920s he added camping and fishing equipment. Still later he added bicycles, sunglasses, cookingware, dishes, watches, and luggage, and broadened the clothing line. By the late 1970s the company offered a fairly wide line of camping, deck, and porch furniture. By the early 1980s Bean also offered a sizeable assortment of casual apparel that was not really meant for outdoors use but could be so used. It was often referred to as "comfortable, well constructed, easy-to-wear clothing for the active person who enjoys the outdoors." The company also added greatly to the shoe line, including "light hiking" products that were upgraded sneakers, and the blanket and linen assortments. Management decided to offer an increased fraction of the clothing items in extra-large and tall sizes.

In the early years L.L. Bean wrote every sales brochure himself in a folksy, personal style, to which most people reacted warmly. He still wrote the copy when his brochures had developed into sizeable catalogs. He converted his informative yet amusing style of writing into a book in 1942 entitled *Hunting, Fishing and Camping*. When the book manuscript was rejected by publishing houses Bean had it privately published, whereupon it sold almost 200,000 copies. Although remaining somewhat folksy and never uptight, the catalog slowly began to take on more of a professional appearance after 1976 when the company added to its staff a professional with commercial art training to design and organize the catalog.

L.L. Bean died in 1967 at the age of 94, while still active in the business, and when sales were $3.5 million. The business press found the company interesting and newsworthy but portrayed it as more of a curiosity and eccentricity than a really serious business. Bean's son succeeded him but died in only a few months, whereupon Bean's grandson, Leon Gorman, took over the business. The only college graduate in the management at the time, the new chief executive and part owner wanted to retain the homey flavor of L.L. Bean's operations while at the same time increase the size and profitability of the company. He expanded the product line and mailing list and rented promising lists from mailing-list brokers. He hired several M.B.A.s for his staff. Gorman moved the manufacturing operation to rented space in 1970 when sales reached $9.9 million. Moving the mail-order operation out, he rebuilt and expanded the three-level store on Main Street in phases until it contained 28,000 square feet of selling area. He built a new complex of structures a few hundred yards away from the store to house the mail-order operations and manufacturing. Some customers were disturbed and annoyed by the store upgrading, for example, carpeting in some areas, that accompanied the expansion.

The organization now made not only the Maine hunting shoe but other handsewn footwear, tote bags, garment bags, and sheepskin covers. Altogether, however, these amounted to a very small fraction of company sales. The rest of Bean's merchandise was bought from over 400 manufacturers, most made to Bean's specifications and about one-fourth bearing the Bean label. There had been an increase in the amount of women's clothing offered. Moreover, quite a few women's clothing items that were merely casual, and not truly of the outdoors-type in a traditional sense, were being stocked. Many other casual garments were presented as unisex in company publications. Executives were quite concerned about going very far with women's casual clothing, fearing damage to the company image because it was for females and because it was not at all rugged. At the same time the company was adding quite a few non-rugged apparel items for men. Oddly enough, the company downplayed books about the outdoors and carried only a small assortment that often suffered from stock outages. Gradually the product mix was beginning to cater to people who fantasized a great deal about outdoors activities as well as those who really participated in outdoors activities. Moreover, it appeared that many users of the Bean catalog were nostalgic for a simpler era of history.

The greatly expanded line of merchandise required a large storage area. The warehouse, serving both the mail-order operations and the store, had merchandise stacked on shelves thirty-three feet tall and was operated by a crew of experienced, expert pickers, a fleet of fork-lift trucks, and a large shipping department. Over two thousand extra employees had to be hired during the pre-Christmas rush. Management had long put great emphasis on speed and accuracy of order filling plus quick refunds on returned merchandise. In a special survey of its readers by *Consumer Reports*, L.L. Bean took first place among mail-order houses.

The mail-order industry in the United States was growing rapidly, in most years about three times as fast as store sales. The average American family received about fifty catalogs a year. The ratio of net profits to sales tended to be about twice as high in mail order as in in-store merchandising. Public confidence in the industry had risen through the years, although there were still some shady operators. In the early days the reason for growth was access to merchandise for consumers living in small towns and rural areas. In recent years the most important reason for the growth was the time that consumers could conserve, provided that they selected right the first time. An important secondary reason was avoidance of surly, lazy store salespersons who knew almost nothing about the merchandise. However, one of the large generalists, Montgomery Ward & Co. which published the first catalog in the United States in 1872, dissolved its catalog operations in 1985 after consistently showing a net loss on them for several years. The three other generalists were J.C. Penney, Sears, Roebuck & Co., and Spiegel, all of them profitable in their mail-order work. The great growth over the past decade had been in the many companies that specialized in only a few lines of goods. Some were in very narrow specialty niches. For example, there were successful mail-order houses for music tapes, games, candy, cheese, fresh fruit, nuts, cookware, china, crystal, needle work, blouses, lingerie, and exotic types of garden plants. Even some nongeneralists had failed, for example the Esprit de Corp and Pier 1 catalog operations. Hallmark, the greeting card company, tried a women's fashion apparel catalog that failed quickly. The mail-order industry had encountered extreme resistance to complex goods, extremely expensive products, and apparel that needed careful fitting.

L.L. Bean's sales were approaching $600 million, up from $205 million in 1983. Among several dozen competitors a few stood out: Eddie Bauer, bought by Spiegel in 1988, Shepler's, Lands End, Patagonia, J. Crew, and Banana Republic. The net worth of the Bean-Gorman family was approximately $450 million. Bean was clearly the largest direct-sales organization in outdoor goods and was among the top ten direct-sales organizations in the United States. However, there appeared to be several routes for possible further expansion.

Freeport was near both the Maine Turnpike and Interstate 95. The store was on the principal street of the town and surrounded mainly by outlet shops seeking to capitalize on the enormous traffic generated by Bean's. The emergence of the many outlet shops had caused some local concern as they replaced several family shops and services. Anyone interested in outdoors activities who drove in that part of the state was likely to stop in to Bean's. People who had not been mail-order customers often became mail-order customers after seeing the store. Moreover, many Bean mail-order customers wanted to see the famous store, which produced about one-tenth of the company's sales revenue. About 90 percent of store customers in the summer came from out-of-state. The store stocked many more items than did the catalog, and would accept telephone requests for products it carried that the catalog did not, provided that they were in stock at the time. This type of demand was not, however, promoted. The store had a large parking lot beside the building and the community operated an extremely large free parking lot one block away. The most prominent feature of the store was the famous trout pond on the ground floor that was quite interesting and attractive, holding the attention of many family members while others in the family shopped. A stuffed deer just inside the entrance was another conversation starter. The store layout, spacious in the sporting goods departments, was very crowded and cluttered everywhere else. There was a small clearance and close-out department as well as a section featuring Down East foods. The front of the enlarged and remodeled store prominently carried two messages: "The store that knows the outdoors" and "An outdoor tradition since 1912." Shopping crowds were greater on rainy days when vacationers cut back on outdoors activities. Although there were several sales desks in the store, check-out lines were often long.

Store personnel were unusually knowledgeable about their merchandise. They consisted mostly of moonlighting farmers, retirees, young backpacking types, and middle-aged local women who enjoyed outdoors activities and casual apparel. Selling behavior was extraordinarily low-pressure. Help was not abundant on the sales floor, but if customers were

168 CHANNELS OF DISTRIBUTION

willing to wait a short while they could have as long a conversation with a knowledgeable salesperson as they wanted. Customers were never rushed. The company invested heavily in employee orientation and refresher training.

Market research conducted by and for the company indicated that Bean's patronage was dominated by people who were highly educated, had far above-average incomes, and were over age thirty-five. Whereas only about 17 percent of adult Americans were college graduates, about two-thirds of Bean customers were college graduates. However, there was a slow trend upward in the share of business accounted for by persons under age thirty-five. Females, who had once been almost trivial in the customer mix, became one-fourth by 1976 and one-half by 1990. In-house analysis showed that the company did rather little volume in the Rocky Mountain and Pacific Coast states. It also showed that the average order by telephone was larger than the average order by mail, which in turn was larger than the average in-store transaction. The company installed a toll-free telephone number in the early 1980s.

Several specialty catalogs were launched to supplement the seasonal versions of the general catalog. These included (1) fly fishing, (2) hunting, (3) home and camp items, (4) spring sporting, (5) winter sporting, (6) women's spring outdoor items, and (7) women's fall outdoor items. Photography, drawings, printing, and descriptions of the merchandise were increasingly more professional looking and less folksy than before. More and clearer colors were used and the printing became sharper.

Advise L.L. Bean, Inc.

GIBSON GREETINGS, INC. (B)

Gibson Greetings, Inc., established in 1850, was the third-largest greeting card manufacturer in the United States and a major manufacturer of gift-wrapping paper, ribbons, bows, tags, and related products (See Gibson case, version A). In addition to the big three, Hallmark, American Greetings, and Gibson, there were several hundred small greeting card manufacturers, many of them quite aggressive. There was continuous tension in the industry about access to retailers, with the small firms accusing the big three of attempting to monopolize floor space and keep retailers from handling the products of the small manufacturers or at least minimize the stock carried and the floor space devoted to them. The large manufacturers took the position that it was a matter of more complete lines of products, more efficient channels of distribution, and better service to the stores. There was also highly aggressive competition among the big three for market access.

This company showed considerable ability to innovate in matters besides products. In late 1982 Gibson introduced electronic reordering, the first in the industry, in a few major retail accounts. It spread to other major retail accounts by 1984. In this computerized reordering service, reorder tickets were converted at store level into electronic data, which were then transmitted to Gibson's central computer. This information was processed and relayed to a company distribution center, where the order was assembled and then shipped to the retailer. On average, three to four days of time in the mail one-way was eliminated. This cut turnaround time for an order by well over 40 percent and simultaneously permitted some reduction of inventory level in the store because less safety stock had to be kept on hand there. The service was not available to stores lacking computerization and very small stores. By 1988 Gibson was offering a system that utilized hand-held electronic units to increase the efficiency of ordering products.

The company operated manufacturing facilities in Cincinnati, Ohio; Kenton County, Kentucky (just across the river from Cincinnati); Berea, Kentucky; and Memphis, Tennessee. Most cards were designed and printed in Cincinnati; and most gift-wrapping merchandise, in Memphis. Gibson had a physical distribution center near Berea, Kentucky, about seventy miles south of Cincinnati. The company opened a new physical distribution center in Kenton County, Kentucky, in 1984. This new facility was built by using the proceeds from industrial revenue bonds. There were also distribution centers in Cerritos, California, and Memphis. Besides the headquarters sales office in Cincinnati, Gibson maintained two sales offices in Texas, two in New York, and one each in California, Pennsylvania, Massachusetts, and Georgia.

Cleo brand commanded retail prices well below Gibson's other gift-wrapping brands. It was sold primarily to mass merchandisers, variety store chains, discount department stores, supermarket chains, and drugstore chains, not to gift shops and conventional department stores. Gibson did not provide merchandising support services or advice for the retailers who handled Cleo brand. Such merchandise was shipped in corrugated paper cartons, which could be used as temporary freestanding displays. They were tall enough that they could be set on the floor but not so tall that they could not be set on a waist-high shelf. Such cartons carried the words "Cleo Wrap" in large clear print. These cartons were shipped directly to stores or to chain-operated central warehouses for subsequent redistribution to branch stores. Many of these retailers carried little or no gift-wrapping material except in the pre-Christmas season.

The large manufacturers of greeting cards and gift-wrapping paper normally provided retailers in the United States with appropriated display fixtures. This custom was really necessary if such merchandise was to be handled well and look presentable. Moreover, retailers needed help in getting more productivity out of limited floor space.

Traditional fixtures for cards and gift-wrapping materials, although supplied by the concerned manufacturer, had had some problems. Drawers at the bottom were for reserve stock. Moving that stock up where it could be seen was seldom done in an orderly, timely manner; shoppers were alienated, countless sales were lost; and some seasonal merchandise did not see the light of day until too late. Moreover, the drawers were often a handy place to put reserves of unrelated goods from nearby departments and also to dump trash. In 1978, Gibson launched a concept that it called the "Everything-Up System." What this amounted to was that Gibson hired dozens of new merchandising personnel to make calls regularly on retailers handling company goods, and these personnel saw to it that no reserves were kept. As part of this concept, the manufacturer reduced the unit packing count that was virtually standard in the industry from twelve to six or sometimes less. Gibson increased frequency of merchandising visits to make sure that displays were kept well supplied and neat. Meanwhile, design work was going on for a new generation of fixtures. In 1980, Gibson brought out drawerless fixtures for everyday cards. Then in 1982, Gibson innovated with "Everything-Up Plus," which was the use of the now inactive, low spaces previously occupied by drawers for sloped displays of other Gibson products such as napkins, paper plates and cups, candles, and gift wrap. This 1982 innovation raised capacity by about 35 percent.

Gibson introduced an innovative store fixture in 1984 that was superior to those provided by the principal competitors. Gibson termed its fixture concept "Everything Cubed." What this concept did was to reduce greatly wasted cubic air space occupied by the fixture. It accomplished this goal in three ways: first, by decreasing the depth of the fixture, moving from twenty-four inches in most cases to twelve inches in most cases; second, by sloping the display front at a steeper angle; and third, by stocking merchandise all the way to the top of the fixture. There was virtually a doubling of the amount that could be shown in the same floor space. Retailer reaction was positive. It should be noted that in stores having large card departments, the Garfield products were assigned their own separate section.

So-called "cross merchandising" interested Gibson's management very much at this time, and it was being further developed. The company wanted to place its products with related products from other manufacturers in the hope of increasing Gibson sales. The argument that Gibson presented to retailers was that such cross-merchandising would increase the sales of both the Gibson products and the related products. Therefore, in every merchandising season or period, Gibson sales representatives would henceforth include product offerings designed to sell outside of the traditional greeting card department of the store; for example, display of Mother's Day cards in the candy department or calendars featuring photographs and drawings of puppies in the pet supply aisle. Moreover, everyday product programs would include offerings such as birthday candles, to be displayed in the cake mix or baked goods department, and gift wrap to be shown with gifts and toys. The company also developed a variety of "outpost" store fixtures to support these cross-merchandising programs. To gain this satellite space in the selected stores and the general cooperation of the merchant over the long run was not going to be easy.

More than 50,000 stores in the United States sold Gibson products, compared to about 37,000 for Hallmark. Gibson's five largest customers accounted for about 27 percent of sales and the largest of these five accounted for about 9 percent of sales. The dominant practice for stores carrying one of the big three of the industry was not to carry the line of any competitor, but there were fairly frequent deviations, especially in department stores and gift shops. Also, fairly frequently a retailer seasonally stocked Cleo wrap near a large permanent display of products made by Hallmark or American Greetings. Gibson and its major competitors provided credit to stores for seasonal merchandise for an average of six months and in a few instances for as long as eleven months. Consistent with industry practice, the company permitted retailers to return unsold seasonal cards, of which there were many.

Gibson employed a direct-field sales force that regularly visited most of the company's customers. For retail accounts that had branches, such visits might be to central offices or district headquarters or both. A much larger merchandising service force called on the stores themselves.

Traditionally, there was a difference between the types of retailers the three leading card makers emphasized. Gibson Greetings, Inc., was a bit more varied and had had a multiple strategy. For a long time the company had cultivated card shops, drugstores, and middle-of-the-road department stores with Gibson brand cards and the rest of the product types the company manufactured while cultivating variety stores, supermarkets, and discount department stores with the Buzza brand. Simultaneously, it tried to reach lower-end stores of several types (supermarkets, discount department stores, and some drugstores) with Cleo brand products. Gibson brand was priced higher than Buzza; and the latter, higher than Cleo. However, the Cleo brand did not have a fully developed line of cards. American Greetings had used supermarkets, drugstores, variety stores, and discount department stores.

Hallmark had emphasized gift shops and conventional department stores and also developed a large network of franchised Hallmark shops that stressed cards but also carried other Hallmark products such as paper party goods, stationery, candles, albums, and coffee mugs. Objectively considered, Hallmark-brand cards were of good quality, but the company had heavily emphasized quality for decades in its public relations work and corporate image advertising. Its crown symbol was extremely familiar to people. Its main promotional slogan, "When you care enough to send the very best," was one of the best known in the nation. Ironically, however, many customers associated that expression with all three of the leading card manufacturers. On the other hand, company identification and prestige had benefited handsomely from its longtime, intermittent television series, "Hallmark Hall of Fame." The name of the program and its content implied something of special quality.

In recent years, a few of the more upscale department stores and a small number that were trading up vigorously had dropped greeting cards even though space productivity and markup rates of cards were attractively high. Retailers normally sold cards at about twice what they paid for them. As one retailing executive put it, "Our store cannot do everything and be everything. Moreover, some merchandise, such as washing machines and greeting cards, does not seem to fit into the image of fashionable merchandise for people and their homes that we want. In addition, a card department makes us look too much like a drugstore or supermarket."

American Greetings had recently altered some of its strategy and was attempting to cultivate gift shops, conventional department stores, and national and regional chains of nondiscount department stores. This manufacturer signed Sears, Roebuck & Co. to carry its cards exclusively whereas Hallmark, anticipating the American Greetings' action, countered by signing up the 2,000-store J.C. Penney chain to carry the Hallmark brand exclusively. Hallmark additionally countered by vastly enlarging its Ambassador-brand line of products (composed of cards, wrapping supplies, and stationery) and pushing hard for placement of Ambassador in the types of stores American Greetings emphasized. Hallmark worked out an arrangement with A & P, Giant Food, and some other supermarket chains. Ambassador brand carried the word "Ambassador" prominently, of course. Hallmark did not legally have to print the work "Hallmark" on Ambassador-brand goods. However, it did so but in a size of print most consumers would not notice and many could not read and in a place where most consumers would not look. American Greetings began to reallocate its product line and called the part of it aimed at grocers and similar retailers "Forget-Me-Not." An arrangement was worked out with Safeway supermarkets. The name "American Greetings" also appeared prominently on the Forget-Me-Not products but in a different typeface.

Advise Gibson Greetings, Inc.

HEAD SPORTS WEAR, INC.

Alex Schuster, an executive of a leading sportswear manufacturer, made a proposal in 1966 to Howard Head, inventor and owner of Head Ski. Schuster proposed: Why not allow skiers to find their entire ski outfit under the Head name? Apply the same standards of quality, design, and engineering to a line of ski wear. The proposal was convincing. Head Ski and Sports Wear, as it was then known, was born, with Alex Schuster as president. Production of quality ski wear under the Head name began in Cockeysville, Maryland. Within four years the company advanced from a newcomer to a solid second place in annual ski wear sales.

Just a year after its ski wear debut, Head Ski and Sports Wear introduced its first line of tennis wear. One reason for the expansion was to achieve a seasonal production balance. Another reason was to apply the same principles of fashionable and functional appeal to sports other than skiing. And for these same reasons, swim and running wear were later added to the sportswear offerings.

The company's rapid growth warranted a new home, and in 1969 it moved to a new corporate headquarters in the newly created town of Columbia, Maryland. In 1970 Head also entered the tennis racquet field, and the hardware division of the company moved its headquarters to Boulder, Colorado. Head became a subsidiary of AMF in 1971. AMF was a conglomerate with annual sales of more than $1.5 billion.

Up to this point the Head Sports Wear collections had always represented top-of-the-line quality and had been priced accordingly. Schuster saw a void between the mid-priced range of ski wear and Head sportswear and he set out to produce a line of ski wear that would have Head's heritage of design and engineered construction, but which would be priced competitively within the mid-price range. The line became Number One Sun—to indicate its Head heritage and also because it would be produced in Hong Kong, although it would be designed by Head people in the United States, as were the other lines. The line grew from a collection of twenty pieces in 1970 to 116 pieces in 1980. In that year the possibility of dropping the Sun line was considered because of the line's drop in sales from $6 million to $4 million in two years. This decision and its implementation are emphasized in the present case.

At the time of Alex Schuster's proposal to Howard Head in 1966, 75 percent of all skis owned in the United States were Head skis, a remarkable market penetration. There was tremendous brand awareness of the name Head, and the decision to expand upon it was a wise one. Also, the personality and charisma of Howard Head, who had become an important figure in this close-knit industry, were complemented by

This case was prepared by Dr. Dee Wewer. Ms. Wewer was vice-president of Head Sports Wear, Inc., from 1979 to 1982.

the equally dynamic and charismatic personality of Alex Schuster. These factors were not taken lightly in the ski industry. Most ski shops were small, privately owned, and operated by people very close to the sport. It was definitely a "family" industry.

Howard Head and Alex Schuster, well aware of this fact, serviced their accounts accordingly. Howard Head sat with every account that wrote an order for Head skis. Alex Schuster became "the" personality in the ski wear industry, known for his parties and personal attention to all the elements of his business. Also, Schuster was considered a progressive merchandiser with innovative designs that ranged from elegant to provocative. Howard Head was a well-known engineer with experience in aircraft design.

Until 1978, Alex Schuster had headed the merchandising department of the sportswear company. He had a superb image within the industry for his ability to know what was "right" in fashion, and he brought a sophistication to ski wear never before equaled. The Sun line had had his attention during its birth and early adolescence, but it began to wane as he lessened his responsibilities in the specific departments and took on more of a managerial role. This alteration of responsibilities was partly caused by the demands of the new owners, AMF.

Besides Head Ski, Head Sports Wear, and Head Tennis Racquets, AMF also owned Tyrolia, an Austrian-based ski binding manufacturer, and several other leisure-oriented businesses. The joint ownership of these companies had some impact on the marketing of their individual products, and this became an important part of many product decisions over the years.

It should also be noted that during the time of the AMF purchase, many ski retailers worried greatly that the personal attention they had received from their entrepreneurial friends, Howard and Alex, would change into a "corporate attitude." This fear received constant attention from Schuster, which won him an even firmer place in the ski family. His attention was forced away from this continuing problem, however, when in 1979 he was sent by AMF to the European division of Head Sports Wear in Munich, Germany, to manage its growth and design.

At this time the management of Head Sports Wear USA was turned over to the executive vice-president, who had never had the exposure and did not have the same image as his forerunner. The "personality" of Head was closely watched by the industry. Every person in management was aware of the "Schuster following," and efforts to be honest, open, friendly, and, above all, service-oriented were established and enforced in order not only to overcome the space created by Schuster's absence but also to take advantage of improving service and quality in any tangible way possible.

Until 1981, Head Sports Wear's revenues were primarily from ski wear sales. However, by the end of the second quarter of 1981, sales had reached a fifty-fifty balance between ski wear on the one hand and sportswear for tennis, swimming, and running on the other.

In the winter of 1980-1981, after reviewing the previous year's sales, production, and delivery of ski wear, both with the Head label and the 1 Sun label, the decision was reached that there was a problem with the demand for the 1 Sun label. Opinions as to the cause of the demand drop varied from lack of promotional funds, poor design, and too much competition to the reality of the poor snow season in the East during the winter of 1979-1980.

The revenue had to be forecasted for 1981, and it was questionable that the 1 Sun label could pull enough in sales for the company to carry the fixed costs previously budgeted to support it. One solution was suggested that became a focal point for creativity in the promotion, design, and budgeting areas: because (1) AMF also owned the company which produced the Tyrolia binding, as well as Head Sports Wear; (2) the Tyrolia name had benefited from a $6 million expenditure in America over the past three years to make the public brand-aware; and (3) the Head Ski Wear line had found its success from the awareness of the Head ski, why not develop a ski wear line and give it the already brand-aware name of Tyrolia?

Most management personnel thought this was a good direction, as long as the continuity between the labels rang true. That is, it would have to be an authentic ski wear line, not a fashion line, in order for the Tyrolia name on both the bindings and the garments to have credibility.

Another major decision was what to do with 1 Sun Ski Wear. Should design continuation for product presentation be cancelled and all efforts be devoted to a new Tyrolia line? If the 1 Sun line were now (November 1980) dropped, would the dealers who heard of it cancel their remaining orders for delivery in December 1980 through March 1981? Would all closeout sales of 1 Sun be cut off if ski retailers knew too soon of the elimination of the line? Closeout goods were those which did not sell during the prime selling period and therefore had to be offered at reduced prices to eliminate inventory before a new line was produced. Would the competition be given too much time for creativity if the company let anyone know too early of the development of the Tyrolia line?

The ski industry had one large national trade show each year, organized by Ski Industries of America, in mid-March in Las Vegas, Nevada. All major manufacturers and dealers participated and did the majority of their buying and selling there. However, Head Sports Wear also maintained permanent showrooms in New York, Los Angeles, and Atlanta, and several sales representatives in the field.

In the past years, 1 Sun had always been introduced to the market a month and a half before the Las Vegas show, whereas the Head Ski line was never introduced until the opening of the show. If it was decided not to produce 1 Sun, yet not introduce Tyrolia too early, what would the ski dealers be told in early February when they asked about the new 1 Sun line?

It was a ski industry practice to advertise and editorialize heavily in the Las Vegas show issues of ski publications, specifically *Ski* and *Skiing* magazines. Both had vast editorial coverage of the new lines to be introduced, and almost all manufacturers advertised their surprises to the industry through these two vehicles. This year, to make matters more difficult, the advertising deadlines for both these magazines were backed up to mid-January. This date was far in advance of the ideal time for Head Sports Wear to introduce Tyrolia, or the news of "no 1 Sun." Could the editorial or advertising staffs of these magazines be trusted with the information of either of these pieces of news? Would keeping back the news regarding the elimination of 1 Sun have ethical overtones? Was it possible, it was considered, to tease the industry with a "Guess what's ahead with Head" campaign, referring to Tyrolia?

The Tyrolia line, if produced, would be dramatically different from the Head or 1 Sun lines. It would be a hardware-oriented line—all-black zippers, buckles, snaps, lining—to represent its birth from the ski binding of the same name. And the colors offered for the line would be those also offered in the bindings, ski-oriented primary colors of red, royal blue, white, black, and bright yellow. The Tyrolia line would have fewer colors and only seventy-eight pieces instead of 1 Sun's 120 pieces. Moreover, it would be a medium-price line. A new brand of ski wear introduced to the industry after two bad snow years was also a major business news story.

After another bad ski winter (this time no snow in the West), should the key dealers across the country be forewarned about the coming of Tyrolia? If they were not and they did not see 1 Sun at the usual introduction time, would they commit their purchase dollars elsewhere? Was this another question of ethics? Considering the family nature of the industry and Schuster's previous image, this was perceived as having extreme importance to dealer-manufacturer relationships.

Head Sports Wear was also wondering what the proper steps of introduction should be for the Tyrolia line. One must remember that little if any research had gone into deciding what the true problems of 1 Sun had been. And the demand for a new ski wear line, even if different in concept, had not been researched. This was a highly argued subject within management, and the decision was made because of "a lack of time for further research or delay."

Advise Head Sports Wear, Inc.

PELKUS'S OAK GROVE MOTEL

Paul and Anna Pelkus owned and operated a motor hotel of seventy rental units in an Ohio community of about 75,000 population. This community had about a dozen other motels. The facility, named Pelkus's Oak Grove Motel, was a few hundred feet away from a busy interstate highway that was completed only a few years before. The motel had a heated swimming pool, a wading pool, black-and-white television in every rental unit, and was fully air-conditioned. The Pelkus' business had no restaurant, but there were eating places within one fourth of a mile.

Mr. and Mrs. Pelkus also owned eight acres of land, for which they paid $46,000, near another Ohio city of about 50,000 population some sixty miles away. The Pelkuses had just begun to consider establishing a second motel on that undeveloped tract when Henry Arliss, a field representative of Biarritz Inns, approached them and inquired if they would be interested in taking franchises for both their old and new locations. He told them that he was thinking of a four-year contract.

In recent years franchising had been adapted to many types of businesses. In addition to the low-priced restaurant, typified perhaps by McDonald's, there were franchising systems in such disparate activities as soft-drink bottling, art galleries, travel agencies, shoe-repair shops, nursing homes, and weight-reduction salons. Many franchisors had developed sophisticated systems of management and had reached great size. There had also been many fly-by-nighters. Perhaps the best known fact was that both the franchisor and the franchisee participated in a common public identity.

Biarritz Inns, Inc., owned motels and also maintained a system under which independent motel operators were franchised to use the Biarritz name. It also had a restaurant chain operating under the name Continental House.

The Biarritz operation was integrated to a considerable degree. There was market research on the geographical area and the particular acreage for each prospective motel. Then there was architectural planning, including building and room plans, planning for furnishings and decorations, brokerage for construction and mortgage financing (but no Biarritz guarantees on financing), central purchasing of operating supplies, operation of a reservation system, training and refresher training of motel personnel, and supervision and monitoring of advertising and public relations. There was considerable inspection, but this was usually announced in advance from headquarters. Considerable physical similarity existed among most of the motels in the chain and all were identified by a standardized sign and the name Biarritz Inn, a properly registered mark.

The motor hotels owned and franchised by Biarritz contained a total of 19,500 rental units and were spread over Ohio, Indiana, Illinois,

Michigan, Wisconsin, Minnesota, North Dakota, South Dakota, Iowa, Nebraska, Missouri, Kansas, Oklahoma, Colorado, New Mexico, and Arizona. In the last year alone 1,101 rental units had been added to the chain's motels. This number included seventy-five units in a new motel in North Dakota, the company's first penetration into that state. Expansion plans for the current year were emphasizing Ohio, Indiana, and Arizona. Biarritz's motels ranged in size from sixty to 290 rental units, and the mean was 112 units. All motels in the chain had air-conditioning, a heated swimming pool, color television, twenty-four-hour switchboard service, room service, restaurant facilities, on-premises parking for all guests, and reservations by teletype.

Biarritz's current franchise agreement specified that the franchisee would pay to the franchisor (a) a one-time fee of $20,000, of which 40 percent was payable on signing the contract and the remainder when construction began or in seven months, whichever was sooner; (b) a royalty of 3.1 percent of gross receipts, payable the first and fifteenth of each month; and (c) a contribution of 8 cents per rental unit per day for advertising. The $20,000 fee was applicable to every location separately.

Motor hotels owned by the chain also paid the 8 cents charge into the advertising fund. National media, local media, and roadside billboards were utilized. Biarritz did not practice cooperative advertising with its franchises. However, it did issue a highly detailed directory that listed all of the Biarritz franchisees and explained how to find them.

Biarritz Inns, Inc., operated food service facilities in all of its motels, but most of these food service facilities were in adjacent buildings. Approximately one fifth of the restaurants in the chain were on sites where no motel of the chain existed. Restaurants were operated in all the states in which motels were operated and California. The restaurants were a separate operating division of Biarritz and all accounting was kept separate from the lodging operation.

Biarritz Inns honored all major credit cards, a point that was extensively featured in its national advertising. In fact, slightly over two thirds of gross rental income in the chain's motels came through credit cards. Pelkus's advertising had been largely on the themes of cleanliness, convenient location, and restfulness. About 60 percent of their rental income was through credit cards.

Expenses, income, and other data for Pelkus's Oak Grove Motel are presented in Exhibits 1 and 2 for 19XX, a representative year.

Arliss called the Pelkuses' attention to the fact that Biarritz motels had an occupancy rate of 73.0 percent the past year and 72.6 percent the year before, a net profit of 13.5 percent of sales, and total operating expenses of 60.0 percent.

The Pelkuses were aware that Biarritz owned around one tenth of the motels in its chain and that the franchisor had bought out two franchised

EXHIBIT 1 Accounting Data for the Oak Grove Motel 19XX

Income	
Room rentals	96 %
Merchandise sales	4
	100 %

Operating Expenses	
Salaries and wages	24 %
Salaries for owners	4
Repairs and maintenance	5
Cleaning and other supplies	3
Heat and electricity	5.5
Laundry	4
Linens and glassware	0.5
Payroll taxes and insurance	6.5
Telephone and telegraph	1.5
Advertising	4.8
Stationery	0.2
Other	3
Total operating expenses	62.0%
Gross operating profit	38.0
Sales	100.0%

Nonoperating Expenses	
Real estate and property taxes	4.6%
Interest	5.5
Insurance	1.9
Depreciation and amortization	14.0
Total nonoperating expenses	26.0%
Net profit	12.0%

EXHIBIT 2 Miscellaneous Data for Oak Grove Motel 19XX

Original investment in motel building	$355,000
Original investment in furniture	$205,000
Original investment in land	$50,000
Occupancy rate	67.0%
Mean daily rate per rental unit rented	$28.50

Biarritz Inns in Chicago last year. Moreover, they knew that several franchises had as many as eight locations operating with Biarritz, which amounted to having chains within a chain.

The Pelkuses were also aware of potential deviations beyond their control. An old friend who managed a franchised sweet shop had told them that a day-old doughnut sold as fresh or a weak cup of coffee served in one shop could lose a customer for the other shops. If a customer was dissatisfied he could blame the entire chain instead of the offender.

Advise the Pelkuses.

POWER TOOLS, INC. (B)

Harvey Beeson had just been named president of the United States Operations Group of Power Tools, Inc., the largest branch of this worldwide company. He was justifiably proud of his new appointment. It meant that he would now sit on the board of directors of this corporation, which was listed in the *Fortune* 500. He believed the promotion was merited because he had overseen the impressive growth of the Consumer Products Division over the last several years. Beeson had started out as a company salesperson about twenty years earlier and later became the head of the Asian-Pacific Division of the organization. Although born in the United State, he was a Canadian citizen. His office was in one of the company's older establishments in the Middle Atlantic states.

Sales of the Consumer Products Division had risen at a compound annual rate that approached 15 percent during the last several years. Beeson had been at the helm of the division while all this rapid growth had occurred. Although the profitability of this division was not as impressive as its sales, profitability too had grown rapidly over the last several years.

However, Beeson knew that all was not as well in the other units under his control. Principally, Beeson was concerned about the serious situation that prevailed in the Air Products Division. He knew that the Air Products Division was not performing profitably and for three years had not met its goals. It was the only unprofitable division in the company.

In order to clarify his understanding, Beeson asked the Air Products Division general manager, Arthur Molnar, to meet with him. Beeson requested that a summary of the current situation be presented to him.

In order to comply with Beeson's request, Molnar first met with two Air Products Division officers, comptroller Bob Roberts and marketing manager Tom Solow. At the conference with Solow and Roberts, Molnar saw a very displeasing picture. The following two viewpoints emerged at the conference.

This case was prepared by Richard Rosecky, Ph. D., who is on the staff of the company being considered.

Marketing's View

Molnar asked Solow to summarize marketing's picture of the situation. Solow portrayed the situation as being a problem thrust upon the Air Products Division from corporate headquarters, which in Solow's view clearly failed to understand the economic characteristics and problems of air-powered tools. A successful small maker of precision power tools located in Ohio, the General Precision Pneumatic Corporation, had been taken over by the much larger Power Tools, Inc., about three years ago. As the marketing manager saw it, the subsidiary had been asked to perform as if it were a rapid-growth company. Solow related how the General Precision Pneumatic product line had been stripped of all the various specialty items that it had and how it had been forced to streamline its product offerings. Worse yet, in Solow's view, General Precision Pneumatic had been forced to drop its established direct-to-the-user method of selling in favor of selling through industrial distributors. Solow stated that the traditional strength of General Precision Pneumatic had been its highly capable sales engineers, who could meet directly with users and potential users and design virtually custom-made products to suit their desires. These sales engineers had been redirected by management to cover the entire nation through a type of middleman, the industrial distributors serving the Electric Tool Division of Power Tools, Inc. In addition, the parent company was so confident that it approximately doubled the capacity of the Ohio plant. Solow stated that he had certainly been able to foresee the disaster that followed. He then explained somberly that division sales dropped rapidly. Solow related that the remaining employees at General Precision Pneumatic, now renamed the Air Products Division of Power Tools, Inc., were disappointed with the entire merger.

Finally, Solow remarked that in his view the marketing policies of a consumer-products-oriented organization would not work when applied to the industrial customers served by the Air Products Division. Solow advocated a return to the limited number of customers who had been served previously by General Precision Pneumatic and a return to the high-profit products that were better suited to the customers' quasi-individual needs.

The Corporate View

Bob Roberts had grown up with the parent company and was clearly an unofficial emissary from its headquarters. When Molnar asked him to present his view, Roberts took the opportunity with apparent relish.

The Air Products comptroller related that he understood the problem quite differently from the view presented by Solow. Roberts stated that the major source of growth in the parent company had been the concept of positive price elasticity of demand for power tools. As Roberts put it, "This concept means that as prices drop, volume in units will increase rapidly, and subsequent dollar sales will increase even faster." Roberts explained that the Consumer Products Division was a clear example of this valuable principle at work.

Roberts related that in the Consumer Products Division, as prices were reduced, great economies of scale in production and marketing generated rapid growth in profits. In addition, there was a greatly expanded market for power tools. In fact, prices for power tools were about one-half the level they had been ten years ago whereas the dollar market was easily two to three times as large.

The Air Products comptroller then explained that the parent firm believed if the very expensive air products were reduced in price and marketed through a channel of distribution that would reach many new users, the same principle would operate. In his eyes, this would have occurred had there been cooperation on the part of General Precision Pneumatic employees. Instead, Roberts related, there had been a small strike, and this difficulty had been followed by considerable personnel turnover in the administrative levels.

A Telephone Conversation

While Roberts and Solow were presenting their points of view to Molnar, a very important telephone call came in for Molnar. It illustrated a problem that contributed further to his perplexing situation.

Paul Fitzgerald, the sales manager for the Automotive Products Division, called to confirm a last-minute plan to increase the production for the division's half-inch air impact wrench. In Fitzgerald's view, the success or failure of his division depended upon the Air Products Division's ability to supply that organization with a reliable and inexpensive air wrench with which he could offer the broader product line that wholesale distributors of automotive products demanded.

The Automotive Products Division sales manager envisaged a sales campaign that would reverse earlier failures on the part of Power Tools, Inc., to consolidate its position in the automotive products market. Just as Power Tools, Inc., had been in the process of gaining an important market share in the automotive marketplace, the Japanese had invaded the air wrench market with very inexpensive products that Fitzgerald described as "inferior or perhaps even cheap." Undeniably, the Japanese had been able to price their products well below the current prices of domestic manufacturers. Worse, they had captured an important part of the market. Fitzgerald was telephoning to be sure that there would be no delay in the latest product redesigns, which would allow costs to be reduced to a level at which the Automotive Products Division would be able at least to meet the prices of the Japanese competition, even if it could not beat this formidable competition.

Molnar's Conference with Beeson

As Beeson had requested, Molnar put together a summary of what he thought of the current situation in the Air Products Division. It was not really a pretty picture to present to his new boss, Molnar thought.

Molnar agreed with Solow that marketing policies that worked with a consumer product would not always work with industrially oriented products. However, Molnar had to agree with Roberts that the considerably reduced prices instituted by Power Tools, Inc., had not been given a real chance to have an impact. There had been great friction between the employees of the General Precision Pneumatic Company and the employees of the new parent company. This had subsided, Molnar thought, as time had progressed. He thought that it really could not be considered a problem today.

In his conference with Beeson, Molnar outlined the situation in simple terms. He related that the concept of altering the General Precision Pneumatic manner of distributing the product from customer representatives to the idea of industrial distributors most likely would not work. He suggested a return to a sales engineer calling upon an industrial user. Molnar also suggested that the pricing strategy put forth by the parent company should be given a chance to work in the Automotive Products Division. He stated, however, that the prices for the Air Products Division output sold directly to industrial users should be increased to reflect the new costs of marketing directly.

Beeson listened intently to the presentation from Molnar, but he was not pleased. He knew that any substantial reduction in the sales of the Air Products Division would most likely mean that division's demise, and that would mean a large loss to the parent company. In his first year as president, Beeson did not want to incur a new loss. On the other hand, Beeson did not need to be told that the situation as it stood could not be sustained for any long period of time. Something simply had to be done. Beeson viewed Fitzgerald's idea of the Automotive Division's pursuit of the air wrench market as a good one. Perhaps it was the only action that would increase the demand on the Air Products Division's factory and thus reduce losses there while stimulating sales in the lagging Automotive Products Division.

Advise Power Tools, Inc.

8

Physical Distribution

UNIVERSAL MOTORS PARTS DIVISION

Six months ago, William Frank, general manager of the parts division of Universal Motors Corporation, began to feel uneasy about certain trends that had been developing in the automotive parts aftermarket. Products in this market fall into two major categories, service parts and accessories. Service parts are those used in repair and replacement, including mechanical, body/frame, and chassis components. Accessories, either appearance or functional items used to improve performance or dress up the car, include fog lights, outside rearview mirrors, or interior floor mats.

Over the past ten years, total aftermarket parts sales in the United States had stabilized in the $70 billion to $80 billion range after growing steadily along with new car sales since World War II. In the last two years, the total number of outlets selling aftermarket parts had declined dramatically, and it was predicted by industry analysts that in five years there would be 20 percent fewer outlets than there are today. Last year

This case was prepared by Robert Krapfel, Ph.D., who is on the staff of the company that is being considered.

the average U.S. car owner spent $405 per vehicle on tires, batteries, accessories, and service parts. In the last three years, service parts sales had increased from $19 billion to $23 billion nationwide.

Like many firms, Universal Motors (UM) had also seen its sales patterns shift to follow population trends. Sales in the South and West were expanding at a faster rate than in the North and East.

The major types of outlets for aftermarket parts are service stations, garages, new vehicle dealers, specialized repair shops (e.g. muffler shops), mass merchandisers, and jobbers. Exhibit 1 shows how market shares of these types of outlets have changed over the last five years.

Fifty-three years ago, the parts division of Universal Motors was established by consolidating the aftermarket service parts warehousing and distribution activities of three marketing divisions. Twelve years ago, the parts division of Universal Motors Corporation became a separate operating division with aftermarket parts responsibility for all six of the North American marketing divisions. This had been done to provide one centralized service parts organization which was devoted entirely to the nationwide distribution of replacement parts to UM dealers. Sales and marketing activities continued to be performed by the marketing divisions, whereas the parts division concentrated on improving service, warehousing, and distribution.

Then, six years ago, sales and marketing functions were also assigned to the parts division, thus giving it total responsibility for marketing and distribution of parts to UM dealers. This move was soon followed by incorporation of all truck division service parts into the parts division system, and finally, two years ago operations were expanded from North America to include all aftermarket parts marketing and distribution activities to UM dealers worldwide. This remains its current status today.

Universal Motors Parts Division (UMPD) and Allied Division are UM's marketing and distribution arms that service the automotive aftermarket. UMPD distributes only to UM dealers, whereas Allied serves independent distributors. Each division maintains its own sales force and network of distribution centers. Many of the parts inventoried are identical; yet, for sales and merchandising reasons, the two divisions operate independently of each other. Also, many of the accessory items sold by both UMPD and Allied are contract-manufactured for UM by independent manufacturers.

In an indirect way UMPD and Allied actually compete because independent jobbers are free to sell to UM dealers, as is shown in Exhibit 2.

William Frank realized that the sales trends he had observed, if continued, would call for adjustments in the distribution system. He called in his director of operations, Dave Hert.

EXHIBIT 1 Percentage Market Shares by Type of Retail Outlet

Year			Type of Outlet			
Number of years ago	Service Stations	Garages	New Car Dealers	Specialized Repair Shops	Mass Merchandisers	Jobbers	Total
5	25	12	30	18	10	5	100
4	24	11	31	17	11	6	100
3	23	10	30	20	14	5	100
2	18	11	29	24	13	5	100
1	21	9	27	22	17	4	100

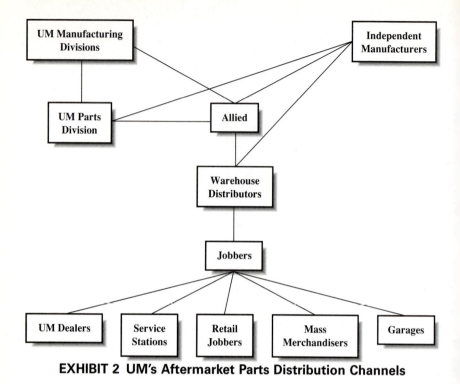

EXHIBIT 2 UM's Aftermarket Parts Distribution Channels

"Dave, I want to re-evaluate our entire operational network. This division needs to operate even better and more efficiently than it has in the past. I know there is no fat to cut, but we have to trim someplace, and I'm depending on you to come up with some answers. Let's get together in thirty days and you show me what you've got."

Hert knew from past experience that such requests from the boss were not to be taken lightly and that completing an entire operational review in thirty days would be no easy task. He worked late that night and the next two deciding what information would be required. On the fourth day after his meeting with Frank, he drafted a memo to each of his twenty-three regional distribution center managers, requesting a selected audit of the previous twelve months' operations.

Specifically, he wanted monthly average figures in each of the following categories.

1. Inbound freight volume in tons, broken down by shipment size. That is, what amount was received in less-than-truckload (LTL) shipments and what amount was received in full truckload (TL) quantities. For both the LTL and TL inbound freight he wanted to know average distance travelled and total freight charges billed. All of this information could be obtained directly from trucking company invoices and internal records.

2. Inventory handled in tons, again in two categories, high versus low turnover items. High turnover items include routine service parts such as spark plugs, oil filters, and shock absorbers. Low turnover parts include sheetmetal and frame parts such as door panels and bumpers. Total inventory carrying costs for each category would also be needed.

3. Outbound freight volumes in tons, reported in the same manner as inbound freight.

Hert asked that the information be in his hands in two weeks. This was pressing things, but he wanted the remaining two weeks to absorb the information and do follow-up if needed.

After one week reports from the field began to come in. Soon twenty of the twenty-three distribution center managers' figures were in hand. Two had not been received because key people were on vacation, and in one location a newly installed minicomputer was experiencing start-up problems. Nevertheless, Hert was satisfied that he would be able to present an accurate picture of the current state of affairs when he met with Frank. Deciding to group the distribution center data by sales regions, he displayed the highest and lowest cost operation in each region. The data for two of these regions appear in Exhibit 3.

Looking at these figures, it was obvious to Hert which operations were most and least costly; yet he still was unsure that the figures clearly pointed to any particular course of action. To get a clearer picture, Hert went back to the original reports and zeroed in on the sources of the inventory carrying costs. He believed these were the most directly controllable and therefore deserved the greatest attention. For each distribution center, he reviewed the figures on the number of employees, total monthly wages, number of cubic feet of storage space in the building, percent of space utilized, and building age. These figures for the Toledo, Indianapolis, Atlanta, and Memphis distribution centers are shown in Exhibit 4.

In the meeting, Frank mentioned that the sales figures continued to be unencouraging and that something would have to be done to reduce operational costs fairly quickly. Hert had been in the industry many years and he knew that it was highly cyclical. Sales often expanded dramatically during the early stages of a business cycle upturn, and he

EXHIBIT 3 Distribution Center Operating Review (for average 30-day period)

	Midwest		South	
	Toledo	Indianapolis	Atlanta	Memphis
Inbound Freight				
LTL				
Volume (tons)	125	260	152	171
Distance (miles)	77	86	380	275
Cost (thousands)	157.85	366.70	901.05	733.59
TL				
Volume	195	196	228	114
Distance	91	88	410	320
Cost	230.68	224.22	1,112.41	434.11
Inventory Carrying				
HIGH TURNOVER				
Amount (tons)	174	319	180	130
Cost (thousands)	22.45	37.64	19.44	11.96
LOW TURNOVER				
Amount	146	137	200	155
Cost	24.82	25.35	26.80	20.30
Outbound Freight				
LTL				
Volume	170	237	304	200
Distance	55	68	40	75
Cost	153.34	264.30	189.70	234.00
TL				
Volume	150	219	76	85
Distance	31	42	62	90
Cost	20.15	119.57	56.07	91.04

did not want to jeopardize the overall ability of the distribution network to respond. The ability to serve customers reliably and on time was still most important in the long run.

After an hour and a half of going over the figures in some detail, Frank turned to Hert and said, "What do you think we should do?"

Advise Universal Motors Parts Division.

EXHIBIT 4 Inventory Carrying Cost Factors

	Midwest		South	
	Toledo	Indianapolis	Atlanta	Memphis
COST FACTOR				
Number of employess	20	26	17	14
Total Average Monthly Wage (thousands)	30.60	39.78	18.79	15.47
Cubic Feet of Storage Space (thousands)	200	275	220	140
Utilization (%)	78	84	87	88
Building Age (years)	12	19	14	6

COLÓN FREE TRADE ZONE

The governments of several nations have authorized the establishment of free trade zones within their borders. This entity is an enclosed policed area in, adjacent to, or near a port of entry, into which foreign products not otherwise prohibited may be brought without formal customs entry or payment of customs duties. It has no resident population, and it is subject to the various other laws of the authorizing jurisdiction, such as those dealing with labor, carrier inspection, public health, and postal service. One international business magazine has referred to the free trade zone entity as a "combination transshipment center and industrial park where a company can enter into the intense competition of world marketing unencumbered by the usual restrictions of import-export business."[1] It is often simultaneously a design for attracting job-producing activities into underdeveloped regions. If products are reshipped out of the free trade zone to foreign destinations, whether or not they have incurred any processing, there is no customs interference or even supervision. Of course, if the goods are reshipped into the interior of the country operating the free trade zone, ordinary regulations and customs duties apply.

Free trade zones, often known as foreign trade zones, are found in a good many places. There are several such operations in the United States: for example New York City, Buffalo, San Francisco, San Jose, Seattle, Honolulu, Toledo, New Orleans, Little Rock, Kansas

[1] "New Life for Free Zones," *International Management*, 18 (March 1963).

City, Charleston (South Carolina), and McAllen (Texas). In addition, such zones are planned for many cities, for example Chicago, Atlanta, Boston, Salt Lake City, Omaha, Louisville, Wilkes-Barre (Pennsylvania), New Bedford (Massachusetts), Portsmouth (Virginia), Port Everglades (Florida), and Bay City and Sault Ste. Marie (Michigan). Some examples of established zones abroad are Monrovia, Liberia; Hamburg, Germany; and Colón, Panama.

Panama

The Republic of Panama links South and Central America. Formerly part of Colombia, Panama achieved independence in 1903. With an area of 29,700 square miles (including the Panama Canal Zone), it is a narrow, curving isthmus extending generally in an east-west direction. It is about fifty miles wide in the vicinity of Colón and Panama City. Its tropical climate is divided into a rainy season extending from mid-May to mid-December and a dry season occupying the rest of the year. The Caribbean side of the country receives about 150 inches of rainfall a year, and the Pacific side receives about seventy inches. Spanish is the official language, but a majority of the population in the two leading cities also speaks English. Many educated persons know a third language. Public sanitation and health conditions in Panama are among the best in the developing world.

The 1990 population of Panama was about 2,200,000, of which about 50 percent was urban. The main cities and their estimated populations are given in Exhibit 1. As in most of Latin America, the rate of population growth in Panama is quite high, in recent years about 3 percent.

There are no foreign exchange controls in Panama, except in an economic crisis. The national unit of currency, the balboa, is at par with the U.S. dollar, and U.S. currency is used throughout the country. The banking services situation tends to be very good. More than seventy foreign banks operate in Panama City, several with branches in Colón. Wages are higher than the average for Latin America but remain at a level only about one third as high as in the United States.

EXHIBIT 1 Population of Major Communities, Panama, 1990 (estimated)

City	Population
Panama City	650,000
Colón	100,000
David	45,000
La Chorrera	30,000
Panama Canal Zone	42,000

The Panamanian economy has always been internationally oriented, and foreign trade and services have always been more important than in the typical Third World nation. Residence papers for foreigners are generally not difficult to obtain. Some U.S. citizens have felt somewhat uneasy about living in Panama because of the former disagreements over the presence of U.S. government and military personnel in the Panama Canal Zone. Other U.S. citizens have felt quite uneasy about living in Panama because of the behavior of the former Noriega regime and the U.S. military action to remove that government in 1989. However, the overwhelming majority of Panamanians have always been hospitable, cordial, and supportive of U.S. citizens and foreigners in general.

Transportation

Panama is unique in its transportation setting. The foremost feature is the 51-mile-long Panama Canal connecting the Pacific and the Atlantic Oceans. An engineering triumph that opened in 1914, the Canal is incapable of handling some U.S. Navy ships today but is wide and deep enough for 96 percent of all the world's ocean-going vessels to use. There are excellent port facilities on both coasts, including modern piers and equipment in Colón that are assigned to the Free Trade Zone. There is a very good international airport at Tocumen, a suburb of Panama City about fifty-one miles from Colón. The airport received a $45 million improvement and enlargement in the late 1970s. Sixty steamship lines and twenty-eight scheduled airlines serve Panama City-Colón. Only the busiest North American, European, and Asian cities equal such numbers. No other Latin American location has access to as many ships, regular schedules, routes, steamship companies, and air carriers.

A good highway and a railroad connect Colón and Panama City, which are fifty miles apart, and an expressway is planned. Rail service to other Latin American nations is unavailable. Motor freight is possible only to the Central American nations by way of the Pan American Highway, which is excellent in some sections and very poor in others. Trucks need about ten and a half hours to reach San Jose, Costa Rica, the next large city and business center to the north. About forty hours of actual driving time is required for a truck to travel from Colón to Guatemala City, which lies at the northern end of Central America. The Pan American Highway connection south to Colombia is in various stages of surveying and construction and will probably open in the mid-1990s. In Colombia the highway will link up with a fairly good existing network in that nation and the excellent highway system of Venezuela to the east. Poor but passable routes are available from Colombia south to the republics down the west coast of South America, Ecuador, Peru, and Chile. The nearest large industrial center, Medellin, Colombia, is on the Pan American Highway. Timing of the completion of the road is dependent mainly on the level of U.S. subsidies and possible money from international lending organizations.

Colón Free Trade Zone

The Colón Free Trade Zone, originally comprising about 120 acres, is in the city of Colón, on the Atlantic coast of the isthmus. The Zone was created in 1948 and actually started operations in 1953. Although a government institution, it is administered by a board of experienced business people. Retail trade is forbidden in this enclave. Warehouse receipts for goods stored there can be used as collateral to borrow money.

The basic law of Panama covering the Free Trade Zone defines the allowable activities as follows:

> to bring in, store, exhibit, unpack, manufacture, put in containers, mount, assemble, refine, purify, blend, alter and, in general, perform operations with and handle all kinds of merchandise, products, raw materials, containers and other articles of commerce, with the sole exception of articles whose importation is prohibited by the law of the Republic.

Physical facilities for operations in the Free Trade Zone can be provided in several ways. First, space can be leased in buildings owned by the Colón Free Trade Zone. One can have a complete building or a portion of a building for a lease period of one to twenty years. Second, one can lease land and erect a building under a twenty-year agreement that has a customer option of renewal. Construction specifications must be approved by the Free Trade Zone. Third, public warehouse space is available in any amount for any time period. Charges for space must be paid at least once a month and are based on total usage. Fourth, in addition to storage, other services such as receiving and checking merchandise, repacking, reshipping, documentation, freight forwarding, and the maintenance of accounting and inventory records are available for reasonable fees.

Various payroll taxes are charged companies who operate in the Colón Free Trade Zone. However, there are several income tax advantages for companies who make sales to customers outside of Panama. The net combined effect of U.S. and Panamanian corporate income taxes is to save the company a sizable fraction of the taxes it would pay if it were conducting this business back in the United States. The saving is not uniform, for the Panamanian corporate income tax, unlike that of the U.S., is divided into twenty-four ascending gradations.

The lowest cost physical distribution may be a sea-air combination. Normal oceangoing vessels may bring the goods in large quantities to the Colón Free Zone, after which small shipments of individual orders may be made by air cargo. In most years the aggregate value of air shipments from the Colón Free Zone exceeds that of ocean shipments. See Exhibit 2.

In an average year, about 600 European, Asian, and North American companies use the facilities of the Colón Free Trade Zone. Examples are presented in Exhibit 3 broken down by industry. About two thirds of the companies using the zone are based in the United States.

In recent years the Free Trade Zone reached the capacity of its 120 acres. Anxious to expand further, it brought about negotiations between the U.S. and Panamanian governments concerning extra space in the Canal Zone, since the town of Colón is an enclave within the Canal Zone. The result was that in 1975 the United States gave the Free Trade Zone an abandoned airport, Old France Field, for a period of ninety-nine years. This 540-acre airfield lies in marshy land on the other side of a saltwater inlet from the existing Free Trade Zone. It has few facilities, but the three hangars were immediately put to use. A causeway several hundred yards long is planned to connect the two tracts of land.

Other Free Trade Zones in the Region

The Colón Free Trade Zone is the largest in the region and one of the largest in the world in terms of monetary value of business conducted. Small zones have been proposed for the cities of Buenaventura and Cali, in southern Colombia a little over 400 miles south of Colón; in Puerto Limón, Costa Rica; and Puerto Cortes, Honduras. Small zones already exist in Managua, Nicaragua; Margarita, Venezuela; San Bartolo, El

EXHIBIT 2 Value of Imports and Re-exports, Colón Free Trade Zone, By Mode of Transportation

	Value of Imports		Value of Re-exports	
	Latest Year	Two Years Ago	Latest Year	Two Years Ago
Air	27.6%	25.5%	60.7%	65.7%
Sea	72.1	74.1	35.7	32.1
Overland	0.3	0.4	3.6	2.2
	100.0%	100.0%	100.0%	100.0%

EXHIBIT 3 Examples of Companies Regularly Using Colón Free Trade Zone

Cosmetic	Beverages	Photographic Equipment
Givenchy	Heineken	Zeiss
Chanel	Ballantine & Sons	Yashica
Dior	Anheuser-Busch	Minolta
Jean Patou	Hiram Walker	Polaroid
Revlon	Courvoisier	Kodak
Colgate-Palmolive	Pedro Domecq	Nikon
Toni	Pepsi Cola	Canon
	Coca Cola	

Electrical and Electronic Equipment	Pharmaceuticals	Foods
Sony	Upjohn	Swift
Sylvania	Pfizer	Gerber
Hitachi	Parke-Davis	McCormick
Mitsubishi	Farbwerke Hoechst	Stokely-Van Camp
Panasonic	Zyma	Kraft
Norelco	Geigy	Heinz
Matsushita	Roche	Beechnut
Schick	Ciba	
	Schering	
	Riker	
	Wyeth	
	Warner-Lambert	

Tobacco	Automotive	Miscellaneous
Phillip Morris	Jeep	McGraw-Hill
American Tobacco	Chrysler	Singer
Brown & Williamson	General Motors	Gillette
P. Lorillard	Toyota	Xerox
Liggett & Myers	Goodyear	3-M
British Tobacco	General Tires	Paper Mate
	Mercedes Benz	

Salvador; Santa Marta, San Andres, Providencia islands, and Barranquilla, Colombia; La Romana, Dominican Republic, and Mayaguez, Puerto Rico; as well as in Oranjestad, Aruba, and Willemstad, Curacao, in the Dutch West Indies. The Mayaquez Zone is fairly aggressive, but it has chosen to specialize. Its forty-four acres of space currently serve

EXHIBIT 4 Distance from Port of Colón and Tocumen International Airport to Selected Cities

	Statute Miles	
City and Region	By Sea	By Air
Latin America and the Caribbean:		
La Guaira, Venezuela (Port of Caracas)	967	850
Maracaibo, Venezuela	797	531
Kingston, Jamaica	634	636
La Romana, Dominican Republic	965	916
Mayaguez, Puerto Rico	1,054	*
San Juan, Puerto Rico	1,142	1,103
Quito, Ecuador	–	633
Guayaquil, Ecuador	897	777
Puerto Limón, Costa Rica	218	253
Puntarenas, Costa Rica	587	362
San Jóse, Costa Rica	–	334
Medellin, Colombia	–	326
Bogotá, Colombia	–	470
Buenaventura, Colombia	458	402
Cali, Colombia	–	435
Barranquilla, Colombia	386	336
Havana, Cuba	1,139	982
Veracruz, Mexico	1,634	1,321
Mexico City, Mexico	–	1,495
Willemstad, Curaçao	803	740
Oranjestad, Aruba	710	702
Managua, Nicaragua	–	507
San Salvador, El Salvador	–	731
Puerto Barrios, Guatemala	897	771
Callao, Peru (Port of Lima)	1,598	1,465
Valparaiso, Chile	3,060	2,943
Rio de Janeiro, Brazil	5,026	3,294
Buenos Aires, Argentina	6,311	3,381
Port of Spain, Trinidad	1,334	1,230
Georgetown, Guyana	1,743	1,484
Port-au-Prince, Haiti	985	817
La Paz, Bolivia	–	1,925
United States:		
Tampa	1,399	1,320
Miami	1,397	1,156
New Orleans	1,598	1,603
Mobile	1,603	1,599
Galveston	1,709	1,753

* Not available.

EXHIBIT 4 *(Continued)*

City and Region	Statute Miles By Sea	By Air
Jacksonville	1,744	1,484
Charleston	1,800	1,657
Norfolk	2,047	2,020
Washington, D.C.	—	2,080
Baltimore	2,240	2,120
New York City	2,272	2,231
Los Angeles	3,402	3,001
San Francisco	3,779	3,322
Seattle	*	3,651
Chicago	*	2,325
Honolulu	5,395	5,245
Canada:		
Toronto	3,975	2,389
Halifax	2,641	2,693
Vancouver	4,678	3,740
St. John (New Brunswick)	2,640	*
Montreal	3,637	2,534
Europe:		
Le Havre, France	5,302	5,283
Antwerp, Belgium	5,516	5,477
Rotterdam, Netherlands	5,522	5,493
Liverpool, U.K.	5,341	5,167
Hamburg, West Germany	5,825	5,699
Zurich, Switzerland	—	5,657
Lisbon, Portugal	4,968	*
Gibraltar	5,038	4,926
Rome, Italy	—	5,903
Madrid, Spain	—	5,064
Barcelona, Spain	5,571	*
Other:		
Tokyo-Yokohama, Japan	8,898	8,419
Hong Kong	10,635	10,084
Manila, Philippines	10,764	10,283
Bombay, India	14,921	9,742
Singapore	12,097	11,687
Melbourne, Australia	9,130	9,022
Wellington, New Zealand	7,491	7,433
Haifa, Israel	7,296	7,303

* Not available.

EXHIBIT 5 Imports from and Re-exports to Leading Countries, Latest Years, Colón Free Trade Zone

Country in Rank Order	$ Amount (in thousands) Imported from	Country in Rank Order	$ Amount (in thousands) Re-exported to
1. Japan	$166,024.7	1. Aruba	$73,741.3
2. United States	93,439.0	2. Brazil	60,055.7
3. Taiwan	61,372.1	3. Venezuela	56,137.7
4. Hong Kong	40,146.4	4. Ecuador	53,793.2
5. Switzerland	29,141.4	5. Colombia[a]	49,616.4
6. United Kingdom	23,574.4	6. United States	35,567.9
7. West Germany	14,708.9	7. Mexico	25,401.7
8. Colombia	13,604.0	8. El Salvador	22,630.6
9. France	12,598.0	9. Chile	22,083.7
10. South Korea	12,012.8	10. Costa Rica	18,725.7
11. Puerto Rico	9,832.9	11. Guatemala	17,002.4
12. Italy	8,274.7	12. Bolivia	16,642.5
13. Spain	7,226.2	13. Nicaragua	15,481.4

[a] Of this amount, $14,905 thousand went to San Andres Island, a possession of Colombia about 120 miles off the Atlantic coast of Nicaragua and 250 miles northwest of Colón.

only eight firms. About six tenths of its business is processing Australian and New Zealand beef and reshipping it. The Mayaguez Zone also manufactures industrial uniforms, towels, and napkins; attaches buttons to ready-made apparel; and makes small amounts of pharmaceuticals. Total value of annual business is about $19 million, versus well over $1 billion in the Colón Free Trade Zone.

Advise the Colón Free Trade Zone, its users, and its potential users.

9

Sales Management

LIBERTY STATESMAN CORPORATION

Liberty Statesman Corporation was a large life insurance company operating throughout the United States and Canada. The manager of the Louisiana-Mississippi district, Cyrus L. Baker, a well-liked native Southerner, had just retired after eight years in that post. His replacement was thirty-six-year-old Lyman J. Danner, who had been with the company six years and with a competitor for about seven years before that. For the past two years Danner, a native of New Jersey, had been manager for his home state for Liberty Statesman Corporation. The results in that territory had pleased top management. Danner, his wife, and three young children immediately moved to New Orleans, where the district headquarters was located.

The first thing Lyman Danner did on arrival in New Orleans was to order the district office refurbished at a cost of about $7,500. He conferred at great length during a series of meetings with an interior decorator on how the project was to be done. After about ten days he started a task that he described to many persons as "the most important for any new district manager, learning the sales force." Simultaneously he investigated the paper-handling and limited bookkeeping activities the district office engaged in, for his observations indicated that things were not smoothly or efficiently handled and that applicable services of Liberty Statesman Corporation's national headquarters office were not being fully utilized. Using the national office for any available services might increase the expertise with which it was done and might save the district office some money, he explained.

Danner was accustomed to being in charge of one of the seven leading districts in the company in terms of sales volume. As he discovered when he began to study the records in his new office, the Louisiana-Mississippi district had never finished in this elite group in any year. The best it had ever done was nineteenth among the thirty-eight districts and that was four years ago. The past year it had been twenty-fourth. It had been rumored in the company that Cyrus Baker was winding down toward his retirement the past two years. Therefore, Danner took the view that his new district had much more potential than the actual sales figures of the past implied. He wondered about trying to transfer in some of the highly able and motivated sales representatives he knew from his old district.

The new manager discussed the idea briefly with Sam Autier, his dependable associate. A Louisiana native, Autier had been assistant district manager for about two years and a salesperson for the company before that. He advised Danner not to waste valuable time and psychic energy even considering the idea, because insurance sales representatives do not transfer as readily as many other types of sales representatives. They are on their own most of the time and can benefit handsomely from a detailed knowledge of and "feel" for the area in which they work. They need networks of contacts and referrals from friends, acquaintances, and customers. Many sales require periodic visits for several years before the sale is consummated. Insurance on one member of the family may lead to insurance on another member.

Danner began to think. He knew all of this as well as Autier did and was embarrassed that he had even brought up such an idea. Perhaps, he reflected to himself, it was symptomatic of his anxiety. But Danner considered that Sam Autier was a good listener and he had to have someone with whom to "bat ideas around." After all, all managers had some ideas that could be improved on. And all people in positions of responsibility need people around them with whom they can talk without entering into commitments and promises.

What he actually said to Sam Autier was: "Of course, you are so right. I was daydreaming. But if I had my druthers, that is about what I would do."

A few days later Danner and Autier, working together, set up a contest to furnish additional incentive for the twenty-eight sales representatives in their district. These salespersons did not represent any other company. There had been no contest in this district for about eighteen months. This one would last three months during the slow season and would be based on percentage increases over the same three months of the previous year. There were to be three prizes. First prize was an all-expense-paid five-day vacation in Montego Bay, Jamaica. The second prize was a $100 U.S. savings bond, and the third prize was a bond of $50. All three winners would be presented handsome certificates on Danner's next field visit to their vicinity. Although uncomplicated, this contest was explained carefully and fully to the salespersons.

As soon as the three-month period was over, Danner eagerly began to examine the results, which are shown in Exhibit 1 for the ten persons with the highest percentage increases. Danner had never conducted a contest with such an outcome. Aggregate sales had gone up only about 4 percent. He was surprised and keenly disappointed and said so, but he gave the three awards anyway. Moreover, Danner immediately announced to the sales force that there would be another contest, the details of which would be given out in a few weeks.

Danner made a field visit swing through Jackson, Oxford, Starkville, Hattiesburg, and Gulfport, Mississippi a few days later. At a party in his honor on this trip there was enough conversation, some of it oblique and some overheard, for Danner to realize that his remarks about wanting to transfer in some sales representatives from his former New Jersey territory had gotten out and had apparently been repeated with some enlargement. There were no scenes at the party and Danner deftly avoided saying anything awkward or embarrassing, despite the strong temptation. Nevertheless, he returned to his New Orleans office perplexed.

Advise Lyman Danner of Liberty Statesman Corporation.

EXHIBIT 1 Selected Results of Sales Contest: The Ten Sales Representatives with the Highest Percentage Increases

Salesman	Location	Sales During Contest	Sales, Same Period Last Year	Percentage Increase
Leary	Shreveport	$800,000	$705,000	13.4%
Caruthers	New Orleans	720,000	650,000	
Bymel	Baton Rouge	640,000	590,000	
Beatty	Jackson	635,000	590,000	
Verier	Lafayette	620,000	581,000	
Sutkin	Lake Charles	481,000	455,000	
Hemingway	Monroe	422,000	400,000	
Rymanson	Ruston	430,000	409,000	
Breaux	Hammond	430,500	410,000	
Belton	Natchitoches	435,750	415,000	

MARY KAY COSMETICS, INC.

Mary Kay Cosmetics, Inc., was giving some careful thought to its policies and practices in sales force management, in particular the recruiting and retention of salespersons. Such reviews, sometimes comprehensive and sometimes not, were done from time to time by all large manufacturers and distributors. However, the direct sales industry tended to need such reviews more frequently than other industries. Some industry observers had been urging a thorough, objective, and detailed examination in the Mary Kay organization. It was one of the largest cosmetics firms in the U.S. direct-sales industry, second only to Avon Products.

The term "direct-sales" usually implied that the product was sold door-to-door, through group meetings usually referred to as "parties," or by telephone. In this industry the door-to-door method was often utilized with advanced announcement or by appointment. Fixed sales routes were often supported carefully by direct-mail advertising timed to arrive shortly before the visit. Among the many well-known organizations whose salespeople went either door-to-door or held parties in the homes of prospective customers were Amway Corporation, Shaklee Corporation, Encyclopaedia Britannica, Tupperware, Electrolux, and Stanley Home Products, the parent of Fuller Brush. In addition, there were hundreds of others, not well-known. The Mary Kay organization did not use the door-to-door technique. Of course, the direct sales cosmetics companies were in competition not just with each other but with the many who distributed through retail shops. Among such firms were Revlon, Estee Lauder, Max Factor, Elizabeth Arden, Helena Rubenstein, Faberge, and L'Oreal.

The Company Founder

The company was established by a woman with an interesting background and personality. Born in a small Texas town, Mary Kay Ash was reared in a family where her mother worked full-time, her father was an invalid, and the girl had primary responsibility from an early age for caring for her father and keeping the house. Her mother was a highly positive, confident person who said to her daughter countless times, "You can do it." Ash gave much of the credit to her mother for making her a self-confident person. A classic overachiever, she also excelled in school. She married at a young age, but she and her two young children soon were abandoned by her husband. Needing employment with flexible hours, she took a job in direct sales with Stanley Home Products, a housewares and cleaning supplies firm using the home party technique. After thirteen successful years with that organization she went with World Gift, a Dallas-based company dealing in decorative accessories where she became the national training director. In her late 40s, Ash retired in 1962 for medical reasons after illness and surgery. Retirement bored her so much, however, that she started to write a book about her business experience. As she wrote Ash became very impressed with how many problems women in particular faced in the world of business. A restless and driving person, she opted to do something about what she had just written. Ash wanted to set up a company in which the management was responsive to what she thought bothered working women, especially working mothers. Among other things the founder had in mind flexible hours, few rules, and ample autonomy for salespersons.

The Company Start-up

Ash decided to develop a skin care products company. It was to be based on a product that had come to her attention ten years earlier while working for Stanley. When conducting a home party she had observed the nice complexions of the women present. Ash discovered that the hostess was a beautician who was using an experimental skin care product on her guests. Following the Stanley party all the people took home samples of the hostess' latest batch of the skin cream. This product derived from a formula that the hostess' father, a tanner, developed when he serendipitously found that some tanning lotions he made and used made his hands look younger than his face. The man then applied these creams to his face regularly and soon his face also began looking smoother and more youthful. The daughter had experimented with her father's product for seventeen years. She prepared small batches and filled any available empty jars and bottles. She sold it to friends and acquaintances with handwritten instructions for using it to best advantage. Ash tried the product herself. Although finding it malodorous and messy, she concluded it was very good. Ash continued to use the product for ten years. With $5,000 from her savings she bought the rights to the formulas and opened a new firm, which she named Beauty, in a storefront in Dallas in 1963. In the meanwhile she had remarried. She planned to handle sales and have her husband handle administration. When the husband suddenly died just days before the planned opening, her children encouraged her to proceed anyway, and her twenty-year old son Richard Rogers stepped into the administrative job. On September 13, 1963 they began with a tiny inventory and nine salespersons who were Ash's personal friends. Ash did not anticipate the venture becoming large or more than regional in sales. However, the company was a major success from the very beginning. The name was changed five years later to its present form.

Evolution of the Company

After rapid growth, Mary Kay, Inc., went public in 1968. Its stock was traded over-the-counter until 1976, at which point it was listed on the New York Stock Exchange. Production was in Dallas, whereas physical distribution centers were located in that city plus Costa Mesa, California;

Tucker, Georgia; Itasca, Illinois; and Somerset, New Jersey. There were also such centers in Canada, Australia, and Argentina. The company entered the British market in 1984 and the German market in 1986. Employment, which does not include self-employed sales representatives, grew quickly and reached about 1200 in the 1980s. These people were engaged in production, laboratory research, office work, warehousing, and shipping. Mary Kay, Inc., contracted out its manufacturing to another Dallas company until 1969. At that time it opened its own facility adjacent to headquarters to take care of manufacturing, warehousing, and product research. This research involved a large staff of technicians and several scientists. Several projects on biological/physical properties of the skin were done collaboratively with universities. The facility was enlarged several times until it reached the size of 275,000 square feet. Sales by 1990 were still well below the production capacity of this facility.

Mary Kay, Inc., bought a 176-acre tract of land in northwest Dallas in 1981 for new production, physical distribution, and administrative facilities. After constructing a manufacturing building and an automated warehouse facility on a portion of this property, management concluded and announced in 1984 that, because of rapidly escalating land values, further development of the land for the company's use represented an underutilization of corporate resources. Approximately seventy nine acres of the portion of the tract not used for company facilities were sold in late 1984 and the remainder, forty three acres, of the unused acreage in 1985. Such transactions generated large amounts of cash.

In late 1985, when Ash and her son Richard Rogers still owned about 29 percent of the stock, the company decided to go private again. They plus several other members of senior management negotiated an almost $400 million leveraged buyout of the company, with the specific purpose of returning the organization to family control. This change was not terribly surprising to most observers, for Ash and Rogers had strong entrepreneurial personalities. Company spokespersons said that the two had always wanted to own the organization again. In addition, the Mary Kay stock price was depressed at the time because of declines in profits at the company, making the total cost attractively low and the necessary cash outlay abnormally small. Some of the cost was met by fifteen-year subordinated debentures. Several banks, led by the Bank of New York, also loaned a significant portion of the funds necessary to these investors.

Through the years the company developed many new products and broadened its line beyond skin care for women to include women's hair care preparations, toiletry items for women, and make-up items such as eye shadow, eyeliner, mascara, lip color, lip gloss, blush rouge, and blusher. In addition, it developed a small line of skin care products and toiletries for men, calling the line Mr. K. Nearly all of the men's

Library and Information Services

Customer name: KUMAR, SANDEEP

Title: Cases in marketing : orientation, analysis, and problems.
ID: 30116003741095
Due: 06-01-11

Total items: 1
11/11/2010 11:15
Checked out: 6

Thank you for using Self Issue.
For queries telephone: 0121 204 4525 or e-mail: library@aston.ac.uk

Late return fines are:
50p per hour for 1 day loans
50p per day for all other Library material

products were purchased by women as gifts. Nevertheless, the women's skin care items continued to be the most important among the almost 150 products, accounting for almost half of sales. Mary Kay, Inc., believed it important to keep the product line small enough that each salesperson could afford to keep an adequate inventory of all products. It wanted each salesperson to be able to supply her customers' needs immediately. The company stood behind the products and readily refunded the price to a dissatisfied user, but this occurred very rarely.

Company Sales Policies and Practices

Mary Kay, Inc., depended on having a very large sales force of persons it termed "beauty consultants." Ash frequently described her organization as a "paid self-improvement program" for family-oriented women. She believed that many, perhaps most, women do not believe in themselves, and thus her organization had to do everything possible to ensure their success both through a good product line and a highly positive program of continuous encouragement and incentives. The encouragement and incentives took the form of money, awards, recognition, and general emotional support. Ash made the statement, "Women will work for recognition when they will not work for money." The company tried to build women's sense of self-confidence and self-worth. It tried to create a corporate climate of acceptance of each person. Most people in the company preferred the term beauty consultant over salesperson because they thought it helped to instill a positive self-image and it called attention to the role of teaching the customer. Good citizenship and the application of the Golden Rule were emphasized. The company founder customarily spoke of three pillars of the beauty consultant's work, allegiance to God, allegiance to family, and allegiance to job, in that order of priority. This was consistent with her personal ideals and the philosophy about women with which she entered this venture. Ash frequently gave eloquent, inspiring speeches to groups of the sales representatives. She had strong leadership qualities and personal charm.

The number of salespersons required by such a company was very large. The total grew rapidly to 7,000 in 1970 and 40,000 in 1978, and then tripled in two years to 120,000 in 1980. It climbed to 196,800 in the mid-1980s, 90 percent of them in the United States, but then went into an unplanned decline. There was a modest turnaround in the late 1980s. In 1989 the number of salespersons was about 175,000. Except for a few hundred men, the sales force was female. Ash had not made a serious effort to recruit men. She often said that God was merely practicing when God created men.

Labor turnover was continuously very high, as in all direct-sales companies, and replenishing the supply of sales labor was a constant headache for the corporation. It was not uncommon for Mary Kay, Inc., to need

30,000 to 40,000 recruits in a year. Other direct-sales organizations were experiencing similar problems. Avon, with about 440,000 salespersons in the United States, was suffering a small decline also and was worried about the future.

At Mary Kay, Inc., the orders of the newest sales representatives were extraordinarily important to overall sales revenues because the average size of their orders, to get them under way, tended to be much larger than the average size of fill-in orders of established sales representatives. A typical initial order was between $2,000 and $3,500. In an average year the total initial orders accounted for 25 to 35 percent of company sales. Stability of the sales force, to the extent it might occur, would thus be a mixed blessing for the company. From this perspective, it would be wise to have quite a few new salespersons constantly and an expanding total sales force, but generally bad to have a declining size of sales force unless one could increase sales volume per salesperson drastically.

Mary Kay employees frequently spoke of the policy of giving each salesperson a commission of 50 percent on sales. However, in reality, each salesperson bought the merchandise and then resold it at prescribed prices equaling twice the salesperson's cost. Thus the employee made earnings equal to half of sales. There were two exceptions: (1) a reduced commission rate for very tiny orders; and (2) an occasional special promotion in which the commission might reach 60 percent. Mary Kay, Inc., did not extend credit to its sales representatives and did not even accept their checks. The company was paid by cashier's check or money order.

Another way for a salesperson to make money was for her to recruit other salespersons. The company strongly encouraged this activity and its executives frequently stated that "At Mary Kay, sales and recruiting go hand-in-hand." If a salesperson successfully recruited she received a prescribed percentage commission on the sales of that person as long as both she and the recruit remained with the company. The percentage varied by number of recruits. If a salesperson recruited twelve other salespersons she received from nine to twelve percent of their sales, depending on sales volume. Salespersons were free to recruit other people anywhere. Many recruited long distances away while on vacation or visiting relatives and friends. A sales unit near the new recruit adopted her. Such professional courtesy was expected throughout the company.

A recruit had to observe three beauty shows (see following), book at least eight shows, and, during her first two weeks on the job, actually conduct at least five such affairs. On meeting these criteria she received a "perfect start" brooch consisting of the signature of Mary Kay Ash in gold with the letters PS attached on a short chain. Each salesperson fitted into one of five ascending levels of rank, each with an impressive title.

The beauty consultants were organized into sales units, each with a sales director. The sales structure was not organized along strict geographical lines but tended to be related to common geographical boundaries. To qualify to be a sales director a person had to have at least twelve active recruits. The number of sales directors varied but tended to be between 4,500 and 5,000 most of the time.

A sales director conducted her own beauty shows but also trained new recruits, led weekly sales meetings, monitored the people in her unit, and furnished assistance, advice, and encouragement to the members of her unit. Fairly often she invited husbands of relatively new recruits to unit sale meetings. This was thought to have the desired effect of building empathy in the husband, making him more understanding and supportive of his wife's time commitment, and generally involving him in the woman's success. The sales director received commissions on her own sales and a reduced commission on the total sales of her unit and on the number of new sales recruits. It was commonplace for a sales director to earn $50,000 per year, but the average was considerably below that figure. The company claimed that it had more women making $50,000 or over than any other company in the world. The sales directors with the most outstanding performance were designated national sales directors, the highest title on the sales career ladder. Each of these sixty national sales directors managed a group of sales directors. The average compensation of a national sales director was well over $100,000 per year. On the corporate level staff there were several national sales administrators who oversaw the work of the national sales directors and sales directors in the field.

Certain factors were working against the recruiting effort. When inflation was low or declining markedly and the economy reasonably prosperous, as it was in the 1980s, the number of women interested in free-lance, part-time beauty consulting to earn some extra money went down. Moreover, the amount of discrimination against women in hiring for full-time jobs was slowly declining in the United States and Canada. Some who would have opted for part-time jobs now began to take full-time jobs. Also, part-time jobs and self-employment lacked the substantial fringe benefits of most full-time jobs. One should also note that some employers began to give some types of full-time employees a modest amount of work schedule flexibility. Also, some people found dependence on commissions rather than a salary, even if it was a small one, highly stressful. In addition, divorce rates were rising. Some women who probably would have chosen to work part-time needed to work full-time.

The "beauty show" was the keystone of the sales efforts. About 65 percent of the sales occurred there and about 35 percent through re-orders that satisfied users placed, often on the telephone, with the sales representatives. The shows were aimed at getting new users. Of course, it was unavoidable that a small percentage of the people at the beauty shows were already users. But even they could be shown new products and the need for greater use of the products they already knew about. The beauty show was envisioned by the company as simultaneously a social experience and a learning experience in which the "guests," as they were called, bought Mary Kay products. The goal size was five or six guests. A larger number reduced individual attention undesirably, but having too many was almost never a problem. The salesperson prepared a written beauty profile for each person, identifying skin type and recommending the appropriate Mary Kay products. Demonstration was emphasized. The company encouraged the salesperson to think of the show as teaching. The party started with skin care and proceeded to make-up, bath items, and hair care products. The party was planned as a smooth paced event of about two hours. The salespersons took orders at the end of the party and handed over the products at that time. There were to be no delays. Credit cards were accepted. Also, at the show the salesperson frequently could secure a booking for a future show at the home of one of the participants. The salesperson was supposed to follow up each beauty show by scheduling a second facial for each guest at the show. Occasionally a customer with an outgoing personality would invite one or more friends to her second facial, the practical result being another show. The hostess of a show was guaranteed at least 10 percent of product sales made at the event. If additional beauty shows were booked with the people in attendance, the percentage rose.

As more and more customers worked full-time, the principal time of the beauty shows had to shift to Tuesday, Wednesday, and Thursday nights. Weekends were not very popular for the parties. A typical married sales representative might be glad not to work on the weekend but often found it a strain to work two or three week nights every week. The sales representative set her own work schedule but naturally had to take into account the preferences and time schedules of her customers and prospects. It was generally believed throughout the direct-sales industry that the party method was most successful among working class, ethnic, and small-town populations where personal relationships were fairly closely knit and loyalty and reciprocity were usually expected.

The fundamental characteristic of the work of the Mary Kay salesperson was "networking." In making her sales she contacted all of her relatives, friends, and neighbors, then new acquaintances, and then the friends and relatives of relatives, friends, neighbors, and acquaintances. She often asked customers to point out potential new customers to her and even to help her to meet them.

The work style of the sales directors was noteworthy in establishing the employment climate. Many demonstrated great empathy for the salespersons. However, there were reports of some who pressed the sales-persons very hard, creating a stressful situation where none was intended if Ash's statements of business philosophy from the 1960s were to be taken seriously.

Mary Kay Ash was particularly charismatic, whether in a small or a large group or leading the entire company. Many observers had fears of the time in the future when poor health or death would take away her leadership. Many other cosmetics companies had gone into steep decline or been bought and gutted after the deaths of their founders, for it was an industry based to a great extent on personality and imagination.

The company was well-known for its sales conferences. They were professionally arranged, elaborate, extremely expensive, and often likened to religious revivals. Many were teleconferences so as to cover regions or the nation. Ash usually addressed the largest meetings and sometimes presented awards. Selected sales conferences were reserved for the better performers. Sizeable sales conferences often used a company theme song. This song began with the words "I've got that Mary Kay enthusiasm up in my head, up in my head, up in my head." It continued at some length with thoughts about enthusiasm in the heart and in the feet and finally with "that Mary Kay enthusiasm all over me" and was sung to the tune of the traditional spiritual "I've got that joy, joy, joy down in my heart."

Awards were numerous and generous. Ash spoke of the need to reward her people with "Cinderella gifts." The most famous award was giving the use of pink Cadillacs for one to two year periods to the best performing sales directors. The pink Cadillac had become closely associated with the name of the company. At times the company had as many as 700 pink Cadillacs loaned out to sales directors. At an intermediate level there was the use of pink Buicks. At still lower levels diamonds, mink coats, and the use of pink Pontiacs were highly popular. The cars had the words "Mary Kay" on the rear glass. Ash often remarked that she had a pink reputation. This stemmed primarily from her initial choice of pink for the packaging materials in 1963. However, bowing to tradition and conservatism, the company had decided early on to package its men's products in chocolate brown accented with silver. Ash initially selected pink because it seemed to her to be noticeable and look nice against the plain white tile so commonly found in bathrooms and because it was a feminine color. Occasionally an outspoken person commented to a Mary Kay sales representative driving a pink Cadillac that it was a tacky thing to do. Such representatives were advised by some executives and long-time successful representatives in the company to answer with this question: "What color of car does *your* company give *you*?"

Although diamond pendants, rings, and earrings were sometimes used, the diamonds were often set in a gold pin with the motif of a bumblebee, which had become a company symbol. Ash was fond of remembering and speaking of detractors. The bumblebee is said to be too heavy and unwieldy to fly, and similar forecasts were made years earlier about the potential of her organization. However, both she and the bumblebee flew well.

Advise Mary Kay Cosmetics.

KRUGER-MONTINI MANUFACTURING COMPANY

The management of Kruger-Montini Manufacturing Company had just entered a new fiscal year and was rethinking its specific policies and general position on transfers of sales representatives. The decision was the responsibility of the sales manager.

Founded many years earlier, this well-established corporation was a medium-sized manufacturer of several related industrial products in rather wide use. The majority of customers were manufacturers and engineering companies. For quite a few years Kruger-Montini did not do its own personal selling. Starting about twenty years ago, it gradually phased out the various intermediaries and manufacturers' agents. After about five years of difficult transition, Kruger-Montini relied strictly on sales representatives who were on the company's payroll and who worked for no one else. Kruger-Montini was not truly national in coverage in its early years but became so nine years ago when it added five sales representatives in one year and relocated thirteen.

The size of the sales force had increased as the company grew and prospered and had now reached thirty-eight. The sales manager had found it necessary to divide his organization into four geographical regions because of span of control difficulties as Kruger-Montini grew. Because the product line was fairly narrow, it was decided that geography, not type of products, would be the best basis for the organization structure. Thus each sales representative sold all products. A contributing reason for deciding against product specialization as the basis for organizing selling efforts was that it would have resulted necessarily in a larger geographical territory for each employee to cover. That would have meant his or her being away from home overnight much more than under the policy adopted. The present sales manager, Henry Rosas, estimated that the average person on his sales force spent six nights a month away from home. This figure was a little lower, he knew, for people in the highly industrialized and densely populated areas of the Northeast, the Michigan, Ohio, Indiana, Illinois, Wisconsin region in the Middle West, and parts of California. The figure was a little higher for his people in all other areas. Rosas estimated that the difference was about five versus eight nights per month. During the past few years the company had noticed a sizable number of its customers relocate to the Sun Belt and many customers open branch factories in those milder climate areas of the nation. The demand for Kruger-Montini's products was slowly becoming more evenly spread across the country, and this trend was expected to continue.

Rosas had been with the organization about three years. He had been a successful salesperson with one company and then assistant sales manager with another company before coming with Kruger-Montini. He had a good personality and was well liked by the sales representatives.

The company had always used a salary-plus-commission pay plan. For the average representative the commission provided 25 percent of his compensation.

Kruger-Montini manufactured nine products, two of which had been introduced only in the past three years. Prior to that three-year period there had been no new product introductions for a great many years. It appeared highly probable that Kruger-Montini would introduce two more new products, closely related to the existing product line, and delete one during the next two years.

During the most recent fiscal year Kruger-Montini had transferred six sales representatives to different territories. In the four years previous to that, the company had transferred seven each year. Each was moved because of company need and/or the assigning of better territories to deserving sales representatives. See Exhibit 1 for earlier years and additional data on size of the sales force and average distances people were transferred. The mean distance of a relocation at Kruger-Montini had shown a downward trend for several years.

EXHIBIT 1 Data on Sales Force of Kruger-Montini Manufacturing Company

	Size of Sales Force	Number Transferred	Mean Distance Transferred (miles)
Latest year	38	6	798
Two years ago	37	7	872
Three years ago	37	7	682
Four years ago	36	7	1122
Five years ago	35	7	1254
Six years ago	34	9	1360
Seven years ago	32	9	597
Eight years ago	32	12	1070
Nine years ago	31	13	793
Ten years ago	26	10	1035
Eleven years ago	25	10	640
Twelve years ago	24	11	510

Every person on the sales force had moved at least once. The longest time in one place anyone on the present sales force had experienced with Kruger-Montini was seven years. Rosas was tentatively thinking about moving from five to seven members of the sales force later this year.

The management did not know much about the geographical preferences of its sales representatives or their family life. Rosas could not legally inquire systematically about whether the spouses were also employed and whether that work was professional and managerial, which might make one less willing to move. Dual careers made it difficult for couples to handle relocations well, and some probably would not consider it at all. However, Rosas and his four regional sales managers had been trying recently to make observations and record facts and inferences about these matters for all the sales representatives. Three of the sales representatives were young, unmarried men who seemed to be mobile and flexible. Three middle-aged men were divorced, and one was a widower. The remaining thirty-one were all married. It appeared that twenty of them had working spouses and that fifteen of these spouses had professional or managerial careers. Rosas also began to understand that most nonworking spouses had developed community ties and that moving for them could also de difficult and unsettling.

The unwritten understanding of personnel at Kruger-Montini had been that turning down a transfer would be suicidal. At the minimum such a rejection would classify a person as unaggressive and unambitious. The U.S. culture for many years had perceived frequent transfers as evidence of fast-track career progress. Staying mobile was a "badge of honor," as business newspapers and magazines usually described it.

No one on the Kruger-Montini sales force had ever declined a transfer until two years ago, as far as Rosas could determine. The sales manager and other headquarters personnel had been surprised and perplexed when Charles Hopkins, a very satisfactory employee, had declined a move from a small, pleasant southeastern city to a much more lucrative territory in another part of the United States. Age thirty-seven and a native of the upper Middle West, Hopkins explained that he liked Kruger-Montini and wanted to continue working for the company but did not want to move. His wife was a business manager in another company, and they had a thirteen-year-old daughter in school.

The costs to relocate a sales representative had been rising quite rapidly. The most recently transferred person was Alex Kendall, a man with a wife and three children. It cost Kruger-Montini $30,880 to move them approximately 2,900 miles from one coast to the other, although the company was not any more generous than the typical American company. Of this amount, $11,475 was to ship household goods, $4,100 was for the pre-move housing search, and $3,680 was for one extra month of this man's average compensation in lieu of incidental expenses. Final travel and temporary living expenses accounted for another $4,550. The remaining costs had to do with company subsidies on the sale of the couple's house and purchase of a replacement house. The management of Kruger-Montini was beginning to note the financial impact of moving costs of the company.

Kruger-Montini also recognized that a transferred sales representative required several months to get work productivity back to normal. The recovery of productivity was much more difficult for people who worked with the public and who needed to understand the characteristics of a market than for other types of workers. A sales representative also needed time to establish rapport with the regular clients.

One managerial colleague whom Rosas respected was outspoken about the issue of moving. Bert Crane, who managed another department at Kruger-Montini and had been with the company about twelve years, believed that if employees were permitted to put down roots in a community they would lose their sense of corporate identity. Loyalties to the geographical community would overcome loyalties to the corporation. He stated that perhaps this had been an unconscious motivation of Kruger-Montini in past years.

Another colleague, Robert Mason, mentioned that a nice compromise might be to confine transfers to the region in which the sales representative was already living. For example, the ten sales representatives in eleven Northeastern states would be transferred only within that region. Mason noted that each region had some lifestyle characteristics that set it apart from the others. He was an experienced manager and had been with the company for about nine years.

Advise Henry Rosas of the Kruger-Montini Manufacturing Company.

10

Advertising and Public Relations

TONKA TOYS

Tonka was established in 1946 by L. E. Baker, Avery F. Crouse, and Alvin F. Tesch in the basement of an abandoned school building in Mound, Minnesota, a western suburb of Minneapolis. It was incorporated on September 18, 1946, as Mound Metalcraft, Inc. The name was changed to Tonka Toys, Inc., in 1956 and Tonka Corporation in 1965.

The three founders and a small number of employees began by producing only two toy designs, a steam shovel and a crane. These items rapidly proved to be quite popular, and very soon demand exceeded production. Other toys were added, and the corporation grew. Tonka was most widely known for its die-cast steel toy trucks. At one time Tonka had about 45 percent of the U.S. market for this type of toy. Without really intending to aim so narrowly, the company appealed principally through the years to a market of boys in the age bracket of two to ten. Two generations of little boys dug up their back yards with Tonka-made trucks, Mighty Crane, Mighty Dozer, and other construction toys. The all-time favorite was the little yellow dump truck.

The high birthrates of the baby boom following World War II helped Tonka very much. This trend line turned down, however, in the early

1960s. There was a baby boomlet in the early 1980s, and it had helped throughout the 1980s, but it would not continue to help, of course. The number of children in the late 1980s and through the 1990s would probably not increase, according to the majority of forecasts from the government, private industry, and universities. A pattern of low birthrates was expected to continue indefinitely. On the other hand, slowly rising real incomes and the growth of two-earner households meant that there was potential to give children more or better toys or both. In addition, more children would be first children. On average, parents spent more on the first child than on later children except when the last child was born many years after its siblings.

Making toys was a relatively risky business. Although sales of the whole toy industry did not show large changes from year to year, the sales of individual toys were extremely volatile. Because a toy manufacturer necessarily had a limited selection of toys in its product line, the sales of a given company were apt to exhibit noteworthy changes from year to year. Until the early 1980s, Tonka tried to combat volatility by emphasizing staple products, that is, those less subject to trends and, especially, fads. Examples of staples were toy boats, airplanes, trucks, and construction equipment. Nevertheless, the average life cycle of a toy truck was only around three or four years. Several new variations of basic products were brought out each year. The tooling necessary to make several new products normally amounted to $1.5 to $3 million in total every year. Two other factors added to the riskiness of the toy manufacturing business. Substantial time was required between the design of a toy and its reaching the shelves of the retailer. Even if the manufacturer guessed right in January, tastes might have changed by the important November-December period. Most toys were exhibited at the industry's Toy Fair held in February every year for buying representatives. Moreover, the industry offered credit on rather generous terms for extended periods of time, and quite a few toy retailers and some wholesaler-distributors were questionable credit risks. For example, recently Tonka had found it necessary to write off as uncollectible the $1.1 million account of a California wholesaler-distributor. The industry was seasonal. Tonka normally did about 64 percent of its sales in the second half of the year. The third quarter was normally slightly better than the fourth quarter.

The toy industry in the United States was composed of about 25 U.S. companies and many importers. Several Oriental sources were becoming important. The main U.S. organizations were Mattel, Inc., Hasbro Bradley, and Coleco Industries, in that order, plus Tonka and Fisher-Price, a subsidiary of Quaker Oats Company. Tonka was the smallest of these major toy operations. Mattel was taken over in 1984 by F. M.

Warburg Pincus as part of a financial restructuring, and it was considered plausible that in a few years time Mattel might be offered for sale. Kenner Parker, a medium size company, was owned by General Mills. Two small but aggressive new toy manufacturers were Axlon, Inc., and Worlds of Wonder, Inc. Both emphasized talking stuffed animals, and the former was beginning to make robotic stuffed animals and dolls. The moving force in Axlon was Nolan Bushnell, the founder and former owner of Atari, Inc. and Pizza Time Theatre, Inc.

As Tonka matured, it made several acquisitions. In October 1963 it purchased Gresen Manufacturing Company of Minneapolis, a maker of pumps, filters, motors, directional control valves, and accessory valves used in hydraulic systems. Tonka sold this subsidiary to Dana Corporation in January 1981. In December 1964, Tonka acquired selected assets of Mell Manufacturing Company, a Chicago producer of outdoor barbecue grills, but sold this subsidiary in 1968. In 1973, Tonka acquired Vogue Dolls, Inc., a small maker of dolls, with the objective of quickly extending its toy line to have more appeal to little girls. However, this attempt did not work out, and the subsidiary was sold in 1976. In December 1973, Tonka acquired Ceramichrome, Inc., a small firm that made paints, stains, glazes, and molds used by ceramics hobbyists. In 1966, Tonka acquired a majority holding in Mercury Tool & Stamping, Rexdale, Ontario. Tonka now had a sizable manufacturing subsidiary in Toronto, Canada, and a small one in Rhodes, Australia.

The average age of boys who played with trucks and other construction toys was going down. Boys of six or eight now tended to want toys that came with a story line. Truly imaginative play emanating from the boy himself was becoming confined to the very young who watched rather little television. In the past, the company's trucks and other construction toys had strong appeal to boys up to about age ten or eleven. Girls had never been significant consumers of Tonka's line of traditional toys.

The president of Tonka, Peter Wimsatt, was dismissed in 1979 following a disagreement with the board of directors. He opposed significant diversification of the product line, which was described by unhappy shareholders as sturdy, reliable, traditional, and dull. Business journalists, securities brokers, and many others continuously described Tonka as "sleepy." In the main, they believed Tonka was facing at best a no-growth future with its present product line and lack of concern for market factors. Instead, the organization had a strong production orientation. Wimsatt went to Ertl Toy Company, located in Dyersville, Iowa, as manufacturing vice-president, and Stephen Shank, the company's thirty-four-year-old chief legal counsel, was elevated to the presidency. The corporation was undergoing a major rethinking about itself and continued to do so for a lengthy time period. In 1982, Shank raided Mattel and hired two marketing executives, including that company's marketing vice-president.

The performance of Tonka had been troubled and uneven in recent years. Sales reached $81.1 million in 1982, but there was a net loss of $2.7 million. In 1983 sales rose to $87.8 million, but there was a net loss of $3.9 million. Losses in 1983 would have been greater if there had not been an extraordinary gain of $3.0 million that year from the reserves related to the termination of the old pension plan for workers and the establishment of a new one. Sales reached $139 million in 1984, and there was a net profit of $5.0 million. Sales surged in 1985 to $244 million, and the net profit was $19.5 million. (See Exhibit 1.)

New Products and the Supporting Advertising and Sales Promotion

Coleco Industries scored the industry's largest hit in 1983 with its Cabbage Patch Kids dolls, and the product continued important for several years. However, in 1984 and 1985, Tonka enjoyed the distinction of having the industry's top-selling new toy, GoBots in 1984 and Pound Puppies in 1985.

The new marketing management people at Tonka did some thinking and conducted some research in trying to identify some breakthrough toys. As part of that process, they studied what was happening in Japan and, in doing so, discovered that GoBots were extremely popular with children in that country. Therefore, Tonka secured a license for the concept from Bandai Company, located in Tokyo, and started producing them. These were small, die-cast metal and plastic action-figure robots having movable arms and legs that could be folded and rearranged, thus converting these little space-age creatures into miniature trucks, sports cars, and other vehicles. Tonka also raised its advertising budget, nearly all the increase going for GoBots. (See Exhibit 2.) The product was a great success, in fact, beyond Tonka's expectations. Having little experience in forecasting sales of hot items and monitoring the actual movement off the retailers' shelves, Tonka decreased production after the pre-Christmas rush season. Demand continued strong, however, and soon demand far exceeded supply. Meanwhile, Hasbro Bradley had introduced Transformers, its version of this product type. More sophisticated at sales forecasting and having a better working relationship between marketing and production processes, Hasbro did not cut back on production and then forged ahead to be number one in the robotics toy market. Tonka had forfeited its lead of several months with this product type. Hasbro attained 40 percent—and Tonka 26 percent—of the market for this type of toy. Matchbox Toys, Ltd., a

EXHIBIT 1 Consolidated Statements of Operations

Tonka Corporation and Subsidiaries
(In millions, except per share data)

	Fiscal Year			
	1985	1984	1983	1
Sales	$244.4	$139.0	$87.8	$8
Cost of goods sold	131.9	93.9	66.5	5
Gross profit	112.5	45.1	21.3	2
Selling, general, and administrative expenses	70.1	33.0	25.8	2
Other (income) expense	2.6	(1.7)	1.9	
Interest expense—Net	3.6	5.5	3.7	
Earnings (loss) before income taxes	36.2	8.3	(10.1)	(
Income taxes	16.7	3.3	(3.2)	(
Earnings (loss) before extraordinary gain	19.5	5.0	(6.9)	(
Extraordinary gain	–	–	3.0	
Net earnings (loss)	19.5	$ 5.0	$ (3.9)	$ (

Consolidated Statements of Retained Earnings
(In millions)

	Fiscal Year			
	1985	1984	1983	1
Retained earnings at beginning of year	$27.3	$22.7	$27.0	$4
Net earnings (loss)	19.5	5.0	(3.9)	(
Dividends	(.4)	(.4)	(.4)	
Retirement of treasury stock	–	–	–	(1
Retained earnings at end of year	$46.4	$27.3	$22.7	$2

EXHIBIT 2 Tonka's Advertising Costs, Recent Years (in millions)

1986	1985	1984	1983	1982	1981	1980
$45.7	$40.2	$13.8	$7.5	$7.5	$6.8	$5.5

well-known British company, also entered this market aggressively with its Voltron.

Hasbro launched an animated miniseries for television in 1984 made by Sunbow Productions, a subsidiary of Griffin Bacal Advertising. This series, featuring Transformers, in time became a weekly, then daily syndicated series. Considerably later, Tonka added its own television miniseries featuring GoBots. Shown on Saturday morning television, this five-part series was made by the successful cartoon producer Hanna-Barbera Productions of Hollywood. As part of the supportive promotion, there were coupons on packages of some snack foods that offered a chance for a free GoBot. Despite the popularity of the GoBots group of products, at the end of 1984 the traditional toys still accounted for almost 60 percent of Tonka's sales.

For 1985, Tonka added twenty-eight new GoBots, and it expanded the television show to a sixty-five-part series. In 1986, Tonka offered its GoBots again but also offered a variation, a line of mechanized Go-Bots with motors. Seventy-eight new television episodes of GoBots were prepared for 1986 to promote this group of toys.

Pound Puppies from Tonka were the industry hit of 1985. They were modeled after the Cabbage Patch Kids dolls. They were individually designed, soft-sculptured dogs that, like Cabbage Patch products, came with optional adoption papers. The puppies were adoptable by means of a mail-in $2 certificate of ownership. Tonka sold more Pound Puppies in 1985 than Coleco sold Cabbage Patch dolls at their peak. As part of the promotion supporting the product, Tonka sponsored a "bark-off" in twelve cities. In this event, children competed for prizes by barking like their favorite dogs.

The line of Pound Puppies was then extended to include Newborns, one-fourth the size of Pound Puppies. Newborns were priced at retail at $8 compared to $20 for Pound Puppies. Tonka anticipated that children would want a litter of Newborns, especially if they had a Pound Puppy. Therefore, the company was counting on multiple-unit sales of the product. Also introduced were a Supreme Pound Puppy, much larger than any Pound Puppy, so as to head the whole group, plus doghouses, carriers, and dog clothing. Pound Purries, a cat version, were introduced as well. Also in 1986, Tonka brought out a set of products promoted solely to girls called Keypers. Soft, sculptured animals with hidden storage compartments, the assortment consisted of a ladybug, a snail, and a turtle, each attached to a carrying case. Another version was a plastic form of Keypers that doubled as a jewelry box and case with a key. An arrangement was reached with Current, Inc., a Colorado manufacturer, to picture soft and plastic versions of Keypers on greeting cards.

On the other hand, Tonka's Star Fairies series of dolls introduced for young girls in 1985 was a distinct disappointment. This product was a small girl doll, in six variations, with wings and wand, and there were accessories. Magical abilities were emphasized. The company supported this group of toys with a syndicated cartoon special, offered back-to-back with another that starred its Pound Puppies, but there was little effect. Tonka felt a little better, however, in that a similar product, Rainbow Brite, did not work out very well for Mattel. Cabbage Patch Kids were still rather popular, but the doll category throughout the industry was slowly declining in size. Nevertheless, Tonka decided to modify the Star Fairies group of products and give it another costly opportunity in 1986. The new version had longer hair and a larger wardrobe selection, but the company was not optimistic. Executives and designers considered girls a more difficult type of customer than boys.

In the spring of 1986 Tonka brought out several more GoBots but shifted its emphasis to a new generation of the basic product concept of transformable robots. This market entry, named the Rocklords line, consisted of boulder-shaped pieces of plastic that unfolded to reveal fantasy figures, many of them highly muscled. The behavioral principle of the product was people's interest in elemental things such as rocks. It was hoped that this principle would also widen the age appeal of the new product group. The introductory advertising campaign, largely on television, used the theme "Rocks that will rock the world." Tonka contracted with Hanna-Barbera to make a full-length movie that featured the Rocklords and seven new GoBot characters. This film was meant for theaters rather than television. Thus, if the movie were successful, people would be paying to watch an extremely long advertisement.

Tonka also launched Legions of Power in 1986. It was a space-age construction set that reminded one of Lego building blocks from Lego System, a Danish organization. It came with a futuristic group of transformable characters.

Corporate Image and Public Relations

Something of Tonka's corporate image was presented in the previous parts of the case. However, there were two problems of corporate image and public relations in a short time period. Each was of such major proportions that most companies of similar size would go for several decades without anything equaling them. The first problem was primarily with employees, the community around metropolitan Minneapolis-St. Paul, politicians, and the state government of Minnesota. Some consumers were concerned also in that they were becoming worried about preservation of jobs in the United States. One could see "Buy American" campaigns emerging. The second problem was primarily with lenders and stockholders, and it also captured the critical attention of many potential investors and some potential lenders.

Location of Production

Tonka Corporation had owned a small plant in Mississauga, Ontario for two decades. Tonka invested in a new plant of 74,256 square feet in Ciudad Juárez, Mexico, in 1982 and shifted some of its manufacturing from Minnesota. There were minor start-up problems. Simultaneously, there was a minirecession in the United States, and the interest in video games drained off some toy sales potential. Like some others, the company operated at a loss in 1982. Nevertheless, Tonka was basically pleased with the Mexican operation. Therefore, in 1983 the company moved the remainder of its domestic production, opening two new plants, each with 187,000 square feet, in El Paso, Texas, directly across the Rio Grande from Ciudad Juárez. The Mound, Minnesota, factory stayed open through 1983, at first as a precaution in case there were major start-up problems in El Paso and later for the sake of orderly wind-down operations. Headquarters remained in suburban Minneapolis. El Paso was a community of about 500,000 population at the western tip of Texas, and Ciudad Juárez was of similar size. Despite being in two nations, these facilities would be operated as one integrated production and physical distribution complex. About 1,200 were employed permanently, 350 of them in Ciudad Juárez and 850 in El Paso. In addition, there were 400 to 500 seasonal workers. By far the most important reason for moving was to achieve lower operating costs. The hourly rate of the production workers hired in El Paso was only 49 percent as high as what Tonka was paying in Minnesota. The wages across the border in the Ciudad Juárez facility were much lower than those in El Paso.

Legislation was adopted in both the United States and Mexico in the 1960s, establishing an in-bond program, creating an opportunity for U.S. firms to use abundant, low-cost labor south of the border. The Mexican government allowed processing, assembling, packaging, or repair facilities or a combination of these in the in-bond area to import parts and processed materials without import taxes provided the finished goods were reexported to the United States or some other foreign country. In turn, the U.S. government allowed the reimportation of the processed, assembled, packaged, or repaired products with only a low tariff applied; and this tariff was applied only to the value that had been added in Mexico. This tariff cost was much lower than the savings in labor costs. Facilities in the program had to be within a specified distance of the U.S.-Mexican border. Over 400 U.S. manufacturers in various industries, such as electronics, apparel, furniture, and automotive parts, decided to participate. This whole idea was a variation on the long-established concept of a free trade zone (also known as a foreign trade zone) but put into a larger context.

Several key items in the Mighty Tonka construction toy group were redesigned in 1983 to reduce their materials costs. Because the materials costs for some products and the labor costs for all products went down, unit production costs declined markedly. When these facts were taken in conjunction with the fact that demand was slightly soft, Tonka decided to decrease the prices of its line of traditional toys substantially in late 1983. This pricing action was taken in order to become more competitive and gain a larger share of this market. The share for such toys rose from about 23 percent to about 30 percent.

In addition, Tonka's management was troubled by trying to match production capacity needs with prudent fixed investment. Like some other corporations from time to time, Tonka became financially vulnerable every time there was a significant decline in sales. This vulnerability was principally because of large fixed investment in manufacturing facilities. The facilities were there, whether needed in total, in the majority, or just a fraction, tying up and using scarce capital. This set of concepts was not appreciated or even understood by consumers. Tonka adopted a policy of moving toward reliance on a combination of its own manufacturing capacity and that of independent suppliers under contract to Tonka. Such a contract might be for any time period from a few months to a few years, or it might be for a definite number of units of product. The new policy was implemented immediately and vigorously. In 1984 and 1985 approximately 40 percent of Tonka's sales came from goods manufactured for the company by others to Tonka's specifications, and this figure was slowly trending upward. Nearly all of the newer products were made in this manner and came from outside North America. The El Paso and Ciudad Juárez plants made the line of traditional toys.

Critics had a field day. Tonka was attacked by critics of all political persuasions for allegedly abandoning its heritage, loyal employees, and the community that helped it get started and grow up. Critics did not note that some employees had not been terribly loyal; that the company's marketing area was widespread, not local, from the beginning; and that some prices were coming down. As with all companies participating in the Mexican-border program, Tonka was also taken to task by liberals for "exploiting" and "abusing" Mexican workers in that it was not paying them as high wages and fringe benefits as it paid American citizens. The same critical comparisons were made between the workers in the El Paso plants, many of whom were American citizens of Mexican ancestry, and the former workers. Critics said virtually nothing then or later about the new contracts for supply from abroad.

Political conservatives got into this situation also. A group called Independent Republicans of Minnesota designed and ran an advertising campaign on the relocation in March 1984. The advertisement, which ran on twenty-seven radio stations spread throughout the state, began with the following highly emotional wording: "Were you there when Tonka left Minnesota for Texas? How many jobs were lost that day? How many tears?" Apparently, sponsors of this campaign were not militantly anti-Tonka but were trying to raise public support for the repeal of a 10 percent surcharge on state income taxes in Minnesota, which was already a high-tax state anyway. The Democratic party in Minnesota opposed the repeal. The overall promotional strategy of the Republican group included the argument that Tonka moved its production because of excessive, unjustified levels of state income tax in Minnesota. The president of Tonka made a public statement that the high income tax "played no part" in the decision.

Financial Scandal

The second trouble spot in corporate image and public relations revolved around an alleged misappropriation of funds discovered by outside auditors. The corporation's financial vice-president was accused of investing about $2 million of Tonka's money in a closely held company with which, according to Tonka's president, Stephen Shank, the financial vice-president had "a close relationship." Also he allegedly received "substantial payments" from that company. Later Tonka described the company as "a personal business venture." That company failed. Shank stated that the financial officer had led Tonka to believe the money was invested in a cash management fund. Using prudent and conservative accounting practices, Tonka recorded the loss and took a $1.3 million charge against corporate earnings. Tonka's earnings were already negative, about $2.6 million, and this action drove the figure to a loss of $3.9 million for 1983. The financial vice-president was fired in early 1984. Tonka also filed a claim with its insurance carrier, Federal Insurance Company, a subsidiary of Chubb Corporation. In late 1984 the insurer paid $1.7 million in settlement of its obligations on the loss, and Tonka recorded an extraordinary gain on its books. Some observers were concerned about inadequate internal controls at Tonka, and some potential buyers of the corporate stock were put off by the whole affair.

Advise Tonka.

EXHIBIT 3 Consolidated Balance Sheets

Tonka Corporation and Subsidiaries
(In millions)

	Fiscal Year-End 1984	1983
Assets		
Current Assets:		
Cash and short-term investments	$ .5	$ 2.0
Accounts receivable–Net	31.6	4.6
Inventories	12.1	14.2
Prepaid expenses and other current assets	3.0	6.5
Assets identified for sale	4.4	–
Total Current Assets	51.6	27.3
Land, Buildings and Equipment		
Land	1.8	3.3
Buildings	10.4	17.1
Equipment	39.9	42.9
Total land, buildings and equipment	52.1	63.3
Less accumulated depreciation	32.0	36.8
Net Land, Buildings, and Equipment	20.1	26.5
Other Assets	.4	.8
Total Assets	$72.1	$54.6
Liabilities and Stockholders' Equity		
Current Liabilities:		
Notes payable	$ 9.8	$ –
Accounts payable	8.7	5.2
Accrued taxes	1.5	1.0
Accrued payroll	2.3	1.4
Accrued advertising	2.8	1.6
Other current liabilities	4.3	7.4
Total Current Liabilities	29.4	16.6
Long-Term Debt	8.2	8.0
Deferred Income Taxes	2.6	2.1
Total Liabilities	40.2	26.7
Stockholders' Equity:		
Common stock	1.4	1.4
Additional paid-in capital	5.0	4.9
Retained earnings	27.3	22.7
Cumulative translation adjustments	(1.8)	(1.1)
Total Stockholders' Equity	31.9	27.9
Total Liabilities and Stockholders' Equity	$72.1	$54.6

NEW YORK METS BASEBALL CLUB

The New York Mets baseball team, a member of the National League, was established in 1962 after New York City had been without a participant in that league for four years. Through 1957 both the old New York Giants and Brooklyn Dodgers represented New York in the National League. At the beginning of the 1958 season, the former became the San Francisco Giants; and the latter, the Los Angeles Dodgers, as professional baseball at last decided to serve the large and lucrative sports markets of California.

The Paysons, a prominent New York business family, founded the Mets and immediately did an unconventional thing. They persuaded Casey Stengel, the seventy-one-year-old baseball veteran, to come out of a one-year retirement to manage the new club. Many considered this action a great coup. Many wondered why the highly successful Stengel would try his hand at the difficult task of building a new team.

One of the most colorful characters in baseball history, Stengel had been a player for several teams, including Philadelphia, Pittsburgh, Brooklyn, Boston, and New York—all in the National League. Later he managed Brooklyn and Boston. Stengel managed the New York Yankees for twelve seasons, 1949 through 1960, in which period they won the pennant ten times and finished in second place once and third place once. He then retired.

Although the talkative Stengel was a man who got much notice from the fans, the media, and the general public and was an acknowledged baseball wizard, the Mets finished in the cellar each of the four years 1962–1965. Because of an injury, Stengel semiretired at that point but served as a vice-president for several more years. He died in 1975.

The Mets' low standings continued. In 1966 under Manager Wes Westrum the Mets finished ninth in the ten-team National League. The 1967 team, managed first by Westrum and then by Salty Parker, finished in last place. The 1968 team, under Manager Gil Hodges, ended the season in ninth place.

The year 1969 brought two major events. First, two teams were added to the National League, Montreal and San Diego, and the league began to play in two divisions, the East and the West. Besides the Mets, the East Division was composed of Chicago, St. Louis, Philadelphia, Pittsburgh, and Montreal. Second, there was what many sportswriters called "the miracle of Flushing Meadows." Under Gil Hodges, the Mets won the National League pennant, beating the Atlanta Braves in the play-offs, and then beat the Baltimore Orioles, winners of the American League, in the World Series by four games to one. They were termed "the Cinderella team" and the "unlikeliest champions in baseball history." The "Amazin' Mets" were called a mystical experience.

In 1970 the Mets finished third in the six-team East Division; and in 1971, fourth, as Gil Hodges continued as manager. In 1972 the Mets finished third. Yogi Berra replaced Hodges, who died before that season. In 1973, Berra's Mets surprised everyone by winning the National League pennant, but they lost to Oakland by four games to three in the World Series. The league championship was achieved with the lowest winning percentage (.509) any champion had ever turned in. After 1973 the Mets again fell into a long period of mediocre to poor performance. In the mid-1980s performance improved.

The founders sold the franchise in 1980 for $21.6 million. The principal purchaser was Doubleday & Co., Inc., a long-established, family-owned book publishing enterprise, based in New York City. Nelson Doubleday, president of the acquiring organization, became chairperson of the board of directors of the Metropolitan Baseball Club of New York, the legally proper name of the Mets. Doubleday bought about 80 percent of the corporate stock, and City Investing Company bought the remaining 20 percent. Although mainly a publisher, Nelson Doubleday had already shown a strong business interest in sports and was a minority stockholder in the New York Islanders hockey team. Doubleday's friend John O. Pickett, Jr., who headed the Islanders and was a major investor in them, had brought about massive improvements in the Islanders, both athletically and commercially.

Nelson Doubleday did not regard the Mets as just a hobby. He was keenly interested and an active administrator, but he left technical-professional baseball decisions to his baseball experts. He was well acquainted with baseball, of course, and attended many of the Mets' games. As a teenager he had been an enthusiastic Dodgers fan. Doubleday was a quiet, reticent man who did not cultivate publicity about himself.

The great-grand-uncle of Nelson Doubleday, General Abner Doubleday, was generally credited with formalizing the sport into the game as it is known today. Although the origins of baseball are obscure, it started in the colonial era of America and had several variations. In 1839, Abner Doubleday, while a college student at West Point, devised at Cooperstown, New York, several basic rules of play and designed the playing field as used today. Some called him the inventor of baseball.

The Mets' playing field was Shea Stadium, a publicly owned facility built specifically for this club and finished in 1964. The first two seasons the Mets played at the Polo Grounds. Shea was in the middle-class Flushing Meadows section of the borough of Queens in New York City. This facility was about seven miles east of midtown Manhattan and was close to two major expressways, the subway, bus lines, and La Guardia Airport. Shea Stadium had a seating capacity of 55,300. Like about half of the National League playing fields, the diamond was perfectly symmetrical at Shea Stadium. The center field line, 410 feet, was about average for National League parks. The left and right center field lines were 371 feet. The left and right field lines were 338 feet.

Attendance at the Mets' home games was highly erratic; but the long-term average was certainly very poor. It had been as high as 2.7 million and as low as 700,000. There had been some improvement in the mid-1980s compared to the late 1970s and early 1980s. (See Exhibit 3.) Low attendance resulted in not only low gate receipts but also low sales of foods, beverages, and souvenirs. From 1977 through 1983 the Mets drew much larger crowds on the road than at home. Undependable attendance remained a source of concern.

The competition was really all other forms of recreation, but the most relevant was other professional sports. The New York City metropolitan area had professional clubs in all major sports, including basketball, hockey, soccer, and football, as well as baseball. There was, naturally, special concern about the other New York baseball club, the Yankees. These crosstown rivals in the American League played in Yankee Stadium in the Bronx in the northwest part of the city, about six miles form Shea Stadium and also the same distance from midtown Manhattan. Built in the early 1920s specifically for baseball, Yankee Stadium had a capacity of 57,545. It was extensively rebuilt in the years 1975–1976, and during this time the Yankees played in Shea. Yankee Stadium had slightly less field depth than Shea Stadium. Both stadiums were lighted. The Mets played some of their home games at night, and the proportion had been slowly rising. The Yankees played about three-fourths of their home games at night. (See Exhibits 1, 2, and 3.)

Professional baseball was considering expansion to more than the present twenty-six cities, fourteen of which were in the American League and twelve in the National League. Many cities wanted teams, but base-

EXHIBIT 1 Mets Home Attendance 1980

Time of Game	Number of Games	Total Attendance	Average Attendance
Daytime Mon.–Thurs.	11	86,904	7,900
Night Mon.–Thurs.	27	285,181	10,562
Daytime Fri.–Sun.	23	450,956	19,606
Night Fri.–Sun.	15	355,618	23,708
Totals	76	1,178,659	15,508

EXHIBIT 2 Mets' Home Game Schedule and Attendance, 1984

Date No.	Game No.	Date	Day	Vs.	Game	Series	Season
1	1	4–17	Tue (D)	Mon	46,637		46,637
2	2	4–18	Wed (D)	Mon	11,147		57,784
3	3	4–19	Thu (D)	Mon	10,705	68,489	68,489
4	4	4–27	Fri (N)	Pha	18,171		89,660
5	5	4–28	Sat (D)	Pha	14,292		100,952
6	6	4–29	Sun (D)	Pha	28,562	61,025	129,514
7	7	5–1	Tue (N)	Chi	13,906		143,420
8	8	5–2	Wed (N)	Chi	11,059	24,965	154,479
9	9	5–4	Fri(N)	Hou	9,717		164,196
10	10	5–5	Sat (N)	Hou	16,895		181,091
11	11	5–6	Sun (D)	Hou	39,294	65,906	220,385
12	12	5–7	Mon (N)	Cin	6,942	6,942	227,327
13	13	5–9	Wed (N)	Atl	8,141		235,468
14	14	5–10	Thu (D)	Atl	6,900	15,041	242,368
15	15	5-22	Tue (N)	SF	14,834		257,202
16	16	5–24	Thu (N)	SF	12,363	27,197	269,565
17	17	5–25	Fri (N)	LA	27,340		296,905
18	18	5–26	Sat (D)	LA	20,051		316,956
19	19	5–27	Sun (D)	LA	26,465	73,856	343,421
20	20	5–28	Mon (D)	SD	36,204	36,204	379,625
21	21	5–31	Thu (N)	StL	7,440		387,065
22	22	6–1	Fri (N)	StL	20,968		408,033
23	23	6–2	Sat (N)	StL	24,879		432,912
24	24	6–3	Sun (D)	StL	13,723	67,010	446,635
25	25	6–11	Mon (N)	Pit	19,596		466,231
26	26	6–12	Tue (N)	Pit	14,255		480,486
27	27	6–13	Wed (N)	Pit	12,124	45,975	492,610
28	28	6–19	Tue (N)	Pha	28,061		520,671
29	29	6–20	Wed (N)	Pha	28,082		548,753
30	30	6–21	Thu (D)	Pha	20,094	76,237	568,847
31	31	6–22	Fri (N)	Mon	39,586		608,433
32	32	6–23	Sat (D)	Mon	46,301		654,734
33	33	6–24	Sun (D)	Mon	22,633	108,520	677,367
34	34	6–28	Thu (N)	Atl	15,077		692,444
35	35	6–29	Fri (N)	Atl	21,458		713,902
36	36–37	7–1	Sun (D)	Atl	8,949	45,484	722,851
37	38	7–2	Mon (N)	Hou	21,923		744,774

ball was a risky business, and the majority of teams were losing money. It was not expected that any new team would be located in or near New York City.

The owner of the Yankee franchise was George Steinbrenner, an outspoken and controversial person who attracted enormous news media attention. This activist owner was the most-discussed person in professional baseball and was fond of proclaiming, "I do it my way." He

EXHIBIT 2 (Continued)

Date No.	Game No.	Date	Day	Vs.	Game	Series	Season
38	39	7–3	Tue (N)	Hou	16,601		761,375
39	40	7–4	Wed (N)	Hou	51,010	89,534	812,385
40	41	7–5	Thu (N)	Cin	14,041		826,426
41	42–43	7–6	Fri (N)	Cin	19,908		846,334
42	44	7–7	Sat (N)	Cin	35,004		881,338
43	45	7–8	Sun (D)	Cin	48,916	117,869	930,254
44	46	7–23	Mon (N)	StL	27,350		957,604
45	47	7–24	Tue (N)	StL	36,749		994,353
46	48	7–25	Wed (D)	StL	37,697	101,796	1,032,050
47	49	7–27	Fri (N)	Chi	51,102		1,083,152
48	50	7–28	Sat (D)	Chi	37,518		1,120,670
49	51–52	7–29	Sun (D)	Chi	50,443	139,063	1,171,113
50	53	8–9	Thu (N)	Pit	27,604		1,198,717
51	54	8–10	Fri (N)	Pit	28,355		1,227,072
52	55	8–11	Sat (N)	Pit	28,326		1,255,398
53	56	8–12	Sun (D)	Pit	36,135	120,420	1,291,533
54	57–58	8–24	Fri (N)	SF	31,834		1,323,367
55	59	8–25	Sat (N)	SF	23,823		1,347,190
56	60	8–26	Sun (D)	SF	22,046	77,703	1,369,236
57	61	8–27	Mon (N)	LA	33,765		1,403,001
58	62	8–28	Tue (N)	LA	25,854		1,428,855
59	63	8–29	Wed (N)	LA	26,290	85,909	1,455,145
60	64–65	8–31	Fri (N)	SD	38,323		1,493,468
61	66–67	9–1	Sat (N)	SD	35,688		1,529,156
62	68	9–2	Sun (D)	SD	36,915	110,926	1,566,071
63	69	9–7	Fri (N)	Chi	46,301		1,612,372
64	70	9–8	Sat (N)	Chi	42,810		1,655,182
65	71	9–9	Sun (D)	Chi	34,956	124,067	1,690,138
66	72	9–10	Mon (N)	StL	9,995		1,700,133
67	73	9–11	Tue (N)	StL	14,968	24,963	1,715,101
68	74	9–12	Wed (N)	Pit	12,876		1,727,977
69	75	9–13	Thu (D)	Pit	6,076	18,952	1,734,053
70	76	9–21	Fri (N)	Mon	15,458		1,749,511
71	77	9–22	Sat (D)	Mon	27,666		1,777,177
72	78	9–23	Sun (D)	Mon	22,171	65,295	1,799,348
73	79	9–24	Mon (N)	Pha	11,071		1,810,419
74	80	9–25	Tue (N)	Pha	13,812		1,824,231
75	81	9–26	Wed (D)	Pha	5,251	30,134	1,829,482

believed strongly that one cannot just call it "the grand old game" and expect people to walk through the turnstiles. Steinbrenner took the long-held mystique of the Yankees and added to it.

A fundamental strategy of the Mets' management and coaching had been joint effort, with emphasis on the team instead of on individual stars. Some cynics believed that this was more of a money-saving device

EXHIBIT 3 Mets' Home Game Schedule and Attendance, 1985

Date No.	Game No.	Date	Day	Vs.	Game	Series	Season
1	1	4–9	Tue (D)	StL	46,781*		46,781
2	2	4–11	Thu (D)	StL	18,864	65,645	65,645
3	3	4–12	Fri (N)	Cin	31,120		96,765
4	4	4–13	Sat (D)	Cin	26,212		122,977
5	5	4–14	Sun (D)	Cin	30,456	87,788	153,433
6	6	4–26	Fri (N)	Pit	31,846		185,279
7	7	4–27	Sat (D)	Pit	24,786		210,065
8	8	4–28	Sun (D)	Pit	36,423	93,055	246,488
9	9	4–30	Tue (N)	Hou	31,558		278,046
10	10	5–1	Wed (N)	Hou	17,973	49,531	296,019
11	11	5–7	Tue (N)	Atl	21,342		317,361
12	12	5–8	Wed (N)	Atl	20,905	42,247	338,266
13	13	5–10	Fri (N)	Pha	46,143		384,409
14	14	5–11	Sat (D)	Pha	29,635		414,044
15	15	5–12	Sun (D)	Pha	32.597	108,375	446,641
16	16	5–17	Fri (N)	SF	23,428		470,069
17	17	5–18	Sat (N)	SF	32,646		502,715
18	18	5–19	Sun (D)	SF	50,369*	106,443	553,084
19	19	5–20	Mon (N)	SD	36,672		589,756
20	20	5–22	Wed (N)	SD	23,468	60,140	613,224
21	21	5–24	Fri (N)	LA	37,124		650,348
22	22	5–25	Sat (D)	LA	40,052		690,400
23	23	5–26	Sun (D)	LA	36,234		726,634
24	24	5–27	Mon (N)	LA	24,458	137,868	751,092
25	25	6–7	Fri (N)	StL	34,490		785,582
26	26	6–8	Sat (D)	StL	36,424		822,006
27	27–28	6–9	Sun (D)	StL	41,431	112,345	863,437
28	29	6–17	Mon (N)	Chi	41,986		905,423
29	30	6–18	Tue (N)	Chi	41,325		946,748
30	31	6–19	Wed (N)	Chi	51,778*		998,526
31	32	6–20	Thu (D)	Chi	37,203	172,292	1,035,729
32	33	6–21	Fri (N)	Mon	38,554		1,074,283
33	34	6–22	Sat (N)	Mon	51,513*		1,125,796
34	35	6–23	Sun (D)	Mon	44,506	134,573	1,170,302
35	36	7–1	Mon (N)	Pit	21,610		1,191,912
36	37	7–2	Tue (N)	Pit	22,651		1,214,563
37	38	7–3	Wed (N)	Pit	46,220*	90,481	1,260,783
38	39	7–18	Thu (N)	Atl	30,496		1,291,279
39	40	7–19	Fri (N)	Atl	36,572		1,327,851

than a strategy. At any rate, the Mets had hired or developed (or both) few widely known performers. The National League's Most Valuable Player Award had never gone to a Met. The same was true for the Home Run Leader Award and the Batting Championship. The most notable exception to the nonstar theme was Tom Seaver, who was voted the National League's Rookie of the Year in 1967 and won the Cy Young

EXHIBIT 3 (Continued)

Date No.	Game No.	Date	Day	Vs.	Game	Series	Season
40	41	7–20	Sat (D)	Atl	35,650		1,363,501
41	42	7–21	Sun (D)	Atl	50,876*	153,594	1,414,377
42	43	7–22	Mon (N)	Cin	27,471		1,441,848
43	44	7–23	Tue (N)	Cin	34,720		1,476,568
44	45	7–24	Wed (D)	Cin	30,154	92,345	1,506,722
45	46	7–25	Thu (N)	Hou	28,421		1,535,143
46	47–48	7–27	Sat (N)	Hou	51,284*		1,586,427
47	49	7–28	Sun (D)	Hou	34,298	114,003	1,620,725
48	50	7–29	Mon (N)	Mon	30,693		1,651,418
49	51	7–30	Tue (N)	Mon	45,118		1,696,536
50	52	7–31	Wed (D)	Mon	26,055	101,866	1,722,591
51	53	8–9	Fri (N)	Chi	44,309		1,766,900
52	54	8–10	Sat (D)	Chi	48,306		1,815,206
53	55	8–11	Sun (D)	Chi	40,311	132,926	1,855,517
54	56	8–12	Mon (N)	Pha	26,577		1,882,094
55	57	8–13	Tue (N)	Pha	31,186		1,913,280
56	58	8–14	Wed (N)	Pha	31,549		1,944,829
57	59	8–15	Thu (D)	Pha	36,663	125,975	1,981,492
58	60	8–20	Tue (N)	SF	31,758		2,013,250
59	61	8–21	Wed (N)	SF	22,450		2,035,700
60	62	8–22	Thu (N)	SF	24,536	78,744	2,060,236
61	63–64	8–23	Fri (N)	SD	45,156		2,105,392
62	65	8–24	Sat (N)	SD	40,863		2,146,255
63	66	8–25	Sun (D)	SD	37,350	123,369	2,183,605
64	67	8–26	Mon (N)	LA	43,063		2,226,668
65	68	8–27	Tue (N)	LA	42,764	85,827	2,269,432
66	69	9–10	Tue (N)	StL	50,195*		2,319,627
67	70	9–11	Wed (N)	StL	52,616*		2,372,243
68	71	9–12	Thu (D)	StL	46,295	149,106	2,418,538
69	72	9–16	Mon (N)	Pha	30,606		2,449,144
70	73	9–17	Tue (N)	Pha	22,440	53,046	2,471,584
71	74	9–18	Wed (N)	Chi	25,424		2,497,008
72	75	9–19	Thu (N)	Chi	26,812	52,236	2,523,820
73	76	9–20	Fri (N)	Pit	33,803		2,557,623
74	77	9–21	Sat (D)	Pit	49,931		2,607,554
75	78	9–22	Sun (D)	Pit	35,679	119,413	2,643,233
76	79	10–4	Fri (N)	Mon	30,910		2,674,143
77	80	10–5	Sat (D)	Mon	45,404		2,719,547
78	81	10–6	Sun (D)	Mon	31,890	108,204	2,751,437

* denotes sellout

award for pitching in 1969, 1973, and 1975. Three Mets players had won the award of National League Rookie of the Year. These were pitcher Jon Matlack in 1972, outfielder Darryl Strawberry in 1983, and pitcher Dwight Gooden in 1984. Gooden won the Cy Young award in 1985. Both Seaver and Matlack moved on to other clubs at much higher salaries.

Management mishandled Seaver's request for contract negotiations in 1977, and tempers flared. Seaver was articulate and witty and enjoyed good relations with the news media. For a short while, he held the extra job of player representative, doing some negotiation and acting in a liaison capacity. This fact plus his stardom hastened his rupture with the Mets' management. Seaver was reacquired from the Cincinnati Reds in 1983, but on January 20, 1984, he was claimed by the Chicago White Sox in a free agent compensation pool.

One of the behavioral principles of sports business management that had emerged in the last decade or so was that good batting is more satisfying to most fans than is good pitching. According to this line of reasoning, finely controlled pitching is appreciated and admired by people who like baseball, but, if given a choice, they would prefer to watch a good display of hitting. Although an active task, pitching was not as active as batting and perhaps not as active as fielding. Contemporary sports fans and journalists seemed to admire action more than those of a generation past. Some purists among baseball fans insist that perfect balance among pitching, batting, and fielding is the goal for which a team should strive.

The conventional wisdom in sports management had always been that a winning team brought out large crowds; and a losing team, small crowds. Commercial success came from a high rate of winning according to tradition. However, recently some people of a more analytical frame of mind had started questioning this idea and called it nothing more than a naive assumption. There was only limited evidence to support the assumption if one gathered the economic data and analyzed them objectively. Many poor teams drew large crowds, and many good teams drew small crowds. This was true even after adjustments for size of the population in the territory around the team and the income levels of that population. A specific example sometimes cited was that of the Yankees in 1977, 1978, and 1979. In the first two of those three years, the Yankees were the world champions. In 1979 the Yankees finished fourth in the American League, but home attendance rose more than 200,000 (9 percent) over 1978. (See Exhibit 4.)

High-quality management of factors other than the team's on-the-field performance could and should overcome most, if not all, of the effect of poor team performance and thus permit the club to earn a satisfactory level of profit. None of this meant that winning games was unimportant. It meant that winning games was not the only factor in the economic success of a team. The conventional wisdom that guided most professional sports businesses was simplistic and out of touch with reality.

One of the most respected voices in athletics, *Sports Illustrated* magazine, noted that the Mets did not understand who their fans were and where these fans came from. The Mets management assumed a prepon-

EXHIBIT 4 Home Attendance by Year, Yankees and Mets

Year	Yankees	Mets
1956	1,491,784	
1957	1,497,134	
1958	1,428,438	
1959	1,552,030	
1960	1,627,349	
1961	1,747,736	
1962	1,493,574	922,530
1963	1,308,920	1,080,108
1964	1,305,638	1,732,597
1965	1,213,552	1,768,389
1966	1,124,648	1,932,693
1967	1,141,714	1,565,492
1968	1,125,124	1,781,657
1969	1,067,996	2,175,373
1970	1,136,879	2,697,479
1971	1,070,771	2,266,680
1972	966,328	2,134,185
1973	1,262,077	1,912,390
1974	1,273,075	1,722,209
1975	1,288,048	1,730,566
1976	2,012,434	1,468,754
1977	2,103,092	1,066,825
1978	2,335,871	1,007,328
1979	2,537,765	788,905
1980	2,627,417	1,178,659
1981*	1,614,353	704,244
1982	2,041,219	1,320,055
1983	2,257,976	1,103,808
1984	1,821,815	1,829,482
1985	2,214,587	2,751,437

* A strike shortened the 1981 season for all teams. The Mets played only 52 home dates and the Yankees 50.

derance of affluent suburbanites from north of the city but finally found, after hiring marketing research consultants, that the fans were mostly working-class people who lived close by in the Brooklyn and Queens portions of the city and from some close working-class suburbs on Long Island. Matthew Levine, president of Pacific Select Corporation, a marketing research and consulting firm retained by the Mets, concluded that the owners prior to Doubleday were among the most disliked owners in sports.[1]

Many observers believed that the Mets had become rather well known, both at home and on the road. Yet that image was not very good. Among the prevailing perceptions of the Mets team were the following recurring descriptions: laughable, juvenile, and inept but occasionally lovable. A large part of the time they were referred to by a diminutive form of their name, the Metsies. Use of the diminutive was sometimes an approval and sometimes a put-down. Nearly all the sports news media consistently expressed the viewpoint, "What's the latest thing the Mets have done to blow the ball game?" Public relations was certainly not used to its potential to assist the organization. The situation was not really poor but needed improvement.

Advise the management of the New York Mets.

DR PEPPER COMPANY

Dr Pepper, formerly a large but only regional producer of a brand holding fifth place in the United States in the soft-drink industry, expanded to national coverage in 1969. By 1981 it had captured third place in the industry after the first place Coca-Cola brand and the second place Pepsi-Cola brand. From 1982 to 1984, 7UP regained the third place, but Dr Pepper and 7UP were of almost identical size and virtually tied for third place among brands. However, Dr Pepper was consistently profitable, and 7UP was not. Dr Pepper regained third place in 1985.

About 800 brands of soft drinks were produced in the United States, but the top ten commanded about three-fourths of the market. Besides the brands just mentioned, important ones included Sprite, Tab, Mello Yello, and Fanta from Coca-Cola Co.; Mountain Dew from Pepsico, Inc.; Royal Crown Cola and Nehi from Royal Crown Company; Sunkist, Canada Dry ginger ale, and Schweppes from Cadbury-Schweppes; Orange Crush and Hires root beer from Procter & Gamble; Shasta; Squirt; Faygo; Nu-Grape; Dad's root beer; and the diet and caffeine-free versions of several of these brands. Pepsi-Cola became the leading brand in the United States in 1985 for a short while after Coca-Cola's patronage was split into Classic Coke and New Coke. Coca-Cola Co. remained the largest soft drink organization, but Pepsico was growing faster. Coca-Cola Classic regained first place as the public showed a strong preference for the old recipe over the new. The industry's unit volume was expected to increase about 5 to 6 percent during the late 1980s and early 1990s.

[1] "More Victories Equals More Fans Equals More Profits, Right? Wrong, Wrong, Wrong," *Sports Illustrated*, April 28, 1980, pp. 34–45.

In 1984 Dr Pepper Company was bought by Forstmann Little & Co., a New York City investment firm backed by several financiers and large pension funds in a leveraged transaction for $623 million. The other aggressive suitor was Castle & Cooke, Inc., producers of Dole brand products. In such a transaction the buyers work largely with borrowed money, pledging assets about to be acquired to secure the new debt. Dr Pepper Company officials were hoping that this maneuver was a way to high growth. In an earlier leveraged buyout, Forstmann Little had purchased Topps Chewing Gum, Inc., Union Ice, and several small firms. Forstmann Little saw in Dr Pepper Company the crucial factors for a profitable buyout: good and fairly predictable cash flow; a loyal base of customers; and, most important, undervaluation of the assets as perceived by the financial publics. This last factor meant that the individual assets of the company were worth more than their combined worth in one company. In other words, it was the *reverse* of the old expression, "The whole is worth more than the sum of its parts." Following the buyout, Dr Pepper's chairperson of the board, W. W. Clements, stayed on, but the president, Richard Armstrong, resigned.

In 1986 Forstmann agreed to sell Dr Pepper to Coca-Cola. The Federal Trade Commission and RC Cola filed suit to block this sale, alleging that there would be too much concentration in the industry and too little competition. The parties cancelled the arrangement. A few weeks later Dr Pepper was sold for $416 million to a group of investors, including Shearson-Lehman Brothers, Inc., several Dr Pepper executives, Cadbury-Schweppes PLC, and Hicks & Haas. Cadbury-Schweppes, a large British maker of candy and beverages, bought about 30 percent of the shares. Hicks & Haas already owned one-third of A & W Beverages, makers of root beer.

The archrival Seven-Up Company became a wholly owned subsidiary of Philip Morris, Inc., in 1981 at a purchase price of $520 million cash. With access to new talent and additional capital, 7UP was expected to become quite aggressive after a year or two of reevaluation and planning under the new ownership. This brand was widely promoted as "the Uncola" by both the old and the new owners. However, 7UP lost money four out of the five years 1981–1985, and Philip Morris sold it to Pepsico, Inc., in January 1986 at a small loss. The FTC and RC Cola filed suit to block this sale, on the same grounds as their complaint against Dr Pepper. The parties cancelled the sale. Schweppes considered trying to buy 7UP. For their own account and a group of investors, Dallas financiers Thomas Hicks and Robert Haas bought 7UP in late 1986 for $240 million. Now Hicks and Haas had very large interests in A&W, 7UP, and Dr Pepper, and constituted the third largest entity in the soft drink industry. They then sold 59 percent of A&W to the public but retained enough ownership to have effective control.

Because different investor groups owned Dr Pepper and 7UP, the two could not be totally merged easily. However, the Dr Pepper management was asked to manage both companies, splitting certain common costs. 7UP paid an annual $5 million fee to Dr Pepper for management direction. Management moved Dr Pepper's production of syrup and concentrate to 7UP's St. Louis plant, which was badly underutilized. 7UP was restored to profitability within a few months. Most business people thought that total merger of the two companies was probable in time.

Soft drinks were clearly a growth industry. Per capita annual consumption in the United States was about forty-seven gallons as of 1989 and rising. The comparable figures in 1987, 1983, and 1980 were only forty-four gallons, thirty-seven gallons, and thirty-four gallons respectively.

Dr Pepper brand enjoyed 5.1 percent of the U.S. market whereas Sugar Free Dr Pepper had 1.0 percent; Sugar Free Pepper Free, 0.1 percent; and Pepper Free, another 0.1 percent. Dr Pepper Company's Welch brand line of fruit-flavored drinks had 0.5 percent. Thus, the company had a total market share of approximately 6.8 percent, selling about 470 million cases annually.

Based in Dallas, Dr Pepper Company had sales of about $225 million in the latest year. Both sales and profits were on a strong trend of improvement. Sales of Dr Pepper Company's products at the retail level were several times the $225 million, of course. Dr Pepper Company made soft drink concentrates and fountain syrups and sold them to about 500 bottlers that were unaffiliated with the company. These franchised firms converted the concentrates to bottled and canned beverages by adding sweeteners and carbonated water. Some bottlers also held franchises for one or more competitive brands, using the same physical facilities. Dr Pepper Company sold fountain syrups to franchised bottlers and wholesale distributors and directly to some fountain accounts, such as fast-food restaurant chains. Until the purchase by Forstmann Little, Dr Pepper was partially integrated vertically, conducting its own bottling operations in ten locations: Dallas-Fort Worth, Los Angeles, Houston, San Antonio, Waco, Corpus Christi, Albuquerque, Mobile, Pensacola, and Washington, North Carolina. When these plants were owned they provided a little over half of company sales dollars and served well over 10 percent of the national demand for Dr Pepper products. All these facilities were in areas where Dr Pepper enjoyed large sales and high brand loyalty. When it was an independent firm, Dr Pepper had a plan to expand the number of its investments in bottling operations. It had purchased the Los Angeles, Houston, Albuquerque, Mobile, Pensacola, and Washington, North Carolina, plants between 1977 and 1983. Forstmann Little divested all these bottling facilities one at a time during its two years of ownership. In a leveraged buyout, the new owners normally pay off part of the debt incurred in buying the organization by selling off selected assets whose loss would not destroy the company but would bring good prices. The dismemberment of the Dr Pepper Company came as a surprise to some of the veteran managers and former shareholders of Dr Pepper.

Although national in scope, Dr Pepper's deepest market penetration was in Texas and California. However, it was also strong throughout the Sun Belt. Because population and incomes were rising a little faster there than in the nation as a whole, Dr Pepper considered itself to be in a fairly promising situation. In addition, in the regions where Dr Pepper was strong, teenagers and young adults comprised a larger share of the population than in the country as a whole. Such age groups consumed more sodas per capita than did middle-aged and elderly people.

Dr Pepper Company bought the exclusive marketing rights to the Welch's line of carbonated soft drinks in late 1981. Started in 1974 by Welch Foods, Inc., this line consisted of several fruit flavors but emphasized grape and strawberry. Welch's was targeted to the traditional users of these sodas, black and Hispanic teenagers, especially for consumption away from home. Dr Pepper company set up a subsidiary, Premier Beverages, Inc., to handle this group of products.

In early 1982, Dr Pepper Company purchased Canada Dry Corp. from Norton Simon, Inc., a conglomerate. Canada Dry made and marketed a successful bitter lemon soda and ginger ale, both successful but not in the top ten sellers. It also had a popular line of mixers, including tonic water and club soda (a sparkling water). Tonic water was occasionally drunk by itself but was usually mixed with vodka or gin. American liquor consumption was slowly shifting toward more "white goods" and less whiskey. Forstmann Little sold Canada Dry to R. J. Reynolds Industries, the tobacco-based conglomerate, a few months after purchasing Dr Pepper Company. Cadbury Schweppes PLC bought Canada Dry and Sunkist from R. J. Reynolds in 1986.

For several years before the purchase of Canada Dry, Dr Pepper Company had been interested in buying Crush International, Ltd., of Vancouver, Canada, whose major products were Orange Crush and Hires root beer. However, giant detergent, toiletries, and food manufacturer Procter & Gamble, looking for further diversification, beat out Dr Pepper Company and bought that organization in 1980. Dr Pepper maintained that its offer was about $2 million higher than Procter & Gamble's but that Crush sold to the other company because of the prospect of lengthy litigation by Procter & Gamble if Crush selected Dr Pepper. It was expected that Procter & Gamble would develop a cola drink soon to add to the acquired line of beverages. Procter and Gamble soon bought an established bottler so as to gain experience with the whole spectrum of soft-drink operations.

Like all soft-drink enterprises, Dr Pepper was vitally concerned about the high and often volatile costs of sugar. The company was expanding its use of high-fructose corn sweetener, which cost much less than traditional sugars. Most other soft-drink organizations were making similar adaptations.

At the head of the Dr Pepper organization was seventy-one-year-old W. W. "Foots" Clements, who worked his way through college by driving a Dr Pepper truck and serving the accounts on a route. After college he worked in sales and later on the corporate marketing staff. He became general sales manager, then president, and finally chief executive and chairperson of the board of directors. In that capacity, he worked mainly on long-range planning. There had been a high turnover in the position of president and chief operating officer. From 1980 to 1982, Charles L. Jarvie, formerly corporate vice-president for Procter & Gamble's Food Products Division filled this position. However, when the national share of the market stopped growing and the product line continued to languish in the northeast (where the share of the market was only 2 percent), he resigned. Jarvie had pushed television network advertising and held a million-dollar lottery, which Clements called "ill-conceived." Richard Q. Armstrong, who had been president of Canada Dry at the time Dr Pepper purchased that organization, replaced Jarvie. Armstrong left immediately when the sale to Forstmann Little was decided. The president and chief operating officer then became fifty-nine-year-old Joe K. Hughes, formerly the Dr Pepper Company's executive vice-president. He had been with the company almost twenty years. That did not work out. By the end of 1984, Hughes was named vice-chairperson of the board without line authority over the president. The new president was John Albers, who had served briefly as executive vice-president. In 1985, Robert Hamlin was appointed vice-president for marketing. He had been Young & Rubicam's account executive for Dr Pepper advertising for many years.

The Dr Pepper beverage was invented in 1885 by a pharmacist working for Wade Morrison, a young druggist, in Waco. Morrison was quite interested in the daughter of Dr. Charles Pepper, a physician. However, Pepper had not allowed Morrison to court his daughter. Morrison thought that surely the father would relent if he named his great new beverage for him. The tactic did not work, but the brand name continued.

Morrison's design objective was to combine a great many of the attractive aromas of the sodas of his day. Therefore, the highly secret formula for this brand had twenty-three ingredients, many of them old-fashioned fruit extracts. There was also a sizeable amount of caffeine. Many people who tried Dr Pepper concluded that cherry was the single most important flavor, but the company indicated several years ago that cherry was not in the formula. Even Clements assumed that there was cherry until he had been with the organization for twenty years. Many people thought they detected prunes. Some people thought the beverage had laxative characteristics, whether or not prunes were included.

Unfortunately, both the name and the taste of Dr Pepper suggested to most people something medicinal or, at least, partly medicinal. Clements readily admitted, "People never knew whether to drink it or rub it on." Besides the simplistic implication of medication, the words, "Dr Pepper" did not seem to convey any particular meaning to people, unlike the names of several competitive soft drinks. In addition, the taste was not easily described. The producer had always had difficulty describing the taste to people in its consumer advertising and in its face-to-face selling to accounts.

Because the Dr Pepper drink was difficult to classify by taste and, in all fairness, could be said to be unique, competitors had worked on the development of items of a similar taste to compete with it. This task became more important as the sales of Dr Pepper grew. Coca-Cola introduced Mr. Pibb in 1972, but it was not very successful. It had only 0.3 percent of the market, but it remained in the product line. Then Coca-Cola introduced Cherry Coke in early 1985, and Royal Crown introduced Cherry R. C. in the spring of 1985. Pepsico launched Cherry Pepsi in Canada in late 1985 and, without test marketing, launched it in Great Britain in January 1986. Later Pepsico introduced the product in the United States. Then 7UP launched a cherry-flavored version of its product. All four organizations publicly stated that these cherry flavored drinks were not aimed at Dr Pepper, but most industry observers, market analysts, and journalists believed otherwise. The cherry emphasis was stronger than in the Dr Pepper products, but there were definite similarities. Coca-Cola had done tests on Cherry Coke for several years. Its research indicted that potential Cherry Coke consumers would be close to the mainstream but willing to be a little different.

Advertising and Sales Promotion

Some of the advertising in the early years of the product was curious. One theme used for many years was a cartoon trademark called "The Old Doc," a character who resembled "Reddy Kilowatt." This theme probably reinforced the suspicion that Dr Pepper was an effective laxative. Later, in 1927, Dallas advertising specialist Earle Racy created the theme "Drink a Bite to Eat at 10, 2, and 4 O'Clock." This was based on a book, *The Liquid Bite*, by a Columbia University professor, Walter H. Eddy. His research into the human diet revealed in-between-meal times when blood sugar reached its low points. The rationale for the theme was that because Dr Pepper metabolized quickly, it restored energy during the valley hours of 10:30 A.M. and 2:30 and 4:30 P.M. This theme was used for more than a quarter of a century. Racy received a $25 bonus for creating this advertising theme. The theme and rationale were so persuasive that J. B. O'Hara, then president of Dr Pepper Company, took the lead for the industry and, in conjunction with the chief executives of several other soft-drink companies, convinced the War Rationing Board to rescind a ruling that would have severely rationed the sugar allowed to the soft-drink industry during World War II.

The advertising and sales promotion of Dr Pepper after it went national was extremely interesting. In 1969 Dr Pepper placed its account with Young & Rubicam, Inc., a large New York advertising agency. This agency attempted to remove the fuzzy and sometimes medicinal image of Dr Pepper and build for it a distinctive image. In the first phase of the long-range plan, the agency introduced this beverage in an audacious manner that was very unconventional: "America's most misunderstood soft drink." Manufacturers and advertising agencies almost never consider any admission of public confusion about a product, preferring to be constantly positive. This musical jingle theme stated, "Dr Pepper, so misunderstood . . . It's not a cola, it's not a root beer, it's something much, much more. . . ." Young & Rubicam wanted to establish that Dr Pepper was different from other soft drinks, and it and the manufacturer were willing to take the risk of approaching the misunderstanding directly. Several television special shows with big-name stars were sponsored by Dr Pepper. This phase ran for more than two years.

The second phase was the "Most Original" theme campaign. This phase sought to position Dr Pepper as a soda in a class by itself. While most major competitors were using variations of the "kids on the beach" sorts of themes, Young & Rubicam developed a series of large-scale, highly theatrical production numbers complete with elaborate singing and dancing routines in the old tradition of producer-director Busby Berkeley. Dr Pepper was promoted as the change-of-pace drink for special people. The social self-confidence of users and those first trying the drink needed to be built up. Phase two also later included the theme, "You've got to try it to love it," followed by the theme "Once you try it you'll love the difference." It was vital to keep talking about trying it, not only because so many people had not done so, but also because the first try did not usually make a convert. The consumer regarded the first few trials as just that. Four to six servings were usually necessary before a person adopted this beverage, if at all. Phase two, which won many awards in the advertising profession, lasted about five years.

By 1977 the manufacturer and Young & Rubicam were ready to go into phase three, which was supposed to position Dr Pepper in the mainstream of the American life-style. They wanted to picture it as the popular beverage for every occasion. They developed "The Pepper," a Pied Piper–like character who danced from town to town and coast to coast leading a joyous crowd in a groundswell of support for this universally enjoyed, admired beverage. A "Pepper" was portrayed as a self-confident, bold, and popular person. David Naughton, an unknown twenty-three-year-old actor, was hired as the Pepper. Emphasis was targeted toward the thirteen-to-thirty-year-old segment of consumers. Advertisements in phase three were less sophisticated and used simpler story lines and songs than in phase two. Naughton's amateur voice was used for the songs. As the Pepper character became more recognizable to viewers, the age target was broadened a little, and celebrities and cartoon characters were built in, for example, Ron Guidry, Charlie Rich, Fred Flintstone, Tweetie Bird, Sylvester, and Popeye.

With the success of company sales, phase three was altered somewhat in 1981 to try to convert nonusers, including specifically those who still had never heard of Dr Pepper and those who knew of it but had not tried it. Naughton was continued, and each new advertisement explored a fanciful facet of his persona. For example, in a thirty-second spot entitled "Sign," he magically produced a rainbow that swirled across the scene to become a glittering Dr Pepper sign. In a sixty-second spot entitled "Whistling," the Pepper was paired with Mickey Rooney in a production number containing only music and a whistle in the sound track. The idea was to encourage viewers to become participants in the commercial. The jingle had become much more familiar to viewers than the jingles of most other advertisers.

With hindsight, both Dr Pepper Company and Young & Rubicam were unhappy with the series of advertising campaigns built around "The Pepper." Awareness of the product rose but share of the market did not. According to the advertising agency, this drink tried to become a soda for the masses. That mass appeal made Dr Pepper's advertising too much like that of Coca-Cola and Pepsi. Psychographic studies showed that consumers who tended to like Dr Pepper's taste were apt to be "inner-directed" rather than "outer-directed" or "other-directed." They did not place a great deal of weight on doing what other people expected them to do, instead emphasizing their own personal values. What is more, Coke and Pepsi already had better-accepted flavors and several times as much money to spend on advertising. Therefore, in 1984, Dr Pepper returned to the advertising strategy that had helped it grow in the 1970s. In 1975 the company had been extremely pleased with the slogan "the most original soft drink ever in the whole wide world." In 1984 and 1985 the company went with a slogan "Hold out for the out-of-the-ordinary." The intended image was that Dr Pepper was the choice of the independent thinker who was looking for an alternative to colas.

The important, costly 1986 and 1987 television campaigns employed the overall theme of "Out of the ordinary. Like you." On radio the Dr Pepper commercials were to be in the style of hit songs of thirty seconds, sixty seconds, and two minutes in length and rendered in the singing styles of several star performers. Each song had a story to tell with Dr Pepper cleverly worked in. Both television and radio were aimed primarily at the youth audiences and stressed two psychological moods, fun and irreverence for the traditional.

For Sugar Free Dr Pepper, now renamed Diet Dr Pepper, there were multiple series of advertisements built around "Stargazers," "Godzilla Too," and "Droids." The theme line was "Diet Dr Pepper, The taste for out of the ordinary bodies." The wording suggested the health benefit of this brand but still tied in with the advertising for the flagship brand. The company had always been cautious about the word "diet" but now felt that the word carried more positive than negative connotations for the consumer.

Robert Hamlin, the company marketing vice-president, tried to sum up the advertising strategy: "Dr Pepper commercials tell a story, often with a twist at the end, and they involve the consumer. This is captivating entertainment value that pays off in long-lasting awareness." Hamlin had been involved in Dr Pepper's advertising since 1977.

Dr Pepper became more aggressive in the mid-1980s and late 1980s with its sales promotions. In-store sweepstakes were organized, one for each quarter of the year with seasonally appropriate premiums and colorful point-of-sale material. Cooperative advertising on radio, on television, and in newspapers was offered to bottlers.

Advise Dr Pepper Company.

UNITED WAY

The United Way[1] was probably the best-known name in the business of charity. It traced its roots back under a series of former names to 1887 in Denver when the first United Community Campaign was organized. From the 1920s through the 1940s the prevailing name was the Community Chest. After that time it was widely known as the United Fund and, in places, United Givers. In the 1970s the designation of United Way became prevalent.

Along the route of development several innovations occurred at the local level. In 1908, in Pittsburgh, the first organized fact-finding group in charity was created. In 1913, Cleveland introduced the concept of

[1] Helpful material can be found in the following: William A. Mindak and H. Malcolm Bybee, "Marketing's Application to Fund Raising," *Journal of Marketing*, 35 (July 1971), pp. 13–18; Ben M. Enis, "Deepening the Concept of Marketing," *Journal of Marketing*, 37 (October 1973), pp. 57–62; Philip Kotler, "Defining the Limits of Marketing," in Boris Becker and Helmet Becker, Eds., *Combined Proceedings of the 1972 Conferences* (Chicago: American Marketing Association, 1972), pp. 48–56; Sidney J. Levy and Philip Kotler, "Beyond Marketing: The Furthering Concept," *California Management Review*, 12 (Winter 1969), pp. 67–73; Philip Kotler and Sidney J. Levy, "Broadening the Concept of Marketing," *Journal of Marketing*, 33 (January 1969), pp. 10–15; David J. Luck, "Broadening the Concept of Marketing—Too Far," *Journal of Marketing*, 33 (July 1969), pp. 53–55; Philip Kotler and Sidney J. Levy, "A New Form of Marketing Myopia: Rejoinder to Professor Luck," *Journal of Marketing*, 33 (July 1969), pp. 55–57; and Philip Kotler, "A Generic Concept of Marketing," *Journal of Marketing*, 36 (April 1972), pp. 46–54.

budgeting for charity fund raising. And, in 1919, Rochester, seeing the need for a permanent name for the movement that had some promotional qualities, coined the name Community Chest.

The underlying concept of the United Way was a federation for seeking contributions. It raised money simultaneously for many good causes, thus cutting down on duplication of fund-raising drives and saving time and frustration for donors. Individual charities within local United Ways received about one fourth of their funding from the annual United Way Campaign on the average. The remainder of funding came from grants and bequests, from government agencies in fees for contracted services, and from supplemental fund-raising drives. These supplemental drives were approved or condoned by the United Way.

By any standard of measurement, charity in the United States was large, totaling about $47 billion in the most recent year. Sources of donations in most years tended to break down in approximately the following shares: individuals, 80 percent; wills of recently deceased individuals, 8 percent; foundations, 7 percent; corporations, 5 percent. Most of the foundations received their original endowments from major entrepreneurs in the business world. Most of the bequests in wills were in the form of securities, real estate, and objects of art rather than cash. Approximately 43 percent of giving went to religious bodies and the rest went to a large variety of civic, welfare, humanitarian, educational, artistic, and health-related organizations. Of the money for nonreligious use, approximately 6 percent, or more than $1.5 billion, was collected and allocated by the United Way. Sources of funds and their shares of contributions to the United Way in the three most recent years are shown in Exhibit 1. This table indicates that this organization received relatively much more from corporations and relatively much less from individuals than did charity at large.

Although large in amounts of money, charity had a difficult time keeping up with inflation throughout the 1970s and early 1980s, and in several years the contributions actually declined when adjusted for inflation. United Way had the same difficulty. In ten of the twelve latest years the percentage increase in collections was less than the inflation rate. In addition, the growth rate in federal spending on the needy was decreased, but absolute amounts continued to rise slightly.

United Way of America was the name for the national movement and for the umbrella organization that maintained national headquarters. Local United Ways were autonomous. Of late the headquarters budget had tended to run a little over $13 million per year. The national level received annual support on the basis of an allocation from the collections of most local United Ways. The national level also received small amounts of money directly from a few people who wanted to support the

EXHIBIT 1 United Way Support By Source, in Percentages, Four Most Recent Years

Source	Latest Year	Two Years Ago	Three Years Ago	Four Years Ago
Corporations	26.5%	27.5%	27.7%	28.4%
Employees and executives	47.6	47.3	46.0	46.1
Education	3.4	3.2	3.1	3.1
Government	7.2	7.2	7.2	7.1
Other nonprofit	1.3	2.0	2.0	1.6
Professions	3.9	3.2	3.1	3.2
Foundations	2.0	1.6	1.5	1.5
Residential	3.1	3.8	3.7	3.9
Other (includes small business)	5.0	4.2	5.7	5.1
	100.0%	100.0%	100.0%	100.0%

headquarters. It received small amounts of program service fees and an extremely small amount of income from rentals and various investments.

The national level was necessary for coordination, long-range planning, and some services to the approximately 2,100 local United Ways in the United States and Canada. Headquarters furnished the local organizations technical support for local campaigns and tried to build and maintain good relations with large corporations. More specific activities had to do with the development and production of films and other materials for use by voluntary solicitors and the media, development and production of planning and budgeting manuals, review of national agency programs, publication of various newsletter series, training of locals in management techniques and fund raising, maintenance of a lending library of pertinent reports, and the execution of public opinion and market research. An example of recent market research was the test marketing in Seattle and Richmond of a telethon format to recruit volunteer labor for local charities.

United Way of America decided that it needed truly year-round communication with its publics instead of just late fall and early winter, the time when most local campaigns were held. This communication should educate and inform people about the United Way, according to C. P. McColough, vice-chairperson of the board of directors. He indicated that they had found a direct correlation between contributor knowledge of United Way and support. The Advertising Council, a social marketing organization formed for the purpose of supporting selected nonprofit causes with the creation and placement of donated professional advertising, became supportive of the United Way. An advertising agency, Bozell & Jacobs, International, volunteered to create the advertising and the National Football League agreed to support the United Way on its televised games. Later the National Hockey League and National Basketball Association agreed to similar arrangements. United Way had to pay production costs of the advertisements, but the electronic and print media contributed the time and space. For example, an elaborate television series with the National Football League cost United Way only $200,000, the cost of producing the advertisements. Some local United Ways began thinking about the purchase of television and radio advertising time.

United Way officials took the lead in establishing the Alexis de Tocqueville Society Award, named for the famous French scholar, author, and admirer of voluntarism. Taking this action meant that some deserving voluntarism leaders would be rewarded, but it also meant that some publicity and positive feelings for voluntarism in general and the United Way in particular would probably result. Recent recipients included the Adams family descendants of President John Adams and Vernon E. Jordan, Jr., executive director of the Urban League and civil rights leader. In a speech accepting this award, Jordan stated that because the voluntary sector provided the opportunity for personal involvement, it constituted the cement binding our society together.

After several scandals in recent years in organizations unaffiliated with the United Way, the United States and some state governments had become concerned about the percentage of funds contributed for charity that were used for charity administration. The United States national average for charitable organizations appears to be just over 20 percent. For the United Way the figure was about 10.5 percent. About 4.6 percent was attributable directly to fund raising and the remaining 5.9 percent was for planning and general management. It was sometimes difficult to classify expenditures perfectly. There was noteworthy hostility and misinformation about the amount of money that went into administration in any charitable organization, especially in geographic areas that had experienced well-publicized scandals. In a few charities unaffiliated with United Way more than 80 percent of funds collected went to administrative costs.

Criticisms of the United Way

Criticisms were always offered against all charitable organizations. Because of its sheer size the United Way seemed to receive a considerable amount of criticism. Some of the criticism was not based on fact, whereas on some other points intelligent, well-informed persons of goodwill could differ.

The fundamental and perhaps unsolvable criticism was that the role United Way assigned itself was inherently arrogant; that is, it ran one campaign on behalf of many worthy causes and then allocated the proceeds among them as it saw fit. Professional envy by administrators in channels undoubtedly played some part in the criticism. This envy was enhanced by the fact that United Way was virtually the only organization with which an employer would cooperate with employee-authorized payroll deduction.

Among the several other criticisms of United Way was that many recipients of United Way money, such as the American Red Cross, Salvation Army, and Boy Scouts, conducted additional fund raising, thus violating the concept of federated fund raising. This was true, but defenders pointed out that these organizations could not carry out their work on the amounts allocated to them from United Way and that they did not want to lose their individual public identities.

Another criticism was that the money a person contributed and designated for a particular charity did not go specifically to that charity, because the bookkeeping involved would be burdensome and the United Way had already reached a tentative agreement in advance with recipients as to the amounts that would be given them. Despite tentative allocations and costly paper work caused by donors specifying recipient charities, the United Way did honor those directions. Because so many people specified nothing and there were offsets, the draft amount and the final amount for each recipient tended to be the same.

Some people believed that United Way was the indirect cause of pressure on employees, because much of its campaign was carried out at places of employment and the payroll deduction was encouraged. Moreover, a certain percentage of one's pay was suggested as the contribution. Although there might have been pressure from some employers, there was infrequent evidence of such pressure, and 100 percent participation in any firm was extremely rare. United Way investigated all such charges. Interestingly enough, only a tiny percentage of employees in small firms donated to United Way.

Another criticism was that the types of services subsidized by the United Way were not the services that were needed the most. According to this line of thought, many needed services were not supported and the United Way was slow to alter its list of recipients. This kind of criticism particularly came from many blacks, and, as a result, in 1975 the National Black United Fund, Inc., was formed. With affiliated groups in about fifteen cities, the national organization set up headquarters of the Black United Way in Los Angeles. The crux of the criticism from blacks was that the set of services supported by United Way did not stress the subjects that mattered the most to blacks: employment, job training, legal assistance, housing, health services, and crime. In a few places whites got into serious dispute about the mix of recipients of United Way funds. For example, in Prince George's County, Maryland, a suburban area near Washington, D.C., the United Way organization split into two groups in the mid-1970s.

An additional criticism was that the United Way employed too many people and compensated them too well. At local and national levels combined there were about 3,500 professionals on the payroll.

Income Tax Developments and Problems

Among the United Way officials and advisors there had long been concern that the structure of personal income tax regulations in the United States was affecting contributions adversely. Instead of itemizing deductions, about 78 percent of taxpayers took the standard deduction (also known as the zero bracket amount), a proportion that had grown of late. People who used the standard deduction had had no financial incentive to donate to any charitable organization, in that their income taxes were unaffected by donations. The federal government had built into the standard deduction an assumed amount of contributions for the typical person. If the person selecting the standard deduction made few or no donations, he or she was automatically ahead financially. In 1981 as part of the overhaul of federal income tax policies this characteristic was changed, effective in 1982, the result largely of intense lobbying by charitable organizations, including the United Way. For tax filings for the years 1981 through 1986, taxpayers who used the standard deduction instead of itemizing their deductions were able to reduce their income tax obligation by a percentage of qualifying donations made during the year. For 1982 and 1983, 25 percent of contributions up to a $100 maximum could be claimed for a top deduction of $25. For 1984 the ceiling rose to $300 and the rate stayed at 25 percent for a maximum deduction of $75. In 1985 the rate went to 50 percent and in 1986 to 100 percent, with no dollar ceilings in either year (except for the traditional limitation to 50 percent of adjusted gross income). This section of the tax code was meant to expire at the end of 1986. The purpose of this provision was financially to motivate people of average income to contribute to charity.

In addition, 1981 reforms in income tax regulations reduced tax rates for all people at all income levels and for corporations. The net impact of the 1981 change was to decrease dollars of tax obligations significantly and the top personal rate to 50 percent. The impact of a planned overhaul in late 1986 was to redistribute tax obligations, eliminate many deductions, and cut the top rate to about 33 percent. Thus, in just five years the whole structure of rates went down dramatically, and the incentive to

EXHIBIT 2 Organization Chart for Headquarters, United Way of America

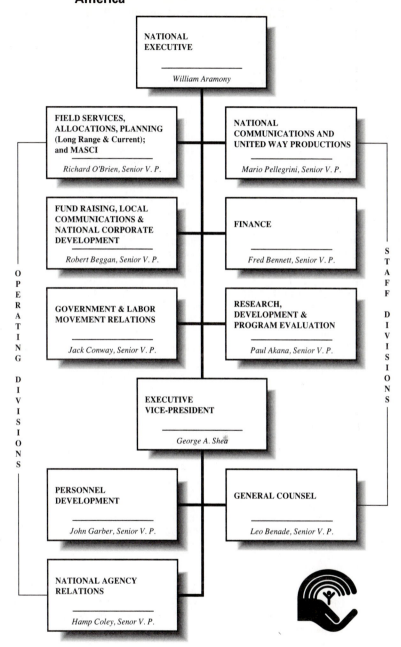

NATIONAL EXECUTIVE

William Aramony

FIELD SERVICES, ALLOCATIONS, PLANNING (Long Range & Current); and MASCI

Richard O'Brien, Senior V. P.

NATIONAL COMMUNICATIONS AND UNITED WAY PRODUCTIONS

Mario Pellegrini, Senior V. P.

FUND RAISING, LOCAL COMMUNICATIONS & NATIONAL CORPORATE DEVELOPMENT

Robert Beggan, Senior V. P.

FINANCE

Fred Bennett, Senior V. P.

GOVERNMENT & LABOR MOVEMENT RELATIONS

Jack Conway, Senior V. P.

RESEARCH, DEVELOPMENT & PROGRAM EVALUATION

Paul Akana, Senior V. P.

EXECUTIVE VICE-PRESIDENT

George A. Shea

PERSONNEL DEVELOPMENT

John Garber, Senior V. P.

GENERAL COUNSEL

Leo Benade, Senior V. P.

NATIONAL AGENCY RELATIONS

Hamp Coley, Senor V. P.

OPERATING DIVISIONS

STAFF DIVISIONS

EXHIBIT 3 A Partial List of Agencies and Services Receiving United Way Allocations

American Diabetes Association
American National Red Cross
American Social Health Association
Arthritis Foundation
Big Brothers
Big Sisters
Boys Clubs
Boy Scouts
Camp Fire Girls
Catholic Charities
Child Adoption Services
Child Guidance Clinics
Day Care Centers
Epilepsy Foundation of America
Family Counseling Services
Foster Care of Children
Girls Clubs
Girl Scouts
Homemaker–Home Health Aide
  Service
Homes for Dependent and
  Neglected Children
Hospitals
Information and Referral Services
Inner City Projects
Legal Aid Services
Leukemia Society of America
Mental Health Services
Medical Clinics
National Association for Mental
  Health
National Association for Retarded
  Citizens
National Association of Hearing
  and Speech Action
National Council on Alcoholism

National Council on Crime and
  Delinquency
National Cystic Fibrosis Research
  Foundation
National Easter Seal Society for
  Crippled Children and Adults
National Hemophilia Foundation
National Kidney Foundation
National Multiple Sclerosis Society
National Recreation and Park
  Associaton
Neighborhood Centers and
  Settlements
Planned Parenthood Services
Residential Treatment Centers for
  Children
Salvation Army
Services for the Aging
Services for the Handicapped
Services for Unwed Mothers
Summer Camps
Temporary Shelters for Children
Travelers Aid
United Cancer Council, Inc.
United Cerebral Palsy Association
United Seamen's Service
United Service Organizations (USO)
United Way Planning Organizations
Urban League
Visiting Nurse Services
Volunteer Bureaus and Voluntary
  Action Centers
Volunteers of America
YMCA
YWCA
YMHA
YWHA

donate for people who itemized their deductions decreased. For example, a person might find his or her effective marginal rate dropping from 53 to about 33 percent. Thus his or her cost to make each $100 contribution to charity would become $67 rather than the old $47. Corporate rates were also cut but not as much.

Advise United Way.

EXHIBIT 4 Themes in Past United Way Campaigns

I gave	Fair share
I care	Do your share
Keep on caring	Be a good neighbor
Suppose nobody cared	Help the unfortunate
Give more	Brighten a life
I give the United Way	It's working
I did not forget	Thanks to you it's working
Open your heart	Thanks to you it works. For all of us
	Now more than ever

ROBERTSHAW CONTROLS COMPANY

Robertshaw Controls company could be traced back to a thermostat device invented by Frederick W. Robertshaw in Pittsburgh in 1899. A prolific inventor who obtained forty-one patents, Robertshaw guided the early growth of the organization. Soon after World War II the Grayson Company, based upon the inventions of John H. Grayson in California, and the Fulton Company, based upon the inventions of Weston M. Fulton in Tennessee, merged with Robertshaw to form the present corporation.

A major participant in the industrial controls industry, Robertshaw manufactured automatic controls and control systems for industry, commercial buildings, and the home. The product line included controls for regulating and measuring temperatures and pressure, for heating and cooling, for appliances, for transportation, and for industrial processes and systems, and instrumentation for other precise control requirements. The company specialized in the applications of the physical sciences, that is, electronics, pneumatics, hydraulics, mechanics, and electromagnetics, to control energy and to enable products to work automatically. It also made a line of clocks and timers for household use, but this represented a very small part of the company's sales. In total, the company manufactured more than 10,000 different products.

The company distributed its industrial products to original equipment manufacturers, contractors, replacement parts wholesalers, governmental agencies, the military, automotive and aircraft manufacturers, shipbuilding yards, public utility service departments, and various other industrial users. The clocks and timers for household use were sold to wholesalers, retailers, and trading stamp companies.

The demand for industrial goods is, of course, derived; the demand depends completely on the demand for the consumer goods produced by the particular industry. For example, there is little need for a new temperature and pressure control system on the production line of a fruit canning factory unless a viable demand exists for the canned fruit.

Manufacturing plants owned and operated by the company included three in Pennsylvania, two in Ohio, four in California, two in Connecticut, one in Tennessee, and one in New Hampshire. In addition, Robertshaw leased and operated two plants in Tennessee and one each in Michigan, Pennsylvania, Georgia, and Virginia. Foreign subsidiary plants were located in Toronto and Oakville, Ontario, Canada; Sydney, Australia; Skelmersdale, England; Reims, France; Amsterdam, The Netherlands; Tokyo, Japan; and Caxias do Sul, Brazil. An affiliate plant was located in Mexico City, Mexico. There were 9,900 employees. Plant size varied from fifty to 1,500 employees. Selling efforts extended to fifty-one nations.

Justifiably proud of its technological expertise and its long tradition of inventions, Robertshaw continued to have a strong commitment to technological advancement. In the latest year inventors in the company were issued eighty-eight patents, compared with sixty-four the previous year and ninety-nine the year before that. The company was consistently among the most prolific firms in the number of patents obtained. Although each manufacturing division conducted some product research and development and was expected to do so, the company operated three facilities devoted exclusively to research and development, one in California and two in Pennsylvania. To permit a more coordinated approach and a cross-fertilization of ideas, the Advanced Technology Forecast Committee was formed in 1974 to monitor advance technological developments that might be utilized in the controls industry and suggest potential new products. This committee consisted of representatives from the research and development, marketing, manufacturing, and patent departments.

In the most recent year the company's sales were $247,145,000, up 27.9 percent from the previous year's $193,280,000. Sales for each of the five most recent years broken down by type of market are presented in Exhibit 1. A five-year summary operating statement of the company is presented as Exhibit 2.

In earlier years Robertshaw Controls Company was organized strictly by product type. There was a manufacturing division for a cluster of related products, and a sales department and an advertising department for the same cluster of products. Manufacturing was still organized by type of product into twelve divisions, but marketing was now organized by type of customer into eight groups. For example, the Industrial Instrument Marketing Group was in Richmond, Virginia, but the products that the customers of this group needed might come from the Grayson Manufacturing Division in Long Beach, California, the Simicon Manu-

EXHIBIT 1 Robertshaw Controls Company Five-Year Sales by Markets

(To nearest million)	Temperature Controls for Homes and Commercial Buildings	Controls for Home Appliances	Industrial Controls and Instrumentation	Transportation Consumer, and Other	Total
Latest year: Volume	$92	$82	$37	$36	$247
Percent of total	37%	33%	15%	15%	100%
Two years ago: Volume	$73	$55	$34	$31	$193
Percent of total	38%	28%	18%	16%	100%
Three years ago: Volume	$64	$60	$34	$32	$190
Percent of total	34%	31%	18%	17%	100%
Four years ago: Volume	$65	$65	$31	$32	$193
Percent of total	34%	34%	16%	16%	100%
Five years ago: Volume	$62	$59	$27	$24	$172
Percent of total	36%	34%	16%	14%	100%

EXHIBIT 2 Robertshaw Controls Company Five-Year Summary of Operations (Amounts in thousands, except per share data), Year Ended December 31

	Latest Year	Two Years Ago	Three Years Ago	Four Years Ago	Five Years Ago
Net sales	$247,145	$193,280	$189,899	$193,335	$172,459
Cost of products sold	194,443	156,701	155,292	150,007	129,217
Equity income (loss)	352	(85)	1,511	2,253	1,245
Other revenue	1,481	871	1,184	1,077	909
Interest expense	1,834	1,963	2,337	1,690	910
Taxes on income	7,607	2,157	1,399	6,780	7,940
Net income	9,382	2,943	5,020	10,438	9,798
Earnings per share of common stock based on average shares outstanding	2.42	.76	1.30	2.70	2.55
Cash dividends per share	.90	.75	.90	.83	.72
Average shares outstanding	3,876,591	3,871,726	3,871,709	3,871,525	3,838,504

256

facturing Division in Holland, Michigan, the Milford Manufacturing Division in Milford, Connecticut, or the Sylphon Manufacturing Division in Knoxville, Tennessee. Without this organizational structure a particular customer or potential customer might be called on by four different Robertshaw sales representatives.

Robertshaw spent $500,000 annually for space purchases for its advertising. Like most other industrial goods firms, the company exhibited a preference for personal selling efforts over advertising. The corporation had used the same advertising agency for ten years and was satisfied with it. Robert W. Pendergast, Robertshaw's corporate director of public relations and advertising, noted that an agency's cooperative attitude was as important as its professional competence.

Perhaps the central difficulty in meeting Robertshaw's advertising needs was that most of the company's products were not highly visible. Most of the time the products were completely hidden and thus unseen by nearly everyone. The company had not engaged in consumer advertising until late in the past year, when it launched a small, limited campaign in selected newspapers and do-it-yourself-type magazines to support its automatic setback thermostat. This was a home control device that had the ability to adjust the temperature at times programmed by the residents.

Some of the advertising effort was decentralized to the eight marketing groups. In addition, each marketing group could retain its own advertising agency. The groups had been using their present agencies for periods of time varying from one to several years. The director of public relations and advertising explained as follows:

> As an arm of marketing, advertising of products and systems now follows the same group approach. Advertising strategies are keyed to portraying Robertshaw as a single source for a variety of controls and systems. Advertising to the chemical process industry, for example, is programmed to present Robertshaw's total instrumentation capability. In the appliance field, advertising backs up the marketing approach wherein appliance makers look to a single Robertshaw representative to supply all their control needs.
>
> Decisions on marketing group advertising objectives, plans, media, and budgets generally are made by the groups themselves. In most cases, however, these plans are formulated only after discussion and consultation with the corporate director of advertising. Budgets are prepared by the groups and submitted to the corporate advertising director for approval. Written permission must be obtained for all additional programs not previously budgeted.

Each marketing group had additional promotional responsibilities, such as participation in appropriate trade shows and exhibitions. The total for all marketing groups combined was usually ten shows-exhibitions per year. Moreover, each marketing group prepared its own product catalog, which required approval from Pendergast.

A sizable amount of the advertising effort was centralized at corporate headquarters. The director of public relations and advertising summarized corporate advertising, media selection, and copy themes in the following manner:

Corporate Advertising

For several years now, Robertshaw's prime corporate objectives have continued to be building a favorable awareness in the financial and investment community. Advertising strategy has centered on creating an understanding among target audiences of our involvement in many and diverse markets. Corporate messages are directed to the decision makers who influence investment decisions, and they also reach individual investors.

Media Choices

To make the most efficient use of our corporate budget, advertising has been concentrated in *The Wall Street Journal*, acknowledged leader in financial circles. Its readership also includes a broad reach among business executives. This provides a "bonus" in awareness among this audience because they are also decision makers in purchasing Robertshaw products as well as potential personal investors. Smaller campaigns are used in *Business Week* to reinforce the message to the general business community, and *Institutional Investor* to reach their audience of major investors.

Copy Themes

Each ad in the campaign spotlights a Robertshaw product and its benefits to the user. Generally the headlines name one or more well-known customers for this Robertshaw control or control system. A closing paragraph points out Robertshaw's diversity, including its international involvement . . . and asks for action by offering more information. Separately and together, these messages convey a picture of leadership in a basic field—controls . . . diversity of markets for a broad base of sales . . . R&D capability . . . proven performance record for blue chip companies. For several years, the ads have also pointed up our ability to perform as the Energy Control Company.

Results

This campaign has fulfilled its objective of contributing to a wider awareness of Robertshaw's total corporate capability. Because the ads talk about specific products, they produce inquiries—particularly on new products and controls that function to provide energy savings.

However, recently the company reexamined its media mix, and it reached a decision to try a different combination of print media. The periodicals chosen had audiences of quite specialized people who were identified with particular types of businesses. The mix consisted of business magazines such as *InTech*, *Appliance*, *Appliance Manufacturer*, *LP Gas*, *Building Supply Home Centers*, *National Home Center News*, and *Hardware Age*. Robertshaw's Consumer Products Marketing Group planned to use the last three named in an attempt to interest retailers and buyers for retail chains who were considered highly relevant to that product line.

The Appliance Controls Marketing Group planned to run the advertisement presented in Exhibit 3 in *Appliance* and *Appliance Manufacturer*. The Consumer Products Control Group planned to run the advertisement presented in Exhibit 4 in *Building Supply Home Centers*, *National Home Center News*, and *Hardware Age*.

Advise Robertshaw Controls Company.

EXHIBIT 3

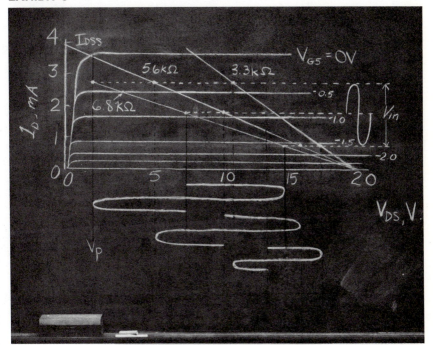

WE SPEAK
THE LANGUAGE.

In fact, at Robertshaw Controls Company, we don't just speak it, we help *invent* it. Just walk down the hallway in any one of our Research and Development departments. You're likely to hear someone say, "{(VDD − V01)/(C × VDD − V01)}." And catch the reply, "Divided by {1 − [(VDD − V01)/(C × VDD − V01)]} × R₂ equals R₁."

Then you might be surprised to learn those are highly imaginative statements — the principles behind many of our recent innovations in electronic oven controls, such as the ERC 4800/5800 for both single and double deluxe ovens. Another innovation is the field-proven HS780 Hot Surface Ignition System.

And all it takes is an inspired connection — mathematics and imaginative insight — to create the invention. In other words, Electronics plus Mind = Innovation.

We've learned that anything is possible with that equation. And we have a history of using it to make amazing things possible in electronic appliance and temperature controls. A history that will continue to become our future.

Call. Find out about another equation we live by at Robertshaw. An equation that can help you fulfill your electronics needs: Talk minus Action = Nothing. In other words, at Robertshaw, we don't just talk, we do.

Robertshaw
CONTROLS COMPANY
Keeping The Spirit Of Invention Alive.
Appliance & Temperature Controls Group
P.O. Box 26544, Richmond, VA 23261, 804-281-0700
The Energy Control Company®

EXHIBIT 4

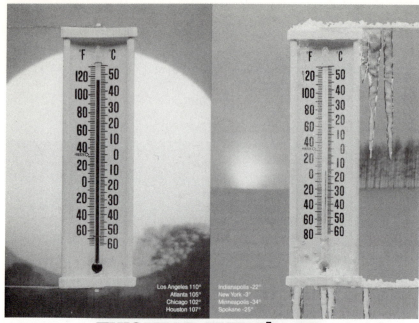

Los Angeles 110°
Atlanta 105°
Chicago 102°
Houston 107°

Indianapolis -22°
New York -3°
Minneapolis -34°
Spokane -25°

THIS YEAR, THERE'LL BE MORE REASONS THAN EVER TO CARRY ROBERTSHAW THERMOSTATS.

When the temperature goes to extremes, the outlook for your thermostat sales turns sunny. And if you're carrying the Robertshaw line, be prepared to set some record highs.

NEW MODELS, SAME HIGH QUALITY.

Robertshaw has rounded out its family of thermostats with more models at more price points to meet every application and customer budget.

So now you can look to one company for high or low-end models—and all points between—with the quality and user-friendly features Robertshaw has built its reputation on. For you: higher profits, *and* more satisfied customers.

We've just introduced two new pre-programmed models—the TX2 and TX10—the ultimates in user-friend-

liness: factory-set heating and cooling temperature settings, easily reprogrammed to suit particular comfort needs.

The T60-1044, pictured, offers advanced features like easy 7-day programmability, 4 program periods per day, temperature override, and vacation hold. It's the best thermostat your customers can buy.

New shape and design create the sleek, contemporary look your customers want.

STRONG DEALER SUPPORT PROGRAM.

New colorful clamshell packaging, P.O.P. displays and a hard-hitting consumer advertising campaign all work hard for you to encourage sales.

So take the ups and downs out of your thermostat profits. Robertshaw selection, quality and features have you covered, all along the line.

Robertshaw
CONTROLS COMPANY
Consumer Products Marketing Group
13625 Neutron Road
Dallas, TX 75244
The Energy Control Company®

See The Complete Line Of Robertshaw Thermostats At Booth #2661 At The Hardware Show in Chicago.

11

Pricing

CROFTON-WAGLEY, INC.

Charles McDowell was worrying about a sales contract that he had counted on signing in a few days but that was now in danger of falling through. He thought, "If only those people in the accounting department and in navigation instrumentation would cooperate sometimes and get a team effort going."

McDowell was a sales representative and contract negotiator in the sales department of Crofton-Wagley, Inc., a large company engaged in the manufacture of electronics, aerospace products, and sophisticated marine equipment. About 80 percent of its sales volume was to the military. Most of the military sales were to the U.S. armed forces, but there was significant business with the military procurement offices of Canada, Australia, and West Germany. Crofton-Wagley's plants were located in California, Texas, and the Middle West, and the company had just opened a small experimental facility in Appalachia following federal government pressure to "spread the jobs around."

Sales volume fluctuated somewhat more from year to year than in most other firms in this type of industry. Sales last year were $499 million, but the year before were $538 million. The ratio of net profit after taxes to sales was a disappointing 2.0 percent in the latest year. Long-term trends are given in Exhibit 1.

EXHIBIT 1 Sales and Profit Trends of Crofton-Wagley, Inc.

Number of Years Ago	Sales	Net Profit After Taxes
1	$499 million	$10,023,000
2	538	12,975,000
3	485	10,045,000
4	456	9,902,000
5	491	10,450,000
6	461	10,076,000
7	485	13,240,000
8	440	13,210,000
9	441	13,230,000

Experienced and age thirty-five, Charles McDowell had been with Crofton-Wagley, Inc. about six years and was with an aerospace company for about seven years before that. He graduated from a well-known university with a BS in a combination engineering-business administration curriculum. In industry he had had experience in product design, product laboratory testing, liaison between various engineering departments and the marketing department, and was currently in sales. He was on a straight salary. McDowell was considered a competent, personable, and loyal employee.

Recently McDowell had been negotiating a sale with Ronninger Corporation for $4 million worth of navigation equipment. He and some others deemed it highly important not just for the large amount of money involved but for the possibility of follow-on orders from Ronninger and also because it would get Crofton-Wagley deeper into civilian markets. The president of the company wanted Crofton-Wagley to be less dependent on military orders.

Crofton-Wagley's pricing had been systematized. This meant that certain procedures adopted a little over a year before had to be followed in determining the asking price. The Crofton-Wagley approach was essentially cost-based pricing. Company practice was to figure the costs involved, then add a small contingency charge (sometimes hidden in slight overestimates of detailed items but sometimes spelled out separately) of about 2 percent of the costs, and then add a markup that averaged 14 percent. Special facilities needed for a specific contract, such as specialized testing equipment or new construction of testing rooms tailor-made for the contract, were charged to the contract and thus became part of the price quoted to the potential customer. The navigation equipment on which McDowell and Ronninger were negotiating required a special testing room that had to be constructed from the ground up. Estimates of cost to construct this room were $135,000, and the special testing equipment would add another $25,000. There seemed to be no significant error in these two estimates that anyone could discover. These two figures were part of the exactly $4 million total figure McDowell was asking the potential customer.

Ronninger had bought similar but technologically less advanced navigation equipment in the past from one of Crofton-Wagley's major competitors, Kingston, Inc. McDowell was able to learn that there had been only one such purchase, but Ronninger Corporation had been happy with the product. This competitor was about the same size as Crofton-Wagley and enjoyed a similar reputation in the industry. However, McDowell and many of his colleagues in the sales areas considered Kingston more aggressive than Crofton-Wagley.

To his great chagrin, McDowell had just learned that Kingston was now trying to obtain the same contract on which he was working. Furthermore, Kingston was quoting a total price of $3,930,000 or $70,000 less than Crofton-Wagley. McDowell had no doubt that this information about the competitor was correct. Said McDowell, "It not only is cheaper than our quotation by one and three-quarters percent but sounds a lot cheaper because it stays below $4 million."

At this point, Charles McDowell approached the senior cost accountant, Louise Bascomb. The cost accounting group had been directed to participate in the paperwork for price quotations in transactions expected to total $2 million or more since the new price setting system had been installed. He attempted to get a special exception to the company's new costing procedure so as to delete from the estimate the $135,000 cost of the construction. Bascomb appeared to want to cooperate but replied in the negative. She called to McDowell's attention that this costing policy was the result of the work of a pricing committee that included the marketing vice-president, the sales manager, two other vice-presidents, and the company president. In vain, McDowell argued that the testing room would still be in place and have some value and usefulness after the sales order had been filled. An immediate appeal to Bascomb's superior, the head of finance and accounting, did not change matters.

Undaunted, McDowell next sought the exclusion of the $25,000 worth of special testing equipment, arguing that this equipment would have a lengthy life and some other potential uses. This line of attack was not successful, however. Next, McDowell began questioning the 2 percent contingency factor, but the reply to that from everyone was a resounding no. It was even added that the company's cost estimating was so imprecise that perhaps the figure of 2 percent should be raised in the future. Finally, McDowell questioned the 14 percent markup but again without positive results.

At this point, these thoughts went through Charles McDowell's mind: "Perhaps Ronninger would pay this price differential just to get what amounts to 'second sourcing' because we all realize that Kingston can give Ronninger just as sophisticated technology as we can. On the other hand, they already know Kingston and Kingston's people quite well. And $70,000 is a lot of money." The term "second sourcing" referred to an idea in which many industrial buyers believed strongly: that is, a company was likely to get into a poor position if over the long run it relied on only one vendor for an important product or category of products. For a very few products that were patentable, there might be only one lawful supplier, of course. For some technical products, however, even when no patent was possible, there might still be only one maker because the demand was so small. Some buyers liked to divide their company's purchases of such an item between two suppliers in an attempt to keep both available. This tactic would insure the buying organization against price exploitation and interruptions resulting from such matters as strikes, fires, and floods.

McDowell then determined again the exact date that the price quotation had to be in the hands of Ronninger Corporation's buyers. He had one week.

Advise Charles McDowell of Crofton-Wagley, Inc.

COLUMBINE DINNER THEATER

The Columbine Dinner Theater was established three years ago in the suburbs of a large city. The founders, Paul Cantwell, Vance Kropatkin, and Luke Archer, now in their late 20s to early 30s, had known each other since college. While there, the first two had majored in drama and the third, in music. All had discovered soon after graduation that few employment opportunities existed in their respective fields and that most relevant jobs available were short-term. Jobs for drama majors were usually for a specific theatrical production and competition for such jobs was extraordinarily vigorous. Primarily because of his long-term view of the labor market, Archer had returned to a university and received a graduate degree in theater arts.

After considerable discussion the three men decided to work together to establish something that would give them economic stability yet professional and personal satisfaction. To begin their own dinner theater business, the three men pooled their savings and borrowed from friends and all of their parents. The loans were all four-year notes secured by the assets of the new company.

Dinner theater is popular in most of the United States and Canada, but no data exist on its real size or growth rate. The industry probably grosses four to five times as much as Broadway. However, it tends to be less important and successful around large cities than around medium-size and medium-large cities. For example, although there were some dinner theaters in those metropolitan areas, the industry had not prospered around New York, Chicago, Los Angeles, Philadelphia, Toronto, and Montreal.

A suitable location was immediately a problem, because they needed a large amount of space for dining, foyer, coat check room, kitchen, restrooms, stage, storage areas for stage sets and costumes, dressing rooms, and parking, and yet they could not pay much. After studying many possibilities they decided to take most of the second floor of a small shopping center. The real estate developer had built the second floor speculatively and had been keenly disappointed when he could not find tenants who wanted more than the first floor space. Luckily most of the second floor had been left without partitions. One partition had to be knocked down and, of course, several partitions built as the theater firm laid out the space for its needs. The dining room floor was laid out on two levels, the rear one about fifteen inches higher than the front one in order to enhance viewing the show. The new company spent $95,000 on the building modifications, of which the owners considered about $87,000 unrecoverable in the event of a change of location. They were able, with the owner's permission, to create a separate outside main entrance for the theater, an emergency exit, and a freight entrance.

The shopping center, known as Colonial Plaza, was rather utilitarian in appearance and tenancy. The occupants included such firms as a hardware store, a drug store, a branch bank, and several professional offices. There were no department, apparel, shoe, or jewelry stores, or restaurants. The shopping center was located on a street in a mixed-use area, but the area was dominated by warehouses and light industry. Crime was minimal and really not a problem. The street and neighborhood were well lighted and kept quite clean.

The new company, temporarily calling itself CKA, took out a four-year lease on the space. The agreement specified a four-year extension at a 32 percent increase in rent if the tenants wanted to exercise the option.

The three owners conferred extensively with each other but specialized in their duties. Cantwell took over business affairs, Archer theatrical production and direction, and Kropatkin the food and beverage service. They talked about this division of labor and decided that it was satisfactory to all three. Although Archer had the most creative work, each man continued to find his type of work satisfying. Cantwell and Kropatkin were able to make some input to the basic theatrical decisions.

The new theater specialized in low budget comedy drama for the first year and began making a modest profit after the first few months. The work was hard and time consuming, but the three owners liked it. Archer gave serious thought during the first year to the potential for musical comedy, which was more challenging to do and more expensive. Moreover, his first marriage had failed. He quickly remarried, this time to a woman who had considerable dramatic and musical talent and interest in theater. Archer's wife Lulubelle had starred in several college shows and community events but had never earned a living as a performer. Archer pressed his co-owners to switch to musical comedy and to start by staging a musical comedy starring Lulubelle. The three owners agreed to switch to musical comedy at the end of the first year and to give Lulubelle a chance.

Musical comedy was the most common form of theater in the United States because it was relatively low cost and appealed to large numbers of people who wanted merely to be entertained, not mentally stimulated. Although comedic drama was popular, the addition of music seemed to most people to add greatly to the fun and made the outing more spirited.

At Archer's suggestion, Lulubelle adopted the stage name of Belle Archer. Both thought her real given name not sophisticated enough. The owners judged the performance satisfactory and attendance normal, and thus assigned her or earmarked for her starring roles in several more productions.

There were already two competitors in the trade territory, both of which were similar to Columbine in facilities, operations, and prices. Called the Eden and the Copacabana, these dinner theaters were two years older than Columbine. Although not spectacular successes, they appeared to be successful and viable. Cantwell, Kropatkin, and Archer were slightly acquainted with the owner-managers of these companies and had attended a few shows there. They went to such events because they enjoyed the performing arts and because they needed to observe the competition from time to time. These owners had also visited Columbine. Another dinner theater existed earlier in this community but, after several years of struggling, failed about the time that the Eden and the Copacabana started.

There was a standard format for dinner theaters. During the theatrical presentation the members of the audience sat at tables where they had just completed their meals. Shows were often divided into two acts, with one intermission, even if the playwright had specified three acts. If the play was not skillfully re-divided, this practice often led to awkward breaks in the dramatic action. Occasionally a production was condensed, either to make for a shorter play or to remove a non-essential but very difficult song, reprise of a song, or dance. Frequently the sets and stage properties were simplified, but often this was artistically justified. Typically the members of the audience arrived early enough to have leisurely drinks, went through a buffet line for dinner, and then watched the show.

The Columbine opened for drinks at 6 P.M., offered the buffet at 7, and began the play at 8:30. The owners insisted on a punctual start to the show. The buffet was taken down at 8:15. There was one intermission, which was planned to be fifteen minutes but occasionally had to be a little longer if heavy or complicated stage props had to be moved. The play ended between 10:45 and 11:15 P.M..

As was universal in the industry, the admission price covered both the dinner and the play, but the beverages were separately priced by the serving. At Columbine the price of admission varied slightly because of different costs of the theatrical productions. For example, recently for one show the admission price was $36.50, but for the previous show it was $38.50. Most of the food was rather plain and simple but abundant. One meat and one seafood were always offered plus vegetables, salads, several types of breads, and desserts. The Columbine put great emphasis on its ice cream and sherbet desserts, which were attractive and good. Unlike those served in the competitive theaters, the vegetables were fresh and not overcooked or heavily sauced. Costs of food did not vary from one play to another. An employee served the meat and seafood, but customers served themselves the other foods. One could go through the line as many times as one desired.

The Columbine had a seating capacity of 210. The local fire safety code did not permit more in this amount of space. The facilities were simple and inexpensive looking if one observed them closely, but there was a pleasant use of color. The dim light that prevailed during most of the evening obscured the lack of luxury.

Performances were each night Wednesday through Sunday. The theater was dark for five weeks from August 1 until early September. The cast for the first autumn show reported for work on September 1 and was in rehearsal for the several days preceding the usual opening around September 5. The year consisted of forty-seven weeks of five performances for a total of 235 performances.

There were six productions during each year, and each was scheduled to run the same number of days. The Columbine had not repeated any play thus far and preferred not to do so. In the most recent year the productions and their admission prices were the following: *Mame* $40.00; *Gentlemen Prefer Blondes* $37.50; *Gigi* $37.00; *Funny Girl* $36.50; *Annie Get Your Gun* $38.50; and *Me and My Girl* $36.50.

Except for the most important lead roles, usually two per play, the actors/singers/dancers were not professionals, and most doubled as servers, which was common in the industry. Nearly all were young and some would go on to have professional theatrical careers. Even the professionals were actually better considered semi-professionals.

The Columbine operated its first year at 67 percent of capacity. The figures for the second year and this latest year were 69 percent and

70 percent respectively. During the first year the mean average night consisted of the following: $423 in drinks and $4935 in admission fees. The corresponding figures for the second year were $435 in drinks and $5147 in admission fees and for the third year $478 and $5439. Sales for the first year were $1,259,131. (See Exhibit 1). There was a 15 percent reduction in admission price for children under 12, but there was hardly ever a child in the audience. Moreover, there was hardly ever a teenager in the audience. Parking was plentiful and free.

The rule of thumb in the dinner theater industry was that the number of drinks sold would be about 2.5 times the number of adult customers, or about 20 percent of all sales revenue. The mean average price of beverages (mixed drinks plus beer and glasses of wine) at Columbine was $3.05 in the most recently completed year.

The three owners drew living allowances throughout the year from the sales revenue. They had agreed that each could draw $48,000 to live on the first year, but they increased this figure to $60,000 for the second and third years. These living allowances completely wiped out the company's profits the first two years. The third year there was a small undistributed profit (i.e., after the living allowances).

Cantwell, Kropatkin, and Archer wanted to try to take an objective look at their business. They were afraid that they had reached an operating plateau almost from the beginning, and that they were at their potential. They were enjoying their work and modest rewards, but they wondered if there was any growth possible for them. They were also aware that most of their friends who lent them money would expect repayment in a timely manner.

Several ideas were discussed by the three men, including raising prices in order to raise prestige and bundling tickets with a discount for buying season admission. The owners had tried to observe and had asked questions of a sizeable number of guests about frequency of coming to the Columbine. It appeared to them that very few came more than twice a year. Another idea was to start offering more difficult shows, including

EXHIBIT 1 Selected Operating Data for Columbine Dinner Theatre

	Latest Year	Two Years Ago	Three Years Ago
Percent of capacity	70	69	67
Mean admission price	$37.67	$35.50	$35.00
Mean admission fees per night	$5439	$5147	$4935
Mean drink revenue per night	$478	$435	$423

some that were musical comedy but with some serious material, such as *West Side Story, South Pacific,* or *Carousel.* Some such shows would cost more to produce than what they did now but not all. Another idea was to seek out non-profit organizations and charities that needed to raise money, then cooperate with them to give them a percentage of the admission price if they held a theater party fund-raising affair at Columbine.

Advise the Columbine Dinner Theater.

DENVER ART MUSEUM

The Denver Art Museum, the major visual arts institution for the Rocky Mountain Region, was founded as an artists' club in 1893. It had no collection and no permanent building. By 1931 it had become the official art institution for Denver, but until 1971 the collection was divided among various locations, including an old mansion and a remodeled automobile showroom.

In 1971 the Denver Art Museum's spectacular six-story building was opened. The striking silver-gray structure, designed by Gio Ponti of Milan and James Sudler of Denver, is located near downtown in the city's Civic Center. The opening of that new building marked a significant boost to the visual arts of the area. According to Thomas Maytham, director of the museum from 1974 to 1983, "In the new building we had a doubled budget, a new board of trustees, quadrupled attendance, and a challenging question: How can we best use this building?"

The answer continued to change, but by most measures the museum had been very successful. The permanent collection numbered 50,000 objects in 1990. The major areas in the collection were Western art, European art, New World art (including Pre-Columbian art), Asian art, native arts (including American Indian art), and contemporary art. The largest single category in the museum's collection was American Indian art, which included more than 20,000 objects and was among the finest assemblages of its type in the world. It had been described as the finest collection of American Indian works in any art museum.

About fourteen major special circulating exhibitions were also shown at the museum each year. These were usually borrowed from other museums or from private collections. The exhibitions ranged in scope from the well-known Armand Hammer collection of European and Ameri-

This case was prepared by Dr. Patricia Stocker, assistant dean, College of Business and Management, University of Maryland, based in part on information provided by Lora L. Witt, director of public relations for the Denver Art Museum.

EXHIBIT 1 Attendance at Selected Temporary Exhibitions (six-week showings)

Armand Hammer Collection	152,106
Masterpieces of French Art	56,836
The Art of the Muppets	115,531
Heritage of American Art	22,531
Frederick Remington: The Late Years	35,000
Silver in American Life	30,000
American Photographers and National Parks	31,045
Museum of Modern Art Collection	40,924
Thyssen-Bornemiza Collection	54,644

can masterpieces and the Thyssen-Bornemiza Collection to "Art of the Muppets" and "Secret Splendors of the Chinese Court," a costume collection. (See Exhibit 1). Among recent exhibitions were "The Bostonians: Painters of an Elegant Age," "Hollywood: Legend and Reality," "Art in New Mexico: Paths to Taos and Sante Fe," and "American Indian Printmaking Today."

The museum also had a number of educational programs, including lectures, tours, films, seminars, and other performing arts. These programs were generally planned around the circulating exhibitions or the museum's permanent collection and were designed to increase the visitors' appreciation of the visual arts. One example is the "Top of the Week" program featuring jazz groups playing in the museum's restaurant area. The program was instituted in 1984, and for eleven consecutive Wednesday nights in 1985, it attracted a total of 12,648 visitors.

Background Information

Although the Denver Art Museum was not strictly a government agency, its assets were held by a Colorado nonprofit educational corporation for the benefit of the public. It served as the official arts agency of the city and county of Denver. (The city and the county are one entity). The museum was managed by an elected, unpaid board of trustees including civic leaders in the community, lawyers, advertising agency executives, professional artists, business managers, and others.

Prior to the imposition of a front-door admission fee to the museum in 1982, attendance at the museum averaged between 500,000 and 600,000 a year (See Exhibit 2), which put it ahead of the Boston, Houston, and Philadelphia art museums. Perhaps more significantly, prior to the admission fee, the museum boasted the highest attendance on a per capita basis of any major art museum in the country. Following the imposition of the front-door fee, attendance dropped dramatically.

EXHIBIT 2 Total Yearly Denver Art Museum Attendance

1972	674,299
1973	527,311
1974	555,058
1975	524,193
1976	527,859
1977	530,000
1978	608,178[a]
1979	466,361
1980	598,648
1981	467,916
1982	291,619[b]
1983	284,034
1984	293,698
1985	334,204
1986	343,614
1987	360,560
1988	288,918

[a] The popular Armand Hammer Collection was included this year.
[b] This was the first year the museum charged an admission fee.

Of the visitors to the Denver Art Museum, about 25 percent came from out of state, another 45 percent came from Colorado but outside of Denver, and the remaining 30 percent from the city and county of Denver. Of those from Colorado but not from Denver, the vast majority were from suburban communities. About 70 percent of museum visitors could be identified as from either Denver or nearby suburban areas. Included in these attendance figures were visits from students as part of the gallery tours led by museum guides. The largest community in the Rocky Mountain region, Denver itself had a population of 500,000, but the population of the metropolitan area was 1,650,000. In the mid- to late-1980s, the population of the area declined slightly as a result of the bleak economy of the city and region.

The Denver Art Museum had been free to the public until January 1, 1982. However, admission fees had been charged for major circulating exhibitions. At that time, the museum had collected an average of $160,000 per year in fees for these special exhibitions.

As of 1990 there were about 19,000 museum members, the majority of these being family memberships at $35 per family per year. The greatest impetus to membership was the free admission granted to members. Among other membership benefits were 10 percent discounts at the museum gift shop, a monthly newsletters about museum activities, and previews of major traveling exhibitions. At each preview showing, light refreshments were served free of charge, and there was a cash bar.

The museum had been more marketing-oriented than most other art museums, with marketing considerations in terms of exhibitions, educational programs, fund raising, and acquisitions of art objects for the permanent collection. The museum's trustees had commissioned a marketing plan in 1983 that focused on the promotional needs of the museum. The museum had traditionally been supported financially by local, state, and federal allocations; gifts from private foundations; and museum memberships. The trend had been toward having a greater percentage of the budget each year raised from private sources. To succeed in this change, the museum had instituted a number of innovative funding ideas, such as the successful museum associates program, for which membership was limited to those individuals who contributed at least $1,500 each year in unrestricted funds for museum support. This was in contrast to restricted funds contributed by individuals and others for specific purposes, such as the support of special exhibitions or the purchase of a specific piece of art for the museum's permanent collection. The museum had also instituted creative benefit events to raise extra dollars. Among the most creative of these events was the annual "Collectors' Choice" benefit at which those attending an expensive benefit party would vote on the particular acquisitions to be purchased by the proceeds of that event. The alternative selections were made by the museum's curators. More than $1.5 million had been raised by this event over the eleven-year period it had been held.

In its solicitation of funds from private foundations, companies, and individuals for restricted uses, the museum had been successful by demonstrating its relationship to the quality of life in Denver and including recognition of the donors, such as associating a special exhibition with the sponsoring organization in the publicity about that exhibition.

The museum also had previously received substantial support from the federal government. In 1984 the museum received about $221,000 from federal sources, including the National Endowment for the Arts, the National Endowment for the Humanities, the Institute for Museum Services, and the National Museum Act of the Smithsonian Institution. Much of this support had come as matching grants. Matching grants generally required the museum to raise $1 for each $1 of the grant. Walter Rosenberry, former chairperson of the museum's board of trustees, explained that these challenge grants had a "tremendously stimulating effect" on private contributions. Federal support for the museum continued to decline through the 1980s as part of the national reduction in support of such activities.

The Funding Crunch

A combination of government funding cuts, inflation, and potential changes in income tax deductions for private contributions forced changes in the museum's funding picture in the 1980s. The museum generated over $1.92 million of its operating budget of $4.3 million in 1984 from grants, gifts, and memberships. The city provided $1.25 million in support. In total, these sources accounted for nearly 75 percent of the museum's budget. The remaining income was generated by front door admission fees ($234,634), interest income from the endowment, educational programs, gift shop income, and volunteer benefits. Unfortunately, these sources declined dramatically, and $50,000 was taken from the museum's endowment in 1984 to meet expenses. It was clear that the gap between revenue and expenses was a continuing problem for the museum.

In 1988 the city of Denver issued $8 million in revenue bonds for the improvement and enlargement of the Denver Art Museum. At the same time, Denver's Scientific and Cultural Facilities District was created by a citizen vote. Revenues from the one-tenth of one percent increase in sales tax in the six-county District were to be used to stabilize and enhance the operations of a broad range of cultural institutions. Under the distribution formula contained in the District plan, the museum was to receive over $2 million during the first years of the District's existence. The importance of this revenue stream cannot be overstated after lean years resulting from a depressed local economy, decreased governmental funding, and rising costs of operation. (At least one major arts institution in Denver had declared bankruptcy in the mid-1980s).

The Second Century Endowment campaign initiated by the museum in 1987 secured pledges which, added to the museum's existing endowment, brought the total endowment to $12 million. Eventually, revenues from the endowment were expected to provide a good measure of stability to the museum's overall financial position.

In the fall of 1989, the museum's Board of Trustees adopted a Capital Improvement Master Plan with two major components: construction of an addition and renovation of the permanent galleries and other public spaces in the museum building. This capital expansion was possible because of the additional dollars from the Scientific and Cultural Facilities District funds.

In 1989 the museum generated $2.4 million of its $7.5 million budget from grants, gifts, and memberships, not including money donated to the endowment. As noted above, the city provided over $1 million, and the new District added another $1.1 million. Other government grants made up $109,000 of the budget. The remaining income continued to be generated by front-door admission fees ($273,552), educational programs, gift shop income, volunteer benefits, and a variety of other sources.

Bridging the Gap

Over the past several years, museum employees had responded to the cuts from funding sources by increasing their solicitations of individuals, corporate, and foundation gifts. They also cut back on the number of traveling exhibitions, putting more emphasis on the museum's own permanent collection. Galleries were temporarily closed on a rotating basis to reduce security expenses.

The museum's retail gift shop was expanded to increase sales, and a small gallery was closed to accommodate this expansion. The museum's management also worked toward establishing a substantial endowment through foundation and individual gifts. Because of the pressure of generating operating expenses and the depletion of the endowment to meet current operating expenses, this effort was largely unsuccessful until the 1987 initiative. Many trustees and staff had felt that the lack of substantial endowment limited the museum's flexibility in meeting unpredictable contingencies.

However, the most noticeable action taken by the museum over the past few years was the institution of an admission fee in January 1982. For about a decade prior to that date, the museum had vigorously opposed the charge as a way to avoid decreasing city and state aid to the museum.

Museum officials had debated not only the imposition of a fee but also what form of admission charge would be most effective in terms of generating the greatest revenue with the smallest drop in attendance. Thomas Maytham, then the director of the museum, suggested as an alternative to a mandatory entrance fee a "recommended contribution" along with a sign saying "Pay what you wish but you must pay something." This flexible type of admission fee was pioneered by New York's Metropolitan Museum of Art, where it had been used with success since 1971. The Metropolitan had signs suggesting certain donations. Several months after the flexible fee was introduced by the Metropolitan Museum, the Art Institute of Chicago adopted the system, which it continues to use.

The Denver Art Museum trustees decided to adopt this "recommended" admission fee. They felt that such a fee would have the smallest impact on attendance. Maytham explained that "while we regret that we must institute the fee, we hope the flexible system will encourage people to come to the museum regardless of their financial means."

"Our two major goals connected with the inauguration of the fee are an increase in critically needed revenue and retention of our healthy attendance goals," he continued. Recommended contributions at the Denver Art Museum started at $2 for adults and $1 for senior citizens and students. Museum members and children under 12 were admitted free. There were no separate charges for special traveling exhibitions, which had previously brought in about $160,000 each year. On Labor Day 1983, the recommended fees increased to $2.50 for adults and in mid-1985 the museum dropped the optional nature of the fee, instituting a standard, required admission fee.

Costs of implementing the fee collection policy were $60,000, which included such items as cash registers and turnstiles. The museum had expected to generate a large increase in memberships following the institution of the admission fee, and such an increase did occur. When the admission fee was instituted in 1982, membership was at 15,000. By mid-1985 membership was 18,500, and museum officials reported 19,500 members in 1990.

The Denver Art Museum admission fee decision relied heavily on the experience at the Metropolitan Museum and Chicago's Art Institute, yet the difference in the Denver Museum and its audience apparently made the flexible fee less successful. Attendance dropped dramatically, by about 40 percent, in the first year after the admission fee was begun. This was alarming to museum officials, who had expected the flexible fee to have less impact on attendance. "With a fixed fee, we'd expected a drop in attendance of 20 to 30 percent at first," a museum official explained, "with rebuilding after that." Unfortunately, even the flexible fee produced a much greater drop in attendance. The drop was of particular concern in terms of the museum's efforts to attract lower-income visitors. It saw its mission as education, and museum officials worried that attendance might become restricted to middle and upper economic classes.

The museum had tried discounting the fixed admission fee heavily through the use of coupons and free days. In addition, it had used more aggressive promotion of the museum's collections and other activities. However, the fee failed to meet its objectives, which were to enhance income significantly for the museum and maintain high attendance figures.

By 1990, then, the Denver Art Museum had finally established a significant source of funding through the Cultural Facilities District, which promised that the building needs of the museum would be met, and had made significant progress toward funding a substantial endowment to meet fluctuating financial needs of the museum. Lewis Inman Sharp, who became museum director in 1989, noted that "firm financial foundation has been set by the trustees, voters of the Scientific and Cultural Facilities District, and innumerable contributors to the Second Century Endowment Fund." However, attendance still was below the desired level both in terms of the educational nature of the institution and in terms of the revenues such admission fees would be expected to generate. In addition, rapidly escalating costs of exhibitions and art work for the permanent collection promised to continue the funding crunch for the museum.

Advise the Denver Art Museum.

WOMEN'S EXERCISE AND FITNESS CENTERS, INC.

Women's Exercise and Fitness Centers was a local chain with nine locations in a large northeastern metropolitan area. Eight of the locations were spaced around the circular Interstate by-pass highway that ran through the suburbs, and the original location was in the heart of downtown. The downtown location was oversubscribed by working women and had a waiting list. The four southside suburban locations were all in relatively affluent communities and had a profitable volume of memberships. The four locations in the northern suburbs were all relatively new and not yet heavily utilized. The company was owned and operated by Anne Martin, a former dancer in her late fifties.

Clients would visit the facilities at any hour between 10 A.M. and 9 P.M. Monday through Friday, and from 10 A.M. to 5 P.M. on Saturday. All locations were open Saturday and closed Sunday, despite the fact that two locations were in suburbs with 15 to 20 percent Jewish population and had some Jewish members. Visits from 10 to 11:30 A.M. were almost entirely from retirees and stay-at-home mothers of nursery school children. School teachers most often came between 3:30 and 5:00 and nurses between 1:30 and 4. Other working women clogged the facilities from 5:30 to 9:00 P.M., the period of greatest use. A minimum of three visits a week, of at least thirty minutes each, was recommended to clients. Dance classes lasted fifteen minutes and were held on the hour. Each woman also had a custom-designed program of weight lifting for at least fifteen minutes.

When founded in 1955, Martin's centers had originally been called "Women's Figure Salons," and until 1979 the emphasis had been on increasing the client's physical attractiveness. "Counselors," usually college students who were dance or physical education majors, were employed at minimum wage. They also received free unlimited use of the facilities and every effort was made to adapt to their school schedules in assigning shifts. The counselors weighed and measured the clients on every fifth visit, exhorted, scolded, and praised them, and adjusted their exercise programs individually. On slow days a counselor would work out with each client.

Many members seemed to enjoy the attention of the counselors, and Martin was careful to select for these jobs only personable young women who related well to others. She also expected the counselors to set an example for clients in maintaining proper weight and a fit appearance. Counselors were required to dress in black leotards and tights and to wear name tags so that they could be readily identified by clients needing assistance on the exercise floor. A ratio of one counselor to five

This case was prepared by Joanne G. Greer, Ph.D., of Loyola College, Baltimore.

clients was maintained. Counselors were rotated from facility to facility every three months, and branch managers were rotated once a year, to prevent any one location from developing an esoteric style of dealing with clients. Martin also made unannounced visits to the nine facilities.

The salons, or centers, were located in shopping plazas with ample free parkings, on or near major traffic arteries. To economize on rent, the suburban locations were in smaller shopping plazas, and often in the least convenient parts of those plazas. Only the downtown location, which catered exclusively to employed women, had showers and lockers. Each of the locations had a changing room with curtained booths and several rest rooms, open hanging space for street clothing, and a secure place for purses. Each facility had several tiny sales offices, an attractive lobby, a private area for counselors, and a large, carpeted and mirrored exercise room. Various kinds of exercise equipment lined the four walls, and the center of the room was kept clear for group activities and for exercise that did not employ equipment. Decor was "feminine," using lots of the color pink and flowers.

For many years Martin's business had grown steadily. This appeared to be the result of a number of factors: (1) Her prices were thought to be more reasonable and her ambience less intimidating when compared with her chief downtown competitor, high-fashion Elizabeth Arden, Inc.; (2) she offered considerable locational convenience, by plowing much of her profit back into additional locations; (3) she trained and encouraged counselors to be friendly and supportive, especially to women who seemed lonely or were very overweight; (4) she used a complicated structure of special rates, discounts, and coupons, combined with effective personal selling, to recruit new members. For example, every November she offered a "Get Ready for the Holidays" promotion, allowing those who signed up for a membership beginning January 1 to start using the facility the day they signed the contract at no extra charge. Counselors were required to learn her personal selling techniques, and those who could not bring in new business were terminated. Counselors who were especially successful were promoted through a series of increasingly impressive managerial titles, and received bonuses and modest pay increases.

Martin utilized only two kinds of advertising, television spots and mail coupons. Except for a telephone number, the television spots were noninformative, utilizing vague statements, such as "Become the woman you've always wanted to be," set to music and featuring shapely young women. They were, however, of professional quality, done by a good local advertising agency. Martin supplied the wording for these advertisements. The coupons offered two free "get acquainted" visits. Martin never gave price information in her advertising or over the telephone.

When a prospective client telephoned to inquire or to arrange for the free visits, counselors made every effort to be both charming and supportive. A specific appointment was made, as soon as possible, and the prospect's telephone number and address were noted for follow-up if she did not come. Prospects were scheduled to visit at slow times, so that the counselors could devote at least forty-five minutes to each one. The prospect was weighed, measured, and escorted to the changing room, to the accompaniment of bright, friendly chatter and much genuinely sound and useful information on diet and exercise. About half an hour was spent in one-on-one exercise instruction, with the counselor taking care to select routines hard enough to be challenging but easy enough for the prospect to complete without aching the next day. Martin devoted considerable effort to teaching counselors how to visually assess a woman's current fitness level and put together a suitable routine from memory, while continuing to entertain the prospect with friendly conversation. Some time was also spent in explaining the equipment and in commenting on the exercise being performed by advanced clients. Finally, the prospect was taken to one of the small private offices to discuss enrollment.

A variety of plans were offered, for three months, six months, one year, two years, and six years. The prospect was told primarily that these plans all permitted unlimited use at any time of day, unlike those of competitors. Martin had never actually checked this out, but she had the impression that her competitors offered time-limited plans with scheduled "classes." Martin preferred that the prospect buy the six-year plan, priced at $60 a month for the first year plus $50 a year renewal thereafter, because it was almost all paid during the first year and few clients used it more than two years. For those who did use it six years, the per month rate figured out to only about $13.00. The per month rates for the three-month and six-month plans were set much higher, at $35 and $30 a month, respectively. Most clients on these two plans used all the time for which they contracted.

If the prospect signed the contract on the first visit, she received a flat 10 percent discount. Twice when Martin needed working capital, she offered by mail an additional 20 percent discount to clients who paid their entire enrollment obligation within ten days. The installment contracts were held by Martin Associates, a small finance company she also owned. Every effort was made to obtain a signed contract on the first visit without applying pressure or deviating from a friendly, concerned stance. Few women who signed a contract later took advantage of the three-day cancellation feature which was required by law. Aware that the decision to enroll was difficult for many reasons, the counselors encouraged prospects to revisit the next day. For the first five visits following enrollment, a counselor stayed with the woman constantly, instructing and encouraging her. For each enrollment they sold, counselors received a commission of 5 percent of the sale.

In the early 1980s, Martin suddenly realized that the competition had become much stiffer. Within two years, three additional competitors, Spa Lady, Swim and Exercise, Inc., and Club Nautilus, had staged grand openings. Of these only Spa Lady advertised prices in dollar figures per month or year. Spa Lady's advertised price for a three-month contract was approximately half of Martin's. Spa Lady also offered diet advice. Martin was aware of the value of this service but was concerned about legal liability issues. She always advised clients to obtain reducing diets from their physicians. Swim and Exercise, Inc. was offering whirlpool, sauna, and swimming pool facilities, none of which was feasible in the spaces currently under long-term lease by Martin. Club Nautilus was coed and emphasized muscle building with the use of complicated machinery. Martin wondered if her clients would have any interest in joining Club Nautilus. She suspected they would not and that they enjoyed the feminine "women only" privacy of her centers and the companionableness of her all-female staff. Many of her clients were over age thirty, and she had attracted many retirees at one of her locations that was close to a suburban retirement community. Some who were exercising under doctor's orders deducted their membership fees on their income tax returns as a medical expense.

To increase volume without overloading facilities, Martin was considering offering a special rate to women over fifty, for long-term enrollments of two to five years good only on weekdays from 11:30 A.M. to 2:30 P.M., the slowest time of the day. Recently she had also expanded the poorly attended noon dance class to a one-hour aerobics class. Two month's attendance at the aerobics class was offered to nonmembers for a flat $39. The only promotion was on 8-1/2 by 11-inch offset-printed flyers posted on location doors. Response was low, and persons buying the package were in poor shape physically and could not handle a full hour of such strenuous exercise as aerobics. The program was quickly redesigned to include a lot of stretching and bending to slow ballet music. The women enjoyed it and several inquired about full membership. The most enthusiasm, however, came from women who were already members and who enjoyed the challenge of the hour-long class in place of the usual fifteen minutes.

Until now, all Anne Martin's clients had to select one branch and use it only. However, she had just decided that she would offer for an additional $20 fee on anyone's contract the right to use all the nine locations. However, Martin did not feel completely at ease with her decision and wondered what use would be made of this offer and what its effects would be on operations.

Swim and Exercise, Inc., had just recently received some unfavorable publicity. Seventy members at one of the three locations had signed a letter to Maria Panos, the consumer advocate reporter on a local evening television news show. This letter stated that the whirlpool and swimming pool had fungus and mold in and around them and that often no staff person showed up to lead the scheduled exercise classes. The owners refused to be interviewed, but Panos succeeded in interviewing a staff member. He remarked spontaneously that he certainly would not pay $800 per year for such services. Panos asked, "But isn't it true that some of the memberships are as much as $1,200 a year?"

Around the nation there had been several bankruptcies of spas and some fraudulent operators of such businesses. To combat fly-by-night operators of spas and exercise salons, local government jurisdictions in Martin's trade area had just put in a requirement that each branch of such a business had to post a small bond. Because she had nine branches, the total bond would be quite substantial. Martin and all her competitors would now have a higher cost of doing business.

Advise Anne Martin.

12

International Marketing

DENTSU ADVERTISING

The Japanese advertising agency Dentsu was one of the most admired of Japanese companies among North American and European business-people. However, its background and manner of operation were not understood well. Even more important, it was not appreciated that Dentsu had some problems and underexploited opportunities.

Dentsu was the largest advertising agency in the world in 1985 if measured in billings to clients, the prevailing way in which business-people and journalists judged the size of an advertising agency. In some people's minds, this corresponded to sales. However, it was really the costs of space and time in the media that the agency bought on behalf of clients whose advertising messages it prepared. In the latest fiscal year, that figure at Dentsu was the equivalent of U.S. $3.5 billion.

An alternative, preferable, and growing way of judging size of advertising agencies was to look at their gross income, that is, revenue (See Exhibit 1.) The Japanese firm's gross income in 1985 placed it just behind Young & Rubicam and Ogilvy Group. Ted Bates & Company, a U.S. agency, was only slightly behind Dentsu and had risen from fifth place in 1980. For the period 1973–1983 the Japanese agency had been first in both billings and gross income, but its share in the billings of the

EXHIBIT 1 World's Largest Advertising Agencies in 1985

Rank	Agency	Home Country	Gross income (in millions)	Billings (in billions)
1.	Young & Rubicam	U.S.	$536.0	$3.58
2.	Ogilvy Group	U.S.	481.1	3.32
3.	Dentsu Inc.	Japan	473.1	3.62
4.	Ted Bates Worldwide	U.S.	466.0	3.11
5.	J. Walter Thompson Co.	U.S.	450.9	3.01
6.	Saatchi & Saatchi Compton Worldwide	Great Britain	440.9	3.03
7.	BBDO International	U.S.	377.0	2.52
8.	McCann-Erickson Worldwide	U.S.	345.1	2.30
9.	D'Arcy Masius Benton & Bowles	U.S.	319.5	2.18
10.	Foote, Cone & Belding	U.S.	284.5	1.90
11.	Leo Burnett Company	U.S.	269.4	1.87
12.	Grey Advertising	U.S.	259.3	1.73
13.	Doyle Dane Bernbach Group	U.S.	231.8	1.67
14.	Hakuhodo International	Japan	198.9	1.53
15.	SSC&B; Lintas Worldwide	U.S.	190.9	1.30
16.	Bozell, Jacobs, Kenyon & Eckhardt	U.S.	173.7	1.22
17.	Marschalk Campbell-Ewald	U.S.	150.1	1.00
18.	Eurocom Group	Several West European nations	129.1	.87
19.	Needham Harper Worldwide	U.S.	127.1	.85
20.	Dancer Fitzgerald Sample	U.S.	121.5	.88

world's ten largest agencies had fallen for six consecutive years. Dentsu was eager to regain first place, lock it in permanently, and improve its financial showing. Dentsu enjoyed its high rank because of domestic dominance. It had rather little foreign business.

There was, however, something of an anomaly in the economic statistics. McCann-Erickson, founded in 1912 and eighth in both gross income and billings, was the largest of three large advertising agencies jointly owned by The Interpublic Group of Companies, Inc., a U.S. holding company. The other two were SSC&B:Lintas, which was fifteenth in both gross income and billings, and Marschalk Campbell-Ewald, which was seventeenth in both gross income and billings. McCann-Erickson alone operated 113 agencies in sixty countries and received 65 percent of its gross income abroad. For several reasons, including tradition, the preservation of corporate cultures, wariness about bigness, and a respect for internal competition, each of the three operated in a quasi-independent manner. If their data had been added together, Interpublic Group would have been the largest in the world in 1985, with $686 million in gross income and $4.6 billion in billings.

Before the eleven-year period of Dentsu supremacy, the largest agency in the world was J. Walter Thompson Co. Young & Rubicam, J. Walter Thompson, and Ted Bates were old, respected U.S. organizations established in 1923, 1864, and 1940 respectively. Typically, Young & Rubicam made about 40 percent of its gross income abroad; and J. Walter Thompson, about 57 percent. The latter was something of a pioneer and in many nations had been the first American advertising agency to go into business.

The advertising industry was going through a pronounced merger trend, but two 1986 transactions in particular were of great significance. First, BBDO, Doyle Dane Bernbach Group, and Needham Harper Worldwide agreed to merge. Their combined 1985 gross income would have been $735.9 million and their billings $5.037 billion. The agreement provided that the new holding company would run two separate and independent international networks of offices and a third subsidiary composed of all the specialty and regional firms of the three. The name of the holding company had not been decided. Second, Saatchi & Saatchi Compton, established in 1970, purchased Ted Bates Worldwide. Their combined 1985 gross income would have been $906.9 million and their billings $6.14 billion. Saatchi's rise had been meteoric. It agreed to let Bates operate quasi-independently and with its present managers.

Several expansion strategies had been followed by U.S.-based advertising agencies. D'Arcy favored joining forces with agencies owned in other countries to establish third companies, which they then owned together. Ted Bates Advertising and BBDO (Batton, Barton, Durstine, & Osborne) mainly purchased existing overseas organizations whereas both J. Walter Thompson and McCann-Erickson expanded abroad mainly by setting up wholly owned subsidiaries. McCann-Erickson also acquired a few foreign agencies. Its acquisition policy was 100 percent or majority ownership wherever local law permitted. The company owned 80 of its 113 agencies around the world. In three Asian countries, Indonesia, South Korea, and Taiwan, the law prohibited foreign ownership interests in an agency, but McCann-Erickson had established "association arrangements" with locally owned and operated agencies. Taken together, the Interpublic Group was the most important advertising business in Asia outside of the Japanese market. All three Interpublic companies shared a joint venture with Matheson-Jardine of Hong Kong and Bermuda in the People's Republic of China. Called Interpublic-Jardine (China) Ltd., it maintained offices in Beijing (Peking), Shanghai, and Guangzhou. This joint venture and Dentsu were the first foreign advertising agencies receiving permits to do business in the People's Republic of China.

Dentsu was founded in 1901, and its name literally translates as "telegraphic communication." The corporate stock was not publicly traded. The two largest shareholders were the two Japanese news services, Kyodo News and Jiji Press. The former was owned, like Associated Press in the United States, by a sizable number of news papers, and the latter was owned principally by an employees' trust.

The Japanese agency was, of course, the largest advertising firm in Japan and was two and one-third times as large as its nearest domestic rival, Hakuhodo, Inc., and over seven times as large as the number three Daiko Advertising. Dai-Ichi Kikaku, based in Tokyo, was fourth. Dentsu was pervasive in the Japanese economy, but Hakuhodo and Dai-Ichi Kikaku were growing much faster than Dentsu. Daiko was rather stable. Founded in 1944 and employing 1,420, Daiko was based in Osaka and had branches in Tokyo, Nagoya, Kobe, Kyoto, and Fukuoka but no overseas branches. Established in 1895 and employing 2,950, Hakuhodo was based in Tokyo and had branches in all large Japanese cities. It had partial ownership in agencies in Hamburg, Düsseldorf, New York, Los Angeles, Singapore, Bangkok, and Kuala Lumpur. Dentsu maintained branches in all large Japanese cities and maintained small offices in London, Paris, Los Angeles, New York, Taipei, Beijing, and Shanghai.

Hakuhodo entered into a joint venture in 1960 with McCann-Erickson. This venture was a pioneering initiative that provided both organizations with great assistance in bridging the gulf separating the U.S. and Japanese cultures. McCann-Erickson Hakuhodo was by far the largest agency there that had majority ownership held by non-Japanese. Other Japanese and U.S. agencies set up several similar arrangements later on in the 1960s and 1970s.

Asahi Advertising, the ninth largest agency in Japan, signed an agreement in 1985 to cooperate with Saatchi & Saatchi Compton. A British organization, Saatchi was the largest agency in Europe, one of the fastest-growing in the world, and one of the most imaginative in its work. Asahi Advertising had annual billings of $194 million and gross income of $30 million.

The majority of Dentsu's Japanese clients did not use it for advertising supporting their exports. Such work constituted no more than 5 percent of Dentsu's billings. The Japanese manufacturers tended to use local, U.S.-based, or European-based agencies for their foreign advertising. In 1966, Dentsu attempted to follow some of its major Japanese clients into the United States and established Dentsu Corporation of America. It did not work out well. Executives later attributed the disappointment to lack of the right personnel for the subsidiary. By 1986 there were forty-eight large Japanese corporations spending about $1.5 billion abroad on advertising every year. About 85 percent of that amount was spent in Western Europe and North America.

It was not until 1981 that Dentsu got together with someone for a joint venture abroad. After years of sporadic dialogue, Dentsu-Young & Rubicam was established. Hakuhodo executives hypothesized that Dentsu's holding back for so long could be explained by corporate personality, managerial style, orientation, and ownership pattern. By personality Dentsu was cautious and conservative. It practiced decision making by consensus, which took a great deal of time but was a revered goal in that culture. As an example of togetherness, observers noticed that as many Dentsu employees as possible climbed Mt. Fuji together annually. Dentsu was domestically rather than internationally oriented in thinking and tradition. Also, there were numerous spokespersons for the owners. On the other hand, Hakuhodo was not conservative, had a cosmopolitan world view, and was closely held by just a few individuals who had similar philosophies and objectives.

The purpose of Dentsu-Young & Rubicam (DYR) was to provide an organization that would let each partner capitalize on reciprocal strengths in markets where they were weak. Dentsu would take Young & Rubicam intensively into Japan and other parts of Asia; and Young & Rubicam would let Dentsu put roots down in Western Europe, the United States, and Latin America. After establishment, it took an abnormally long time for this joint venture to organize itself and begin seriously to conduct business. The president of Dentsu was appointed chairperson of the board and an American was appointed president and chief executive officer of DYR. The firm opened branches in New York, Tokyo, Los Angeles, Kuala Lumpur, Singapore, Hong Kong, and Melbourne. Among the first clients signed up were Pacific Southwest Airlines and Hawaiian Punch. By 1985 the venture was doing over $330 million in billings in the United States, Japan, Malaysia, Singapore, Hong Kong, and Australia; and among foreign agencies it ranked seventh in Malaysia, fourth in Singapore, third in Hong Kong, and twenty-ninth in Australia.

If an advertising agency could attract a client from its own country abroad, there was interesting potential at home as well as abroad. An important example was that of McCann-Erickson, which years earlier got its foot in the door providing service to Coca-Cola in some foreign countries before D'Arcy, which held the Coca-Cola account at home, expanded into other nations. Coca-Cola subsequently shifted to McCann-Erickson.

The corporate culture of Dentsu was quite noteworthy in ways other than what has already been mentioned. At its core was an interlocking set of connections throughout the Japanese economy. The company constantly tried to improve this set. The agency recruited many of its employees from the families of Diet (Congress) members. There was in essence an "old boy" network. This network was so intricate that some people had term   it the "Tsukiji CIA" after the section of Tokyo in which the organization was located.

There were sometimes complaints in Japanese business circles that Dentsu was favored by the media. To be specific, it was alleged that on occasion when time and space were scarce, Dentsu could always get whatever its clients needed. Moreover, in all periods Dentsu could obtain the most desirable time and space. This set of feelings, whether always true or not, assisted Dentsu in holding clients. In addition, many corporate advertising managers reasoned that if Dentsu conducted a campaign for them and it did not succeed, then they would not be blamed, for others would feel that if Dentsu could not do it, nobody could. If they hired another agency and the campaign failed, the company superiors would ask why they had not hired Dentsu.

Japanese industry traditionally put much more emphasis on personal selling and healthy, harmonious relationships with the other member firms in the channel of distribution than on advertising. In that country, the fraction of the gross national product (GNP) spent on advertising in a typical year was about 1 percent, compared to about 2.1 percent in the United States (See Exhibit 2.)

The Japanese economy, although quite healthy, was showing some signs of maturation. The economy was growing, but the long-term rate of growth was slowing. As part of this trend, the growth in national spending on advertising was slowing. In recent years that growth rate was only about one-half as much as in the 1970s. In addition the mix of promotion showed a small but noteworthy change (See Exhibit 3.) There was an increase in clients' requests for Dentsu to help with sales promotion. This term, of course, referred to a miscellany of promotional activities such as contests, sweepstakes, cents-off coupon offers, and short- and long-term exhibitions. Sales promotion work had risen to about 15 percent of Dentsu's billings. Instead of the traditional 15 percent commission on media time and space, sales promotion by an advertising agency was paid for by negotiated fees. The clients negotiated aggressively. Such fees were running only 5 to 8 percent of the cost of the services rendered. Sales promotion work was labor-intensive and thus costly to furnish a client. The sales promotion services rendered to some clients were loss leaders, offered mainly to keep their high commission billings on the books. Overall, Dentsu was netting only about 5.6 percent on gross income and about 10 percent on shareholders' equity. Interpublic Group was making over 18 percent on shareholders' equity.

There were at least two extremely important differences in professional practices, from an ethical viewpoint, between Japanese advertising agencies on the one hand and all American and most European agencies on the other hand. First, it was considered perfectly all right in Japan for an

EXHIBIT 2 Advertising Expenditures as a Percent of GNP in Selected Countries

Argentina	1.3	Pakistan	.1
Australia	1.8	Peru	.6
Austria	1.0	Philippines	.4
Belgium	.6	Portugal	.2
Brazil	.7	Puerto Rico	1.8
Canada	1.3	Saudi Arabia	.1
Chile	.8	Singapore	1.0
Colombia	1.0	South Africa	1.7
Denmark	1.3	South Korea	.7
Finland	1.8	Spain	.8
France	.8	Sri Lanka	.2
Greece	.3	Sudan	.1
Hong Kong	.7	Surinam	.3
India	.3	Sweden	1.1
Indonesia	.2	Switzerland	1.4
Ireland	.8	Syria	.3
Israel	.7	Taiwan	1.3
Italy	1.3	Thailand	.3
Japan	1.0	Trinidad & Tobago	.6
Kenya	.4	Turkey	.3
Luxembourg	.6	United Kingdom	1.8
Malaysia	.5	Uruguay	.5
Mexico	.6	United States	2.1
Netherlands	1.8	Venezuela	1.0
New Zealand	1.8	West Germany	.8
Norway	1.5		

agency to serve two or more clients who were in direct competition with each other. In the United States and most other developed economies, an advertising agency avoided this practice, regarding it as a conflict of interest although local laws did not prohibit it. Even if a Western advertising agency were to assign most personnel to work exclusively on just one client account, rather inefficient and a rarity, the organization would still suspect that some commercially valuable information would leak between these groups of staff members, and also simple observation would provide significant insights into the rival's plans and accomplishments. Even the sharing of equipment could offer opportunities for leakage. Also, of course, the agency's top managers would inevitably have some degree of conflict in overseeing the work of their employees even if there were substantial delegation of authority.

Second, Japanese agencies could have ownership interests in media. Although this was not totally unknown in Europe, it was uncommon

EXHIBIT 3 Breakdown of Billings by Agency by Media Type[a]

	Dentsu	Hakuhodo	Daiko	DYR
Newspapers	23%	18.3%	32%	5.6%
Magazines	5	6.2	4	22.8
Business publications	Included in other	Included in other	Included in other	4.8
Farm publication	Included in other	Included in other	Included in other	0.3
Outdoor	14	Included in other	Included in other	0.7
Transit	Included in other	Included in other	Included in other	0.2
Television	42	43.6	34	43.8
Radio	4	3.6	4	5.2
Direct mail	Included in other	Included in other	Included in other	13.3
Yellow Pages	Included in other	Included in other	Included in other	0.5
Point of purchase	Included in other	Included in other	17	Included in other
Sales promotion	Included in other	12.7	Included in other	Included in other
Other	12	15.6	9	2.8

[a] Dai-Ichi Kikaku is not available.

there and did not exist in the United States. Dentsu owned 3 percent of the stock of Tokyo Broadcasting System, the largest privately owned telecaster in Japan. It also owned small fractions of the Yomiuri Group's television operations, Mainichi Shimbun, a major newspaper, and eleven other newspapers.

Employees of Dentsu numbered 5,700, about 17 percent of whom were female. Salaries and wages were average for the advertising industry in Japan, but bonuses, paid twice a year, were quite generous even by Japanese standards. The Japanese culture and some other cultures, especially in Asia, were characterized by modest salaries but also by the expectation of significant bonuses once or twice a year and quite a few recreational benefits paid for by the employer was well as the normal vacation, retirement, and health insurance benefits. The employer saw bonuses as a way of building and keeping morale high and rewarding some people for particularly fine work performance. The bonus could be linked directly to the work, instead of building it into the base salary. In twice-a-year bonus systems like that of Dentsu, the reward could come without a long passage of time intervening, thus putting a good psychological principle into practice. In most situations the bonsuses were optional with the management, not required. Of course, the reputation of a company could be damaged easily if it wandered too far from cultural expectations unless some other employers began to do the same. All forms of compensation together amounted to about 60 percent of all Dentsu revenue, well above the corresponding figure in North American and European agencies. In Japan there was also the expectation of lifetime employment with the same firm. This expectation was strong, and it was part of the thinking of both employer and employee. Only a tiny percentage of employees violated this idea.

The Japanese government was interested in expanding Japanese-based service businesses abroad. In part, this was because of a desire to move toward balance, but there was another reason. If tariffs should rise against foreign products or strict quotas be imposed on many foreign products that Japan exported in large quantities or both, then the provision of services, such as advertising, could help take up the slack.

Advise Dentsu.

LEVI STRAUSS & COMPANY

The management of Levi Strauss & Company, the largest U.S. apparel maker, was concerned about the amount of counterfeiting of its products, principally abroad. This problem had been around a very long time, but there had not been much progress. It meant lost sales, chiefly in other countries.

Development of the Company and Product[1]

Levi Strauss, born in Germany in 1829, immigrated to the United States at the age of seventeen, unable to speak any English. After a short stay in New York City he became a peddler in Kentucky, going from farm to farm with a pack on his back. He moved to San Francisco in 1853 during the tumultuous era when that young community served the gold prospecters of northern California. He joined his brother-in-law David Stern and older sister Fanny. Strauss and Stern established a store selling dry goods and household furnishings on an extension of one of the piers at the harbor. They obtained their merchandise from Strauss' brothers Jonas and Louis in New York and from auctions of merchandise arriving speculatively in San Francisco by ship. Goods were scarce and prices and profits very

---

[1] For the very early history of the organization and product see: E. Cray, *Levi's* (Boston: Houghton Mifflin, 1978): Strauss v. Elfelt, U.S. Circuit Court, District of California. 1211, 1874; and Strauss v. King, U.S. Circuit Court, Southern District of New York, 276, 1877.

high in this frontier, boom situation. By the early 1860s the firm changed from retail to wholesale, supplying hundreds of small stores, especially in the gold and silver fields. Brothers Jonas and Louis, still living in New York City, and brothers-in-law William Sanlein and David Stern were partners with Levi in this business. Although the youngest, Levi had the best head for business among the group and assumed leadership. They considered naming the firm Strauss Brothers. However, they named it Levi Strauss & Company because, by coincidence, there was already an unrelated dry goods firm just a few blocks away called Strauss Brothers.

The garment known as "jeans" today originated in Reno, Nevada in 1870, the invention of a tailor, Jacob Davis. Born in Latvia in 1831 as Jacob Youphes, he immigrated to New York at the age of twenty-three and then moved to San Francisco. He lived in various western towns and did many jobs before settling in Reno and opening a tailoring shop. One day a woman asked him to make a pair of work pants for her husband, a woodcutter, who could not find anything large enough in the stores. She emphasized the sturdiness of the cloth as well as the size. It was a common problem for laborers not to be able to get sturdy, dependable clothing. Workers had long complained that their trousers came apart, especially where the pockets were sewn to the trousers. Even Davis had tried to develop special stitches to keep the pants pockets from ripping, but without success. The strongest fabric he had in the shop was ten-ounce duck twill, from which he made wagon covers, horse blankets, and tents. It was difficult to work with, but he had had ample experience with it. Davis used rivets on the front straps of the horse blankets that he produced. After sewing the custom ordered pants he noticed the rivets beside him. It occurred to him to fasten the pants pockets with the rivets. That first pair of pants was off-white, the only color he had in stock and the one normally used for products made from that type of cloth. In the months following he made several more pairs of these pants for other laboring men, teamsters, and surveyors. He tried unsuccessfully to buy other colors of the fabric. Finally he was able to locate some in blue from Strauss. Each pair of pants was a walking advertisement for Davis among men who needed sturdy outdoor clothing. The tailor was now selling the pants as fast as he could make them.

Davis realized that he was onto something very important commercially. He wanted to patent his product, but his wife refused to let him spend the money for the application after two other costly patents that did not pay off. Moreover, he had no means or funds with which to distribute the new product. On July 2, 1872 Davis had a friend write Levi Strauss, because Davis did not trust his own command of English. Davis offered to give Strauss half the patent rights for the Pacific Coast areas if Strauss would arrange for and pay for the patent costs. Noting how much of the blue cloth he had sold Davis recently, Strauss readily agreed. The first application was rejected in Washington, D.C. for the reason that similar rivets had been used during the Civil War to hold soldiers' boots together. It took almost a year and three revisions before the patent was issued. It was for a "fastening for pocket-openings whereby the sewed seams are prevented from ripping or starting from frequent pressure. . . . by the placing of the hands in the pockets . . ." Davis did not attempt to get a patent on the use of rivets for all seams in clothing, which might have prevented getting any patent at all.

Davis sold quite a few pairs of the patented pants from his Reno shop. However, both he and Levi Strauss came to realize that their scale of operation could multiply if they worked together. Davis moved to San Francisco. He sold half of the full patent rights to Strauss and became production manager, while Strauss took on the marketing of the pants. Davis insisted on calling them pantaloons, but Strauss insisted on calling them overalls. They began to emboss the words "Levi Strauss & Company" on the edge of the metal buttons.

At first the two men used the cottage industry method. Davis saw that the fabric was cut properly and then distributed all materials to women working in their homes. All production was in off-white heavy duck. They considered using the sweat shops of New York City, where the work could be done more cheaply, but rejected the idea because transportation costs would more than wipe out the labor savings. Soon thereafter they brought the workers together into a factory. Because the owners were not familiar with the concept of dividing the labor tasks by specialization, each worker made the complete garment. Within a year the factory was making over 100,000 units annually. Demand grew rapidly and was dispersed through several states. The owners thus asked brothers Jonas and Louis to open a factory in New York City to make the same product. This smaller facility opened in 1877.

Copying came early. Two other California firms began making the same product in September 1873. Strauss sued both A.B. Elfelt of San Francisco and Kan Lun of San Jose in early 1874 for patent infringement and won the disputes.

Strauss avoided the ultra-cheap labor of the Chinese immigrants in San Francisco. Thus the company's labor costs were well above other northern California apparel makers. This extra cost was reflected in the higher prices that Strauss had to charge. The company was highly motivated constantly to provide better quality and more durability in order to justify this higher price to the customers.

As production and sales grew. Strauss realized it would be better off to standardize the characteristics of the fabric used. It came to rely on one New England mill, Amoskeag. This way it was able to get one quality of cloth and dependable color. Although an assortment of colors was available, Strauss decided on an indigo blue fabric, so named because the dye came from the indigo plant, and an off-white fabric. The fabric chosen by Strauss was the heaviest and strongest produced in the United States at the time. Thus Strauss offered a choice of blue denim or white duck pants. The design was set: tight-fitting, low in the hips, and straight-legged so as to tuck into a laborer's work boots. In addition, there were six suspender buttons and, somewhat later, belt loops as well.

The Strauss organization needed a brand and a trademark. In 1873 Jacob Davis did something interesting. He tried to match the copper color of the rivets by using orange linen thread for the stitching. Then to distinguish the pants from competitors the factory sewed in two curving Vs on the back pockets. However, the company did not register this stitching design as a trademark until 1942. The company also tacked to the seat of the pants an oilcloth guarantee. This piece of cloth showed two teamsters whipping a pair of horses in an unsuccessful effort to pull apart a pair of the riveted pants, displayed the name of Levi Strauss & Company, and carried the promise of a new pair free if the present one ripped. The brand name was "Two Horse Brand." In 1886 this cloth label was replaced by one made of leather and affixed with orange linen thread.

Sales and production grew rapidly, and the San Francisco factory was expanded. Later, Levi Strauss bought out his partners. Now it was he plus four of his Stern nephews. When the patent expired in 1890 after its seventeen-year life there were suddenly many lawful competitors of essentially the same product. Strauss then expanded the product line to offer various qualities so as to compete effectively. Levi Strauss died a rich bachelor in 1902, leaving the firm to his four Stern nephews.

The company lost its San Francisco facilities in the devastating earthquake of 1906, but it carried on from some branch facilities in Oakland across the bay and quickly rebuilt in San Francisco. The Wall Street panic of 1907 hurt virtually all companies, including Strauss. The company began to put more emphasis on its Sunset brand of men's dresswear manufactured by others to its orders and on its Two Horse brand clothing rather than on its wholesaling of a wide line of clothing and dry goods. In 1912 Simon Davis, son of the inventor and now production manager of Strauss, designed the koverall. This was a one-piece, button-up-the-front overall of blue denim for children. The promotional work had the theme "The Kind of Klose That Keep Kids Kleen." It was a huge success and the company's first product to be distributed nationwide, but it was also widely copied. In 1916 Strauss successfully sued J.C. Penney Company, Inc., to keep that organization from using the work "koverall" on any garment that it might order manufactured for itself.

Gradually the important administrative jobs drifted into the hands of non-family members as the wealthy owners began to spend less time in the business and more time in recreation and philanthropy. There was a great falling out between Davis and the Stern family over Davis' lack of knowledge and concern about costs and pricing. One of the Stern men still active in the business passed the leadership on to Walter Haas, his son-in-law. An outsider, Milton Grunbaum, was appointed factory superintendent at age thirty. Unionization came peacefully in 1935 and relations with the union were good, but the company refused to add the union label to the garments. This policy continued indefinitely.

Curiously the jeans were distributed in New Zealand, Mexico, and several Pacific islands when most of the United States had never heard of them. This was because of the natural trade connections between the U.S. Pacific coast and points west and south.

Grunbaum became more and more important in the company. In answer to complaints from consumers he made two changes in the famous jeans, one his own idea and one his quick implementation of the president's idea. He found a way to cover the copper rivets on the back pockets so that they would stop scratching things the wearer leaned against. Yet the company had to mount a large advertising campaign to reassure customers that the rivet was actually still there. Second, the company removed the rivet from the crotch. For years company officials had laughed off this set of complaints. However, one day the company president, Walter Haas, crouched close to a campfire in the mountains and the flames heated the crotch rivet in his jeans. The top administration finally got the customer message. From then on the crotch rivet was removed from the product specifications.

During the 1930s the Strauss Company managed to get its products in a few prestigious stores. Abercrombie and Fitch, the world famous sporting goods store, added Levis in order to serve its well-to-do urban customers who discovered the newly created dude ranch. In connection with this merchandising movement, Chris Lucier, the only talented merchant on the Strauss staff, ran its famous advertisement: "Guaranteed to shrink, guaranteed to fade." In 1935 the company added the little red tab with the word "Levi's" on the right rear pocket. This was registered with the U.S. government. In order to protect the whole concept, the company used an assortment of colors but red for most units. This policy was for the purpose of keeping other manufacturers from imitating the tab in another color. Strauss sponsored an exhibit in the 1939 International Exposition, or world's fair, on Treasure Island in San Francisco Bay. This mechanical rodeo attracted visitors from all over North America and later went on a nationwide tour itself. This marked the beginning of large scale, nationwide promotion for Strauss. Sales at that time were only $3.2 million, down somewhat because of the Great Depression.

The Strauss Company had continued calling the jeans "double X, lot 501 waist overalls." It was the consumers and a few of the retailers who began referring to the product as LEVI'S pants. After many decades the company finally adopted the commercially valuable name that everyone else by then was using.

Sales grew during World War II despite material shortages. War factory workers judged the jeans just the thing to wear. Costs of many inputs rose. However, because of wartime price controls the company could not raise its jeans prices and thus did not make a profit on the growing demand. To save materials for the war effort the suspender buttons, belt loops, and cuffs disappeared. After the war only the belt loops reappeared. Factories for defense goods, disproportionately located in California, drew workers from all over the United States. They spread word of the jeans and took some back to other parts of the country. Servicemen from the West spread the word about the jeans while stationed in other regions of the United States and overseas. Slowly and unevenly the company's principal product was gaining a national reputation and a fledgling reputation abroad. A pair of LEVI'S was a very valuable item on the postwar black market in Europe.

Growth of the organization was spectacular for several years following World War II and rapid for several decades. By 1950 sales were $22 million; and they reached $137 million by 1965. Strauss withdrew from the wholesaling business in 1954 to concentrate on manufacturing its several clothing items. Film stars James Dean and Marlon Brando usually appeared in blue jeans, thus stimulating public interest in this type of product and helping to establish it as a sort of youthful protest against the neat and traditional clothing that prevailed. Jeans became symbolic of the right of teenagers to decide on their own clothing. For at least a decade there was a running battle with school officials, most of whom banned jeans. By 1960 Strauss had adopted pre-shrunk fabric and made a zipper fly, both features insisted on by people living in the eastern United States. The Strauss product line was expanded and the number of factories increased. The company went public and was listed on the New York Stock Exchange in 1971, at which time annual sales were $432 million. However, in 1985, when sales were about $3 billion, it went private again in a leveraged buyout.

The Counterfeiting Problem

Levi Strauss & Company's products were sold in about seventy-five countries and its trademarks were some of the most readily recognized in the world. For the most part, the company had reacted to overseas inquiries until recent years, rather than taking the initiative to cultivate foreign markets. Strauss entered western Europe and Canada in 1961, but the Canadian venture was under the name Great Western Garment Company because Strauss had bought three-fourths of that firm. About a decade later Strauss started a second Canadian company, this time under the name Levi Strauss. Strauss reached these overseas markets through a variety of means: exporting; licensing arrangements; joint ventures; and solely owned branches.

The International Division was created in 1971 and was organized by geographical area of the world: Europe; Latin America; Canada; and Asia/Pacific. Europe was the largest. Foreign sales were only $4 million, or 3 percent of sales, in 1965. Foreign demand now provided almost 40 percent of total sales and this fraction was growing. Goods for foreign consumption were redesigned as little as possible, but different physical characteristics such as height and girth made changes in the size assortment necessary. Although it was now doing well in Europe, in 1973 and 1974 Levi Strauss & Company suffered large losses there, misjudging fashion trends and ethnic preferences and not controlling the product mix and levels of inventory or the production schedules. In addition, at that time it had just replaced independent European distributors with its own company employees. Levi Strauss & Company had evolved into a maker of fashions as well as basic clothing, especially as perceived abroad.

A counterfeit was a spurious mark used in connection with goods that was identical with or substantially indistinguishable from a registered mark. Counterfeits were marketed as the identically trademarked product, thus defrauding the customer and the trademark owner. There might also be bodily harm or physical damage to the consumer. For example, a fake Chevron fertilizer used on African coffee plantations caused extensive crop damage. This act even damaged Chevron's reputation for quality, although the product was not genuine. Some people never learned that it was a counterfeit. There had been many problems with fake pharmaceuticals and automotive parts. These problems always loomed on the horizon for any firm engaging in foreign trade.

There was a small amount of counterfeit merchandise that was not shoddy or defective. Once in a great while such products were physically equal to the copied products. However, even in these cases the consumer and trademark owner were defrauded, because the consumer was not getting the real item implied by the seller or the warranty on the product, and because the trademark owner was losing the sale.

The U.S. government estimated that U.S. firms lost to foreign counterfeiters around $8 billion in sales annually. The offenders could be found throughout the world but were concentrated in East Asia and Latin America. The sales of counterfeits were in Asia, the Middle East, Africa, and Latin America, but seldom in Europe. Among the industries most hurt by this problem were the manufacturers of jeans, shirts, software, books, and musical recordings. The affected U.S. companies also strongly suspected that a few U.S. companies worked with illicit overseas organizations to copy their products. A small amount of such illicit goods found their way into the United States but most were distributed abroad. The overseas counterfeiters were very difficult to find, because they tended to change locations from time to time, often used the cottage industry arrangement, and sometimes changed their choice of brand copied.

At least half of the Third World nations paid only lip service to trademark protection. They saw in counterfeiting a relatively fast way to establish demand for their output and further industrialize their economies. A very few countries that had been offenders earlier, such as Japan, had stopped counterfeiting. The offending countries absorbed the domestic demand for the brand and also exported to other countries, including sometimes the home country of the trademark holder.

Of course, a manufacturer should attempt first to protect its trademarks by properly registering them with the governments of the jurisdictions where they marketed or would market the products. And they should show an encircled R beside the mark to indicate registration. There were many cases on record in which naive or careless U.S. firms did not even try to protect their trademarks.

Under the English common law heritage of the United States, registration of the mark with the government was not necessary. The firm that adopted the mark and used it first in commerce owned it. By the 1940s it was commonly expected in U.S. business circles that a firm would also register the mark with the U.S. Patent and Trademark Office, but this action was still not absolutely necessary. The individual states of the United States also specifically protected trademarks without registration. Registration was vital in the great majority of countries, however. Otherwise the first person or firm to register the mark owned it. Several U.S. firms had had to buy back their marks in foreign countries from first registrants. Under a proposed international treaty on the topic, the United States would need a change from English common law to the principles observed by most of the rest of the world, but the United States was far from ready to sign this treaty. The United States was pressing the approximately 100 member nations of the General Agreement on Tariffs and Trade to increase the protection of trademarks, patents, and copyrights both informally and through amendments to the GATT treaty. The United States passed additional legislation, the Trademark Counterfeiting Act, in the mid-1980s. Under this statute counterfeiting became a crime in the United States, not just a civil matter, and involved jail sentences and large fines. Moreover, seizure of counterfeit goods in the hands of retailers was authorized. Under both the statutes and the common law the owners of trademarks had to make some clear effort to police the use of their rights by others.

Proper care of a trademark did not deter the counterfeiters or governments in dozens of countries. Yet it constituted a legal basis for specific action if a counterfeiter could be identified and such a legal action seemed feasible in that jurisdiction. Some aggrieved trademark holders used field investigators and then local lawyers to represent them. Most trademark owners preferred simply to pressure the offending companies to stop, rather than to bring a lawsuit and gain a formal legal decision and, in some jurisdictions, be awarded damages. When lawsuits were won the results might not be attractive. In one well-known situation Union Carbide, a large U.S. company, sued three counterfeiters and won. The suit took two years and cost over $50,000. The three convicted firms received a fine of less than $1000. A few countries did not even permit a foreign entity to sue unless it had a branch in that country. A few U.S. and European firms had found that foreign licensees were a weak link in trademark protection. Licensees might not carefully protect the mark.

Levi Strauss & Company had attempted to protect its valuable trademarks and had pursued many investigations and lawsuits. Nevertheless, it seemed clear that its trademarks were being copied abroad.

Advise Levi Strauss & Company.

13

Legal Environment
of Marketing

A NOTE ON STUDYING THE LEGAL CASES

Three recent Court cases are included in this section on the legal environment of marketing. All are decisions of the U. S. Supreme Court.

It is extremely helpful to the student of marketing to become familiar with legal thinking, to pinpoint the issues, and to understand how the comparison of points of law is carried out. Look for the points of law being rejected, those being accepted, those given priority, and those raised on which the Court takes no position. Determine the important precedents set by the cases. Try to reconstruct the reasoning that led to the overturning of a lower court or regulatory agency decision or a Supreme Court decision from past years.

Note the ambiguity of statutes that the Court is trying to interpret and enforce. Attempt to determine the role of economic, political, psychological, and sociological beliefs in the decision. Laws operate in a behavioral milieu. Law is not a science in the conventional sense of that term.

Many courts and individual judges have been accused of being social and economic engineers, whereas many others regard their roles more narrowly as interpreters and clarifiers of law. Many judges seek to establish the executive or legislative intent and motivation. Do these cases reflect engineering or strict constructionism? Closely related to this question is what and how much respect is demonstrated in each of these cases for the executive and legislative branches of the government? This deals with the classic dilemma of the *separation of powers* doctrine, that is, separation of authority among the executive, legislative, and judicial branches of government.

What and how much respect is shown for the *division of powers* doctrine, which is sometimes called the *federalism* doctrine? This deals with the split of authority between the national government and the state governments. Does the case perhaps treat rights delegated to the states by the federal government, as opposed to state rights specified in the U. S. Constitution? What rights are irrevocable?

Dissents by judges are common. Note if they occur and their extent. Do they apply to peripheral areas or go to the heart of the case? Dissents often give rise to reversals, partial reversals, or reinterpretations by judges sitting on the same court later. Do you think there is a good basis for overturning the decision in these cases? If so, explain your reasoning. Suppose that you were asked to challenge the decision. Organize your arguments from the case and add other ideas and facts of your own. Present them persuasively and anticipate the counterarguments.

Often a decision in a legal case is accompanied by one or more concurring opinions by judges who voted with the majority. Even a unanimous opinion may be accompanied by one or more concurring opinions. These concurring opinions may deal with a secondary issue in the case or the central issue, but the holder of the concurring opinion believes it is necessary to distinguish his or her line of reasoning, the stream of precedents, and/or the level of his or her doubt or conclusiveness on the issue from those of colleagues. The concurring rationale of the judge(s) may imply the difference in degree to which he or she (they) may be willing to carry an idea or an interpretation. A judge who concurs on one case will not always concur on a similar case later, but the concurring opinion provides clues to that judge's future decision making.

Suppose that you were called by the U. S. government or a concerned company as an expert on marketing to support the legal decision. Organize the thoughts of the case into a presentation. Add ramifications and implications, using your present background and expertise in marketing.

Consider the practical effects of each case on the marketing policies and practices of the companies involved. What changes in the organizations will be necessary if the decision stands and is implemented? If an overturning or reversal is expected in the long term, what changes must be made for the short term? What new broad marketing strategies will be necessary, as opposed to narrow specific changes? What will be the effects on the day-to-day operating policies?

MAINE v. TAYLOR ET AL.
477 U.S. 131

APPEAL FROM THE UNITED STATES COURT OF APPEALS FOR THE FIRST CIRCUIT

Opinion of the Court

BLACKMUN, J., delivered the opinion of the Court, in which BURGER, C. J., and BRENNAN, WHITE, MARSHALL, POWELL, REHNQUIST, and O'CONNOR, J. J., joined. STEVENS, J., filed a dissenting opinion, *post*, p. 152.

JUSTICE BLACKMUN delivered the opinion of the Court.

Once again, a little fish has caused a commotion. See *Hughes* v. *Oklahoma,* 441 U. S. 322 (1979); *TVA* v. *Hill,* 437 U. S. 153 (1978); *Cappaert* v. *United States,* 426 U. S. 128 (1976). The fish in this case is the golden shiner, a species of minnow commonly used as live bait in sport fishing.

Appellee Robert J. Taylor (hereafter Taylor or appellee) operates a bait business in Maine. Despite a Maine statute prohibiting the importation of live baitfish,[1] he arranged to have 158,000 live golden shiners delivered to him from outside the State. The shipment was intercepted, and a federal grand jury in the District of Maine indicted Taylor for violating and conspiring to violate the Lacey Act Amendments of 1981, 95 Stat. 1073, 16 U. S. C. §§3371–3378. Section 3(a)(2)(A) of those Amendments, 16 U. S. C. §3372(a)(2)(A), makes it a federal crime "to import, export, transport, sell, receive, acquire, or purchase in interstate or foreign commerce . . . any fish or wildlife taken, possessed, transported, or sold in violation of any law or regulation of any State or in violation of any foreign law."

Taylor moved to dismiss the indictment on the ground that Maine's import ban unconstitutionally burdens interstate commerce and therefore may not form the basis for a federal prosecution under the Lacey Act. Maine, pursuant to 28 U. S. C. §2403(b), intervened to defend the validity of its statute, arguing that the ban legitimately protects the State's fisheries from parasites and nonnative species that might be included in shipments of live baitfish. The District Court found the statute constitutional and denied the motion to dismiss. *United States* v. *Taylor,* 585 F. Supp. 393 (Me. 1984). Taylor then entered a conditional plea of guilty pursuant to Federal Rule of Criminal Procedure 11(a)(2), reserving the

---

[1] "A person is guilty of importing live bait if he imports into this State any live fish, including smelts, which are commonly used for bait fishing in inland waters." Me. Rev. Stat. Ann., Tit. 12, §7613 (1981).

right to appeal the District Court's ruling on the constitutional question. The Court of Appeals for the First Circuit reversed, agreeing with Taylor that the underlying state statute impermissibly restricts interstate trade. *United States* v. *Taylor,* 752 F. 2d 757 (1985). Maine appealed. We set the case for plenary review and postponed consideration of Taylor's challenges to our appellate jurisdiction. 474 U. S. 943 (1985).

I

Maine invokes our jurisdiction under 28 U. S. C. §1254(2), which authorizes an appeal as of right to this Court "by a party relying on a State statute held by a court of appeals to be invalid as repugnant to the Constitution, treaties or laws of the United States." Appellee, however, contends that this provision applies only to civil cases, and that, in any event, Maine lacks standing to appeal the reversal of a federal conviction. These contentions both relate to the unusual procedural posture of the case: an appeal by a State from the reversal of a federal conviction based on a violation of state law. We consider them in turn.

First, despite its procedural peculiarities, this case fits squarely within the plain terms of §1254(2): Maine relies on a state statute that the Court of Appeals held to be unconstitutional. Although statutes authorizing appeals as of right to this Court are strictly construed, see, e.g,. *Silkwood* v. *Kerr-McGee Corp.,* 464 U. S. 238, 247 (1984), nothing in the language or legislative history of §1254(2) suggests that its scope is limited to civil litigation. In arguing for such a limitation, appellee relies principally on the fact that §§1254(1) and (3)—which authorize discretionary review of cases from the Courts of Appeals by writ of certiorari and certification, respectively—both apply explicitly to "any civil or criminal case."[2] Since this express language is absent from §1254(2), appellee contends that Congress must have intended this Court's appellate jurisdiction over cases from the courts of appeals to remain limited

---

[2] Section 1254 reads in full:

"Cases in the courts of appeals may be reviewed by the Supreme Court by the following methods:

"(1) By writ of certiorari granted upon the petition of any party to any civil or criminal case, before or after rendition of judgment or decree;

"(2) By appeal by a party relying on a State statute held by a court of appeals to be invalid as repugnant to the Constitution, treaties or laws of the United States, but such appeal shall preclude review by writ of certiorari at the instance of such appellant, and the review on appeal shall be restricted to the Federal questions presented;

"(3) By certification at any time by a court of appeals of any question of law in any civil or criminal case as to which instructions are desired, and upon such certification the Supreme Court may give binding instructions or require the entire record to be sent up for decision of the entire matter in controversy."

to civil cases, as indeed it was limited prior to the 1925 enactment of §1254's predecessor.[3]

We find the argument unconvincing. While some statutes governing this Court's jurisdiction, such as §§1254(1) and (3), expressly apply to both civil and criminal cases, others are explicitly limited to civil actions. See, e.g., 28 U. S. C. §§1252 and 1253. The absence of *either* sort of provision from §1254(2) hardly demonstrates that Congress had only civil cases in mind, and we see no reason to read such a limitation into the straightforward and unambiguous terms of the statute. This is not a situation where "the sense of the statute and the literal language are at loggerheads," or where adherence to the plain terms of the statute " 'would confer upon this Court a jurisdiction beyond what "naturally and properly belongs to it." ' " *Heckler* v. *Edwards,* 465 U. S. 870, 879 (1984), quoting *Florida Lime & Avacado Growers, Inc.* v. *Jacobsen,* 362 U. S. 73, 94 (1960) (Frankfurter, J., dissenting), in turn quoting *American Security & Trust Co.* v. *District of Columbia,* 224 U. S. 491, 495 (1912). Section 1254(2) serves to ensure that a state statute is struck down by the federal judiciary only when it is found invalid by this Court, or when the parties acquiesce in the decision of a lower federal court. Federal nullification of a state statute is a grave matter whether it occurs in civil litigation or in the course of a criminal prosecution, and review by this Court is particularly warranted in either event.[4]

Appellee's second jurisdictional argument is based on the fact that the only appellant before this Court is the State of Maine—only an intervenor in the District Court—not the United States, which brought the

---

[3] Congress in 1925 amended §240(b) of the Judicial Code to read as follows:

"Any case in a circuit court of appeals where is drawn in question the validity of a statute of any State, on the ground of its being repugnant to the Constitution, treaties, or laws of the United States, and the decision is against its validity, may, at the election of the party relying on such State statute, be taken to the Supreme Court for review on writ of error or appeal; but in that event a review on certiorari shall not be allowed at the instance of such party, and the review on such writ or error or appeal shall be restricted to an examination and decision of the Federal questions presented in the case." Act of Feb. 13, 1925, §1, 43 Stat. 939.

Until then, appeals were allowed as of right from decisions of the courts of appeals only in civil cases involving more than $1,000, and not arising under the diversity, admiralty, patent, or revenue jurisdiction of the federal courts. See Act of Mar. 3, 1891, §6, 26 Stat. 828.

The relevant portion of the 1925 Act was added on the floor of the Senate, and the debates surrounding the amendment contain no suggestion that it was intended to apply only in civil cases. See 66 Cong. Rec. 2753–2754, 2757, 2919–2925 (1925).

[4] Even if this case fell outside the scope of 28 U. S. C. §1254(2), we would still have discretion under 28 U. S. C. §2103 to grant review by writ of certiorari. See *Doran* v. *Salem Inn, Inc.,* 422 U. S. 922, 927 (1975); *El Paso* v. *Simmons,* 379 U. S. 497, 502–503 (1965).

original prosecution.[5] Since the United States and its attorneys have the sole power to prosecute criminal cases in the federal courts, appellee contends that Maine may not seek review of the Court of Appeals' reversal of his conviction. By statute, however, Maine intervened with "all the rights of a party," 28 U. S. C. §2403(b),[6] and appeals may be taken to this Court under §1254(2) by any "party relying on a State statute" held invalid under federal law by a Court of Appeals. We previously have recognized that intervenors in lower federal courts may seek review in this Court on their own, so long as they have "a sufficient stake in the outcome of the controversy" to satisfy the constitutional requirement of genuine adversity. *Bryant* v. *Yellen,* 447 U. S. 352, 368 (1980); see also, *e.g., Diamond* v. *Charles,* 476 U. S. 54, 68 (1986). Maine's stake in the outcome of this litigation is substantial: if the judgment of the Court of Appeals is left undisturbed, the State will be bound by the conclusive adjudication that its import ban is unconstitutional. See, *e.g., Stoll* v. *Gottlieb,* 305 U.S. 165 (1938). And although private parties, and perhaps even separate sovereigns, have no legally cognizable interest in the prosecutorial decisions of the Federal Government, cf., *e.g., Diamond* v. *Charles, supra,* at 64–65; *Linda R. S.* v. *Richard D.,* 410 U. S. 614, 619 (1973), a State clearly has a legitimate interest in the continued enforceability of its own statutes, see *Diamond* v. *Charles, supra,* at 65; *Alfred L. Snapp & Son, Inc.* v. *Puerto Rico ex rel. Barez,* 458 U. S. 592, 601 (1982). Furthermore, because reversal of the judgment of the Court of Appeals would result in the automatic reinstatement of appellee's guilty plea, the controversy before us clearly remains live notwithstanding the Federal Government's decision to abandon its own appeal.[7] We turn to the merits.

---

[5] The United States filed a timely notice of appeal to this Court, App. 311, but later moved in the Court of Appeals to dismiss its appeal. *Id.,* at 313. This was "[b]ecause the Acting Solicitor General determined that other cases were entitled to priority in selecting the limited number of cases the government would ask this Court to review." Brief for United States 14–15. The Court of Appeals granted the Government's motion. App. 315.

[6] Title 28 U. S. C. §2403(b) provides:
"In any action, suit, or proceeding in a court of the United States to which a State or any agency, officer, or employee thereof is not a party, wherein the constitutionality of any statute of that State affecting the public interest is drawn in question, the court shall certify such fact to the attorney general of the State, and shall permit the State to intervene for presentation of evidence, if evidence is otherwise admissible in the case, and for argument on the question of constitutionality. The State shall, subject to the applicable provisions of law, have all the right of a party and be subject to all liabilities of a party as to court costs to the extent necessary for a proper presentation of the facts and law relating to the question of constitutionality."

[7] The United States advises us that it does not intend to seek dismissal of the indictment if Maine prevails in this Court. See Brief for United States 17, n. 17.

II

The Commerce Clause of the Constitution grants Congress the power "[t]o regulate Commerce with foreign Nations, and among the several States, and with the Indian Tribes." Art. I, §8, cl. 3. "Although the Clause thus speaks in terms of powers bestowed upon Congress, the Court long has recognized that it also limits the power of the States to erect barriers against interstate trade." *Lewis* v. *BT Investment Managers, Inc.*, 447 U. S. 27, 35 (1980). Maine's statute restricts interstate trade in the most direct manner possible, blocking all inward shipments of live baitfish at the State's border. Still, as both the District Court and the Court of Appeals recognized, this fact alone does not render the law unconstitutional. The limitation imposed by the Commerce Clause on state regulatory power "is by no means absolute," and "the States retain authority under their general police powers to regulate matters of 'legitimate local concern,' even though interstate commerce may be affected." *Id.,* at 36.

In determining whether a State has overstepped its role in regulating interstate commerce, this Court has distinguished between state statutes that burden interstate transactions only incidentally, and those that affirmatively discriminate against such transactions. While statutes in the first group violate the Commerce Clause only if the burdens they impose on interstate trade are "clearly excessive in relation to the putative local benefits," *Pike* v. *Bruce Church, Inc.*, 397 U. S. 137, 142 (1970), statutes in the second group are subject to more demanding scrutiny. The Court explained in *Hughes* v. *Oklahoma,* 441 U. S., at 336, that once a state law is shown to discriminate against interstate commerce "either on its face or in practical effect," the burden falls on the State to demonstrate both that the statute "serves a legitimate local purpose," and that this purpose could not be served as well by available nondiscriminatory means. See also, *e.g., Sporhase* v. *Nebraska ex rel. Douglas,* 458 U. S. 941, 957 (1982); *Hunt* v. *Washington State Apple Advertising Comm'n,* 432 U. S. 333, 353 (1977); *Dean Milk Co.* v. *Madison,* 340 U. S. 349, 354 (1951).

The District Court and the Court of Appeals both reasoned correctly that, since Maine's import ban discriminates on its face against interstate trade, it should be subject to the strict requirements of *Hughes* v. *Oklahoma,* notwithstanding Maine's argument that those requirements were waived by the Lacey Act Amendments of 1981. It is well established that Congress may authorize the States to engage in regulation that the Commerce Clause would otherwise forbid. See, *e.g., Southern Pacific Co.* v. *Arizona ex rel. Sullivan,* 325 U. S. 761, 769 (1945). But because of the important role the Commerce Clause plays in protecting the free flow of interstate trade, this Court has exempted state statutes from the implied limitations of the Clause only when the congressional direction to do so has been "unmistakably clear." *South-Central Timber Development, Inc.* v. *Wunnicke,* 467 U. S. 82, 91 (1984). The 1981 Amendments of the Lacey Act clearly provide for federal enforcement of valid state and foreign wildlife laws, but Maine identifies nothing in the text or legislative history of the Amendments that suggests Congress wished to validate state laws that would be unconstitutional without federal approval.

Before this Court, Maine concedes that the Lacey Act Amendments do not exempt state wildlife legislation from scrutiny under the Commerce Clause. See Reply Brief for Appellant 3, n. 2. The State insists, however, that the Amendments should lower the *intensity* of the scrutiny that would otherwise be applied. We do not agree. An unambiguous indication of congressional intent is required before a federal statute will be read to authorize otherwise invalid state legislation, regardless of whether the purported authorization takes the form of a flat exemption from Commerce Clause scrutiny or the less direct form of a reduction in the level of scrutiny. Absent "a clear expression of approval by Congress," any relaxation in the restrictions on state power otherwise imposed by the Commerce Clause unacceptably increases "the risk that unrepresented interests will be adversely affected by restraints on commerce." *South-Central Timber, supra,* at 92.

In this case, there simply is no unambiguous statement of any congressional intent whatsoever "to alter the limits of state power otherwise imposed by the Commerce Clause," *United States* v. *Public Utilities Comm'n of California,* 345 U. S. 295, 304 (1953). In arguing to the contrary, Maine relies almost exclusively on the following findings in the Senate Report on the Lacey Act Amendments:

> "It is desirable to extend protection to species of wildlife not now covered by the Lacey Act, and to plants which are presently not covered at all. States and foreign government are encouraged to protect a broad variety of species. Legal mechanisms should be supportive of those governments." S. Rep. No. 97–123, pp. 3–4 (1981).

Maine reads this passage, particularly the last sentence, to direct federal courts to treat state wildlife laws more leniently. We find this interpretation not only less than obvious but positively strained; by far the more natural reading of the last sentence is that it refers only to the availability of federal investigative and prosecutorial resources to enforce *valid* state wildlife laws. The passage certainly does not make "unmistakably clear" that Congress intended in 1981 to alter in any way the level of Commerce Clause scrutiny applied to those laws. Maine's ban on the importation of live baitfish thus is constitutional only if it satisfies the requirements ordinarily applied under *Hughes* v. *Oklahoma* to local regulation that discriminates against interstate trade: the statute must serve a legitimate local purpose, and the purpose must be one that cannot be served as well by available nondiscriminatory means.

III

The District Court found after an evidentiary hearing that both parts of the *Hughes* test were satisfied, but the Court of Appeals disagreed. We conclude that the court of Appeals erred in setting aside the findings of the District court. To explain why, we need to discuss the proceedings below in some detail.

A

The evidentiary hearing on which the District Court based its conclusions was one before a Magistrate. Three scientific experts testified for the prosecution and one for the defense. The prosecution experts testified that live baitfish imported into the State posed two significant threats to Maine's unique and fragile fisheries.[8] First, Maine's population of wild fish — including its own indigenous golden shiners — would be placed at risk by three types of parasites prevalent in out-of-state baitfish, but not common to wild fish in Maine. See *e.g.,* App. 39–55.[9] Second, nonnative species inadvertently included in shipments of live baitfish could disturb Maine's aquatic ecology to an unpredictable extent by competing with native fish for food or habitat, by preying on native species, or by disrupting the environment in more subtle ways. See, *e.g., id.,* at 59–70, 141–149.[10]

The prosecution experts further testified that there was no satisfactory way to inspect shipments of live baitfish for parasites or commingled species.[11] According to their testimony, the small size of baitfish and the

---

[8] One prosecution witness testified that Maine's lakes contain unusually clean water and originally supported "a rather delicate community of just a few species of fish." App. 57. Another stressed that "no other state . . . has any real landlocked salmon fishing. You come to Maine for that or you live in Maine for that." *Id.,* at 137.

[9] Two of these types of parasites were found in appellee's confiscated shipment of golden shiners. See *United States* v. *Taylor,* 585 F. Supp. 393, 395–396 (Me. 1984).

[10] Although appellee's shipment was not found to contain any fish other than golden shiners, it did contain "some polliwogs and . . . some crustacean crawfish." App. 69. There was testimony suggesting that these could pose the same ecological risks as nonnative fish. See *id.,* at 70.

[11] The expert who examined appellee's shipment testified that, although his inspection of the shipment revealed only two of the three parasites he described as prevalent in baitfish outside Maine, "I certainly could not put my signature on a certificate to say that [none of the third parasite] was present in that lot." *Id.,* at 85.

large quantities in which they are shipped made inspection for commingled species "a physical impossibility." *Id.*, at 81.[12] Parasite inspection posed a separate set of difficulties because the examination procedure required destruction of the fish. *Id.*, at 81–82, 195. Although statistical sampling and inspection techniques had been developed for salmonids (*i.e.*, salmon and trout), so that a shipment could be certified parasite-free based on a standardized examination of only some of the fish, no scientifically accepted procedures of this sort were available for baitfish. See, *e.g.*, *id.*, at 71, 184, 193–194.[13]

Appellee's expert denied that any scientific justification supported Maine's total ban on the importation of baitfish. *Id.*, at 241. He testified that none of the three parasites discussed by the prosecution witnesses posed any significant threat to fish in the wild, *id.*, at 206–212, 228–232, and that sampling techniques had not been developed for baitfish precisely because there was no need for them. *Id.*, at 265–266. He further testified that professional baitfish farmers raise their fish in ponds that have been freshly drained to ensure that no other species is inadvertently collected. *Id.*, at 239–240.

Weighing all the testimony, the Magistrate concluded that both prongs of the *Hughes* test were satisfied, and accordingly that appellee's motion to dismiss the indictment should be denied. Appellee filed objections, but the District Court, after an independent review of the evidence, reached the same conclusions. First, the court found that Maine "clearly has a legitimate and substantial purpose in prohibiting the importation of live bait fish," because "substantial uncertainties" surrounded the effects that baitfish parasites would have on the State's unique population of wild fish, and the consequences of introducing nonnative species were similarly unpredictable. 585 F. Supp., at 397.[14] Second, the court concluded that less discriminatory means of protecting against these threats were currently unavailable, and that, in particular, testing procedures for baitfish parasites had not yet been devised. *Id.*, at 398. Even if procedures

[12] The shipment intercepted in this case contained approximately 158,000 fish, with about seventy specimens to the pound. *Id.*, at 80.

[13] According to the prosecution testimony, the design of sampling and inspection techniques must take into account the particular parasites of concern, and baitfish parasites differ from salmonid parasites. See *e.g.*, *id.*, at 184, 193–194. Appellee's expert agreed. *Id.*, at 237, 265–267. There was also testimony that the physical layout of bait farms makes inspection at the source of shipment particularly difficult, and that border inspections are not feasible because the fish would die in the time it takes to complete the tests. *Id.*, at 75–79.

[14] For several reasons, the District Court discounted the testimony of appellee's expert that baitfish parasites did not pose so serious a threat as disease organisms found in salmonids. The court noted that "considerable scientific debate" surrounded even the threat posed by salmonid diseases, that appellee's expert testified largely about the effects that baitfish parasites had in commercial hatcheries rather than in the wild, and that he was unfamiliar with northeast fisheries. 585 F. Supp., at 397.

of this sort could be effective, the court found that their development probably would take a considerable amount of time. *Id.*, at 398, n. 11.[15]

Although the Court of Appeals did not expressly set aside the District Court's finding of a legitimate local purpose, it noted that several factors "cast doubt" on that finding. 752 F. 2d, at 762. First, Maine was apparently the only State to bar all importation of live baitfish. See *id.*, at 761. Second, Maine accepted interstate shipments, of other freshwater fish, subject to an inspection requirement. Third, "an aura of economic protectionism" surrounded statements made in 1981 by the Maine Department of Inland Fisheries and Wildlife in opposition to a proposal by appellee himself to repeal the ban. *Ibid.* Finally, the court noted that parasites and nonnative species could be transported into Maine in shipments of nonbaitfish, and that nothing prevented fish from simply swimming into the State from New Hampshire. *Id.*, at 762, n. 12.

Despite these indications of protectionist intent, the Court of Appeals rested its invalidation of Maine's import ban on a different basis, concluding that Maine had not demonstrated that any legitimate local purpose served by the ban could not be promoted equally well without discriminating so heavily against interstate commerce. Specifically, the court found it "difficult to reconcile" Maine's claim that it could not rely on sampling and inspection with the State's reliance on similar procedures in the case of other freshwater fish. *Id.*, at 762.[16]

Following the reversal of appellee's conviction, Maine and the United States petitioned for rehearing on the ground that the Court of Appeals had improperly disregarded the District Court's findings of fact. The court denied the petitions, concluding that, since the unavailability of a less discriminatory alternative "was a mixed finding of law and fact," a reviewing court "was free to examine carefully the factual record and to draw its own conclusions." *Id.*, at 765.

---

[15] While the District Court approved the Magistrate's general finding that "there are no obviously workable alternatives to the outright prohibition of importation," *id.*, at 398, neither the court nor the Magistrate made any specific finding as to whether Maine could adequately protect against the inadvertent introduction of nonnative species by allowing baitfish to be imported only from professional bait farmers using freshly drained ponds. There was conflicting evidence on this point. Appellee's expert suggested that such methods largely eliminated the problem of commingled species, App. 239–240, but a prosecution witness testified that complete success was "unlikely." *Id.*, at 170. See also *id.*, at 150 (prosecution testimony that shipments cannot be screened reliably for commingled species because "[t]his is a business. You have living material that you have to move; you can't hold them in tanks and this kind of thing for any length of time"). We are in no position to resolve this factual dispute, and we conclude in any event that the District Court's findings regarding parasites adequately support the constitutionality of the challenged statute.

[16] The court also noted that "a restriction on the number and size of importations would be less restrictive than a total ban," 752 F. 2d, at 762, but it identified no reason to believe that such a restriction would protect against parasites and commingled species as effectively as a ban.

B

Although the proffered justification for any local discrimination against interstate commerce must be subjected to "the strictest scrutiny," *Hughes* v. *Oklahoma,* 441 U.S., at 337, the empirical component of that scrutiny, like any other form of factfinding, "is the basic responsibility of district courts, rather than appellate courts,' " *Pullman-Standard* v. *Swint,* 456 U. S. 273, 291 (1982), quoting *DeMarco* v. *United States,* 415 U. S. 449, 450, n. (1974). As this court frequently has emphasized, appellate courts are not to decide factual questions *de novo,* reversing any findings they would have made differently. See, *e.g., Anderson* v. *Bessemer City,* 470 U. S. 564, 573 (1985); *Zenith Radio Corp.* v. *Hazeltine Research, Inc.,* 395 U. S. 100, 123 (1969). The Federal Rules of Criminal Procedure contain no counterpart to Federal Rule of Civil Procedures 52(a), which expressly provides that findings of fact made by the trial judge "shall not be set aside unless clearly erroneous." But the considerations underlying Rule 52(a)—the demands of judicial efficiency, the expertise developed by trial judges, and the importance of firsthand observation, see *Anderson, supra,* at 574–575—all apply with full force in the criminal context, at least with respect to factual questions having nothing to do with guilt. Accordingly, the "clearly erroneous" standard of review long has been applied to nonguilt findings of fact by district courts in criminal cases. See *Campbell* v. *United States,* 373 U. S. 487, 493 (1963); 2 C. Wright, Federal Practice and Procedure § 374 (2d ed. 1982). We need not decide now whether all such findings should be reviewed under the "clearly erroneous" standard, because appellee concedes that the standard applies to the factual findings made by the District Court in this case. See Tr. of Oral Arg. 27. We note, however, that no broader review is authorized here simply because this is a constitutional case, or because the factual findings at issue may determine the outcome of the case. See *Bose Corp.* v. *Consumers Union of United States, Inc.,* 466 U. S. 485, 501 (1984); *Pullman-Standard* v. *Swint,* 456 U. S., at 287.[17]

No matter how one describes the abstract issue whether "alternative means could promote this local purpose as well without discriminating against interstate commerce," *Hughes* v. *Oklahoma,* 441 U. S., at 336, the more specific question whether scientifically accepted techniques exist for the sampling and inspection of live baitfish is one of fact, and the District Court's finding that such techniques have not been devised cannot

---

[17] In support of its conclusion that it "was free to examine carefully the factual record and to draw its own conclusions," *id.,* at 765, the Court of Appeals cited *Bacchus Imports, Ltd.* v. *Dias,* 468 U. S. 263 (1984), and *Boston Stock Exchange* v. *State Tax Comm'n,* 429 U. S. 318 (1977). The question in each of these cases was whether a given set of facts amounted to discrimination forbidden by the Commerce Clause; in neither case did this Court reject underlying factual findings made by the trial court. Indeed, there were no such findings to reject—the facts were stipulated in *Bacchus,* see 468 U. S., at 269, and *Boston Stock Exchange* was decided on a motion to dismiss, see 429 U. S., at 320.

be characterized as clearly erroneous. Indeed, the record probably could not support a contrary finding. Two prosecution witnesses testified to the lack of such procedures, and appellee's expert conceded the point, although he disagreed about the need for such tests. See App. 74–75, 184, 265–266. That Maine has allowed the importation of other freshwater fish after inspection hardly demonstrates that the District Court clearly erred in crediting the corroborated and uncontradicted expert testimony that standardized inspection techniques had not yet been developed for baitfish. This is particularly so because the text of the permit statute suggests that it was designed specifically to regulate importation of salmonids, for which, the experts testified, testing procedures had been developed.[18]

Before this Court, appellee does not argue that sampling and inspection procedures already exist for baitfish; he contends only that such procedures "could be easily developed." Brief for Appellee 25. Perhaps this is also what the Court of Appeals meant to suggest. Unlike the proposition that the techniques already exist, the contention that they could readily be devised enjoys some support in the record. Appellee's expert testified that developing the techniques "would just require that those experts in the field . . . get together and do it." App. 271. He gave no estimate of the time and expense that would be involved, however, and one of the prosecution experts testified that development of the testing procedures for salmonids had required years of heavily financed research. See *id.,* at 74. In light of this testimony, we cannot say that the District Court clearly erred in concluding, 585 F. Supp., at 398, n. 11, that the development of sampling and inspection techniques for baitfish could be expected to take a significant amount of time.

More importantly, we agree with the District Court that the "abstract possibility," *id.,* at 398, of developing acceptable testing procedures, particularly when there is no assurance as to their effectiveness, does not make those procedures an "[a]vailabl[e] . . .] nondiscriminatory alternativ[e]," *Hunt,* 432 U. S., at 353, for purposes of the Commerce Clause. A State must make reasonable efforts to avoid restraining the free flow of commerce across its borders, but it is not required to develop new and unproven means of protection at an uncertain cost. Appellee, of course, is free to work on his own or in conjunction with other bait dealers to develop scientifically acceptable sampling and inspection procedures for golden shiners; if and when such procedures are developed, Maine no

---

[18] The statute provides: "This commissioner *may* grant permits" for the importation of freshwater fish upon an application that describes the fish and their source and includes "[a] statement from a recognized fish pathologist, from a college or university, from a state conservation department or from the United States Fish and Wildlife Service, certifying that the fish . . . are from sources which show no evidence of viral hemorrhagic septicemia, infectious pancreatic necrosis, infectious hematopoietic necrosis, Myxosomo cerebralis or other diseases which may threaten fish stocks within the State." Me. Rev. Stat. Ann., Tit. 12, §7202 (1981) (emphasis added). The listed diseases all were identified at the hearing before the Magistrate as salmonid disorders. See App. 193.

longer may be able to justify its import ban. The State need not join in those efforts, however, and it need not pretend they already have succeeded.

C

Although the Court of Appeals did not expressly overturn the District Court's finding that Maine's import ban serves a legitimate local purpose, appellee argues as an alternative ground for affirmance that this finding should be rejected. After reviewing the expert testimony presented to the Magistrate, however, we cannot say that the District Court clearly erred in finding that substantial scientific uncertainty surrounds the effect that baitfish parasites and nonnative species could have on Maine's fisheries. Moreover, we agree with the District Court that Maine has a legitimate interest in guarding against imperfectly understood environmental risks, despite the possibility that they may ultimately prove to be negligible. "[T]he constitutional principles underlying the commerce clause cannot be read as requiring the State of Maine to sit idly by and wait until potentially irreversible environmental damage has occurred or until the scientific community agrees on what disease organisms are or are not dangerous before it acts to avoid such consequences." 585 F. Supp., at 397.

Nor do we think that much doubt is cast on the legitimacy of Maine's purposes by what the Court of Appeals took to be signs of protectionist intent. Shielding in-state industries from out-of-state competition is almost never a legitimate local purpose, and state laws that amount to "simple economic protectionism" consequently have been subject to a "virtually *per se* rule of invalidity." *Philadelphia* v. *New Jersey,* 437 U. S. 617, 624 (1978); accord, *e.g., Minnesota* v. *Clover Leaf Creamery Co.,* 449 U. S. 456, 471 (1981).[19] But there is little reason in this case

---

[19] This rule has been applied not only to laws motivated solely by a desire to protect local industries from out-of-state competition, but also to laws that respond to legitimate local concerns by discriminating arbitrarily against interstate trade, for "the evil of protectionism can reside in legislative means as well as legislative ends." *Philadelphia* v. *New Jersey,* 437 U. S., at 626. The Court has held, for example, that New Jersey may not conserve the disposal capacity of its landfill sites by banning importation of wastes, see *ibid.,* and that Oklahoma may not fight depletion of its population of natural minnows by prohibiting their commercial exportation, see *Hughes* v. *Oklahoma,* 441 U. S. 322 (1979). In each case, out-of-state residents were forced to bear the brunt of the conservation program for no apparent reason other than that they lived and voted in other States. See *Philadelphia* v. *New Jersey,* 437 U. S., at 629; *Hughes,* 441 U. S., at 337–338, and n. 20. Not all intentional barriers to interstate trade are protectionist, however, and the Commerce Clause "is not a guaranty of the right to import into a state whatever one may please, absent a prohibition by Congress, regardless of the effects of the importation upon the local community." *Robertson* v. *California,* 328 U. S. 440, 458 (1946). Even overt discrimination against interstate trade may be justified where, as in this case, out-of-state goods or services are particularly likely for some reason to threaten the health and safety of a State's citizens or the integrity of its natural resources, and where "outright prohibition of entry, rather than some intermediate form of regulation, is the only effective method of protecti[on]." *Lewis* v. *BT Investment Managers, Inc.,* 447 U. S. 27, 43 (1980).

to believe that the legitimate justifications the State has put forward for its statute are merely a sham or a "*post hoc* rationalization." *Hughes,* 441 U. S., at 338, n. 20. In suggesting to the contrary, the Court of Appeals relied heavily on a 3-sentence passage near the end of a 2,000-word statement submitted in 1981 by the Maine Department of Inland Fisheries and Wildlife in opposition to appellee's proposed repeal of the State's ban on the importation of live baitfish:

> " '[W]e can't help asking why we should spend our money in Arkansas when it is far better spent at home? It is very clear that much more can be done here in Maine to provide our sportsmen with safe, home-grown bait. There is also a possibility that such an industry could develop a lucrative export market in neighboring states.' " 752 F. 2d, at 760, quoting Baitfish Importation: The Position of the Maine Department of Inland Fisheries and Wildlife, App. 294, 309–310.

We fully agree with the Magistrate that "[t]hese three sentences do not convert the Maine statute into an economic protectionism measure." App. To Juris. Statement E–6, n. 4.[20] As the Magistrate pointed out, the context of the statements cited by appellee "reveals [they] are advanced not in direct support of the statute, but to counter the argument that inadequate bait supplies in Maine require acceptance of the environmental risks of imports. Instead, the Department argues, Maine's own bait supplies can be increased." *Ibid.* Furthermore, the comments were made by a state administrative agency long after the statute's enactment, and thus constitute weak evidence of legislative intent in any event. See *ibid.*[21]

The other evidence of protectionism identified by the Court of Appeals is no more persuasive. The fact that Maine allows importation of salmonids, for which standardized sampling and inspection procedures are available, hardly demonstrates that Maine has no legitimate interest in prohibiting the importation of baitfish, for which such procedures have not yet been devised. Nor is this demonstrated by the fact that other States

---

[20] The District Court did not address appellee's argument that the import ban was protectionist, because it did not believe that appellee had objected to the Magistrate's rejection of that argument. See 585 F. Supp., at 395, n. 5. The Court of Appeals disagreed, concluding that appellee's objections to the Magistrate's recommended decision incorporated all the arguments included in his motion to dismiss. See 752 F. 2d, at 760, n. 7. In the objections he filed with the District Court, appellee did not specifically contend that the statute was protectionist, but he concluded by asking that the indictment be dismissed "[f]or the reasons stated herein and *also for those reasons stated in Defendant's Memorandum of Law in Support of Motion to Dismiss.*" Defendant's Objection to the Magistrate's Recommended Decision on Defendant's Motion to Dismiss Indictment 4 (Mar. 12, 1984) (emphasis added). Because we think the Magistrate was clearly right to reject the argument that Maine's bait statute constitutes economic protectionism, we need not decide whether this catchall language sufficed to preserve the argument for later review. Cf. *Thomas* v. *Arn,* 474 U. S. 140, 148–149 (1985).

[21] The import ban was originally enacted in 1959. See 1959 Me. Acts, ch. 112.

may not have enacted similar bans, especially given the testimony that Maine's fisheries are unique and unusually fragile.[22] Finally, it is of little relevance that fish can swim directly into Maine from New Hampshire. As the Magistrate explained: "The impediments to complete success . . . cannot be a ground for preventing a state from using its best efforts to limit [an environmental] risk." *Id.*, at E–10, n. 8.

IV

The Commerce Clause significantly limits the ability of States and localities to regulate or otherwise burden the flow of interstate commerce, but it does not elevate free trade above all other values. As long as a State does not needlessly obstruct interstate trade or attempt to "place itself in a position of economic isolation," *Baldwin v. G.A.F. Seelig, Inc.*, 294 U. S. 511, 527 (1935), it retains broad regulatory authority to protect the health and safety of its citizens and the integrity of its natural resources. The evidence in this case amply supports the District Court's findings that Maine's ban on the importation of live baitfish serves legitimate local purposes that could not adequately be served by available nondiscriminatory alternatives. This is not a case of arbitrary discrimination against interstate commerce; the record suggests that Maine has legitimate reasons, "apart from their origin, to treat [out-of-state baitfish] differently," *Philadelphia v. New Jersey*, 437 U. S., at 627. The judgment of the Court of Appeals setting aside appellee's conviction is therefore reversed.

It is so ordered.

JUSTICE STEVENS, dissenting.

There is something fishy about this case. Maine is the only State in the Union that blatantly discriminates against out-of-state baitfish by flatly prohibiting their importation. Although golden shiners are already present and thriving in Maine (and, perhaps not coincidentally, the subject of a flourishing domestic industry), Maine excludes golden shiners grown

---

[22] Although Maine's flat statutory ban on the importation of all live baitfish is apparently unique, Minnesota prohibits the use of imported minnows for bait purposes "[e]xcept as otherwise specifically permitted," Minn. Stat. §101.42, subd. 6 (1984), and several other States require administrative approval for the importation and introduction of any live fish, see, *e.g.*, Utah Code Ann. §23–15–12 (1984); Va. Code §28.1–183.2 (1985); Wis. Stat. §29.535 (Supp. 1985); cf. S. D. Codified Laws §41–14–30 (1977) (minnows may be transported "into or through South Dakota" only pursuant to a 12-hour permit). Other States have granted authority to their wildlife agencies to prohibit the importation of particular species. See, *e.g.*, Ala. Code §9–2–13 (1980); N. C. Gen. Stat. §113–160 (1983); cf. Nev. Rev. Stat. §503.310(1) (1985) ("The [state wildlife] commission is empowered to regulate or prohibit the use of live bait in fishing to the end that no undesirable species of fish intentionally or unintentionally may be introduced into the public waters of this state").

and harvested (and, perhaps not coincidentally, sold) in other States. This kind of stark discrimination against out-of-state articles of commerce requires rigorous justification by the discriminating State. "When discrimination against commerce of the type we have found is demonstrated, the burden falls on the State to justify it both in terms of the local benefits flowing from the statute and the unavailability of nondiscriminatory alternatives adequate to preserve the local interests at stake." *Hunt* v. *Washington State Apple Advertising Comm'n,* 432 U. S. 333, 353 (1977).

Like the District Court, the Court concludes that uncertainty about possible ecological effects from the possible presence of parasites and nonnative species in shipments of out-of-state shiners suffices to carry the State's burden of proving a legitimate public purpose. *Ante,* at 142–143, 148. The Court similarly concludes that the State has no obligation to develop feasible inspection procedures that would make a total ban unnecessary. *Ante,* at 147. It seems clear, however, that the presumption should run the other way. Since the State engages in obvious discrimination against out-of-state commerce, it should be put to its proof. Ambiguity about dangers and alternatives should actually defeat, rather than sustain, the discriminatory measure.

This is not to derogate the State's interest in ecological purity. But the invocation of environmental protection or public health has never been thought to confer some kind of special dispensation from the general principle of nondiscrimination in interstate commerce. "A different view, that the ordinance is valid simply because it professes to be a health measure, would mean that the Commerce Clause of itself imposes no restraints on state action other than those laid down by the Due Process Clause, save for the rare instance where a state artlessly discloses an avowed purpose to discriminate against interstate goods." *Dean Milk Co.* v. *Madison,* 340 U. S. 349, 354 (1951). If Maine wishes to rely on its interest in ecological preservation, it must show that interest, and the infeasibility of other alternatives, with far greater specificity. Otherwise, it must further that asserted interest in a manner far less offensive to the notions of comity and cooperation that underlie the Commerce Clause.

Significantly, the Court of Appeals, which is more familiar with Maine's natural resources and with its legislation than we are, was concerned by the uniqueness of Maine's ban. That court felt, as I do, that Maine's unquestionable natural splendor notwithstanding, the State has not carried its substantial burden of proving why it cannot meet its environmental concerns in the same manner as other States with the same interest in the health of their fish and ecology. Cf. *ante,* at 151, n. 22 (describing less restrictive procedures in other States).

I respectfully dissent.

BROWN-FORMAN DISTILLERS CORP. *v.*
NEW YORK STATE LIQUOR AUTHORITY
476 U.S. 573

APPEAL FROM COURT APPEALS OF NEW YORK

MARSHALL, J., delivered the opinion of the Court, in which BURGER, C. J., and POWELL and O'CONNOR, JJ., joined, and in all but n. 6 of which BLACKMUN, J., joined. BLACKMUN, J., filed a concurring opinion, *post*, p. 586. STEVENS, J., filed a dissenting opinion, in which WHITE and REHNQUIST, JJ., joined, *post*, p. 586. BRENNAN, J., took no part in the consideration or decision of the case.

JUSTICE MARSHALL delivered the opinion of the Court.

The State of New York requires every liquor distiller or producer that sells liquor to wholesalers within the State to sell at a price that is no higher than the lowest price the distiller charges wholesalers anywhere else in the United States. The issue in this case is whether that requirement violates the Commerce Clause of the Constitution.

I

New York extensively regulates the sale and distribution of alcoholic beverages within its borders. The State's Alcoholic Beverage Control Law (ABC Law) prohibits the manufacture and sale of alcoholic beverages within the State without the appropriate licenses, ABC Law § 100(1) (McKinney 1970), and regulates the terms of all sales, §§ 101-a to 101-bbb (McKinney 1970 and Supp. 1986). Distillers and their agents may not sell to wholesalers in New York except in accordance with a price schedule filed with the State Liquor Authority. § 101-b(3)(a). The distiller or agent must file the price schedule before the 25th day of each month, and the prices therein become effective on the first day of the second following month. The schedule must contain a precise description of each item the distiller intends to sell, and a per-bottle and per-case price. All sales to any wholesaler in New York during the month for which the schedule is in effect must be at those prices.

Briefs of *amici curiae* urging reversal were filed for the Distilled Spirits Council of the United States, Inc., by *David W. Ichel* and *Russell W. Shannon;* for the Distillers Somerset Group Inc. by *Bartlett H. McGuire* and *James D. Liss;* for the United States Brewers Association, Inc., et al. by *Jeffrey Ives Glekel, Timothy G. Reynolds, Lawrence J. Block, Jerome I. Chapman,* and *William F. Allen;* and for the Wine Institute by *Arnold M. Lerman, Daniel Marcus,* and *Roy T. Englert, Jr.*

Briefs of *amici curiae* urging affirmance were filed for the National Conference of State Legislatures et al. by *Benna Ruth Solomon;* and for Wine and Spirits Wholesalers of America, Inc., by *Michael Whiteman, Douglas W. Metz,* and *Abraham Tunick.*

This litigation concerns § 101-b(3)(d) of the ABC Law, which requires any distiller or agent that files a schedule of prices to include an affirmation that "the bottle and case price of liquor to wholesalers set forth in such schedule is no higher than the lowest price at which such item of liquor will be sold by such [distiller] to any wholesaler anywhere in any other state of the United States or in the District of Columbia, or to any state (or state agency) which owns and operates retail liquor stores" during the month covered by the schedule. Violation of the statute may lead to revocation of a distiller's license and the forfeiture of bond posted by the distiller in connection with the license, § 101-b(6). Twenty other States have similar affirmation laws.[1]

Appellant Brown-Forman Distillers Corp. (Brown-Forman) is a distiller that owns several brands of liquor that it sells in New York and in other States. Beginning in 1978, appellant has offered its wholesalers cash payments, or "promotional allowances," which are credited against any amounts due appellant.[2] Appellant intends for wholesalers to use these allowances for advertising; however, the amount of the allowance a wholesaler receives is not tied to the quantity either of the wholesaler's advertising or of its purchases of appellant's products. The amount of a particular wholesaler's allowance does depend on its past purchases and projections of future purchases, but accepting the allowance does not constitute an agreement to purchase any particular quantity of Brown-Forman products. The allowances, therefore, are unconditional, lump-sum payments to all wholesalers, in every State except New York, that purchase Brown-Forman brands.

Appellant offered the promotional allowance to its New York wholesalers, but the Liquor Authority determined that the ABC Law prohibited

---

[1] These States differ in the time reference for the affirmation price. Some require the distiller to set a price that is no higher than the lowest price charged *previously* anywhere in the United States, see, *e.g.,* Ariz. Rev. Stat. Ann. §4-253(A)(Supp. 1985). Others, like New York, require the affirmed price to be no higher than the lowest price that will be charged during the *current* month. See ABC Law §101-b(3)(d).

There are 18 States, known as "control" States, that purchase all liquor that will be distributed and consumed within their borders. The control States use a standard sales contract that requires the distiller to warrant that the price the distiller charges to the State is no higher than the lowest price offered anywhere else in the United States. See Brief for Appellant 5, n. 4.

[2] The Federal Bureau of Alcohol, Tobacco and Firearms (BATF), upon appellant's request, ruled that appellant's promotional allowance does not violate the Federal Alcohol Administration Act, 27 U. S. C. §§201-211. See §205(b) (prohibiting "paying or crediting [any] retailer [of alcoholic beverages] for any advertising" if done to induce the retailer to purchase alcohol from the person providing such payment or credit to the exclusion in whole or in part of other distillers or producers). Some of the features of appellant's promotional allowance program described herein were required by BATF in order to ensure that the program would not violate the Act. See Juris. Statement 4.

such payments.[3] The Authority also determined, however, that the payment of promotional allowances to wholesalers in other States lowered the effective price of Brown-Forman brands to those wholesalers, and thus violated § 101-b(3)(d) of the ABC Law.[4] The Liquor Authority accordingly instituted license revocation proceedings against appellant.

Appellant sought review of the Liquor Authority's ruling in the state courts, asserting that it was both arbitrary and unconstitutional. Appellant contended that it could not possibly file a schedule of prices that reflected precisely the "effective price" charged to wholesalers in other States, because there was no one "effective price." Each participating wholesaler could pay a different effective price in a given month depending on the amount of Brown-Forman product it had purchased during that month. Moreover, appellant argued, other States did not treat the promotional allowances as discounts. Were New York to force appellant to reduce its prices in that State, appellant would be charging a lower price to New York wholesalers than the price recognized by other States, thereby forcing appellant to violate the affirmation laws of those States. Appellant contended that the only way to avoid this dilemma was to stop offering promotional allowances, unless other States chose to alter their affirmation laws. By effectively forcing appellant to discontinue a promotional program in other States where that program was legal, appellant argued, New York's regulation violated the Commerce Clause. Appellant also argued that the affirmation law on its face directly regulated interstate commerce in violation of the Commerce Clause.

The Appellate Division of the New York Supreme Court rejected these arguments, 100 App. Div. 2d 55, 473 N. Y. S. 2d 420 (1984), as did the New York Court of Appeals, 64 N. Y. 2d 479, 479 N. E. 2d 764 (1985). The Court of Appeals concluded, first, that the Liquor Authority's decision to consider the promotional allowances as a discount was supported by substantial evidence. Second, the court held that the ABC Law as applied does not violate the Commerce Clause, rejecting as speculative appellant's contention that it cannot comply simultaneously with the affirmation laws of New York and of other States. Finally, the court held that the affirmation law, on its face, does not violate the Commerce Clause. We noted probable jurisdiction limited to the question whether the ABC Law, on its face, violates the Commerce Clause, 474 U. S. 814 (1985). We now reverse.

---

[3] See § 101-b(2)(b) (prohibiting "any discount, rebate, free goods, allowance or other inducement of any kind whatsoever" except for quantity and prompt-payment discounts of specified amounts).

[4] See § 101-b(3)(g) (in determining lowest price, "appropriate reductions shall be made to reflect all discounts . . . and all rebates, free goods, allowances and other inducements").

II

This Court has adopted what amounts to a two-tiered approach to analyzing state economic regulation under the Commerce Clause. When a state statute directly regulates or discriminates against interstate commerce, or when its effect is to favor in-state economic interests over out-of-state interests, we have generally struck down the statute without further inquiry. See, *e.g., Philadelphia* v. *New Jersey,* 437 U. S. 617 (1978); *Shafer* v. *Farmers Grain Co.,* 268 U. S. 189 (1925); *Edgar* v. *MITE Corp.,* 457 U. S. 624, 640–643 (1982) (plurality opinion). When, however, a statute has only indirect effects on interstate commerce and regulates evenhandedly, we have examined whether the State's interest is legitimate and whether the burden on interstate commerce clearly exceeds the local benefits. *Pike* v. *Bruce Church, Inc.,* 397 U. S. 137, 142 (1970). We have also recognized that there is no clear line separating the category of state regulation that is virtually *per se* invalid under the Commerce Clause, and the category subject to the *Pike* v. *Bruce Church* balancing approach. In either situation the critical consideration is the overall effect of the statute on both local and interstate activity. See *Raymond Motor Transportation, Inc.* v. *Rice,* 434 U. S. 429, 440–441 (1978).

A

Appellant does not dispute that New York's affirmation law regulates all distillers of intoxicating liquors evenhandedly, or that the State's asserted interest—to assure the lowest possible prices for its residents—is legitimate. Appellant contends that these factors are irrelevant, however, because the lowest-price affirmation provision of the ABC Law falls within that category of direct regulations of interstate commerce that the Commerce Clause wholly forbids. This is so, appellant contends, because the ABC Law effectively regulates the price at which liquor is sold in other States. By requiring distillers to affirm that they will make no sales anywhere in the United States at a price lower than the posted price in New York, appellant argues, New York makes it illegal for a distiller to reduce its price in other States during the period that the posed New York price is in effect. Appellant contends that this constitutes direct regulation of interstate commerce. The law also disadvantages consumers in other States, according to appellant, and is therefore the sort of "simple economic protectionism" that this Court has routinely forbidden. *Philadelphia* v. *New Jersey, supra,* at 624.

If appellant has correctly characterized the effect of the New York lowest-price affirmation law, that law violates the Commerce Clause. While a State may seek lower prices for its consumers, it may not insist that producers or consumers in other States surrender whatever competitive advantages they may possess. *Baldwin* v. *G. A. F. Seelig, Inc.,* 294 U. S. 511, 528 (1935); *Schwegmann Brothers Giant Super Markets* v. *Louisiana Milk Comm'n,* 365 F. Supp. 1144 (MD La. 1973), aff'd, 416 U. S. 922 (1974). Economic protectionism is not limited to attempts to convey advantages on local merchants; it may include attempts to give local consumers an advantage over consumers in other States. See, *e.g., New England Power Co.* v. *New Hampshire,* 455 U. S. 331, 338 (1982) (State may not require "that its residents be given a preferred right of access, over out-of-state consumers, to natural resources located within its borders"). In *Seelig, supra,* this Court struck down New York's Milk Control Act. The Act set minimum prices for milk purchased from producers in New York and in other States, and banned the resale within New York of milk that had been purchased for a lower price. Justice Cardozo's opinion for the Court recognized that a State may not "establish a wage scale or a scale of prices for use in other states, and . . . bar the sale of the products . . . unless the scale has been observed." *Id.,* at 528. The mere fact that the effects of New York's ABC Law are triggered only by sales of liquor within the State of New York therefore does not validate the law if it regulates the out-of-state transactions of distillers who sell in-state. Our inquiry, then, must center on whether New York's affirmation law regulates commerce in other States.

B

This Court has once before examined the extraterritorial effects of a New York affirmation statute. In *Joseph E. Seagram & Sons, Inc.* v. *Hostetter,* 384 U. S. 35 (1966), the Court considered the constitutionality, under the Commerce and Supremacy Clauses, of the predecessor to New York's current affirmation law. That law differed from the present version in that it required the distiller to affirm that its prices during a given month in New York would be no higher than the lowest price at which the item had been sold elsewhere during the *previous* month. The Court recognized in that case, as we have here, that the most important issue was whether the statute regulated out-of-state transactions. *Id.,* at 42–43. It concluded, however, that "[t]he mere fact that [the statute] is geared to appellants' pricing policies in other States is not sufficient to invalidate the statute." The Court distinguished *Seelig, supra,* by concluding that any effects of New York's ABC Law on a distiller's pricing policies in other States were "largely matters of conjecture," 384 U.S., at 42–43.

Appellant relies on *United States Brewers Assn.* v. *Healy,* 692 F. 2d 275 (CA2 1982), summarily aff'd, 464 U. S. 909 (1983), in seeking to distinguish the present case from *Seagram.* In *Healy,* the Court of Appeals for the Second Circuit considered a Connecticut price-affirmation statute for beer sales that is not materially different from the current New York ABC Law. The Connecticut statute, like the ABC Law, required sellers to post prices at the beginning of a month, and proscribed deviation from the posted prices during that month. The statute also required brewers to affirm that their prices in Connecticut were as low as the price at which they would sell beer in any bordering State during the effective month of the posted prices. The Court of Appeals distinguished *Seagram* based on the "prospective" nature of this affirmation requirement. It concluded that the Connecticut statute made it impossible for a brewer to lower its price in a bordering State in response to market conditions so long as it had a higher posted price in effect in Connecticut. By so doing, the statute "regulate[d] conduct occurring wholly outside the state," 692 F. 2d, at 279, and thereby violated the Commerce Clause. We affirmed summarily.

C

We agree with appellant and with the *Healy* court that a "prospective" statute such as Connecticut's beer affirmation statute, or New York's liquor affirmation statute, regulates out-of-state transactions in violation of the Commerce Clause. Once a distiller has posted prices in New York, it is not free to change its prices elsewhere in the United States during the relevant month.[5] Forcing a merchant to seek regulatory approval in one State before undertaking a transaction in another directly regulates interstate commerce. *Edgar* v. *MITE Corp.*, 457 U. S., at 642 (plurality opinion); see also *Baldwin* v. *G. A. F. Seelig, Inc.*, 294 U. S., at 522 (regulation tending to "mitigate the consequences of competition between the states" constitutes direct regulation). While New York may regulate the sale of liquor within its borders, and may seek low prices for its residents, it may not "project its legislation into [other States] by regulating the price to be paid" for liquor in those States. *Id.*, at 521.

That the ABC Law is addressed only to sales of liquor in New York is irrelevant if the "practical effect" of the law is to control liquor prices in other States. *Southern Pacific Co.* v. *Arizona ex rel. Sullivan*, 325 U. S. 761, 775 (1945). We cannot agree with New York that the practical effects of the affirmation law are speculative. It is undisputed that once a

---

[5] The Liquor Authority may "for good cause shown" permit a distiller to change its prices during a particular month, ABC Law § 101-b(3)(a), and New York speculates that the Authority would permit a distiller to lower its prices in other States in a given month so long as the distiller also lowers them in New York. However, whether to permit such a deviation from the statutory scheme is a matter left by the statute to the discretion of the Liquor Authority.

We would not solve the constitutional problems inherent in New York's statute by indulging the dissent's assumption that the Authority will be sensitive to Commerce Clause concerns. Certainly New York could not require an out-of-state company to receive a license from New York to do business in other States, even if we were quite sure that such licenses would be granted as a matter of course. Similarly, New York simply may not force appellant to seek regulatory approval from New York before it can reduce its prices in another State. The protections afforded by the Commerce Clause cannot be made to depend on the good grace of a state agency.

distiller's posted price is in effect in New York, it must seek the approval of the New York State Liquor Authority before it may lower its price for the same item in other States. It is not at all counterintuitive, as the dissent maintains, *post,* at 588, to assume that the Liquor Authority would not permit appellant to reduce its New York price after the posted price has taken effect. The stated purpose of the prohibition on price changes during a given month is to prevent price discrimination among retailers, see ABC Law §§ 101-b(1), (2)(a). That goal is in direct conflict with the dissent's view of the "whole purpose" of the ABC Law, and we have no means of predicting how the Authority would resolve that conflict. We do know, however, that the Liquor Authority forbade appellant to reduce its New York prices by offering promotional allowances to New York retailers, precisely because the Authority believed that program would violate the price-discrimination provisions. App. to Juris. Statement 50a. The dissent would require us to assume that other States will adopt a flexible approach to appellant's promotional allowance program, *post,* at 589, despite New York's refusal to do so.

Moreover, the proliferation of state affirmation laws following this Court's decision in *Seagram* has greatly multiplied the likelihood that a seller will be subjected to inconsistent obligations in different States. The ease with which New York's lowest-price regulation can interfere with a distiller's operations in other States is aptly demonstrated by the controversy that gave rise to this lawsuit. By defining the "effective price" of liquor differently from other States, New York can effectively force appellant to abandon its promotional allowance program in States in which that program is legal, or force those other States to alter their own regulatory schemes in order to permit appellant to lower its New York prices without violating the affirmation laws of those States. Thus New York has "project[ed] its legislation" into other States, and directly regulated commerce therein, in violation of *Seelig, supra.*[6]

III

New York finally contends that the Twenty-first Amendment, which bans the importation or possession of intoxicating liquors into a State "in violation of the laws thereof," saves the ABC Law from invalida-

---

[6] While we hold that New York's prospective price affirmation statute violates the Commerce Clause, we do not necessarily attach constitutional significance to the difference between a prospective statute and the retrospective statute at issue in *Seagram.* Indeed, one could argue that the effects of the statute in *Seagram* do not differ markedly from the effects of the statute at issue in the present case. If there is a conflict between today's decision and the *Seagram* decision, however, there will be time enough to address that conflict should a case arise involving a retrospective statute. Because no such statute is before us now, we need not consider the continuing validity of *Seagram.*

tion under the Commerce Clause. That Amendment gives the States wide latitude to regulate the importation and distribution of liquor within their territories, *California Liquor Dealers Assn.* v. *Midcal Aluminum, Inc.,* 445 U. S. 97, 107 (1980). Therefore, New York argues, its ABC Law, which regulates the sale of alcoholic beverages within the State, is a valid exercise of the State's authority.

It is well settled that the Twenty-first Amendment did not entirely remove state regulation of alcohol from the reach of the Commerce Clause. See *Bacchus Imports, Ltd.* v. *Dias,* 468 U. S. 263 (1984). Rather, the Twenty-first Amendment and the Commerce Clause "each must be considered in light of the other and in the context of the issues and interests at stake in any concrete case." *Hostetter* v. *Idlewild Bon Voyage Liquor Corp.,* 377 U. S. 324, 332 (1964). Our task, then, is to reconcile the interests protected by the two constitutional provisions.

New York has a valid constitutional interest in regulating sales of liquor within the territory of New York. Section 2 of the Twenty-first Amendment, however, speaks only to state regulation of the "transportation or importation into any State . . . for delivery or use therein" of alcoholic beverages. That Amendment, therefore, gives New York only the authority to control sales of liquor in New York, and confers no authority to control sales in other States. The Commerce Clause operates with full force whenever one State attempts to regulate the transportation and sale of alcoholic beverages destined for distribution and consumption in a foreign country, *Idlewild Bon Voyage Liquor Corp., supra,* or another State. Our conclusion that New York has attempted to regulate sales in other States of liquor that will be consumed in other States therefore disposes of the Twenty-first Amendment issue.

Moreover, New York's affirmation law may interfere with the ability of other States to exercise their own authority under the Twenty-first Amendment. Once a distiller has posted prices in New York, it is not free to lower them in another State, even in response to a regulatory directive by that State, without risking forfeiture of its license in New York. New York law, therefore, may force other States to either abandon regulatory goals or to deprive their citizens of the opportunity to purchase brands of liquor that are sold in New York. New York's reliance on the Twenty-first Amendment is therefore misplaced. Having found that the ABC Law on its face violates the Commerce Clause, and is not a valid exercise of New York's powers under the Twenty-first Amendment, we reverse the judgment of the New York Court of Appeals.

It is so ordered.

JUSTICE BRENNAN took no part in the consideration or decision of this case.

JUSTICE BLACKMUN, concurring.

I join the Court's opinion (except for its footnote 6), but I would go further and overrule *Joseph E. Seagram & Sons, Inc. v. Hostetter,* 384 U. S. 35 (1966). *Seagram* is now a relic of the past. It was decided when affirmation statutes were comparatively new and long before the proliferation of overlapping and potentially conflicting affirmation statutes that has taken place in the last two decades. I see no principled distinction that can be drawn for constitutional analysis between New York's current prospective statute and the same State's retroactive statute upheld in *Seagram,* and I doubt very much whether any Member of this Court would be able to perceive one. Either type, despite one's best efforts at fine-tuning, operates to affect out-of-state transactions and violates the Commerce Clause. Our failure to overrule *Seagram* now merely preserves uncertainty and will breed or necessitate further litigation. We should face reality and overrule *Seagram.*

JUSTICE STEVENS, with whom JUSTICE WHITE and JUSTICE REHNQUIST join, dissenting.

Speculation about hypothetical cases illuminates the discussion in a classroom, but it is evidence and historical fact that provide the most illumination in a courtroom. Forgoing the support of a record developed at trial, appellant Brown-Forman Distillers Corporation (Brown-Forman) contends that New York's Alcoholic Beverage Control (ABC) Law § 100 *et seq.* (McKinney 1970 and Supp. 1986) is an unconstitutional burden on interstate commerce "on its face." Over 20 years ago this Court unanimously refused to invalidate the predecessor of New York's present statute on precisely the same ground. As Justice Stewart then explained:

"The mere fact that § 9 is geared to appellants' pricing policies in other States is not sufficient to invalidate the statute. As part of its regulatory scheme for the sale of liquor, New York may constitutionally insist that liquor prices to domestic wholesalers and retailers be as low as prices offered elsewhere in the country. The serious discriminatory effects of § 9 alleged by appellants on their business outside New York are largely matters of conjecture. It is by no means clear, for instance, that § 9 must inevitably produce higher prices in other States, as claimed by appellants, rather than the lower prices sought for New York. It will be time enough to assess the alleged extraterritorial effects of § 9 when a case arises that clearly presents them." *Joseph E. Seagram & Sons, Inc. v. Hostetter,* 384 U. S. 35, 43 (1966).

Two decades have elapsed since those sentences were written. In the interim, Brown-Forman has been selling its products in more than 30 States, including New York. Yet at no time did it introduce any evidence tending to prove that New York's ABC Law affected the price of its products in any other State.[1]

In lieu of evidence about the actual impact of the New York statute, the Court speculates that the ABC Law prevents price competition in transactions involving Brown-Forman's products in other States. See *ante*, at 579–580, 582. This result is not a necessary consequence of the operation of the New York law. To begin with, so far as New York is concerned Brown-Forman may maintain its selling price in other States or may increase it—either is consistent with Brown-Forman's promise to give New York wholesalers its "lowest price." §101–b(3)(d). Only if Brown-Forman reduces its prices outside of New York would it violate its affirmation. But in that event, the State allows it to extend the same discount to its New York customers "for good cause shown and for reasons not inconsistent with the purpose of this chapter." §101–b(3)(a).[2] There is nothing in the record to suggest that the State Liquor Authority would ever object to a price *reduction* to conform to a lower out-of-state price, and it is counterintuitive to assume that it would. The whole purpose of the law, after all, is to provide New York consumers with the lowest prices that can be obtained. Consistent with this purpose, the State Liquor Authority has, in a similar situation, "offered to grant approval ... to offer a cash discount in New York equivalent to the product discounts [the distiller] would offer in other states." *Joseph E. Seagram & Sons, Inc.* v. *Gazzara*, 610 F. Supp. 673, 678, n. 5 (SDNY), appeal docketed, No. 85–7547 (CA2, July 1, 1985). The administrative flexibility demonstrated by the State Liquor Authority thus belies the Court's assumption to the contrary. See *ante*, at 582, n. 5. It also demonstrates the wisdom of the *Seagram* Court's unwillingness to "presume that the Authority will not exercise that discretion to alleviate any friction that might result should the ABC Law chafe against" a provision of the Federal Constitution. *Seagram & Sons, Inc.* v. *Hostetter*, 384 U. S., at 46 (rejecting Supremacy Clause challenge predicated on federal antitrust laws). Cf. *id.*, at 51. The presumption of constitutionality applied in *Seagram* not only accords with tradition—agencies are frequently charged with rectifying questionable applications of necessarily general rules—it is also

---

[1] The record does show that Brown-Forman's promotional allowances "effectively lowered the price to wholesalers in Massachusetts below the affirmation price in New York" in a manner "designed to circumvent the New York State Alcoholic Beverage Control Law." App. to Juris Statement 51a. This evidence, however, surely does not provide any basis for distinguishing this case from the *Seagram* case.

[2] The Connecticut statute invalidated on its face in *United States Brewers Assn., Inc.* v. *Healy*, 692 F. 2d 275 (CA2 1982), summarily aff'd, 464 U. S. 909 (1983), had no escape clause. See 692 F. 2d, at 276–277, nn. 3, 5, 6, and 7. The Second Circuit panel construed the Connecticut statute "to control the minimum price that may be charged by a non-Connecticut brewer to a non-Connecticut wholesaler in a sale outside of Connecticut." *Id.*, at 282.

consistent with the respect due state administrative organs responsible for the operation of a state law whose constitutionality is challenged on its face. Cf. *United States* v. *Vuitch,* 402 U. S. 62, 70 (1971).[3] And if the State Liquor Authority were in fact to allow Brown-Forman to extend discounts given outside the State to its customers in New York, there is no reason to suppose that those other States would in turn refuse to allow Brown-Forman to credit the value of its promotional allowances against its list prices in order to comply with the statutory recording obligations in those States.[4]

Even if these open questions are all resolved in the Court's favor, its conclusion that the ABC Law trenches on interstate commerce does not follow from *Baldwin* v. *G. A. F. Seelig, Inc.,* 294 U. S. 511 (1935), the authority on which it primarily relies. Decided 30 years before *Seagram,* that case invalidated the New York Milk Control Act on the ground that it was designed to inflate milk prices in order to protect New York producers from out-of-state competition, see 294 U. S., at 519—a classic illustration of economic provincialism.[5] By contrast, the New York ABC Act was designed to keep the prices of liquor down in order to give New York consumers the benefit of out-of-state competition. See 384 U. S., at 38–39, and n. 9. The obvious infirmity of the statute struck down in *Seelig* thus says nothing about the constitutionality of the statute before us.

---

[3] This discussion indulges the Court's unstated assumption that price changes are not preceded by sufficient lead time to comply with the 35-day notice provision of the ABC Law. Again, however, there is nothing in the record to indicate that Brown-Forman has ever found it necessary to make a price change that could not be preceded by sufficient notice. *Amicus curiae* Wine & Spirits Wholesalers of America, Inc., informs us that the 18 States with liquor monopolies "perhaps typically" require suppliers "to warrant that quoted prices will remain in effect for a minimum of 90 days." Brief for Wine and Spirits Wholesalers of America, Inc., as *Amicus Curiae* 9,, n. 6. If, as a result of such contracts, prices in this industry are changed quarterly or at other infrequent intervals and are normally preceded by an announcement that the effective date of the change will be two or more months in the future, the statute would not have any inhibiting effect whatsoever on Brown-Forman's pricing decisions.

[4] "In making this argument, appellant assumes, and properly so, that other States will enforce their liquor laws. But appellant also requires us to assume that other States enforce their laws without regard for reality, and this we are unwilling to do.

"... It is certainly reasonable to expect that other States will recognize that the prices on appellant's New York schedules have been adjusted, because of New York's statutory requirements, to take into account the effect of credits enjoyed by wholesalers elsewhere—credits which the other States receiving the tangible benefits of appellant's program apparently have already chosen not to consider in determining the affirmed price.

"... It would require us to engage in mere speculation were we to declare, on such a tenuous basis, the lowest-price affirmation statute unconstitutional as applied." 64 N. Y. 2d 479, 489–490, 479 N. E. 2d 764, 769–770 (1985)(citations omitted).

Moreover, such possible consequences in States other than New York would seem to provide as good a reason for invalidating those States' laws as it does for striking down New York's statute.

[5] Seelig had purchased milk from Vermont farmers at a competitive price—instead of the New York regulated price—and was therefore denied a license to resell that milk in New York. *Baldwin* v. *G. A. F. Seelig, Inc.,* 294 U. S., at 520. As Justice Cardozo explained, Seelig "may keep his milk or drink it, but sell it he may not." *Id.,* at 521.

Moreover, as Judge Friendly observed, "[f]or some of us who were 'present at the creation' of the Twenty-First Amendment, there is an aura of unreality in [the] assumption that we must examine the validity of New York's Alcoholic Beverage Control Law (ABC Law) just as we would examine the constitutionality of a state statute governing the sale of gasoline"—or, I would add, of milk. *Battipaglia* v. *New York State Liquor Authority,* 745 F. 2d 166, 168 (CA2 1984), cert. denied, 470 U. S. 1027 (1985). The statute in *Seelig* regulated an article of commerce that New York had no power to exclude from the State;[6] the statute challenged here, in contrast, regulates the sale of a product that the Twenty-first Amendment expressly authorizes New York to exclude entirely from its local market.[7] As Justice Stewart explained for a unanimous Court in *Seagram:*

"Consideration of any state law regulating intoxicating beverages must begin with the Twenty-first Amendment, the second section of which provides that: 'The transportation or importation into any State, Territory, or possession of the United States for delivery or use therein of intoxicating liquors, in violation of the laws thereof, is hereby prohibited.' As this Court has consistently held, 'That Amendment bestowed upon the states broad regulatory power over the liquor traffic within their territories.' *United States* v. *Frankfort Distilleries,* 324 U. S. 293, 299 [1945]. Cf. *Nippert* v. *Richmond,* 327 U. S. 416, 425, n. 15 [1946]. Just two terms ago we took occasion to reiterate that 'a State is totally unconfined by traditional Commerce Clause limitations when it restricts the importation of intoxicants destined for use, distribution, or consumption within its borders.' *Hostetter* v. *Idlewild Liquor Corp.,* 377 U. S. 324, 330 [1964]. See *State Board of Equalization* v. *Young's Market Co.,* 299 U. S. 59 [1936]; *Mahoney* v. *Joseph Triner Corp.,* 304 U. S. 401 [1938]; *Ziffrin, Inc.* v. *Reeves,* 308 U. S. 132 [1939]; *California* v. *Washington,* 358 U. S. 64 [1958]. Cf. *Indianapolis Brewing Co.* v. *Liquor Comm'n,* 305 U. S. 391 [1939]; *Joseph S. Finch & Co.* v. *McKittrick,* 305 U. S. 395 [1939]." 384 U. S., at 41–42.[8]

[6] "New York has no power to project its legislation into Vermont by regulating the price to be paid in that state for milk acquired there. So much is not disputed. New York is equally without power to prohibit the introduction within her territory of milk of wholesome quality acquired in Vermont, whether at high prices or at low ones. This again is not disputed." *Ibid.*

[7] New York's ABC Law complies with the letter and spirit of the Twenty-first Amendment. The New York law imposes a condition precedent to importation of liquor into the State pursuant to the literal terms of the Amendment, and it does so "for the purpose of fostering and promoting temperance in th[e] consumption [of alcoholic beverages] and respect for and obedience to the law." §101–b(1). Cf. *Bacchus Imports, Ltd.* v. *Dias,* 468 U. S. 263 (1984).

[8] The Court's Twenty-first Amendment analysis, unsupported by any citation to authority, appears to be at war with itself. I simply cannot understand how the Twenty-first Amendment gives New York *no* right to condition access to *its* market on compliance with a "lowest price" affirmation (because to do so affects liquor sales in other States), and yet at the same time gives other States authority "to purchase brands of liquor that are sold in New York." *Ante,* at 585. By reading the Twenty-first Amendment broadly to encompass any interstate regulation of liquor, but removing the constitutional shield when the faintest economic ripples begin to flow outside state boarders, the Court has, at least in the interdependent national liquor market in which Brown-Forman participates, gutted the constitutional provision.

Of more recent vintage, see *Capital Cities Cable, Inc. v. Crisp*, 467 U. S. 691, 712–713 (1984); *California Retail Liquor Dealers Assn.* v. *Midcal Aluminum, Inc.*, 445 U. S. 97, 110 (1980).

It may well be true that the network of statutes that have spread across the Nation since the Court's decision in *Seagram* has created "so grave an interference with" interstate commerce as to exceed the "wide latitude for [state] regulation" under the Twenty-first Amendment and to make "the regulation invalid under the Commerce Clause." 384 U. S., at 42–43. If that be the case, however, there should be ample evidence available to a concerned litigant to prove that this consequence has in fact developed. Until that is done, I believe we have a duty to adhere to the ruling in *Seagram*. Accordingly, I respectfully dissent.

UNITED STATES *v.* AMERICAN COLLEGE OF PHYSICIANS
475 U. S. 834

CERTIORARI TO THE UNITED STATES COURT
OF APPEALS FOR THE FEDERAL CIRCUIT

MARSHALL, J., delivered the opinion for a
unanimous Court. BURGER, C. J., filed a concurring
opinion, in which POWELL, J., joined, *post*, p. 850.

JUSTICE MARSHALL delivered the opinion of the Court.

A tax-exempt organization must pay tax on income that it earns by carrying on a business not "substantially related" to the purposes for which the organization has received its exemption from federal taxation. The question before this Court is whether respondent, a tax-exempt organization, must pay tax on the profits it earns by selling commercial advertising space in its professional journal, *The Annals of Internal Medicine.*

I

Respondent, the American College of Physicians, is an organization exempt from taxation under §501(c)(3) of the Internal Revenue Code.[1] The purposes of the College, as stated in its articles of incorporation, are to maintain high standards in medical education and medical practice; to

---

Robert A. *Saltzstein* and *Joseph J. Saunders* filed a brief for American Business Press as *amicus curiae* urging reversal.

Briefs of *amici curiae* urging affirmance were filed for the American Association for the Advancement of Science by *John D. Lane;* for the American Medical Association et al. by *George A. Platz, Frank V. Battle, Jr., J. Timothy Kleespies,* and *Kathleen R. Curtis;* and for the American Society of Association Executives by *George D. Webster* and *Frank M. Northam.*

[1] Title 26 U. S. C. §501(c)(3) exempts from taxation entities "organized and operated exclusively for religious, charitable, scientific, testing for public safety, literary, or educational purposes," with certain restrictions on their activities, including prohibition of political activity.

encourage research, especially in clinical medicine; and to foster measures for the prevention of disease and for the improvement of public health. App. 16a. The principal facts were stipulated at trial. In furtherance of its exempt purposes, respondent publishes *The Annals of Internal Medicine (Annals),* a highly-regarded monthly medical journal containing scholarly articles relevant to the practice of internal medicine. Each issue of *Annals* contains advertisements for pharmaceuticals, medical supplies, and equipment useful in the practice of internal medicine, as well as notices of positions available in that field. Respondent has a long-standing policy of accepting only advertisements containing information about the use of medical products, and screens proffered advertisements for accuracy and relevance to internal medicine. The advertisements are clustered in two groups, one at the front and one at the back of each issue.

In 1975, *Annals* produced gross advertising income of $1,376,322. After expenses and deductible losses were subtracted, there remained a net income of $153,388. Respondent reported this figure as taxable income and paid taxes on it in the amount of $55,965. Respondent then filed a timely claim with the Internal Revenue Service for refund of these taxes, and when the Government demurred, filed suit in the United States Claims Court.

The Claims Court held a trial and concluded that the advertisements in *Annals* were not substantially related to respondent's tax-exempt purposes. 3 Cl. Ct. 531 (1983). Rather, after finding various facts regarding the nature of the College's advertising business, it concluded that any correlation between the advertisements and respondent's educational purpose was incidental because "the comprehensiveness and content of the advertising package is entirely dependent on each manufacturer's willingness to pay for space and the imagination of its advertising agency." *Id.,* at 535. Accordingly, the court determined that the advertising proceeds were taxable.

The Court of Appeals for the Federal Circuit reversed. 743 F. 2d 1570 (1984). It held clearly erroneous the trial court's finding that the advertising was not substantially related to respondent's tax-exempt purpose. The Court of Appeals believed that the trial court had focused too much on the commercial character of the advertising business and not enough on the actual contribution of the advertisements to the education of the journal's readers. It held that respondent had established the requisite substantial relation and its entitlement to exemption from taxation. *Id.,* at 1578. We granted the Government's petition for certiorari, 473 U. S. 904 (1985), and now reverse.

II

The taxation of business income not "substantially related" to the objectives of exempt organizations dates from the Revenue Act of 1950, Ch. 994, 64 Stat. 906 (1950 Act). The statute was enacted in response to perceived abuses of the tax laws by tax-exempt organizations that engaged in profit-making activities. Prior law had required only that the profits garnered by exempt organizations be used in furtherance of tax-exempt purposes, without regard to the source of those profits. See *Trinidad v. Sagrada Orden de Predicadores,* 263 U. S. 578, 581 (1924); *C. F. Mueller Co. v. Commissioner,* 190 F. 2d 120 (CA3 1951); *Roche's Beach, Inc. v. Commissioner,* 96 F. 2d 776 (CA2 1938). As a result, tax-exempt organizations were able to carry on full-fledged commercial enterprises in competition with corporations whose profits were fully taxable. See Revenue Revision of 1950: Hearings before the House Committee on Ways and Means, Vol. I, 81st Cong., 2d Sess., 18–19 (1950) (hereinafter cited as 1950 House Hearings) (describing universities' production of "automobile parts, chinaware, and food products, and the operation of theatres, oil wells, and cotton gins"). Congress perceived a need to restrain the unfair competition fostered by the tax laws. See H. R. Rep. No. 2319, 81st Cong., 2d Sess., 36–37 (1950).

Nevertheless, Congress did not force exempt organizations to abandon all commercial ventures, nor did it levy a tax only upon businesses that bore no relation at all to the tax-exempt purposes of an organization, as some of the 1950 Act's proponents had suggested. See, *e.g.,* 1950 House Hearings, at 4, 19, 165. Rather, in the 1950 Act it struck a balance between its two objectives of encouraging benevolent enterprise and restraining unfair competition by imposing a tax on the "unrelated business taxable income" of tax-exempt organizations. 26 U. S. C. §511(a)(1).

"Unrelated business taxable income" was defined as "the gross income derived by any organization from any unrelated trade or business . . . regularly carried on by it . . . ." §512(a)(1). Congress defined an "unrelated trade or business" as "any trade or business the conduct of which is not substantially related . . . to the exercise or performance by such organization of its charitable, educational, or other purpose or function constituting the basis for its exemption . . . ." §513(a). Whether respondent's advertising income is taxable, therefore, depends upon (1) whether the publication of paid advertising is a "trade or business," (2) whether it is regularly carried on, and (3) whether it is substantially related to respondent's tax-exempt purposes.

III

A

Satisfaction of the first condition is conceded in this case, as it must be, because Congress has declared unambiguously that the publication of paid advertising is a trade or business activity distinct from the publication of accompanying educational articles and editorial comment.

In 1967, the Treasury promulgated a regulation interpreting the unrelated business income provision of the 1950 Act. The regulation defined "trade or business" to include not only a complete business enterprise, but also any component activity of a business. Treas. Reg. § 1.513–1(b), 26 CFR § 1.513–1(b) (1985) (first published at 32 Fed. Reg. 17657 (1967)).[2] This revolutionary approach to the identification of a "trade or business" had a significant effect on advertising, which theretofore had been considered simply a part of a unified publishing business. The new regulation segregated the "trade or business" of selling advertising space from the "trade or business" of publishing a journal, an approach commonly referred to as "fragmenting" the enterprise of publishing into its component parts:

"[A]ctivities of soliciting, selling, and publishing commercial advertising do not lose identity as a trade or business even though the advertising is published in an exempt organization periodical which contains editorial matter related to the exempt purposes of the organization." 26 CFR § 1.513–1(b) (1985).

In 1969, Congress responded to widespread criticism of those Treasury regulations[3] by passing the Tax Reform Act of 1969, Pub. L. 91–172, 83 Stat. 487 (1969 Act). That legislation specifically endorsed the Treasury's concept of "fragmenting" the publishing enterprise into its component activities, and adopted, in a new § 513(c), much of the language of the regulation that defined advertising as a separate trade or business.

"Advertising, etc., activities . . . an activity does not lose identity as a trade or business merely because it is carried on . . . within a larger complex of other endeavors which may, or may not, be related to the exempt purposes of the organization." 26 U. S. C. § 513(c).

The statute clearly established advertising as a trade or business, the first prong of the inquiry into the taxation of unrelated business income.

---

[2] The 1967 Treasury regulations at issue in this case, published in final form at 32 Fed. Reg. 17657 (1967), have not been amended in pertinent part since their promulgation, and references to those regulations herein are to the current version.

[3] See, *e.g.,* Moore, Current Problems of Exempt Organizations, 24 Tax L. Rev. 469, 476 (1969); Middleditch & Webster, The new unrelated business income Regs: what they mean; how to cope with them, 28 J. Tax. 174, 178 (1968); Webster, New proposals change definition of unrelated business income, 27 J. Tax. 42, 43 (1967); Weithorn & Liles, Unrelated Business Income Tax: Changes Affecting Journal Advertising Revenues, 45 Taxes 791, 798 (1967). See also Tax Reform, 1969: Hearings before the House Committee on Ways and Means, 91st Cong., 1st Sess., 1129, 1184, 1223 (1969). Numerous bills were introduced in the 90th Congress, 1st Session, in an unsuccessful attempt to overturn the regulations, even before they became final. See, *e.g.,* H. R. 8765; H. R. 8766; H. R. 9103; H. R. 9468; H. R. 9661; H. R. 9763; H. R. 10150; H. R. 10997; H. R. 10998; H. R. 11491; H. R. 11492. And several years later, two federal courts struck down the 1967 regulations as exceeding pre-1969 statutory authority, insofar as they required the "fragmentation" of publishing activities. See *American College of Physicians* v. *United States,* 209 Ct. Cl. 23, 29, 530 F. 2d 930, 933 (1976); *Massachusetts Medical Society* v. *United States,* 514 F. 2d 153, 154 (CA1 1975).

The presence of the second condition, that the business be regularly carried on, is also undisputed here. The satisfaction of the third condition, however, that of "substantial relation," is vigorously contested, and that issue forms the crux of the controversy before us.

B

According to the Government, Congress and the Treasury established a blanket rule that advertising published by tax-exempt professional journals can never be substantially related to the purposes of those journals and is, therefore, always a taxable business. Respondent, however, contends that each case must be determined on the basis of the characteristics of the advertisements and journal in question. Each party finds support for its position in the governing statute and regulations issued by the Department of the Treasury.

In its 1967 regulations, the Treasury not only addressed the "fragmentation" issue discussed above, but also attempted to clarify the statutory "substantially related" standard found in §513(a). It provided that the conduct of a tax-exempt business must have a causal relation to the organization's exempt purpose (other than through the generation of income), and that "the production or distribution of the goods or the performance of the services from which the gross income is derived must *contribute importantly* to the accomplishment of [the exempt] purposes." Treas. Reg. §1.513–1(d)(2), 26 CFR §1.513–1(d)(2) (1985) (emphasis added). In illustration of its new test for substantial relation, the Treasury provided an example whose interpretation is central to the resolution of the issue before us. Example 7 of Treas. Reg. §1.513–1(d)(4)(iv) involves "Z," an exempt association formed to advance the interests of a particular profession and drawing its membership from that profession. Z publishes a monthly journal containing articles and other editorial material that contribute importantly to the tax-exempt purpose. Z derives income from advertising products within the field of professional interest of the members:

"Following a practice common among taxable magazines which publish advertising, Z requires its advertising to comply with certain general standards of taste, fairness, and accuracy; but within those limits the form, content, and manner of presentation of the advertising messages are governed by the basic objective of the advertisers to promote the sale of the advertised products. While the advertisements contain certain information, the informational function of the advertising is incidental to the controlling aim of stimulating demand for the advertised products and differs in no essential respect from the informational function of any commercial advertising. Like taxable publishers of advertising, Z accepts advertising only from those who are willing to pay its published rates. Although continuing education of its members in matters pertaining to their professions is one of the purposes for which Z is granted exemption, the publication of advertising designed and selected in the manner of ordinary commercial advertising is not an educational activity of the kind contemplated by the exemption statute; it differs fundamentally from such an activity both in its governing objective and in its method. Accordingly, Z's publication of advertising does not contribute importantly to the accomplishment of its exempt purposes; and the income which it derives from advertising constitutes gross income from unrelated trade or business." § 1.513–1(d)(4)(iv), Example 7.

The Government contends both that Example 7 creates a *per se* rule of taxation for journal advertising income and that Congress intended to adopt that rule, together with the remainder of the 1967 regulations, into law in the 1969 Act. We find both of these contentions unpersuasive.

Read as a whole, the regulations do not appear to create the type of blanket rule of taxability that the Government urges upon us. On the contrary, the regulations specifically condition tax exemption of business income upon the importance of the business activity's contribution to the particular exempt purpose at issue, and direct that "[w]hether activities productive of gross income contribute importantly to the accomplishment of any purpose for which an organization is granted an exemption depends *in each case* upon the facts and circumstances involved," § 1.513–1(d)(2) (emphasis added). Example 7 need not be interpreted as being inconsistent with that general rule. Attributing to the term "example" its ordinary meaning, we believe that Example 7 is best construed as an illustration of one possible application, under given circumstances, of the regulatory standard for determining substantial relation.

The interpretative difficulty of Example 7 arises primarily from its failure to distinguish clearly between the statements intended to provide hypothetical facts and those designed to posit the necessary legal consequences of those facts. Just at the point in the lengthy Example at which the facts would appear to end and the analysis to begin, a pivotal statement appears: "the informational function of the advertising is incidental to the controlling aim of stimulating demand for the advertised products." The Government's position depends upon reading this statement as a general proposition of law, while respondent would read it as a statement of fact that may be true by hypothesis of "Z" and its journal, but is not true of *Annals*.

We recognize that the language of the Example is amenable to either interpretation. Nevertheless, several considerations lead us to believe that the Treasury did not intend to set out a *per se* statement of law. First, when the regulations were proposed in early 1967, the Treasury expressed a clear intention to treat all commercial advertising as an unrelated business. See Technical Information Release No. 889, CCH 1967 Stand. Fed. Tax Rep. ¶6557. When the regulations were issued in final form, however, following much criticism and the addition of Example 7, they included no such statement of intention. 32 Fed. Reg. 17657 (1967). Second, a blanket rule of taxation for advertising in professional journals would contradict the explicit case-by-case requirement articulated in Treas. Reg. §1.513–d(d)(2), and we are reluctant to attribute to the Treasury an intention to depart from its own general principle in the absence of clear support for doing so. Finally, at the time the regulations were issued, the 1950 Act had been interpreted to mean that business activities customarily engaged in by tax-exempt organizations would continue to be considered "substantially related" and untaxed. See Note, The Macaroni Monopoly: The Developing Concept of Unrelated Business Income of Exempt Organizations, 81 Harv. L. Rev. 1280, 1291 (1968). A *per se* rule of taxation for the activity, traditional among tax-exempt journals, of carrying commercial advertising would have been a significant departure from that prevailing view. Thus, in 1967 the idea of a *per se* rule of taxation for all journal advertising revenue was sufficiently controversial, its effect so substantial, and its statutory authorization so tenuous, that we simply cannot attribute to the Treasury the intent to take that step in the form of an ambiguous example, appended to a subpart of a subsection of a subparagraph of a regulation.

It is still possible, of course, that, regardless of what the Treasury actually meant by its 1967 regulations, Congress read those regulations as creating a blanket rule of taxation, and intended to adopt that rule into law in the 1969 Act. The Government appears to embrace this view, which it supports with certain statements in the legislative history of the 1969 Act. For example, the Government cites to a statement in the House Report, discussing the taxation of advertising income of journals published by tax-exempt organizations.

> "Your committee believes that a business competing with taxpaying organizations should not be granted an unfair competitive advantage by operating tax free unless the business contributes importantly to the exempt function. It has concluded that by that standard, advertising in a journal published by an exempt organization is not related to the organization's exempt functions, and therefore it believes that this income should be taxed." H. R. Rep. No. 91–413, pt. 1, p. 50 (1969).

Similar views appear in the Senate Report:

> "Present law.—In December 1967, the Treasury Department promulgated regulations under which the income from advertising and similar activities is treated as 'unrelated business income' even though such advertising for example may appear in a periodical related to the educational or other exempt purpose of the organization.

"General reasons for change. — The committee agrees with the House that the regulations reached an appropriate result in specifying that when an exempt organization carries on an advertising business in competition with other taxpaying advertising businesses, it should pay a tax on the advertising income. The statutory language on which the regulations are based, however, is sufficiently unclear so that substantial litigation could result from these regulations. For this reason, the committee agrees with the House that the regulations, insofar as they apply to advertising and related activities, should be placed in the tax laws." S. Rep. No. 91–552, p. 75 (1969).

Based on this language, the Government argues that the 1969 Act created a *per se* rule of taxation for advertising income. The weakness of this otherwise persuasive argument, however, is that the quoted discussion appears in the Reports solely in support of the legislators' decision to enact §513(c), the provision approving the fragmentation of "trade or business." Although §513(c) was a significant change in the tax law that removed one barrier to the taxation of advertising proceeds, it cannot be construed as a comment upon the two other distinct conditions—"regularly carried on" and "not substantially related"—whose satisfaction is prerequisite to taxation of business income under the 1950 Act. Congress did not incorporate into the 1969 Act the language of the regulation defining "substantial relation," nor did the statute refer in any other way to the issue of the relation between advertising and exempt functions, even though that issue had been hotly debated at the hearings. See, *e.g.,* Tax Reform, 1969: Hearings before the House Committee on Ways and Means, 91st Cong., 1st Sess., 1113, 1118, 1192, 1241 (1969). Thus, we have no reason to conclude from the Committee Reports that Congress resolved the dispute whether, in a specific case, a journal's carriage of advertising could so advance its educational objectives as to be "substantially related" to those objectives within the meaning of the 1950 Act.

It is possible that the Committees' discussion of advertising reflects merely an erroneous assumption that the "fragmentation" provision of §513(c), without more, would establish the automatic taxation of journal advertising revenue. Alternatively, the quoted passages could be read to indicate the Committees' intention affirmatively to endorse what they believed to be existing practice, or even to change the law substantially. The truth is that, other than a general reluctance to consider commercial advertisements generally as substantially related to the purposes of tax-exempt journals, no congressional view of the issue emerges from the quoted excerpts of the Reports.[4] Thus, despite the Reports' seeming

---

[4] Indeed, different excerpts suggest that perhaps the House Committee did not construe the statute as creating a *per se* rule. In its explanation of §513(c), the House Report states that "the advertising contained in a publication of an exempt organization *may* be subject to the tax under section 511 even though the editorial content of the publication may be related to the exempt purposes of the organization." H. R. Rep. No. 91–413, pt. 2, p. 26 (1969) (emphasis added).

endorsement of a *per se* rule, we are hesitant to rely on that inconclusive legislative history either to supply a provision *not* enacted by Congress, see *Commissioner* v. *Acker,* 361 U. S. 87, 93 (1959); 1 J. Mertens, Law of Federal Income Taxation §3.29 (Weinstein rev. 1985), or to define a statutory term enacted by a prior Congress. See *SEC* v. *Sloan,* 436 U. S. 103, 121 (1978); *United States* v. *Price,* 361 U. S. 304, 313 (1960). Cf. *TVA* v. *Hill,* 437 U. S. 153, 193 (1978). We agree, therefore, with both the Claims Court and the Court of Appeals in their tacit rejection of the Government's argument that the Treasury and Congress intended to establish a *per se* rule requiring the taxation of income from all commercial advertisements of all tax-exempt journals without a specific analysis of the circumstances.[5]

IV

It remains to be determined whether, in this case, the business of selling advertising space is "substantially related"—or, in the words of the regulation, "contributes importantly"—to the purposes for which respondent enjoys an exemption from federal taxation. Respondent has maintained throughout this litigation that the advertising in *Annals* performs an education function supplemental to that of the journal's editorial content. App. 7a. Testimony of respondent's witnesses at trial tended to show that drug advertising performs a valuable function for doctors by disseminating information on recent developments in drug manufacture and use. *Id.,* at 27a, 38a, 43a. In addition, respondent has contended that the role played by the Food and Drug Administration, in regulating much of the form and content of prescription-drug advertisements, enhances the contribution that such advertisements make to the readers' education. All of these factors, respondent argues, distinguish the advertising in *Annals* from standard commercial advertising. Respondent approaches the question of substantial relation from the perspective of the journal's subscribers; it points to the benefit that they may glean from reading the advertisements and concludes that that benefit is substantial enough to satisfy the statutory test for tax exemption. The Court of Appeals took the same approach. It concluded that the advertisements performed various "essential" functions for physicians, 743 F. 2d, at 1576, and found

---

[5] This conclusion is consistent with the Treasury's own approach to analogous problems. See, *e.g.,* Rev. Rul. 82–139, 1982–2 Cum. Bull. 108 (advertisements in county bar journal; no *per se* rule); Rev. Rul. 72–431, 1972–2 Cum. Bull. 281 (exempt organization's sale of mailing lists to commercial advertisers; no *per se* rule). Our objection of the *per se* rule renders it unnecessary for us to address respondent's alternative argument that any such rule should apply only to associations organized under §501(c)(6) of the Internal Revenue Code.

a substantial relation based entirely upon the medically related content of the advertisements as a group.

The Government, on the other hand, looks to the conduct of the tax-exempt organization itself, inquiring whether the publishers of *Annals* have performed the advertising services in a manner that evinces an intention to use the advertisements for the purpose of contributing to the educational value of the journal. Also approaching the question from the vantage point of the College, the Claims Court emphasized the lack of a comprehensive presentation of the material contained in the advertisements. It is commented upon the "hit-or-miss nature of the advertising," 3 Cl. Ct., at 543, n. 3, and observed that the "differences between ads plainly reflected the advertiser's marketing strategy rather than their probable importance to the reader." *Id.,* at 534. "[A]ny educational function [the advertising] may have served was incidental to its purpose of raising revenue." *Id.,* at 535.

We believe that the Claims Court was correct to concentrate its scrutiny upon the conduct of the College rather than upon the educational quality of the advertisements. For all advertisements contain some information, and if a modicum of informative content were enough to supply the important contribution necessary to achieve tax exemption for commercial advertising, it would be the rare advertisement indeed that would fail to meet the test. Yet the statutory and regulatory scheme, even if not creating a *per se* rule *against* tax exemption, is clearly antagonistic to the concept of a *per se* rule *for* exemption for advertising revenue. Moreover, the statute provides that a tax will be imposed on "any trade or business the *conduct* of which is not substantially related," 26 U. S. C. §513(a) (emphasis added), directing our focus to the manner in which the tax-exempt organization operates its business. The implication of the statute is confirmed by the regulations, which emphasize the "manner" of designing and selecting the advertisements. See Treas. Reg. §1.513–1(d)(4)(iv), Example 7, 26 CFR §1.513–1(d)(4)(iv), Example 7 (1985). Thus, the Claims Court properly directed its attention to the College's conduct of its advertising business, and it found the following pertinent facts:

"The evidence is clear that plaintiff did not use the advertising to provide its readers a comprehensive or systematic presentation of any aspect of the goods or services publicized. Those companies willing to pay for advertising space got it; others did not. Moreover, some of the advertising was for established drugs or devices and was repeated from one month to another, undermining the suggestion that the advertising was principally designed to alert readers of recent developments [citing, as examples, ads for Valium, Insulin and Maalox]. Some ads even concerned matters that had no conceivable relationship to the College's tax-exempt purposes." 3 Cl. Ct. at 534 (footnotes omitted).

These facts find adequate support in the record. See, *e.g.,* App. 29a–30a, 59a. Considering them in light of the applicable legal standard, we are bound to conclude that the advertising in *Annals* does not contribute importantly to the journal's educational purposes. This is not to say that the College could not control its publication of advertisements in such a way as to reflect an intention to contribute importantly to its educational functions. By coordinating the content of the advertisements with the editorial content of the issue, or by publishing only advertisements reflecting new developments in the pharmaceutical market, for example, perhaps the College could satisfy the stringent standards erected by Congress and the Treasury. In this case, however, we have concluded that the Court of Appeals erroneously focused exclusively upon the information that is invariably conveyed by commercial advertising, and consequently failed to give effect to the governing statute and regulations. Its judgment, accordingly, is

Reversed.

CHIEF JUSTICE BURGER, with whom JUSTICE POWELL joins, concurring.

Most medical journals are not comparable to magazines and newspapers published for profit. Their purpose is to assemble and disseminate to the profession relevant information bearing on patient care. The enormous expansion of medical knowledge makes it difficult for a general practitioner—or even a specialist—to keep fully current with the latest developments without such aids. In a sense these journals provide continuing education for physicians—a "correspondence course" not sponsored for profit but public health.

There is a public value in the widest possible circulation of such data, and advertising surely tends to reduce the cost of publication and hence the cost to each subscriber, thereby enhancing the prospect of wider circulation. Plainly a regulation recognizing these realities would be appropriate. Such regulations, of course, are for the Executive Branch and the Congress, not the courts. I join the opinion because it reflects a permissible reading of the present Treasury regulations.

14

Social Responsibility

NATIONAL PEACH COUNCIL

Among the several pesticides used on agricultural crops was dibromochloropropane, usually termed DBCP. This chemical was widely used on fruit trees, cotton, and soybeans to combat wormlike nematodes and some other pests that imperil these crops. A total of about 30 million pounds of this pesticide was produced and marketed annually by several companies. The three main suppliers were Dow Chemical Company, Shell Oil Company, and Occidental Chemical Company. Dow sold this product under the trade name Fumazone, Shell under the trade name Nemagon Soil Fumigant, and Occidental under the trade names Green Light, Garden Fume, and CHA-KEM-CO.

Evidence of the effect of DBCP on people working closely with it came to light in at least three locations in August. In Dow Chemical Company's DBCP plant at Magnolia, Arkansas, there was evidence of sterility in twelve male workers, whereas in Shell's installations in Denver and Mobile, sixteen of twenty-one male workers tested after exposure to the chemical showed abnormally low sperm counts. The Oil, Chemical, and Atomic Workers Union filed complaints with the government, especially the Occupational Safety and Health Administration (OSHA), a unit of the Department of Labor, and the Environmental Protection

Agency. These agencies imposed emergency restrictions on the handling of the substance and began studying the imposition of permanent restrictions or a banning of the product. The manufacturers of the product voluntarily halted its production.

Following the reaction of OSHA to the DBCP health threat, the executive secretary of the National Peach Council, Robert K. Phillips, sent the letter reproduced as Exhibit 1 and dated September 12 to Dr. Eula Bingham, assistant secretary of labor for Occupational Safety and Health. A few days later the National Cancer Institute, a federal agency, released the results of a research project in which it was shown that large doses of DBCP caused cancer in laboratory rats and mice. Phillips did not have advance knowledge of these research results. According to Phillips, someone employed by OSHA gave a copy of his September 12 letter to a *New York Times* reporter on September 26. That newspaper and the news wire services carried portions of the letter on September 27.

There followed considerable news coverage about the product, the manufacturers, the workers, and the proposal from the National Peach Council. Phillips stated that the suggestion was made in good faith and with sincerity. He noted further that people might think he was speaking tongue in cheek but he definitely was not. Phillips stated to the press "All these government agencies overdo everything. I know they carry things to extremes. They should at least consider alternatives to banning this material." He added that "After all, people take some kind of chance every day."

In mid-November Phillips made the following statement:

It is . . . only in the last few years that peach producers, and many others in agriculture have come to the somewhat belated realization that Congress can and will pass laws which allow Federal *bureaucrats* powers which would have been undreamed of only a few years ago.

The situation which has developed in Washington requires more checking and more direct contact than ever before, and it seems the situation will build more in that direction.

That is just one of the reasons that National Peach Council, as an organization which speaks only for the nation's peach industry, is so important to each and every peach grower.

Eula Bingham replied to Phillips on November 21, ten weeks after Phillips had written her. Her letter arrived on November 25 and is reproduced as Exhibit 2.

On December 13 Phillips added the following:

It [Bingham's letter] is a nice enough letter, but does not in my opinion serve as an answer to the letter I wrote to her on September 12.

EXHIBIT 1 Letter from National Peach Council to OSHA

National Peach Council

Dr. Eula Bingham
Assistant Secretary for Occupational
  Safety and Health
U.S. Department of Labor
Washington, D.C. 20210

Recently we received the interesting DOL news release concerning worker exposure to DBCP.

It appears to us that you and Secretary Marshall may have overreacted, or at least that is your public posture.

While involuntary sterility caused by a manufactured chemical may be bad, it is not necessarily so. After all, there are many people who are now paying to have themselves sterilized to assure they will no longer be able to become parents.

How many of the workers who have become sterile were of an age that they would have been likely to have children anyway? How many were past the age when they would want to have children? These, too, are important questions.

If possible sterility is the main problem, couldn't workers who were old enough that they no longer wanted to have children accept such positions voluntarily? They would know the situation, and it wouldn't matter. Or could workers be advised of the situation, and some might volunteer for such work posts as an alternative to planned surgery for a vasectomy or tubal ligation, or as a means of getting around religious bans on birth control when they want no more children.

We do believe in safety in the work place, Dr. Bingham, but there can be good as well as bad sides to a situation.

Above all, please don't try to get a ban on the manufacture and sale of the chemical DBCP, because that would cause some losses of agricultural production which would be serious.

Sincerely,

Robert K. Phillips
Executive Secretary

EXHIBIT 2 Letter from OSHA to National Peach Council

Office of the Assistant Secretary

Mr. Robert K. Phillips
Executive Secretary
National Peach Council
Post Office Box 1085
Martinsburg, West Virginia 25401

Dear Mr. Phillips:

In response to your letter of September 12 regarding the sterilization of workers, I can think of no situation where the material impairment of an employee's health or reproductive capacity as a result of exposure to a toxic substance could be regarded as beneficial. The right to have children is a fundamental human right entitled to serious protection under the Occupational Safety and Health Act of 1970. There is no comparison between involuntary sterilization resulting from exposure to a chemical in the workplace and voluntary sterilization achieved by a medical procedure. Voluntary sterilization involves a conscious, deliberate choice by a man or woman to end one's reproductive capability. It also involves medical supervision in order to control any other adverse health consequences. Moreover, the reproductive period varies between men and women and between individuals. Therefore, it would be inappropriate for an employer or the government to make any general assumptions regarding the end of an individual employee's reproductive capability. Instead, the Occupational Safety and Health Administration (OSHA) must set standards which assure that no employee will suffer material impairment of health of functional capacity during the entire lifetime.

Sterility is only one hazard of exposure of 1,2-Dibromo-3-Chloropropane ("DBCP"). Degenerative changes occur in several organs of the body, and there is also a cancer hazard. OSHA intends to treat DBCP as a carcinogen because well-designed studies have demonstrated the carcinogenicity of DBCP in both sexes of two mammalian species at multiple-dose levels. Therefore, the Agency's decision to issue an emergency temporary standard is based not only on the sterilant effects of DBCP but also on other serious health effects, including the carcinogenicity of DBCP.

In light of the serious health effects from worker exposure to DBCP, I believe that the issuance of an emergency temporary standard was necessary and appropriate to protect employees from this grave danger.

Please be assured that your letter has been included in the official record of the permanent standard for DBCP.

Sincerely,

Eula Bingham
Assistant Secretary
Occupational Safety and Health

Dr. Bingham certainly deserves praise for the recent moves to wipe out a large number of trivial job-safety standards and loosen enforcement standards. At least there is progress in that direction.

The National Peach Council

The National Peach Council was an agricultural federation representing the interests of growers of fresh market peaches throughout the United States. Established in 1942, it was the only peach farmers trade association of national scope in the United States, and had 6,300 members and associate members. The latter were manufacturers of equipment and supplies needed by this industry, sales agencies, and other interested firms. Production and per capita consumption of fresh peaches had exhibited small decreases for several years.

The council had various activities. For example, it published a monthly newspaper and employed a professional home economist to assist in its educational public relations efforts to increase the use of fresh peaches. The Council also held a large national convention lasting four days once a year at which there were speeches, panels, and technical papers on horticulture and the economics of the industry. The latest convention, held in San Antonio, included sessions on peach tree disease control, nursery certification, use of computers and aerial photography in orchard management, chemical and mechanical thinning of fruit, evaporative cooling to delay blooming, herbicides in orchard floor management, peach varieties by production area, peaches and competitive fruits around the world, and wholesale and retail marketing. Another activity of the Council was the preparation and dissemination of news releases and direct contact with the U.S. Department of Agriculture. For example, many growers found that their peaches were not selling one mid-August. When these growers notified the National Peach Council, that organization Mailgrammed factual but promotional information to the major networks. The organization also contacted the Plentiful Foods section at the Department of Agriculture, which prepared a radio news release and got it out immediately rather than using the regular release system, which would have required seven to ten days.

One recent interesting activity of the National Peach Council was participation in the planning of proposed enabling legislation known as the Freestone Peach Research and Education Act. This proposed statute called for a plan of action and a nongovernmental board to oversee the resulting program of research and promotional education. Research would be on all phases of the production and marketing of freestone peaches. The promotional education would consist of preparation and dissemination of materials to households, institutional food buyers, restaurant chains, teachers, and others. Costs would be met by assessments on fresh peaches marketed. Rates of half a cent per bushel to several cents per bushel were being considered. Under the proposed enabling legislation the plan of action would have to go to a referendum among freestone peach farmers. The federal government would only monitor that the resulting work adhered to the statutes and the guidelines established by the plan of action that had been approved by a vote of the growers.

Occupational Safety and Health Administration

The Occupational Safety and Health Administration was a relatively new agency, but had quickly established itself as an activist group. It was considered unreasonable, arbitrary, capricious, and indifferent to cost by much of the business community. A survey of Congressmen's opinions of OSHA conducted by the White House revealed several criticisms, including harassment of business organizations, too many forms, and unnecessary paperwork. Even liberal Senator George McGovern (Democrat, South Dakota) attacked OSHA for "overregulation of small business [and] nitpicking enforcement."

Advise the National Peach Council.

FIRENZE GROCERY STORES[1]

Anthony Firenze opened a grocery store near Rhode Island Avenue in northeast Washington, D.C., in the late 1940s. The neighborhood could be characterized as middle-middle class. Firenze prospered and in the late 1950s opened a second store in northwest Washington in an affluent area west of Rock Creek Park.

Both stores were in areas of high-density population. Although the areas were zoned for land use, there were within easy walking distance

[1] Some publications that would assist in dealing with the problems of this case include the following: Donald E. Sexton, Jr., "Comparing the Cost of Food to Blacks and to Whites," *Journal of Marketing*, 35 (July 1971), pp. 40–46; Lola M. Ireland, Ed., *Low Income Life Styles* (Washington, D.C.: Department of Health, Education, and Welfare, 1966); Joseph B. Mason and Charles S. Madden, "Food Purchases in a Low-Income Negro Neighborhood: The Development of a Socio-Economic Behavioral Profile as Related to Movement and Patronage Patterns," in Fred C. Allvine, Ed., *Combined Proceedings of 1971 Conferences* (Chicago: American Marketing Association, 1971), pp. 634–639; Leonard Berry and Paul Solomon, "Generalizing About Low-Income Food Shoppers: A Word of Caution," *Journal of Retailing*, 47 (Summer 1971), pp. 41–51, 92; Leonard Berry, "The Low-Income Marketing System: An Overview," *Journal of Retailing*, 48 (Summer 1972), pp. 44–63, 90; Lawrence Feldman and Alvin Star, "Racial Factors in Shopping Behavior," in Keith Cox and Ben Enis, Eds., *A New Measure of Responsibility for Marketing* (Chicago: American Marketing Association, 1968); Arieh Goldman, "Do Lower Income Consumers Have a More Restricted Shopping Scope?" *Journal of Marketing*, 40 (Jan. 1976), pp. 46–54; Gerald Hills, Donald Granbois, and James M. Patterson, "Black Consumer Perceptions of Food Store Attributes," *Journal of Marketing*, 37 (April 1973), pp. 47–57; Hiram Barksdale and Warren French, "Response to Consumerism: How Change is Perceived by Both Sides," *MSU Business Topics*, 23 (Spring 1975), pp. 55–67.

single-family homes, duplexes, small apartment buildings, and large apartment buildings. Each store was located on a bus route and each was to be within walking distance of new subway stations then under construction. About 45 percent of the households in the trade territory of the northeast store owned an automobile.

Firenze had paid off the mortgage on the northeast building and had only one more year of mortgage payments on the northwest building. Both buildings were well constructed and in good condition. Each had been set up on a twenty-year life basis for purposes of depreciation accounting. Most of the northeast store's patronage came from a radius of about six blocks, whereas that of the northwest store was a little more spread out.

The census tract in which the northeast store was opened had been 100 percent white in 1940 and 98 percent white in 1950. During the 1950s it was obvious to Firenze that many blacks were moving into the neighborhood. This trend was a cause for temporary anxiety on the part of Firenze and other businesspeople in the area, but they immediately discerned that the blacks moving in were almost all middle-class federal government employees. The transition for residents, both black and white, was not easy but was accomplished with no violence and little overt rancor. The 1960 census showed that the tract was 52 percent white, but by 1970 this figure had declined to about 10 percent. A similar trend had occurred in adjoining areas of the city. One adjoining tract was only 5 percent white. Anthony Firenze observed that most of the whites in the vicinity appeared to be in their late fifties or older, and that many of them were retired.

An additional trend had taken place. Some of the middle-class blacks had moved out and had been replaced by lower-middle-class and lower-class blacks. This trend was beyond Firenze's ability to measure, but he suspected that about 60 to 70 percent of the original blacks had moved on to more expensive neighborhoods in the city or into the suburbs. In addition, the physical condition of most rental housing units in the vicinity showed considerable deterioration. Apparently the landlords were not performing maintenance adequately or at least not up to the level of past years. Several commercial buildings were not being maintained well, but the commercial structures were not deteriorating as rapidly as were the residential buildings. Two small businesses had relocated out of the neighborhood because of vandalism.

The number of grocery stores in the city belonging to corporate chains had declined from ninety-one to forty-two over the past ten years. For example, A&P, the nation's sixth largest chain, had six stores then but had only one now. Grand Union, which operated throughout most of the northeastern United States, closed all of its District of Columbia locations. In the city's northeast quadrant the number of chain supermarkets declined from twenty-three to nine over the ten-year period. The corresponding figures in the other quadrants were as follows: northwest, fifty-four to twenty-two; southwest, one to two; southeast, thirteen to eight.

Firenze was perplexed by the disappointing net profits of his northeast store for the past two years. This was rather galling to him for several reasons. First, it was his first store and he was sentimentally attached to it. Second, he gave this store just as much attention as he gave the northwest location. Third, with a sales volume of $700,000, the northeast store did about as much business as the $730,000 of the northwest store. The operating statements for the fiscal year just completed are presented as Exhibit 1.

From time to time Firenze did some comparison shopping, principally to gain perspective on prices but also to gain other merchandising ideas. In his most recent comparisons he found a long-standing situation to be continuing. His prices were slightly higher than the four chain stores located within a one-mile radius. On the average his prices were 3.5 percent higher than in those stores. For his price comparison he utilized a "shopping basket" of thirty specified items, a measurement popularized

EXHIBIT 1 Operating Statements for Firenze Stores, Most Recent Year

	Northeast Store	Northwest Store
Net sales	$700,000	$730,000
Cost of goods sold	595,000	606,630
Gross profit on sales	$105,000	$123,370
Expenses		
Property taxes	5,300	5,600
Advertising	7,300	7,600
Wages	49,900	48,900
Inventory shrinkage	8,770	7,010
Electricity, heat, water, trash removal, telephone, etc.	4,200	4,220
Salary to Anthony Firenze	10,000	10,000
Insurance	1,200	800
Depreciation on building	0	3,600
Depreciation on fixtures	950	975
Mortgage interest expense	0	2,705
Office expenses	1,950	1,650
	$ 89,570	$ 93,060
Net profit before income taxes	$ 15,430	$ 30,310

EXHIBIT 2 Population and Age in District of Columbia

	1980	1970	1960	1950
White	171,768	209,272	345,263	517,865
Black and all other races	466,565	547,238	418,693	284,313
	638,333	756,510	763,956	802,178
Median age for whites	N/A	41.0	40.0	34.4
Median age for Black and all other races	N/A	25.1	27.1	29.6

Source: 1980 Census of Population.

by some officials in the federal government and several consumer groups. Using the same technique Firenze had determined that his prices were about 4 percent below other owner-managed grocery stores within a one-mile radius in the northeast. None of these chain or independent stores, including Firenze, offered home delivery or charge accounts. The prices in Firenze's northeast store were identical to those in his northwest store. Because his profits in the northeast were lower than in the northwest, Firenze was seriously considering charging more in his northeast store than in the northwest store for identical items.

Advise Anthony Firenze.

EXHIBIT 3 Population in District of Columbia, 1980, by Quadrant

Quadrant	Total	White	Black	Other	Median Age
Northeast	150,738	14,573	134,635	1,530	31.2
Northwest	301,032	132,462	154,768	13,802	33.7
Southeast	159,923	14,972	143,610	1,341	26.9
Southwest	26,640	9,761	15,833	986	28.8
Total	638,333	171,768	448,906	17,659	31.1

Source: 1980 Census of Population.

15

Planning and Forecasting

IMPERIAL LAWNS, INC.

Imperial Lawns, Inc., was established slightly over nine years ago in the northern suburbs of a large city. The founders and present owners were Stephen Nolan and George Pleshette, both age twenty-three at the time and just out of college. The first two years were extremely difficult for the owners as they got the firm going and looked for customers. Sales figures are given in Exhibit 1. Both men graduated from the agricultural college of the state university, Nolan majoring in agronomy, and Pleshette in horticulture, with strong supporting study in chemistry and biology. Agronomy is the agricultural science that studies relationships between soils and plant life and seeks improved methods of soils management and crop production.

The lawn care industry in the United States was a rather recent phenomenon but was estimated now to be a $1.5 billion per year business. This type of service, often called turf management, typically was provided by small firms. Approximately 5,000 companies averaged about $300,000 in sales per year. There was one large firm in the industry, Chem-Lawn, based in Ohio, which was estimated to do about $98 mil-

EXHIBIT 1 Price, Customer, and Sales Data, Imperial Lawns, Inc.

| Year | Nine-month Service | | | | Winter Service | | | | | Total | |
	Price	No. of Customers	Sales	% Change	Price	No. of Customers	Sales	% Change		Sales	% Change
Latest Year	$240	2,067	$496,080	11.9	$80	201	$16,080	94.9		$512,160	13.4
Two years ago	220	2,015	443,300	11.2	73	113	8,249	92.3		451,549	12.1
Three years ago	198	2,013	398,574	11.3	66	65	4,290	110.3		402,864	11.8
Four years ago	180	1,990	358,200	16.5	60	34	2,040	–		360,240	18.4
Five years ago	160	1,921	307,360	34.8	–	–	–	–		307,360	34.8
Six years ago	152	1,500	228,000	39.8	–	–	–	–		228,000	39.8
Seven years ago	145	1,125	163,125	69.1	–	–	–	–		163,125	69.1
Eight years ago	137	704	96,448	24.6	–	–	–	–		96,448	24.6
Nine years ago	131	591	77,421	–	–	–	–	–		77,421	–

lion in sales annually. Nationally, about 6.1 percent of households in single-family, detached houses used a lawn care service. A typical company always fertilized the lawn and treated it for weeds and, if necessary, debugged it and reseeded it. Imperial Lawns, Inc., like most other companies, did not provide mowing.

The chemicals applied were either in pellet or liquid form in this industry. Imperial used the liquid form, which the company considered safer for the customers and their pets. In addition, the liquid form worked faster in helping the lawn.

In some ways lawn care was a luxury service. Some people considered it extravagant. Homeowners who would order and read government-issued pamphlets and/or contact their local Agricultural Extension Service advisor and would read and follow the instructions on lawn care products available in countless stores could provide the service for themselves. However, some customers disliked yard work, some had allergies, and some had too little time to learn about or look after their own lawns. An advertising theme that Imperial used often was "Imperial works while you play." Interestingly enough, some people who enjoyed gardening and had a knowledge of lawns nevertheless used a lawn service. The reason many gave was that lawn care was not as creative and satisfying as the care of flowers, shrubbery, and trees. Most real estate people believed that an attractive lawn added to the market value of a house, and the figure usually given by such persons was 2 to 3 percent.

The most persuasive argument for a lawn service and the one used the most in primary promotion was that in the pricing of lawn fertilizers, herbicides, fungicides, and insecticides, there was a large quantity discount. Small sales were priced much higher per pound than were bulk sales. In addition, of course, lawn care organizations bought at wholesale rather than retail prices. The net effect was that the chemical supplies alone for an individual consumer for a nine-month period would probably cost approximately $120 for an average-size lawn. The incremental cost to buy the lawn service from Imperial was thus about $120.

For this $120 increment the homeowner's lawn received the right things in the right quantities at the right times and the homeowner was relieved of the shopping, labor, scheduling, and the necessity of owning a spreader, which came in varying weights and qualities but averaged about $50 at retail. Virtually no homeowners applied these chemicals in liquid form, because they were wet, messy, usually malodorous, and best applied with a sprayer under pressure. Imperial used a large pressurized sprayer with a long hose attached to the truck.

Fertilizers needed to be selected to suit the types of grass and soils. Herbicides, which were chemicals designed to kill or discourage weeds and undesirable types of grasses, had to be measured properly or harm might come to the lawn. In addition, they had to be applied at just the right time or they would have little effect, and allowances had to be made for how sunny or shady the various parts of the yard were.

About half of the northern, northwestern, northeastern, and eastern suburban population was in Cabot County, which Nolan and Pleshette considered their trade territory. Both lived in Cabot County, which had a population of 497,200, according to the professional planners and statisticians in the county government. Their annual estimates of economic and demographic data for the county tended to be of high quality. For example, virtually all these planners' relevant estimates for December 31, 1979 were proved true in the April 1980 national census of population and housing.

Cabot County's population and that of the entire metropolitan area were rising but more slowly than the national average. The annual population growth rates for the nation, the metropolitan area, and the county were approximately 0.9, 0.7, and 0.8 percent, respectively. Such rates were expected to continue until the mid-1990s, after which the national rate would probably decline. It appeared likely that the rates for the metropolitan area and the Cabot County portion of the metropolitan area would stay almost constant. Average household income was about 20 percent higher in Cabot County than for the city and the remainder of the suburbs. The county had about 167,000 dwelling units, of which about 110,300 were detached single-family houses and about 7,000 were townhouses. Nolan and Pleshette aimed at the people in the detached single-family houses. They had noticed in the last two or three years that most of the newly constructed houses were on slightly smaller lots. The typical Cabot County lot contained 11,000 square feet.

Nolan and Pleshette estimated that about 5,750 households in the county subscribed to a lawn care service at an average nine-month price of about $240. They also estimated that about 580 households in the county subscribed to winter service at an average of $80. These were also the prices charged by Imperial.

Nolan and Pleshette's organization was the oldest and largest in the lawn care business in Cabot County and enjoyed a good reputation. Two companies preceded Imperial but failed many years ago. Sales of Imperial Lawns, Inc., in the most recent year were $512,160, of which $16,080 came from sales of winter service to 201 families. Of these 201, all but three also took the nine-month service. Imperial's winter lawn care service was begun four years ago and was furnished during the annual downtime for this industry, December through February.

Five other such companies operating in Cabot County each did a smaller sales volume in the county than did Imperial. However, two of these five were larger than Imperial in that they operated also in the city and/or the other suburban counties. One was Chem-Lawn. All five competitors started providing winter service in Cabot County the same year as Imperial. The national figure for use of winter lawn service was estimated to be about 1.5 percent.

The scientific rationale for the winter service was that the root system of the lawn could grow and gain strength when the top was dormant. When mild weather returned, the lawn would be healthier and more beautiful. The following message was used by Imperial in its advertising of the winter service:

> Heavy nitrogen fertilization of grasses during the winter months will promote a stronger root system. The root system is vital to turfgrass development because it is responsible for nutrient and water uptake and also anchors plants in the soil. Development of the root system depends on cooler soil temperatures. Therefore it is important to have a readily available supply of nitrogen in the soil during periods of cool soil temperatures to enhance this growth.

Mainly because of the climate and the natural soil conditions, fine lawns were harder to develop and maintain in this metropolitan area than in most others. Moreover, many people unknowingly abused their lawns by poor watering practices. They watered too lightly, too often, erratically, or at night, all of which were bad. Also some people mowed their grass too short or let it grow tall and then cut it short, sending the grass into shock.

The nine-month service consisted of five lawn treatments, not spaced quite evenly for unavoidable scientific reasons. The winter service consisted of one treatment, but it required about one-fourth longer to perform than did the treatments during the nine-month period. After each treatment the Imperial representative left a short prepared note explaining what was done on that visit. The representative added a comment if he or she thought the height of the grass was inappropriate to its health, or if the chemical just applied needed water or the avoidance of water for a certain time period.

The average time required for a treatment during the nine-month period was twenty-six minutes. When one took into account the driving time between the houses, one person and his or her truck could cover fifteen accounts in a typical eight-hour workday during the nine-month period. Imperial owned four route trucks, all modern and in excellent condition. For customers who had outdoor dogs and/or fences with gates that were kept locked, it was necessary for the driver to telephone ahead and make arrangements.

Advise Imperial Lawns, Inc.

WALKER FURNITURE

Wayne and Lorna Walker owned and operated a store dealing in furniture and small appliances in the inner city of a large metropolitan area. They were black, as was the great majority of the population within a radius of several miles of their store. There was a sizable Hispanic neighborhood fairly near.

This establishment did not look large, but it was about the average size for furniture stores in the United States. It provided an income that the owners found satisfactory and met their drive for independence. However, they wanted to build their business and were looking to the future. They had in mind two routes for growth. One was to keep offering the present range of merchandise with no shift in relative emphasis within the line. Better personal selling and friendly service would be stressed. The other route for growth was to give additional emphasis to a product category that was already handled but that was uncommon for this type of store, wood-burning stoves. This type of merchandise appeared to have an interesting future.

Stoves had originally been stocked because some customers and potential customers who moved to this metropolitan area had rural Southern backgrounds, were quite familiar with the product, and liked it. Others saw this product as a necessity to supplement the heating systems that were too small in capacity, inefficient, or undependable in older city homes. Sometimes the purpose was to heat an extra room that was added or a newly finished basement or attic. A few customers were interested in an authentic-looking wood-burning stove to complement Early American family room or den furniture.

The stoves stocked by Walker's came in plain utilitarian models, historical reproductions, and Scandinavian-style decorator models. Stove manufacturers in recent years had made utilitarian stoves more compact. Some were as small as twelve inches wide by nineteen inches long and twenty inches tall, exclusive of legs. Many utilitarian stoves were made in the United States but some came from Scandinavia. In recent years, four Scandinavian stove producers, Jotul, Lange, Trolla, and Morsa, had substantially increased their exports to the United States. Their products included utilitarian and decorator models. Stoves were extremely popular for heating homes in the Scandinavian countries, as well as in several other European countries. In the United States, reproductions were made of several period stoves, including Victorian and Early American, such as the famous Franklin stove.

Scandinavian-style decorator stoves were available either with or without a frontal opening for viewing the fire. Those stoves with the view thus constituted combination fireplace-stoves and offered an aesthetic advantage, for fireplaces seemed to create an intimate focal point in a room. The image of flames and flickering light was emotionally as well as physically warm. However, stoves with the view of the fire cost more. These decorator stoves came in a range of colors, usually orange, red, yellow, gold, or black, and were finished in enamel or enameled porcelain. Such stoves were conical, barrel shaped, and trapezoidal in shape. The stoves were particularly favored by customers who enjoyed modernistic decor. Many of the Scandinavian-style decorator stoves were now made in other countries as well, including the United States. Of late, several large chains, including J. C. Penney, Montgomery Ward, and Sears, Roebuck, had added these stoves to their lines but at much lower prices than what had been prevalent previously for Scandinavian-style decorator stoves.

Because their working capital and floor space were both limited, in a store whose merchandise was bulky, the Walkers carried only nine to twelve stoves at a time. In addition, they had to be conscious of inventory turnover in all departments, and they tried to keep inventory turnover high. This frequently meant that they did not have in stock the model of stove that a customer wanted. Thus, some of the stove sales consisted of orders that were delivered to customers several weeks later. The Walkers observed with great interest that in January and February of the three most recent years they sold out of stoves, despite raising the planned stock level appreciably each year. Sales of stoves had reached the point that they were bringing in about 7 percent of overall sales. Store sales are presented in Exhibit 1 and sales of stoves, in units and dollars, are presented in Exhibit 2. All stoves in stock were displayed.

The Walkers estimated that during the period when they were out of stoves in the most recent year about forty-eight to fifty shopping parties inquired about stoves. One sale was made to these shoppers for later delivery. The firm's experience had been that about one third of the people who discussed stoves with the store personnel purchased a stove from Walker's. The store owners estimated that out-of-stock conditions had caused no significant amount of lost stove sales except in the most recent year. Stoves occupied a selling area measuring fifteen by twenty and a half feet.

EXHIBIT 1 Walker Furniture Store Sales

Most recent year	$300,004
Two years ago	272,950
Three years ago	250,215
Four years ago	230,203
Five years ago	209,501
Six years ago	196,968

EXHIBIT 2 Sales of Stoves, Walker Furniture Company

	Utilitarian Models		Reproduction Models		Scandinavian Style Decorator Stoves	
	Units	$ Sales	Units	$ Sales	Units	$ Sales
Latest year	10	2,507	20	4,905	17	14,260
Two years ago	6	1,498	13	3,121	13	10,901
Three years ago	5	1,124	7	1,575	8	6,322
Four years ago	5	1,050	6	1,264	5	3,704
Five years ago	4	798	5	1,020	5	3,518
Six years ago	3	567	4	781	1	695

One store in the metropolitan area, Rosansky's, sold nothing but stoves. It was widely known in the mercantile community that this firm sold more than 1,500 stoves per year. Another company with two locations specialized in stoves and fireplace equipment and appeared to be doing extremely well.

The Walkers had given some thought to expanding the space that was devoted to the display of stoves. Of course, it was possible to rearrange floor space and give the stoves a more prominent location without giving them more space. They also considered converting a small adjacent storage area measuring about twelve by eighteen feet to expansion of the stove department. It would be inconvenient to sacrifice this storage area but the firm had enough storage space in a warehouse building not far away. The total selling area of the store was currently about 4,500 square feet.

Financial institutions were more willing than ever to make loans in the inner city for people to buy houses and to improve the houses they already owned. Several large churches in the inner city had become involved in housing in recent years through loans from the federal government. Operating on a nonprofit basis, the churches built a number of houses, but primarily they rehabilitated old houses. Architects had determined that 60 to 75 percent of the housing stock of the inner city was structurally quite good. Expenditures for new plumbing, new electrical wiring, new or improved heating, and insulation and storm windows, plus decorating touches, would put them in very good condition. The former practice of indiscriminately tearing down large numbers of buildings seemed to be ending. Lately there was a strong feeling that urban renewal probably should preserve communities to the extent possible. In the Walkers' area, a federally sponsored program was making twenty to thirty abandoned houses a year available to inner city homesteaders for the nominal price of $1. Local families were chosen by lot and had to commit themselves

EXHIBIT 3 Cost of Fuels per Million BTUs

Fuel Type	Cost per Million BTUs
Natural gas	$ 3.05
Fuel oil	4.80
Electricity	
Without heat pump	8.00
With heat pump	5.60
Wood	
Stove	3.90
Fireplace	22.00

Source: Energy Research and Development Administration.

to renovate the house and live in it a minimum of five years. Both white and black families were participating enthusiastically in this program.

Exhibit 3 presents the approximate cost per million BTUs[1] for natural gas, fuel oil, electricity, and wood in the Walkers' metropolitan area; these figures were very near the national average. A heat pump made electric heating much cheaper, but it was still more costly than gas or fuel oil. The data indicated that a fireplace was quite inefficient. Coal is not included in the exhibit because almost everyone objected to the labor, dust, and odor involved in using this fuel. Many wood-burning stoves would, however, also burn coal if desired. The prices of natural gas, fuel oil, and electricity were expected to rise more rapidly than the overall Consumer Price Index, but the price of wood was expected to rise in line with the CPI. The CPI had been rising from 5 to 7 percent each year and was expected to rise at a rate of 4 to 5 percent in the next one or two years.

Experts in forestry management indicated that a sizable fraction of U.S. homes could be shifted to the use of wood for heat without interfering with other current uses of wood and without harvesting more than the annual forest growth, thus assuring no net resource depletion. Proven reserves of natural gas were quite low. It was time-consuming and troublesome to get a new building connected to a natural gas distribution system in some parts of the United States, including the area where the Walkers lived.

Advise Walker Furniture.

---

[1] BTU = British Thermal Unit, a standard measure of heat generated.

16

Marketing Programs (Overview)

MACK TRUCKS, INC.

Mack Trucks, Inc., one of the world's most famous names in truck manufacturing, was facing several problems of varying severity. The picture of the Mack bulldog, wearing the collar with the word "Mack" on it and carrying the promotional themes of toughness and "bulldog protection," was one of the best-known trade symbols in the commercial art field. A statue of the dog, over twenty feet tall, stood in front of headquarters. Moreover, the expression "built like a Mack truck" had taken its place in American colloquial English. Almost 300,000 Mack trucks were on the road in the United States.

The truck-building industry was not generally considered a growth industry. In fact, Mack executives characterized it as "mature" and felt that the long-run growth of any company in this industry had to come at the expense of the competitors. It was fully expected that, around the world, several truck makers would have to go out of business during the 1990s. Mack showed significant losses in three of the last five years: 1985, 1986, and 1989.

This organization, now employing about 8,000 people, compared to 12,200 in 1985, maintained headquarters in Allentown, Pennsylvania; truck assembly plants in Macungie, Pennsylvania; Winnsboro, South

Carolina, Oakville, Ontario, and Richlands, Australia; and a power-train plant in Hagerstown, Maryland. A plant in Hayward, California was eliminated in 1983. The company operated engineering development and test laboratories at Allentown, Pennsylvania, and Hagerstown, Maryland. The latter was on a site that included a three-quarter mile, banked, oval test track on sixty-two acres, leading to a 1,100-foot-long skid path with thirteen lanes and three different road surfaces. This site included space for off-road testing also. Mack operated parts distribution centers in Baltimore, Atlanta, Dallas, Chicago, Hayward (California), Toronto, Vancouver, and Antwerp (Belgium). In New Bern, North Carolina, and Middletown, Pennsylvania the company operated the Mack Remanufacturing Centers, where worn Mack diesel engines, transmissions, water pumps, injection pumps, cylinder heads, and other items were remanufactured to "like new" standards. For example, an engine was completely disassembled and high-wear items were replaced with new parts.

Mack owned and operated seventeen sales and service branches in the United States in 1988, compared to twenty-three in 1985. It owned two parts stores and five used truck centers in the United States. Mack acquired many trucks as trade-ins at its company-owned sales branches. The historical average was about fifty trade-ins for every 100 new trucks sold at these branches. There were 250 independently owned sales and service outlets and 450 independently owned service centers in 1988. The corresponding figures in 1985 were 242 and 503. Mack also supplied parts to fifty-two independently owned parts outlets in the United States. Mack's Canadian subsidiary operated a network of sales, parts, and service facilities scattered through that country. Mack considered that it had greater distributor strength in the East and the South than elsewhere in the United States. In recent years, Mack had converted many of its own sales and service branches to independent ownership. Mack maintained inventory on 83,000 different parts through its regional parts distribution centers. Adequate stocks of parts were highly important to its customers, all of whom were business users of trucks. Company sales and operating results are presented in Exhibit 1 and a recent balance sheet in Exhibit 2.

Most Mack truck sales were to customer order rather than from stock. Extremely large business customers who were probably going to need many hundreds of units sometimes observed or even participated in Mack's product development. For example, one of the manufacturer's largest customers was United Parcel Service (UPS), and they had had a good relationship for many years. Equipment specialists from UPS evaluated Mack's Ultra-Liner model in the prototype stages and suggested modifications and specifications. Subsequently UPS bought 830 of these units.

EXHIBIT 1 Mack Trucks, Inc. Operating Statements

	For The Years Ended December 31		
	1988	1987	1986
	(in thousands except per share amounts)		
Revenues:			
Net sales......................	**$2,102,228**	$1,857,748	$1,711,844
Interest income................	**77,274**	68,682	76,834
Other..........................	**8,493**	4,744	8,252
Total Revenues...............	**2,187,995**	1,931,174	1,796,930
Cost and Expenses:			
Cost of sales....................	**1,902,459**	1,699,846	1,567,554
Depreciation and amortization of property.....	**29,619**	28,249	29,604
Selling, general and administrative expenses......	**154,908**	137,120	136,852
Interest expense...............	**56,307**	47,638	53,888
Provision for special early retirement costs........	**—**	—	33,732
Total Costs and Expenses....	**2,143,293**	1,912,853	1,821,630
Income (Loss) Before Income Taxes and Extraordinary Items.	**44,702**	18,321	(24,700)
Provision for Income Taxes...........................	**19,761**	13,397	9,404
Income (Loss) Before Extraordinary Items..........	**24,941**	4,924	(34,104)
Extraordinary Items.............	**6,845**	(834)	3,535
Net Income (Loss)................	**$ 31,786**	$ 4,090	$ (30,569)
Income (Loss) Per Common and Common Equivalent Share:			
Income (loss) before extraordinary items...........	**$ 0.84**	$ 0.16	$ (1.18)
Extraordinary items.............	**0.23**	(0.02)	0.12
Net Income (Loss)................	**$ 1.07**	$ 0.14	$ (1.06)

A new manufacturing plant, costing over $80 million and extremely modern and efficient in design, had long been planned for the late 1980s; and the old Allentown plant, built in 1926 and excessively costly to operate, was to be closed down. There had been very little modernization of plant and equipment since the mid-1960s. The planned new factory,

EXHIBIT 2 Mack Trucks, Inc. Balance Sheets

Assets	December 31	
	1988	1987
	(in thousands)	
Current Assets:		
Cash and short-term investments............	$ **81,475**	$ 70,466
Refundable taxes............................	**2,297**	14,462
Trade accounts, finance and notes receivables:		
Accounts....................................	**611,473**	519,716
Less unearned finance fees................	**38,700**	30,336
Less allowance for uncollectible accounts...................................	**9,379**	10,056
Trade accounts, finance and notes receivable - net..........................	**563,394**	479,324
Inventories..................................	**393,847**	380,668
Deferred income taxes	**36,794**	39,859
Prepaid expenses............................	**3,408**	5,589
Total current assets.......................	**1,081,215**	990,368
Long-Term Finance Receivables:		
Accounts....................................	**365,141**	266,382
Less unearned finance fees.................	**37,721**	25,010
Less allowanced for uncollectible accounts...................................	**3,639**	3,889
Long-term finance receivables - net..........	**323,781**	237,483
Sundry Investments...........................	**12,400**	6,328
Property - at cost	**518,839**	484,799
Less accumulated depreciation and amortization...............................	**255,914**	246,757
Property - net.............................	**262,925**	238,042
Other Assets................................	**4,001**	3,259
Total	**$1,684,322**	$1,475,480

it was figured, would cut production costs for a new truck line by 20 to 25 percent. Location of the manufacturing facility was in doubt for a long time, a fact that contributed considerably to the employee relations problems of the firm as well as to the community and general public relations problems. There was great pressure from the Pennsylvania state and local governments to place Mack's new investment in the Allentown vicinity.

EXHIBIT 2 *(Continued)*

Liabilities and Shareholders' Equity	December 31	
	1988	1987
	(in thousands)	
Current Liabilities:		
Notes payable – banks..........................	$ **44,170**	$ 25,289
Current portion of long-term debt..............	**94,869**	94,061
Accounts payable...............................	**157,379**	189,698
Other accrued liabilities........................	**194,357**	177,027
Total current liabities.........................	**490,775**	477,075
Long-Term Debt:		
Notes and loans.................................	**594,377**	410,205
Obligations under capital leases................	**7,756**	7,801
Total long-term debt.........................	**602,133**	418,006
Other Liabilities and Deferred Credits:		
Deferred income taxes..........................	**37,293**	39,140
Deferred gain on disposal of capital............		
assets...	**11,800**	8,614
Accrued termination and restructuring.........		
costs..	**4,819**	40,587
Other...	**6,320**	5,138
Total other liabilities and deferred credits....	**60,232**	93,479
Contingent Liabilities and Commitments.........	**–**	–
Redeemable Preference Shares...................	**5,978**	4,711
Shareholders' Equity:		
Common stock, par value $1 per share - authorized, 100,000,000 shares; issued, 30,594,033 and 30,527,713 shares at December 31, 1988 and 1987, respectively	**30,594**	30,527
Additional paid-in capital......................	**317,145**	316,385
Retained earnings..............................	**185,586**	153,800
Equity adjustment from foreign currency translation.....................................	**3,143**	(7,333)
	536,468	493,379
Less: Treasury stock at cost (1,016,952 and 1,009,958 shares at December 31, 1988 and 1987, respectively).............................	**11,264**	11,170
Shareholders' equity............................	**525,204**	482,209
Total..	**$1,684,322**	$1,475,480

The old plant suffered not only from obsolete equipment and too little mechanization but from high hourly labor rates as well. The top management referred to the labor arrangement in this plant as "high button shoes." United Auto Workers labor costs there were about $23 per hour, including cost of fringe benefits. Moreover, the union contract with the United Auto Workers specified a maze of over ninety separate job classifications and very limited ability for a worker to move voluntarily between classifications to perform work or for the management to move the worker even if the tasks were similar. The company asked the union for concessions of $3.85 per hour and said that, without such a concession, it would construct the new plant outside of Pennsylvania. Both the Middle West and the South, especially the Carolinas, had been under consideration.

The reduction requested was the amount that Mack calculated it overpaid compared to its most direct U.S. competitors, Paccar, Freightliner, and Volvo-White Truck Corporation. Other noteworthy competitors were General Motors, Ford, and International Harvester, which had renamed itself Navistar. Because the United States represented almost one-third of the world's total truck market, new competitors had come in. Daimler-Benz of West Germany bought Freightliner, based in Portland, Oregon, in 1981; and AB Volvo, of Sweden, bought bankrupt White Motor, based in Greensboro, North Carolina, the same year. Volvo also took over much of the heavy truck making operations of General Motors. The Japanese truck makers, Nissan, Isuzu, Hino, and Mitsubishi, were now entering the market, too. Volvo and Renault had announced the long-run intention to try several joint projects.

After about a year of negotiation, Mack set a deadline in early 1986 for the union to accept the reduction in the pay package. Straw votes and polls in the union's local branches in Pennsylvania and Maryland implied strongly that a majority of the workers were willing to accept the cut. The leadership, especially at the national level, was opposed, because it was ego-involved and it feared a domino effect across the country. The Maryland plant workers were involved in the dispute not only through wages and fringe benefits but also in two other ways. First, if the Maryland workers did not accept compensation reductions, Mack would definitely start "outsourcing" (this practice is explained and developed later in the case) some items now made in Hagerstown, and the number of jobs in the facility would be decreased correspondingly. Regardless of union action on the proposed pay cut, some outsourcing would be considered. Second, a relocation of the Allentown plant to any point at great distance from Hagerstown would make it tempting to Mack to move Hagerstown activities closer to the proposed plant gradually. Hagerstown and Allentown were only 170 miles apart. In addition, a reduction of the size of the Hagerstown plant might bring it down to the point where it could not enjoy any economies of scale, and then it might be tempting to eliminate it.

The union offered only to make some of the work rules more rational and economical and to decrease compensation temporarily in Pennsylvania and Maryland, the savings going directly into an account to pay the cost to construct the new Allentown plant. Mack waited for five days after the deadline, and then it decided to relocate the Allentown facility to Winnsboro, South Carolina, a town of about 4,000 population about thirty miles north of Columbia. It also announced that it would start purchasing several of the items it was making at Hagerstown. The 3,100 jobs at the Maryland factory were scheduled to decline by 40 to 60 percent. An arbitrator ruled that Mack's workers in Pennsylvania and Maryland had the right to transfer to the South Carolina plant. About 400 workers took advantage of this opportunity. The company then decided to retain the Hagerstown plant and committed $100 million to its modernization but, as indicated, with far fewer employees.

The company and the U.A.W. negotiated a five and a half year collective bargaining agreement in April 1987, providing the employees with substantial job security improvement in return for wage reductions and productivity improvements. The U.A.W. repudiated the agreement shortly thereafter, whereupon Mack sued the union. The lower court and then the appeals court ruled in favor of Mack. Then the U.S. Supreme Court in February 1989 declined to hear a further appeal from the union.

The Winnsboro plant started up in August 1987 but did not become fully operational until 1989. The United Auto Workers, the same union that represented the employees in Pennsylvania and Maryland, launched an emotional organizing effort among the Winnsboro workers. After a tumultuous drive, during which production was frequently disrupted, this union won the right in an April 1989 election to represent the Winnsboro workers. South Carolina state officials, who had worked hard to persuade Mack to come to that state, where dismayed by the labor unrest and were fearful that it would harm the attractiveness of their state to industry.

In trying to get the new plant fully operational rather quickly, Mack strained the ability of its parts suppliers to deliver. Thus there were significant delays in completing many hundreds of almost finished trucks. The company had to place these vehicles, at times as many as 1,200, in an open field adjoining the new factory. In addition, the computerized system providing information on parts inventories broke down. The company had to move tens of thousands of parts in its warehouses just to establish manually how many it had of each and thus how many more to order.

In 1988 the company had to transfer production of some models from Winnsboro to the Macungie and Oakville plants temporarily. In an attempt to catch up with its production schedule Mack even shipped some partially assembled trucks to dealers and paid them to finish the work. Some dealers joked that Mack's Winnsboro production workers were so poor and the company's quality control had slipped so much that they had to finish many of the trucks anyway, and so why not get paid for it. Dealer relations had deteriorated significantly. In 1989 Mack suffered very large expenses to honor warranties on products badly made in the early months of the Winnsboro plant.

Founded in 1900 as Mack Brothers, the company later offered its stock to the general public. Then, in 1967, it became a subsidiary of the Signal Companies, which were based in La Jolla, California. In 1979, while Mack was still a Signal subsidiary, Regie Nationale des Usines Renault, a French organization, bought into Mack, investing $50 million for a 10 percent common stock interest. Renault at that time also acquired convertible subordinated debentures for $65 million, which in 1982 it converted into an additional 10 percent of Mack's common stock. Then, in 1983, through complex transactions pursuant to a stock and warrant purchase agreement, Renault purchased more shares from Signal and a fifteen-year warrant to purchase still more shares. Thus, Renault had paid $228 million beyond the first $50 million and then owned 41.9 percent of the stock. Of the amounts Renault paid, $94 million went directly to Mack. Renault bought more shares on the open market during 1987 and 1988, so that currently Renault owned almost 45 percent of the stock. The previous chairperson of the board at Mack, John Curcio, was head of Mack's international operations in 1979 and helped persuade Renault to invest in Mack. In 1983, Signal sold all but 10.6 percent of its Mack holdings to the general public, for which it received an aggregate of $144 million. The Signal Companies were later absorbed by Allied. The resulting firm, named Allied-Signal, was mainly in chemicals.

If it exercised all its rights under existing agreements, Renault could buy enough stock to take majority control if it so chose. In practical terms, however, it was impossible to get enough stockholders to agree on any policy position to swing a majority vote against someone who owned over four-tenths of the stock. Therefore, Renault had been in control for several years but generally had taken a hands-off attitude. To the dismay of some stockholders, in mid-1990 Renault indicated it would probably buy more shares.

In 1983, Mack issued 2,020,202 shares of its Series A Cumulative Preferred Stock for a purchase price of $33,333,333. This stock was redeemable at the option of Mack at any time at the price of $16.50 per share plus accrued dividends; and it was convertible into common stock at a rate of $16.21 per share, subject to antidilution adjustments. Signal had the right to require Renault to purchase this preferred stock if it had not been previously redeemed by Mack or if Renault had the right to purchase these shares from Signal at any time. In either case, the purchase price would be $33,333,322 plus accrued dividends.

Founded as a private enterprise, Renault had been a French government-owned corporation since 1946. The usual but not totally proved explanation for the nationalization was punishment for Renault's alleged cooperation with the German authorities who had occupied France during World War II and the extremely large amounts of war goods Renault supplied the German military forces during the occupation. With its private enterprise heritage, Renault performed well after nationalization for a time and intermittently well thereafter for many years. By the mid-1980s it was incurring heavy losses, in fact, the equivalent of over U.S. $1 billion per year. Under conservative, moderate, liberal, and, ironically, socialist government regimes, Renault had experienced severe labor relations problems. The reasons for the losses revolved around inadequate management, questionable decisions on the composition of the product line, and, in particular, the French government policy of keeping many thousands of workers for whom the company had no need at all. Moreover, in addition to its investment in Mack, Renault had owned 46 percent of American Motors and had had an option to buy more. Instead, Renault sold American Motors to Chrysler.

When moderates and conservatives were again in the majority in the French National Assembly in the late 1980s Renault was authorized to reduce its costly work force and reorganize itself. It was told to reach the breakeven point as quickly as possible and then to seek modest profits. These changes at Renault suddenly affected Mack. Renault began to play a much larger role in the decision making at Mack and one of its executives stated that "heads would roll" at Mack. Renault caused the 1989 termination of the contract of John Curcio, the chairman of the board, president, and chief executive, and the hiring of Ralph Reins, who had good experience in the automotive parts operations of Rockwell International and ITT. Together Renault and Reins fired most of the upper-level management. Curcio was temporarily reassigned to repair the damaged relations with frustrated dealers, but many dealers resisted this arrangement and some judged it very inappropriate, and thus Curcio was terminated completely.

Mack made sixteen lines of domestic "on" and "on-off" highway trucks and tractors, including a line of fire truck chassis units. The company's lines of trucks and tractors were distinguished by features such as cab style (conventional or cab-over-engine), size (engine compartment, frame, and axle size), and use-related design characteristics (highway or in-city tractor, dumper-mixer, all-wheel-drive snowplow, all-wheel-drive block hauler and mixer, refuse hauler). Models within each line were distinguished by such feature options as engines, transmissions, axles, frames, front-axle placement, and gross vehicle or gross combination weight.

Vehicles generally consisted of a chassis and cab without a body. Cab and chassis units were designed to accommodate many different types of bodies and trailers, including dry and refrigerated vans; dumps; concrete mixers; block haulers; liquid tanks; powder-hopper tanks; stake, flatbed, front-side, and rear-loading refuse bodies; well-servicing equipment platforms; and beverage vans. Mack also made cab and chassis units designed especially for extra-heavy-duty hauling, such as oil field, logging, and coal hauling. Truck tractors were used primarily on highways by long-distance freight carriers of dry and liquid cargoes. Mack engineered and built its trucks to meet the requirements of the industries in which they were to be used. Annual models were not produced. However, improvements, refinements, and modifications were made whenever deemed advantageous.

The U.S. truck-building industry suffered from overcapacity in class eight trucks, that is, equipment with gross vehicle weight of over 33,000 pounds. The classification system was created by the Motor Vehicle Manufacturers Association. Often called "heavy-duty trucks," class eight carried about three-fourths of the freight in the United States. Mack itself, one of the largest of the twelve producers of such trucks in the United States, suffered from overcapacity, and such trucks were its principal business.

Total U.S. demand for class eight trucks dropped for several years after peaking in 1979. The general strength of the U.S. economy pulled demand up sharply for heavy trucks in 1984. Class eight units sold by the entire industry rose 79 percent over 1983, and classes six and seven combined rose 45 percent. The industry's exports of heavy-duty trucks declined slightly from 1983 to 1984. In 1984 Mack sold worldwide 29,003 class eight units, an increase of 103 percent over the 14,300 of 1983, and 5,778 medium-duty (classes six and seven) units, an increase of 63 percent over 1983, thus outperforming the industry. U.S. demand for class eight trucks fell in 1985 but rose in 1986, 1987, and 1988. Total U.S. industry class eight capacity was about 230,000 units in the late 1980s. U.S. deregulation of the trucking (i.e., freight carrying by truck) industry had led to more efficient hauling; and aggressive competition from railroads plus the lack of growth in U.S. manufacturing kept demand for large trucks down. The average selling price of a class eight truck declined for five consecutive years starting in 1981. In 1985 that average price was $54,000. The percentage breakdown between Mack's sales of new trucks and sales of parts and service is given in Exhibit 3.

Mack sold 27,469 class eight vehicles during 1988, a rise of 16 percent over 1987 unit sales of 23,697. Of these 1988 sales 22,300 vehicles were sold in the United States, compared to 19,000 in 1987. Mack's share of the U.S. market for heavy trucks was 14.6 percent in 1988 and 14.0 percent in 1987. See Exhibit 4.

The company's share of the U.S. market for truck classes six and seven (medium duty) combined was 7.3 percent in 1983, 8.2 percent in

**EXHIBIT 3 Sales of Mack Trucks, Inc.
by Major Type by Year**

Year	Trucks	Parts and Service
1988	77%	23%
1985	77	23
1984	77	23
1983	69	31
1982	72	28
1981	75	25
1980	77	23
1979	80	20

1984, 6.4 percent in 1985, 8.0 percent in 1986, 6.8 percent in 1987, and 5.6 percent in 1988. Mack's product offering was termed the Mid-Liner series, the best-selling import in the United States in this size range. It was built in France by Renault Vehicles Industriels, a wholly owned subsidiary of Renault. Mack was the exclusive distributor of the Mid-Liner in the United States, Canada, and several Central American and Caribbean countries. Mack did not make or sell trucks lighter than class six.

With a product named the FR-1 coach, Mack reentered the inter-city bus market in 1984. Introduced in Europe by Renault in 1983, this rather advanced product had an aluminum and stainless steel structure and electronic technology. It was assembled with a Mack diesel engine and transmission. In 1986, Volvo-White closed down its U.S. bus manufacturing operation, which was located in Chesapeake, Virginia.

Two interesting new products were launched in 1988. At the beginning of that year the company brought out the Mack Baby 8, a conventional model truck to serve the lighter end of the heavy-duty market. It was

**EXHIBIT 4 Mack's Unit Sales in Class 8 Trucks in United States
and Share of the Market by Year**

Year	Unit Sales	Share of Market
1988	22,300	14.6%
1987	19,000	14.0
1986	16,600	14.7
1985	23,800	18.5
1984	25,400	17.5
1983	12,200	15.0
1982	13,100	Not available

developed jointly with the Renault staff. After five years of planning and an investment of $60 million in research, development, and testing Mack launched an even more important new product at the end of 1989. The CH600 model truck was aimed at the over-the-road market and was to replace the R model introduced in 1965. It featured a larger, more comfortable cab and improved fuel efficiency. However, the product was introduced with an old model engine, a major disappointment to many potential customers. A new engine, planned to be available in June 1989, was delayed when the supplier had trouble making its pistons. When the new engines were finally available in late September 1989 the demand for trucks had declined badly. Mack had a backlog of 3,400 unsold units of the new product, most with the old engine.

The new Japanese competitors in truck manufacturing had entered the market with small and midsized trucks and, in Mack's estimation, were not expected to do much with class eight trucks right away. Mack officials noted that makers of class eight trucks in the United States had kept quality up better than Detroit had done in the late 1970s and early 1980s with passenger cars. Furthermore, the Japanese had had very little experience using or making heavy-duty trucks, a product type little used outside of the United States, Canada, and Australia. The Japanese were doing fairly well making earthmoving equipment and farm tractors. Mack and other U.S. and European firms building large trucks in the United States were reasonably optimistic about competing well against the Japanese companies.

Mack had a wholly owned subsidiary in the United States, Mack Financial Corporation (MFC), engaged in financing the sale of trucks to customers. MFC, in turn, had a wholly owned subsidiary in Canada. Varying by year, from 11 to 17 percent of Mack's new truck sales in the United States and Canada were so financed. The service was available on trucks sold by both company-owned branches and independent dealers. Mack had another subsidiary, Mack Americus, Inc., which financed the purchase by distributors of replacement parts and certain of the company's short-term unsecured retail truck receivables. Mack also owned Mack Leasing System, Inc., which acquired vehicles from the company and in turn leased them to users who preferred not to buy. The leasing operation was begun in 1987.

The company had long been a highly integrated manufacturer. It had made nearly all its own parts, such as front and rear axles, axle housings, axle shafts, support frames, engines, and transmissions, and did not offer such components to any other manufacturer. This high degree of manufacturing integration gave rise to the expression "all-Mack," "the all-Mack truck," and occasionally "Mack-Mack." The first two of these expressions had been widely used, and the third was occasionally used in company advertising, personal selling, and public relations. According to company officials, "Mack's greatest strength has always been the design and production of the total vehicle . . . the concept of balanced design." This strongly implied supplying from within the company. Nearly all competitors used outsourcing, that is, buying some key components from outside suppliers. All U.S. competitors for class eight vehicles used outsourcing for engines, transmissions, and rear-axle carriers. Contrary to laypeople's expectations, outsourcing was often cheaper than making one's own parts because the outside supplier was a specialist and also gained large economies of scale by making a larger number of units than the customer organization needed to make for itself. Such parts makers served multiple manufacturing customers. The mass component manufacturers, which produced for both truck and carmakers, included at least five U.S. firms: Eaton Corporation of Cleveland; Dana Corporation of Toledo; Cummins Engine Company of Columbus, Indiana; and two conglomerates, Rockwell International of Pittsburgh and TRW Inc. of Cleveland. All of them had foreign as well as domestic plants.

Mack was in the process of reducing its manufacturing integration and had already set up contracts with several parts-manufacturing specialists. It cost about $3,500,000 to close down selected parts-making operations in Allentown, but savings from outsourcing were estimated at $30 million per year. This included the termination of several hundred workers. Some of these new arrangements called for just one supplier of certain components, and others called for two suppliers. The new corporate policy was to "review its component manufacturing program periodically to determine which components it will continue to manufacture and which it will purchase from vendors." Some components were manufactured for Mack by single source suppliers, several under the terms of long-term supply agreements covering cabs, carriers, axles, frame and drive line assemblies, and paint and finish coatings. The paint producer provided all paint warranties on the trucks.

Most Mack trucks contained Mack-built major components, such as engine and transmission, front axles, and single and tandem rear axles (including the gear-drive carriers). However, if specified by a customer, Mack was willing to substitute major components made by other firms. The company had a long-range objective of developing "a high degree of interchangeability of basic components among its truck models," which would permit flexibility in adapting models to a wide range of uses and reduce the size and complexity of parts inventories.

In recent years, the research and development effort on the powertrain, that is, the engine, transmission, and rear-axle carriers, was on two fronts. First and more emphasized, there was work that management described as "evolutionary," taking products and product concepts to higher levels. This was perfecting what was already done well. Examples were the new engines in the company's six-cylinder, eleven-liter series and a six-cylinder, twelve-liter engine. Evolutionary work was very much influenced by scheduled and forecast future rises in government standards for emissions controls. Second, there was research and development that management described as "revolutionary," the increased application of electronic controls. Such electronics had to do mainly with engine fuel controls, vehicle instrumentation, a road-speed governor, and a transmission-shifting system. In addition, there was considerable work on redesign to make the trucks meet new regulations of the U.S. Environmental Protection Agency on noise and exhaust emissions. Mack and the entire industry urged the E.P.A. to order a reduction in the sulphur level in diesel fuel. Such a decrease would help the truck-building firms to meet emissions standards. Without such a decrease there would be extremely costly engine modifications in 1991 and 1992. Such costs would, of course, make U.S. trucks less competitive abroad. Very few countries had any emissions requirements at all.

Mack's products were regularly exported to seventy-four countries, down from the figure of eighty in the mid-1980s. Canada and Australia were the principal foreign markets, but Mack's sales there were supplied almost entirely from the company's production in those two countries. Total foreign sales accounted for about 22 percent of company sales in most years. About five percent of Mack's U.S. production was exported. Sales of Mack products abroad were made through seventy-two franchised distributors and branches located or selling in seventy-four countries and occasionally through independent agents not under franchise. These representatives abroad received a commission, the rate of which varied based on the amount of the representative's involvement in transactions or local custom on rates or both. On the whole, Mack's exports made a higher rate of profit than did domestic sales, mainly because of higher prices the company could usually command abroad. However, Japanese truck makers were steadily chipping away at the overseas markets Mack had long enjoyed, and European truck makers were noteworthy competitors. Mack was especially strong in Canada, Australia, and Venezuela.

Much of the organization's export volume was in the form of CKD (completely knocked down) chassis shipped for assembly in the country of destination, with varying degrees of local content added. In 1988 CKD assembly operations were conducted in three foreign nations by local firms, but Mack had an ownership interest in two of them. The corresponding figures in 1985 were seven and three.

From 1983 to 1985, Mack Trucks Australia Pty, Ltd., the wholly owned Australian subsidiary, delivered 1,000 eight-ton trucks to the Australian army, beating twenty-four other builders for the contract. The major criterion for winning was projected life-cycle cost. Using one standard chassis and both Australian and U.S. content, several vehicle variations were made for this contract. The company received the Defence Industry

Quality and Achievement Award from the Australian government. With the encouragement of the host government, the Australian subsidiary had plans to develop exports of its own, but probably they would not be military vehicles.

Advise Mack Trucks, Inc.

POLAROID CORPORATION

Polaroid Corporation, based in Cambridge, Massachusetts, designed, manufactured, and marketed worldwide a line of products stemming from its inventions. This line was almost entirely in the photographic field. The products included instant cameras and film, light-polarizing filters and lenses, and diversified chemical and optical products. Polaroid produced more than forty types of film in eight different formats and in a variety of emulsion characteristics. The main products of the company were used in amateur and professional photography, industry, science, medicine, and education.

There was considerable concern about the well-being of the company and its future although it was still profitable. Sales were weak; profits, low; and the trends, not encouraging. See Exhibits 1 through 4 for data. About one-third of the company's workers had been dismissed. Nevertheless, Polaroid had almost two-thirds of the world's sales of instant cameras and instant film and had a hoard of cash of several hundred million dollars. Moreover, it held about 150 patents and continued to win some new patents from time to time.

Development of Polaroid and Its Corporate Culture

Edwin H. Land established Polaroid in 1937, when he was twenty-eight years old. He was universally acknowledged to be an inventor of impressive talent and skill, one of the best physicists of his generation. He was also well prepared in chemistry and could make creative and useful ties between physics and chemistry. Land founded and built up the company around his own inventive work. He began by inventing new solutions to very old problems in the field of light polarization. Land invented additional optical devices for the U.S. military effort in World War II, and in 1948 he introduced his famous Land camera for instant photographs. A prolific professional, Land was second only to the legendary Thomas A. Edison in the number of U.S. patents issued to him. Over his career Land received dozens of awards from scientific societies and honorary degrees from twelve universities. He still found time to teach a course occasionally at M.I.T. in Cambridge.

EXHIBIT 1 Polaroid Corporation's Operating Statements in Recent Years (dollar amounts in millions except per share data)

	1985	1984	1983	1982	1981	1980	1979	1978
CONSOLIDATED STATEMENT OF EARNINGS								
Net sales								
United States	$ 779.3	$ 743.5	$ 730.1	$ 752.5	$ 817.8	$ 791.8	$ 757.2	$ 817.
International	515.9	528.0	524.4	541.4	601.8	659.0	604.3	559
Total net sales	1295.2	1271.5	1254.5	1293.9	1419.6	1450.8	1361.5	1376.
Cost of goods sold	756.0	735.2	698.3	769.6	855.4	831.1	876.8	778
Marketing, research, engineering, and administrative expenses	505.6	492.6	462.1	472.6	520.8	483.9	449.4	418.
Total costs	1261.6	1227.8	1160.4	1242.2	1376.2	1315.0	1326.2	1196.
Profit from operations	33.6	43.7	94.1	51.7	43.4	135.8	35.3	180
Other income	28.9	39.5	32.5	45.5	49.2	25.4	13.3	20
Interest expense	22.3	20.9	26.5	35.5	29.9	17.0	12.8	5
Earnings before income taxes	40.2	62.3	100.1	61.7	62.7	144.2	35.8	194.
Federal, state and foreign income taxes (credit)	3.3	36.6	50.4	38.2	31.6	58.8	(.3)	76
Net earnings	36.9	25.7	49.7	23.5	31.1	85.4	36.1	118
Earnings per share	$ 1.19	$ .83	$ 1.61	$ .73	$ .95	$ 2.60	$ 1.10	$ 3.
Cash dividends per share	$ 1.00	$ 1.00	$ 1.00	$ 1.00	$ 1.00	$ 1.00	$ 1.00	$ .9
Average shares outstanding (in thousands)	30,959	30,959	30,959	32,144	32,855	32,855	32,855	32,85

EXHIBIT 2 Polaroid Corporation and Subsidiary Companies Consolidated Balance Sheet December 31, 1984 and 1983 (in millions)[a]

Assets		1984	1983
Current assets	Cash and short-term investments	$ 350.2	$ 366.5
	Receivables, less allowances of $9.4 ($8.6 in 1983)	269.7	241.0
	Inventories	344.9	372.4
	Prepaid expenses	74.6	62.2
	Total current assets	1,039.4	1,042.1
Property, plant and equipment	Land	11.9	11.9
	Buildings	200.6	197.3
	Machinery and equipment	645.9	617.0
	Construction in process	47.7	31.3
	Gross property, plant and equipment	906.1	857.5
	Less accumulated depreciation	599.5	580.5
	Net property, plant and equipment	306.6	277.0
	Total assets	$1,346.0	$1,319.1
LIABILITIES AND STOCKHOLDERS' EQUITY			
Current liabilities	Short-term debt	$ 82.6	$ 66.9
	Payables and accruals	126.6	116.4
	Compensation and benefits	71.1	68.2
	Federal, state and foreign income taxes	24.9	21.6
	Total current liabilities	305.2	273.1
	Long-term debt	124.5	124.4
Stockholders' equity	Common stock, $1 par value, authorized 36,000,000 shares, issued 32,855,475 shares	32.9	32.9
	Additional paid-in capital	122.0	122.0
	Retained earnings	808.3	813.6
	Less treasury stock, at cost, 1,896,300 shares	963.2	968.5
	Total stockholders' equity	916.3	921.6
	Total liabilities and stockholders' equity	$1,346.0	$1,319.1

[a] 1985 not available

EXHIBIT 3 Number of Consumer Cameras Sold by Polaroid Corporation by Year

Year	Number (in millions)
1988	3.5
1987	3.8
1986	4.4
1985	3.5
1984	3.6
1983	3.8
1982	4.0
1981	5.6
1980	6.6
1979	7.3

In 1980 the founder retired as chief executive officer and director of research and in 1982 as chairperson of the board of directors. He chose not to keep a seat on the board although, with 8.3 percent of the company stock, he was the largest individual shareholder. However, Land continued to express opinions from time to time and was known to hold some views rather strongly.

Land built a technological empire and yet a supportive, warm, almost family-style corporate culture. It was his policy (Polaroid Corporate Personnel Policy # 251) that anyone who had been employed for ten years with Polaroid had a job for life. There was rapid growth at Polaroid, inventions came quickly and frequently, and there was an extremely high esprit de corps. Land envisioned the company as a gathering place for talented scientists and engineers to exchange ideas and invent products "that bring science and technology to bear on filling . . . a deep human need." He spoke of making Polaroid "a noble prototype of industry." Land added, in one of his most famous pronouncements. "We're not here to make profits. . . . We're here to make innovation." Yet many former employees alleged that over the years a country club, minimum-work attitude began and finally took over the organization.

The founder disapproved of the acquisition of products invented or developed by people outside the Polaroid family and of companies that would have made logical—and often needed—additions to Polaroid's lines of goods and services. He disdained joint ventures. Land even disapproved of Polaroid's conducting basic research or product development work anywhere but in the headquarters laboratories in Cambridge although the organization had become multinational. He thought poorly of present and potential industrial and commercial applications of Polaroid goods and ideas and did not encourage them. Somewhat incongruously

**EXHIBIT 4 Polaroid Corporation and Subsidiary Companies
Consolidated Statement of Changes in Financial Position
Years ended December 31, 1984, 1983, and 1982
(in millions)[a]**

Source and use of funds	1984	1983	1982
Source of funds			
Net earnings	$ 25.7	$49.7	$23.5
Items not requiring current outlay of funds			
Depreciation of property, plant, and equipment	50.8	51.8	62.2
Write-downs of property, plant, and equipment	–	–	18.6
Other	.7	.1	.1
Funds derived from operations	77.2	101.6	104.4
Disposals of property, plant, and equipment	1.7	3.1	1.8
Total source of funds	78.9	104.7	106.2
Use of funds			
Additions to property, plant, and equipment	82.7	50.1	31.5
Cash dividends	31.0	31.0	31.9
Purchase of common stock for treasury	–	–	46.9
Total use of funds	113.7	81.1	110.3
Increase (decrease) in working capital	$(34.8)	$23.6	$ (4.1)
CHANGES IN COMPONENTS OF WORKING CAPITAL			
Current assets – increase (decrease)			
Cash and short-term investments	$(16.3)	$33.0	$ 1.7
Receivables	28.7	(20.8)	(27.7)
Inventories	(27.5)	(14.2)	(26.1)
Prepaid expenses	12.4	2.3	(7.9)
Total change in current assets	(2.7)	.3	(60.0)
Current liabilities – (increase) decrease			
Short-term debt	(15.7)	19.2	21.6
Payables and accruals	(10.2)	7.9	11.0
Compensation and benefits	(2.9)	(9.6)	12.7
Federal, state, and foreign income taxes	(3.3)	5.8	10.6
Total change in current liabilities	(32.1)	23.3	55.9
Increase (decrease) in working capital	$(34.8)	$23.6	$ (4.1)

[a] 1985 not available

for a man of such sophisticated scientific expertise, Land was extremely enthusiastic about amateur photography and managed the corporation so as to try to be preeminent in that field. Land saw photography as "the most elegant of arts." He made it clear that he did not think of photography as a toy or mere hobby and did not want others to do so. He wanted people to be seriously interested in photography and make it part of their lives.

Although Polaroid Corporation had been willing, of course, to talk to industrial, commercial, medical, and educational organizations about its products and adaptations of them for nonconsumers, the corporate culture did not encourage promotional initiative. The sales force was not aggressive by normal business standards. Sales representatives normally waited for prospects to contact them. The advertising was unusually educational in tone although creative and typically interesting.

Polaroid's International Involvement

Polaroid Corporation owned manufacturing subsidiaries in Enschede, Holland, where it employed about 900 people, and Vale of Leven, Scotland, where it employed slightly over 1,000 people. In Holland, Polaroid made pack film, integral film, and film backs for industrial cameras; and in Scotland, cameras, pack film, and sunglasses. In conjunction with the manufacturing plant in Holland, Polaroid operated its International Distribution Center to supply products to most of its foreign-marketing subsidiaries. The majority of Polaroid products for non-U.S. markets came from these two factories and flowed through this physical distribution center. The company closed a film-manufacturing facility in Ireland in 1982 and wrote off a loss of $20 million on the plant and equipment in so doing. The overseas manufacturing facilities received batteries, all light-sensitive materials and receiving sheet, some chemicals, and some components from the U.S. manufacturing plants of the company and selected components from the Far East made specifically for Polaroid, and they purchased some materials locally.

By the mid-1970s, shortly after major international currencies went off fixed rates of exchange, Polaroid found it advisable to create its Monetary Control Center in Holland to manage its exposure to changes in values of the many currencies in which it did business. Nevertheless, it lost money on foreign currency exposure during the period 1979–1984. The net after-tax effect of foreign currency exchange amounted to losses of $5.4 million in 1984, $4.8 million in 1983, $1.7 million in 1982, $1.3 million in 1981, $0.6 million in 1980, and $1.0 million in 1979.

The company first entered foreign markets with exports of its sunglasses. Then in 1959 it established its first subsidiaries outside the

United States, Polaroid Canada, Inc., and Polaroid G.m.b.H. in West Germany. Approximately 42 percent of Polaroid's sales came from abroad each year from 1981 through the mid-1980s compared to 44 percent in 1979 and 45 percent in 1980. See Exhibit 4. The extremely high foreign exchange rate of the U.S. dollar in the early and mid-1980s hurt Polaroid's exports of products, components, and supplies; but, of course, it was impossible to determine exactly how much.

Polaroid had an extensive marketing effort abroad through its wholly owned subsidiaries in twenty-one countries: Canada, West Germany, Italy, France, Holland, United Kingdom, Switzerland, Belgium, Holland, Sweden, Norway, Denmark, Austria, Spain, Singapore, Japan, Hong Kong, Australia, New Zealand, Panama, and Brazil. Polaroid also had such an organization in Puerto Rico. Most of the wholly owned marketing subsidiaries did business only within the territorial limits of the country where located and attempted to be part of the local business community. The company also marketed abroad through unrelated selected distributors in more than 100 other nations.

Polaroid created the European Marketing Council at the end of 1982 to address common concerns among the Polaroid marketing subsidiaries located in the European Economic Community. The council was designed to deal with policies and issues in marketing, and "marketing" was envisioned to include public affairs. In nearly all years since the 1960s Europe accounted for about 60 percent of Polaroid's foreign sales, and most of that figure was in countries having membership in the European Economic Community, sometimes known as the European Common Market.

With over $100 million sales per year, Japan was the most important country for Polaroid's foreign sales. Polaroid set up Nippon Polaroid Kabushiki Kaisha (NPKK), its wholly owned marketing subsidiary, in 1960. It maintained headquarters and a central distribution center in Tokyo and branch offices in Osaka, Nagoya, Sendai, Sapporo, Hiroshima, and Fukuoka. NPKK marketed Polaroid products through an exclusive distributor, Konishiroku Photo Ind. Co. Ltd., maker of Konica brand cameras, to more than 12,000 retail stores. However, the Japanese market was different in that nonconsumer sales accounted for almost one-half of Polaroid sales in that nation. Staffed almost entirely by Japanese nationals, NPKK used traditional Japanese operating practices, such as measurement of performance of the group rather than the individual, considerations of age and seniority in advancement, and lifetime employment. Japan was doubly important to Polaroid in that in 1983 the company established in Tokyo a special subsidiary, Polaroid Asia/Pacific Ltd., to monitor and oversee all Polaroid activities in Asia and the South Pacific.

The Current Situation

In the early and middle 1980s, sales of instant cameras and instant film, the life blood of Polaroid Corporation, declined for six consecutive years. Sales of such cameras declined both in the United States and abroad but declined by a slightly lower percentage abroad than in the United States.

Some people spoke of Polaroid as having a mid-life crisis. In all fairness, the majority of high-tech firms seemed to have gone through a mid-life crisis in which they had to find themselves, and it was perhaps inevitable that all high-tech organizations would do so. Many, of course, had not survived such an experience.

As Land departed in 1982, the company was reorganized, and there were many changes in the ranks of management. Two vice-presidents left as Land left. They were the executive vice-president and director of world-wide marketing and the vice-president and director of the Patent Department. William J. McCune, Jr., an engineer who had joined the company in 1939 at the age of twenty-four, became chairperson of the board, president, and chief executive officer. McCune had become vice-president for engineering while still in his thirties, then executive vice-president in 1969, president and chief operating officer in 1975, and president and chief executive officer in 1980. He relinquished the position of president (only) in 1983 in favor of I. M. Booth, who became president and chief operating officer. An engineer, Booth had joined the company in 1958 at the age of twenty-seven and in 1975 had been named assistant vice-president and assistant to the president, in 1976 vice-president and assistant to the president, in 1977 senior vice-president, in 1980 executive vice-president, and in 1982 executive vice-president and chief operating officer. Sheldon Buckler, a scientist, who had joined Polaroid in 1964 at the age of thirty-three, remained as executive vice-president. Buckler had been appointed assistant vice-president in 1969, vice-president of the research division in 1972, group vice-president in 1975, senior vice-president in 1977, and executive vice-president in 1980.

Sales of nonconsumer products were given high priority by the new or newly elevated executives. By 1985 such markets constituted about 40 percent of Polaroid sales. The new top management also decided that not all research had to be centralized in Cambridge. Land, now conducting basic research in his own private laboratory, the Rowland Institute for Science in Cambridge, let it be known that he did not like the diversification of products and market segments at Polaroid. The new top management also raised the percentage of sales devoted to research and development. This figure became 10.6 in 1984 compared to 9.8 in 1983, 9.1 in 1982, and 8.5 in 1981. However, the proportion of R&D

devoted to basic research declined while the proportion devoted to direct product development and improvement increased.

The new top management made several acquisitions. In 1982, Polaroid bought a 25 percent interest in Image Resource Corporation, whose product line made print images from video cassette recorders and from computer screens. However, in its long tradition of not trusting anyone else to develop a new product, Polaroid decided to develop such products itself and in 1985 sold its interest in Image Resource Corporation for about one-third of what it had paid. In 1983, Polaroid bought 1984 Inc., a research and development firm specializing in single-mode fiber optics but without any goods in actual production, in order to gain its expertise and patents. In 1984, Polaroid acquired a 20 percent interest in Sage Technology, Inc., a California-based maker of plateroom chemistry and imaging products used in printing processes. Also in 1984, Polaroid bought a 30 percent interest in Advanced Color Technology, Inc., a Chelmsford, Massachusetts, maker of ink-jet printers for color graphics, and bought an additional 8 percent in 1985. Founded in 1980, Advanced Color Technology made products priced around $6,000 used principally with computers.

In another management innovation at Polaroid, the company began in 1985 to market an 8-mm video camera-recorder for Toshiba. The latter was a very large Japanese corporation engaged mainly in electronics.

Although the new top management was aiming at a partial reorientation of Polaroid's marketing efforts so as not to be so dependent on the ultimate consumer and was doing reasonably well in moving toward that objective, the corporation was still extremely dependent on instant photography. By 1986 almost 90 percent of company sales were still in instant photography. Several new markets and potential adaptations of the company's products were being developed, but they did not diversify the company out of instant photography significantly. The diversification sought was to go in two directions, more nonconsumer sales and less dependence on instant photography, but there was sizable progress on only the former.

The entire amateur portion of the photographic industry, not just instant photography, slumped in the early and middle 1980s. In part, this was because of recession in nearly all the world. The United States recovered far faster than the rest of the world. The slump was also because consumers were becoming rather blasé about instant photography. Many simple 35-mm cameras were brought to the market by competitors at a variety of prices. In addition, film-developing service for consumers became widely and conveniently available and cheaper than in former times. Most U.S. consumers had access to storefront developing service in a fraction of a day. This new fact of life discouraged interest in instant photography. In addition, some outspoken consumers disparaged instant photography as suitable for only the unsophisticated dabbler.

Over 90 percent of U.S. households already owned at least one camera, and a sizable fraction had multiple units. A few business analysts had described cameras as a "sunset industry." This was rather exaggerated, but the industry certainly had problems. Although the recession of the early 1980s and all recessions had hurt the industry because cameras are basically a luxury item and purchase is infinitely postponable, the more powerful, long-term factor was probably the near saturation in several affluent countries, including the United States, West Germany, and Japan. Cameras were a type of product with a very long functional life. Thirty years' use was not uncommon. If consumers were going to judge it worthwhile to replace their old cameras or upgrade or add another unit, a stream of genuine innovations seemed necessary. Moreover, several Japanese companies were aggressively cultivating the U.S. market for the first time and were entering the European markets. U.S.–based organizations had long been faced with competition from many European and several other Japanese camera makers.

Ernst Leitz Wetzlar G.m.b.H., the West German manufacturer of Leica brand equipment, and Hasselblad of Sweden were probably the most prestigious camera companies in the world. The German firm was primarily engaged in making binoculars and scientific instruments, such as microscopes. Leica cameras were important in World War II, and the Allies spent a great deal of scientific and espionage effort to obtain and copy the most advanced versions of Leica cameras and other Leica optical goods. Other prominent European companies were Rollei and Zeiss-Ikon, both West German.

Several camera makers had recently brought out a new generation of equipment often referred to as "smart cameras." They were 35-mm models that automatically set aperture openings and shutter speed, adjusted the focus, rewound the film, and even activated a flash attachment. Most models were priced under $100. Minolta, a large Japanese organization, introduced a "talking" camera. With an electronically synthesized voice, this camera, priced about $200, told the user for example, when film required reloading. In addition, many improvements had been introduced throughout the camera industry in the inexpensive lines, even those lines under $40.

Eastman Kodak made an extremely important product introduction in May 1982 and called it the Disc. Sandwich-thin and small enough to go in a shirt pocket, the product was described in promotion as "decision-free." This fully automatic camera, which virtually allowed the user simply to point and shoot, replaced several heavier, cumbersome Kodak models. Because of its thinner body, it was easier to handle for most people and less likely to be jiggled while the shutter was pressed. The product took its name from the film format, a disc with fifteen exposures that rotated automatically after each exposure. Because of the generic nature of the word, it appeared that it was going to be difficult for Eastman Kodak to assert and keep legal rights to the term "Disc." By 1983, Konica, Minolta, Continental, Ansco, Keystone, and several other makers introduced similar products, most at lower prices; and Eastman brought out three additional models of the basic product. The various brands of disc-type cameras, ranging from about $30 to $150 in price, accounted for an impressive 21 percent of the U.S. camera market by 1984.

Sony of Japan began marketing a total electronic photographic system at a premium price, approximately $800 for the Mavica camera and almost $1,000 for the optional printer, in 1983. The Mavica was similar to the thin disc cameras and contained a magnetic disc that could hold up to fifty exposures. Sony's early introduction of this product to the market surprised other camera companies although the technology was not terribly surprising. Several companies, such as Polaroid, had been researching these concepts. Electronic photography, also known as "video imaging," converts light into electronic impulses that can be viewed on a television screen instead of photographic paper. Such impulses can be easily stored on magnetic tapes and are potentially more versatile for consumer than chemical photography because the images can be modified and put back into storage. Sony brought out its prototype in 1981 but did not ship it to commercial outlets until late 1983. Sony then offered a color version in 1985. Both Eastman Kodak and Polaroid had developed experimental models but were waiting to see the public reaction to the Sony product. Polaroid's top executives saw that photography and electronics would increasingly be used together. This would be of extreme importance in industrial, technical, and medical photography and of some yet-to-be-determined use in amateur photography. Unlike the Sony model, Eastman's experimental model was not completely electronic but still used film.

The overall market for electronic photography would probably grow more quickly if an electronics company joined with a camera company to develop much lower-price models. Such work would merge electronic and chemical technologies. No company really had adequate expertise in both at this time.

Some interesting changes occurred in advertising and sales promotion. Polaroid terminated Doyle Dane Bernbach as its domestic advertising agency for consumer photography in 1982 after a thirty-year relationship. The company said, "It's easier to get fresh ideas from a new agency." Polaroid hired the much smaller Ally & Gargano, Inc., to handle this work, which constituted nearly half of its advertising budget. This budget, which had been at $97 million, was cut by the new top management to $88 million per year. Polaroid left the industrial and professional photography account with Doyle Dane Bernbach. The company then hired the Ogilvy & Mather advertising agency to handle its new video cassette and computer diskette products. It was one of Doyle Dane Bernbach's smaller client accounts, but the dismissal was intriguing to the advertising industry because that agency had won innumerable awards from the advertising industry for creative excellence in advertising, including a sizable number of advertisements done for Polaroid products. Polaroid was one of Ally & Gargano's large client accounts.

Promotional tie-ins with air carriers were tried with some success. This work was with Delta in late 1982 and TWA in late 1984 and early 1985. Each purchaser of selected Polaroid cameras got a coupon entitling him or her to one-fourth off any TWA coach flight, domestic or foreign, except the London route, through April 30, 1985, or between October 15, 1985, and March 15, 1986, including fares that might be already discounted. For many people this meant that a $20 Polaroid 600-series camera produced a $200 to $250 saving on a foreign flight. The promotion was a success for Polaroid but not for TWA. With hindsight, TWA regretted that the offer had not been limited one to a customer and to the least popular routes.

Another type of promotion, simultaneously a public service, was the Polaroid Education Product. Started in 1979, this ongoing endeavor explored the relation of visual experience to children's learning. Project staff developed "curricula which apply the immediacy and simplicity of instant photography to the basic skills that determine how children perceive themselves and understand their relationship to the world and to those in their lives." School teachers were offered numerous exercises in natural science, mathematics, social studies, and language arts — all utilizing instant pictures. The instant photographic records of the children's gently guided inquiry served as visible, sharable evidence of their expanding interest and accomplishment. This built on the principles that rapid feedback and tangible evidence are more important when students are young. Using Polaroid cameras and film, well over one million U.S. and Canadian children had participated in the Polaroid Education Project, and large amounts of goodwill had been created, as well as widened familiarity with parts of Polaroid's product line.

The Patent Dispute with Eastman Kodak Company

Eastman Kodak introduced a camera and film for instant photography in April 1976, thus ending Polaroid's monopoly position. Polaroid filed a lawsuit against Eastman six days later in a U.S. district court, charging that Eastman was thus infringing several Polaroid patents. The action asked for an injunction against Eastman to halt all sales and that Polaroid be awarded treble damages and reimbursement of all legal costs of the action. Eastman countersued and counterclaimed, seeking a declaratory judgment that the Polaroid patents identified in Polaroid's complaint and several other Polaroid patents were invalid and not infringed. Eastman alleged that Polaroid's own designs were nothing more than new patents on Eastman's own patented processes. The complex trial of the issues was not completed until February 26, 1982, and no judgment was rendered at that time.

From 1957 to 1969, Polaroid had shared some of its instant color secrets with Eastman. Apparently, Polaroid, then much smaller, needed the technical know-how of the industry leader to make negatives for its pull-apart instant prints. In the trial, Polaroid charged that Eastman stole some of the proprietary technology that it learned during those years. Moreover, it alleged that Eastman "reverse-engineered" certain features of the Polaroid SX-70 after that camera was introduced in 1972. This term referred to the practice of taking a competitor's product, tearing it apart, and determining how to get the same result differently. An innovation, the SX-70 produced a color print without requiring the user to strip "garbage," as it was called in the photographic industry, or apply chemicals.

The complex five-month trial was completed in September 1985 after more than nine years of litigation and over $10 million in legal costs for Polaroid. The judge ruled in favor of Polaroid. She issued an injunction October 11, 1985, ordering Eastman to withdraw its instant cameras and film from the market by January 9, 1986. Eastman appealed at once.

Under a new arrangement of the U.S. judicial system, the Eastman appeal went to the Court of Appeals for the Federal Circuit, a new institution established in 1982 in Washington, D.C. This new tribunal was needed to bring logic and consistency to patent disputes. Many federal courts and individual judges were friendly to patent protection, many were unfriendly, and many were totally unqualified for the complex technical disputes about which they were rendering decisions. The lack of understanding by judges contributed to the inexcusable length of such disputes. Despite inconsistencies, in the United States only about 30 percent of patents survived competitors' challenges.

Out of this untenable judicial situation came a solution. All appeals of patent cases from federal district courts had to come to this special-ized court composed of fifteen specialized judges. This court was to handle patent disputes, customs disputes, and claims against the U.S. government. The creation of the specialized court meant not only future consistency and predictability but probably also that patents would be upheld more often and thus become of more economic worth.

Another reason for the prediction that patents would hold up more often under challenge in the future had to do with the perennial U.S. government policy rivalry between antitrust forces and pro-patent forces. Antitrust enthusiasts wanted more and keener domestic competition and perceived patents as essentially damaging to the process of competition. Historically, no other country had pursued as vigorous an antitrust policy as the United States. The highly aggressive and successful competition from firms in Japan, Europe, and the newly industrializing countries such as South Korea, Taiwan, and Singapore, however, was forcing the U.S. government to give more attention to the international competitive process and less to the domestic competitive process. Thus there was need and empathy for better protection of patents of U.S. firms in order to make the U.S. economy stronger in the world business arena.

At the appeals hearing, Polaroid stated, "They saw the SX-70, and they copied it." Eastman's attorney, Francis T. Carr, placed the different-looking Eastman and Polaroid products side by side in the courtroom and stated, "If Kodak is a clone of the SX-70, I hope Kodak never gets into biotechnology." Polaroid noted that it was referring to the working internal principles, not the looks.

Eastman's attorneys noted the phenomenon of "inventing around existing patents," also known as "designing around existing patents." This expression describes the situation in which one firm is able to accomplish essentially the same product objective as another firm in a somewhat similar manner without exact copying and thus without infringing the patent. When a patent is granted, the ideas, techniques, and approximate drawings go on public record for all to see if they wish. Eastman maintained that the U.S. Patent Office encouraged "innovating and designing around."

One day before it was to take effect, the appeals court declined to overturn the injunction. So on January 9, 1986, there were 16.5 million Eastman instant cameras with no further source of film. Moreover, Eastman and retailers had millions of dollars tied up in unsalable inventory, and the manufacturer had a $230 million investment in plant and equipment for instant cameras and instant film to close down. Several hundred Eastman workers were without jobs. Polaroid declined to manufacture film for the obsolete Eastman cameras, a dubious public relations posture. Fuji Photo, a Japanese company, made film compatible with Eastman's instant camera but did not offer that film in the United States. The question of how much the damages would be and whether they would be trebled remained to be settled in more litigation. What is more, the appeals court had not ruled on the merits of the case. If the appeal on merits failed, as was extremely likely, Eastman could ask the U.S. Supreme Court to hear an appeal, but, of course, had no right to be heard. In fact, it seemed likely, based on earlier public statements from

Eastman, that that company would not even attempt to appeal the appeals court decision. A Supreme Court reversal of the appeals court was considered extremely unlikely. And once the ill will of the consumers and retailers had been incurred at the time of the market withdrawal, it would be quite difficult to get back into this product market.

Faced with 16.5 million irate consumers, Eastman within twenty-four hours offered three options. First, each consumer could exchange his or her camera, most purchased for $30 or less, for $50 worth of company coupons, or, second, for a telephoto disc camera currently selling for $50. Third, the consumer could exchange the camera for one share of Eastman Kodak corporate stock, which closed that day on the New York Stock Exchange at $47.50. Eastman offered to reimburse retailers for inventory and encouraged them to send it back immediately. Many consumers tried to speculate, but within a day Eastman Kodak had imposed a limit of three per household.

The several types of costs involved in this lost dispute were quite substantial for Eastman, as was the future loss of sales of instant cameras and film, about $300 million per year. Eastman had about one-fourth of the instant camera market in the United States, versus 40 percent in 1977. However, this annual loss of sales amounted to only about 3 percent of Eastman's total sales. On the other hand, over $1 billion of Polaroid's sales per year, about 90 percent of that company's annual sales, were involved in the dispute. Eastman Kodak, with $10.6 billion per year in sales, was many times more product-diversified than smaller Polaroid. Despite the long, heated controversy, it was not clear if Eastman had ever turned a profit on the instant camera in ten years and, indeed, if it had recovered its research and development costs on this product. The fragmentary evidence that leaked out suggested that Eastman had sustained a loss on instant photography.

A few days after the court decision in January 1986, Eastman Kodak announced that it was reentering the 35-mm market, a quality segment from which it withdrew in the United States in 1970. It unveiled two cameras of that type, priced at $200 and $130 at retail. These two battery-powered, fixed-lens cameras offered automatic loading, focus, exposure, and flash functions. Eastman Kodak decided not to make these new products itself although it did not say so publicly for some time. Instead, it would use manufacturers in the Orient that already supplied Eastman Kodak with the 35-mm cameras it sold under its own name in Southeast Asia. Moreover, Eastman Kodak acknowledged that it was suffering from many serious internal problems, sluggish sales, and low profits and that it would need to dismiss permanently about 10 percent of all its employees.

Advise Polaroid Corporation.

ADOLPH COORS COMPANY

One of the largest, oldest, and most interesting brewers in the United States was the Adolph Coors Company. It faced a perplexing set of circumstances, opportunities, and problems as an organization and was part of an industry that showed great structural change, extensive modifications of traditional consumer behavior, and public relations problems.

The U.S. Beer Industry

After the prohibition era, about 750 brewing companies went into business in the United States. Of course, many failed quickly, and the number of firms kept going down. However, the industry underwent a massive shakeout and restructuring between the late 1960s and the late 1980s. Over sixty brewers disappeared, some by closing down and some by merging with stronger organizations, leaving the industry rather highly concentrated in ownership. Among those remaining, a few were in difficulty, a few faced significant problems, and some others faced problem-laden opportunities.

For a long time fourth in size behind Anheuser-Busch, Inc., Jos. Schlitz Brewing Company, and Pabst Brewing Company, Coors fell to number five as the seventh-ranked Miller Brewing Company of Milwaukee surged into second place in the late 1970s. Formerly independent, Miller had been acquired by Philip Morris, Inc., the tobacco-based firm, in 1970 and had been given needed fixed investment, working capital, and marketing expertise for growth. Coors fell to sixth in 1981 as G. Heileman Brewing Company expanded.

In late 1981 the then number 4 producer, G. Heileman, attempted to take over number 3 Schlitz, which was in difficulty with declining sales and profits. Schlitz had been number one in the United States until 1957, when Anheuser-Busch surpassed it. The Schlitz brand was in severe difficulty for several reasons, perhaps the most important of which was an ill-considered change in the recipe, or brewing formula. A second reason was the greater sophistication of marketing at arch-rival Miller. Schlitz agreed to the proposed takeover. However, the Antitrust Division of the U.S. Justice Department was displeased with the additional ownership concentration that the deal would bring to the brewing industry and with the potential for significantly reduced competition. When the Justice Department announced that it would file suit to block the acquisition, it was canceled. This government action surprised many people because, in a much larger and more important merger about two months earlier, Du Pont had acquired Conoco. The reason for the different government posture was that, without the Du Pont action, Conoco, an important oil, natural gas, and coal producer, would have been taken over by Seagram, a Canadian corporation. In mid-1982 seventh-ranked Stroh Brewing Company took over the ailing Schlitz. Thus, the rank order became the following for the next few years: Anheuser-Busch, Miller, Stroh-Schlitz, Heileman, Pabst, Coors.

Heileman, of La Crosse, Wisconsin, had been one of the fastest-growing companies in the country, but Schlitz would have been Heileman's first nationally distributed brand. In an unusual strategy, Heileman operated a network of regional brewers offering over thirty brands. Among its better-known brands were Carling Black Label and National Bohemian along the East Coast, Rainier in the Northwest, and Blatz and Old Style in the Middle West and parts of the East. Colt 45 Malt Liquor, Blatz, Mickey's Malt Liquor, and Weinhard were also popular brands belonging to Heileman. In the late 1980s Heileman acquired Pittsburgh Brewing, maker of the successful Iron City brand, and Christian Schmidt Brewing. Heileman's fundamental strategy was to revitalize the acquired regional brands, gradually bring in some of its other regional brews, and then promote heavily. Heileman decided to take Colt 45 national and did so successfully. In 1987 Bond Corporation of Australia bought Heileman for $1.2 billion. However, by 1990 the Australian parent was having severe financial difficulties at home.

There were only a very few other important brewing organizations. Genessee Brewing Company, Joseph Huber Brewing Company, and Hudepohl-Schoenling Brewing Company were noteworthy regional corporations. Genessee made about 2,400,000 barrels in the latest year. Hudepohl made several popular brands in Cincinnati and distributed them in a few states. With a capacity of 500,000 barrels per year in its Monroe, Wisconsin, plant, Huber made Augsburger brand beer, a Bavarian-style favorite in the Middle West.

A number of tiny local breweries had started up and were referred to in the trade as "boutique breweries," or microbrewers, or both. By common consent, the term was confined to those making only 10,000 barrels or less per year. Interestingly, Coors had spillage of almost 70,000 barrels per year. The number of small brewers was variable, but it averaged about thirty. Prominent examples were Sierra Nevada of Chico, California; Anchor Brewery of San Francisco; and Independent Ale of Seattle, the three that got the movement going in the 1970s. Other examples were Kessler of Helena, Montana; Samuel Adams (Boston Beer) of Boston; Reinheitsgebot (approximate translation: legal code of purity) of Plano, Texas; New Amsterdam of New York City; William S. Newman Brewing Company of Albany, New York; White Tail of Fordyce, Arkansas; Chesapeake Bay of Virginia Beach, Virginia; Hibernia Dunkel Weizen Fest of Eau Claire, Wisconsin; Snake River of Caldwell, Idaho; Boulder Brewing of Longmont, Colorado; Wild Goose of Cambridge, Maryland; and Grant's Imperial Stout of Yakima, Washington. White Tail added 10 percent rice to give crispness, and Imperial was the strongest beer offered in North America. Chesapeake Bay called its Munich-style lager Chesbay Amber and distributed it in the eastern parts of Pennsylvania, Maryland, Virginia, and North Carolina. All boutique beers were high-priced, usually above prestige imports, and all taken together held less than one percent of the U.S. market. Whether some of these operations were just fun and hobbies or serious enterprises remained to be seen. A few, such as Anchor, were outgrowing their placement in this category. Anchor Brewing, owned by Fritz Maytag, heir to the Maytag home appliance fortune, made about 50,000 barrels of Anchor Steam, Anchor Porter, Anchor Wheat, Liberty Ale, and Old Foghorn annually and distributed it in thirty states.

Another interesting development in the industry was the brew pub, a combination of a restaurant and a microbrewery. Whether it was here to stay or only a fad of a few years was yet to be determined. In the mid-1980s there were only about twenty in the United States and Canada, but by 1990 there were about 200. This type of business tried to meet the intense desire for a neighborhood bar and meeting place with a further miniaturization of the boutique brewery but without the elevated social status of the boutique brewery. The output, usually under 1,500 barrels per year, was almost always sold only in-house. The owners were always proud of the product and gave it great care and attention. They sometimes tailored the characteristics of the beer to the clientele. In some jurisdictions the brew pub could also sell brands it did not make. Most brew pubs sold food, and most jurisdictions required them to sell food. Although the brew pub was common in parts of Europe, it was made possible in North America only when laws began to change. Both the United States and Canada changed federal regulations requiring that beer be kegged before it was sold, a procedure which had been adopted to reduce the risk that the brewer would not pay federal taxes on the product. Also, some states began to remove the policy requiring separate ownership of breweries and retailers. Because the cost to make a serving of beer in a brew pub was normally no more than about 10 cents, the net profits of well-managed brew pubs were extraordinarily high. The potential number of brew pubs in North America was estimated to be 12,000 to 16,000.

Many beer drinkers preferred to consume regional or local beers for various reasons, such as perceived unique taste, desire to enjoy local color, a wish to support local business and thus local jobs, or avoidance of beers that were thought to be mass-appeal, mass-produced goods. In the case of the boutique beers there was also a strong prestige factor for most brands. However, it was well understood in the industry and had been demonstrated experimentally countless times that most beer consumers could not recognize their favorite brands in blindfold tests that compared several brands. The majority of taste differences among popular U.S. brands were imaginary or too slight for the average beer consumer to detect.

The total demand for beer in the United States rose rather rapidly in the 1950s, 1960s, and 1970s, but the growth rate slowed down markedly in the early 1980s. Despite an increasing population, in 1984 there was a small consumption decrease, the first in over three decades. This was followed by small increases in 1985 and 1986. The year 1987 saw a small decrease but 1988 a small increase. There was a small decrease in 1989. The demand for light beer was still growing but not enough to offset the decrease in demand for regular beer. The sales of packaged beer were still growing very slightly, but the sales of draft beer were declining. (See Exhibit 1). Draft, which was, of course, consumed on premises, had been particularly hurt by great public concern and consumer awareness of the amount a person had consumed just before driving. Most of the industry was pessimistic and believed that there would be very little growth throughout the 1990s.

There had been significant production overcapacity in the industry. Most large and medium-size firms built in the late 1960s and 1970s as though the high-growth trend line of the industry would go on indefinitely. This was despite the clear demographic evidence that the age distribution of the U.S. population would no longer be as encouraging for this industry after the early 1980s. In late 1984, Miller Brewing decided to write down part of the value of a new $450 million brewery in Trenton, Ohio, because some of it was not needed then and would not be needed in the future. The amount was $140 million after income tax effects. In 1985, Stroh abandoned its Detroit headquarters brewery, the oldest and least efficient facility in that company, because of lack of need. Although there was clearly overcapacity in the industry, there might still be some construction of new breweries. This was primarily because some of the unused capacity was poorly located in relation to the geographical demand patterns. Beer was bulky, heavy, and costly to transport long distances. A secondary reason was that a few plants were underautomated and required too much expensive labor.

EXHIBIT 1 U.S. Beer Sales by Segment and Year in Percentages of Barrels

Segment	1981	1983	1985	1987	1988	1989
Domestic						
Superpremium-priced	6.9	6.3	4.1	2.9	2.6	2.4
Premium-priced	51.6	47.0	43.7	41.7	40.8	40.2
Popular-priced	21.4	21.3	24.4	23.6	23.2	22.8
Light	13.8	18.5	20.5	24.0	25.6	27.0
Malt Liquor	3.2	3.5	3.0	2.8	2.8	2.9
Imports	2.9	3.4	4.3	5.0	5.0	4.7

There were several reasons for the lack of growth in the brewing industry, among them the decrease in the number of people in the traditionally heaviest per capita beer-consumption stage of the life cycle. This stage was from the drinking age to age thirty-four, especially from the drinking age to age twenty-four. The U.S. population was much older on average than a generation earlier. The older people became, the less beer they consumed. Second, the minimum drinking age was being raised in almost every state to twenty-one under extreme pressure from the federal government and the threat of cancellation of federally provided subsidies and matching funds for many programs if the states did not do so. There certainly were violations of the age requirement, but retailers, restauranteurs, and bar owners were anxious not to lose valuable licenses and had become rather careful. Third, there was greater concern about physical fitness and being "in shape." Fourth, there was a ground swell of public concern about misuse of alcoholic beverages, including the weak products such as beer. The Mothers Against Drunk Driving organization was influential and effective. A broad coalition of groups ranging from the Consumer Federation of America to the National Parents and Teachers Association was pushing hard for a legal ban on television and radio advertising of all alcoholic beverages similar to that imposed on cigarettes in 1969. According to William K. Coors, chairperson of the board of Coors Brewing, "The image of the alcohol beverage industry is the greatest challenge facing brewers today." He went on to argue that sanctions against advertising have little influence on the alcohol abuser. "This is an individual behavior problem, the solution to which is to teach people how to accommodate the pressure and stress of everyday life without the crutch of alcohol." He added that sanctions would reduce the consumption of alcohol by responsible users. Coors was a leader in "Drink safely" messages placed on point-of-purchase displays and packages. The large U.S. and Canadian brewers established and funded the Alcohol Beverage Medical Research Foundation at Johns Hopkins University School of Medicine in Baltimore.

Anheuser-Busch launched an interesting product in 1984 in response to criticism of the industry. Called L.A., for low alcohol, it was the first such beer from a major company. This product was difficult to place with accounts. Sports facilities looked promising, for managers of stadiums and arenas were anxious to prevent and control rowdyism. Tiger Stadium in Detroit decided to offer only low-alcohol beers. Following that breakthrough, several other sports complexes added L.A. to their assortment. Michael Roarty, marketing vice-president of Anheuser-Busch, noted that there was a problem getting people to try L.A. However, when Anheuser-Busch could get people to try it, the repeat sale rate was almost twice what this company normally experienced with a new product.

The brewing industry's promotion targeted to college-age people proved to be especially upsetting to critics and some executives in the industry itself. This part of the industry's promotional efforts was criticized for poor taste as well as possibly raising the risk of abuse. Included were advertising, personal selling, and sales promotion practices such as chug-a-lug contests and wet T-shirt competitions. These practices raised the ire of William Coors. He said that he personally thought they were "outrageous" and that everyone else in the company agreed with him. He doubted that the members of the industry would cooperate to change them.

Peter Coors delivered a major speech to the National Beer Wholesalers Association annual convention, in which he talked about both the abuse and tastefulness issues. Coors dared wholesalers

> to be even more responsive to societal concerns about the proper use of alcoholic beverages. . . . It is our challenge for all three tiers of the industry to promote beer properly and with good taste and common design to enhance the credibility of the product and its quality. . . . Ideally, we need to be so good at what we do that we are never placed in the position of having to run around putting out fires. If we are sensitive to our many publics and listen to what they are telling us, we can take action that will never let the fires get started in the first place. We're fully aware of the intense competitive environment in which we operate, but the industry can unite in common purposes.[1]

Pabst Brewing was an old, established firm with headquarters in Milwaukee, but it had been suffering from sluggish sales and profits and high managerial turnover for a decade. An offer by Pabst to buy Schlitz for a larger sum of money than Heileman proposed was rejected by the Schlitz board of directors. Much of the business public and brewing industry saw this rejection as a slap in the face for Pabst and a commentary on how Pabst's future was perceived. Pabst itself was clearly vulnerable to a takeover, dissolution, or splitting up. Its marginal performance grew worse, but in 1983 it acquired Olympia Brewing Company in Tumwater, Washington, which held about 3 percent of the U.S. market. Olympia had viable subsidiaries, Hamm's in Minneapolis and Lone Star in San Antonio.

In 1983, G. Heileman Brewing Company was poised to make a friendly takeover of Pabst to save it from two aggressive, unfriendly bidders, Paul Kalmanovitz and Irwin Jacobs. Kalmanovitz owned Falstaff Brewing Company, Pearl Brewing Company, and General Brewing Co. The Antitrust Division of the U.S. Justice Department agreed at the end of 1984 to a complex arrangement by which Heileman was to

---

[1] *Beverage World* (December 1985), p. 53.

acquire within a reasonable time period about two thirds of Pabst. However, Heileman was required to give up the Tumwater brewery and the Olympia, Hamm's, and Olde English 800 Malt Liquor brands to S&P of Vancouver, Washington, the Kalmanovitz holding company. Thus, by 1986 the rank order of the largest U.S. brewing companies was the following: Anheuser-Busch, Miller, Heileman, Stroh-Schlitz, and Coors.

Coors had been eager for some time to improve its sales and profits and move up in the industry rankings. For the company to climb to fourth or third place and lock in that rank without marketing nationwide intensively would be a noteworthy accomplishment. Coors' coverage of many markets was quite thin, and it had little more than a token presence in a number of states. Some concerned people thought it was more realistic to approach the corporate objective another way, that is, seek an extraordinary penetration of selected geographical markets and high-brand loyalty among a hard core of consumers.

During the period 1986 through 1988 Coors sales grew faster than Stroh's or Heileman's, and by 1989 Coors was in fourth place in the industry after Anheuser-Busch, Miller, and Stroh. During 1988 and 1989 Stroh saw its sales and share of the market decline. By the middle of 1989 Stroh had about 10 percent of the market, versus about 9 percent for Coors. In addition, Stroh had never really got over the financial strain imposed by its 1982 purchase of Schlitz. Morale of its management deteriorated. Stroh put out feelers for the sale of the company and then publicly sought a partner. Coors made a tentative offer to purchase all of Stroh's brands, five of Stroh's seven breweries, and two container facilities. The transaction was subject to review by the Anti-Trust Division of the Justice Department, but an affirmative answer was expected by mid-1990. The majority of commentators considered the price of $425 million fair. Bond considered trying to buy Stroh but decided against it. For anti-trust reasons, Anheuser-Busch and Miller could not consider buying Stroh. Pabst filed an anti-trust complaint against the proposed acquisition. In early 1990 Coors decided not to formalize the offer to Stroh, because the declining market shares of Stroh's brands and Coors' evaluation of the Stroh brewing facilities did not support the tentatively agreed price. However, the two companies continued to talk from time to time about this matter. Molson of Canada expressed some interest in acquiring Stroh, as did Interbrew of Belgium. Thus, as the 1990s started, the rank order in the industry was Anheuser-Busch, Miller, Stroh, Coors, Heileman, Pabst. Anheuser-Busch had 42 percent, Miller 22 percent, Stroh 10 percent, Coors 9 percent, Heileman 7.5 percent, and Pabst 2.5 percent. The top six now accounted for 93 percent of the industry volume.

The proposed acquisition of Stroh would create a complex product line for Coors. Stroh's Schlitz Malt Liquor, the dominant brand in that category, would fill a void in the Coors line. The flagship products, Coors and Coors Light, would compete head to head with Stroh's and

EXHIBIT 2 Largest Brewing Companies in the United States and Their Share of U.S. Market

Company	1980	1982	1984	1985	1989
Anheuser-Busch	28.2%	32.4%	35.0%	37.0%	42.0%
Miller	20.9	21.5	20.5	20.5	22.0
Stroh	13.9	12.6	13.1	12.9	10.0
Coors	7.8	6.5	7.2	8.0	9.0
G. Heileman	7.5	7.9	9.2	8.9	7.5

Stroh's Light, unless, as the industry suspected, these two Stroh products were confined to the Midwest. Coors had never done very well in most of the Midwest; whereas Stroh's enjoyed great strength in that region, its home base. Stroh's Old Milwaukee would go directly against Coors' new product Keystone in the popular price category. It seemed likely that if Keystone did not have great success in a very short time, it would be dropped in favor of the well-established Old Milwaukee, Stroh's biggest seller with 3.7 percent of the U.S. market. Old Milwaukee Light had a respectable one percent of the market. Stroh's other products, Schlitz, Schlitz Light, Piels, Goebel, Schaefer, Signature, Erlanger, White Mountain Cooler, and others would be tricky questions for retention and positioning.

Beer Imports

Imported beers in 1989 amounted to 8.8 million barrels, or 4.7 percent of the American market. This category did not include beers made in the United States under license from foreign brewing concerns, such as Lowenbrau. Imported beer competed with domestic premium and super-premium beers. Imports share of the market rose rapidly until 1987 and 1988, when they peaked at 5.0 percent. In 1971 the figure was only 0.6 percent, but it rose to 2.9 percent in 1981, 3.2 percent in 1982, 3.4 percent in 1983, 3.9 percent in 1984, 4.3 percent in 1985, and 4.7 percent in 1986. The bulk of market analysts had been drastically wrong when they forecasted that the import segment would total about 10 percent by 1991. The reasons for a change in the trend line were as follows: (1) domestic brewers had launched some interesting new brands; (2) stricter laws about driving under the influence of alcohol affected eating and drinking places, where the bulk of sales of foreign brands occurred; and (3) the national economy slowed somewhat in 1989, making many consumers resistant to the premium prices of foreign brands.

Heineken from Holland was the leading foreign-made beer. Imported since 1933 by Van Munching & Company of New York, it held about 26 percent of the import market in 1989, compared to 31 percent in 1985 and 40 percent in 1981. Corona Extra from Mexico was number two with almost 14 percent, compared to only 0.2 percent in 1982. Beck's from Germany was third with 9 percent. Molson Golden from Canada with 8 percent was fourth, compared to 15 percent and second place in 1983. Other highly important ones were Moosehead from Canada with 5 percent, Labatt from Canada with almost 5 percent, Amstel Light from Holland with 3.6 percent, and Foster from Britain with 2.4 percent. An Irish import, Guinness-Harp; a German Import, St. Pauli Girl; a Japanese import, Sapporo; and Four Mexican Imports, Dos Equis, Carta Blanca, Tecate, and Bohemia all did well but much less than the brands mentioned earlier. Moosehead had had a meteoric rise in the United States in the early 1980s that was doubly impressive in view of the fact that the other Canadian brands suffered a decrease in the United States. That brand had now leveled off but maintained a good share. Moosehead was a small company and did not even have nationwide distribution in Canada. It was imported by All Brands Importers, Inc., of New York City, a subsidiary of Heublein, Inc., the large distiller. The importer had taken the initiative and done all the planning. Grizzly was a new import from Canada but was made by Heineken in Canada. Maccabee from Israel had just entered the U.S. market. Exotic brews were now being imported from such places as Ivory Coast, Congo, Thailand, Venezuela, and the People's Republic of China. In total, there were about 250 foreign brands imported. G. Heileman Brewing Company became the U.S. distributor of Hacker-Pschorr beers from Munich, West Germany, in 1985, and Anheuser-Busch became the U.S. importer-distributor of highly regarded Carlsberg and Carlsberg Elephant beers from Denmark in 1986.

Americans bought imported beer for three major reasons: prestige, variety, and flavor. Beer was often perceived as a blue-collar beverage. Accordingly, many people, certainly not the majority, in the middle and upper classes found it psychologically necessary to separate themselves from the blue-collar consumers by choice of brands. The same thinking or emotional process sometimes applied to domestic higher-priced beers. Nearly all imports had a heavier, stronger, and more distinctive flavor than American beers. Most foreign tourists in the United States and a small percentage of Americans were contemptuous of U.S. beers, regarding them as caramel-colored carbonated water. American commentators and writers on food and beverages almost all agreed that American beers were bland by prevailing world standards and were rather similar to each other. In addition, there was some speculation but no evidence that some ethnic groups in the United States might begin to look favorably on beers from foreign cultures with which they partially identified.

Curiously enough, the physical characteristics of the vast majority of beers produced in the United States and Canada made them harder, not easier, to produce than the beers from other countries. This refers to knowledge of chemistry, extreme precision in the blending, perfect consistency, and meticulous quality control. Finn Knudsen, director of brewing research and development for Coors Brewing, stated that it took greater skill to make North American lighter-flavored beers consistently than to make European beers. He had twenty-four years of brewing experience, including ten in Europe. As a general principle, the lighter a beer is in flavor, color, and calories, the more difficult is the manufacturing process. Carelessness and inconsistency could not be masked. Yet almost no North American consumers had any inkling of this principle.

The Coors Company

For many years, Coors was the only large brewer in the United States that was not national in scope. Based in Golden, Colorado, a suburb of Denver, this organization distributed its output in only sixteen states, all of them in the West or the western edge of the Middle West, at the beginning of the 1980s. At that time it covered all the West except Oregon and Alaska. In the early 1980s it gradually added one to three states each year. Then in 1983, Coors added Florida, Georgia, North Carolina, South Carolina, Alabama, Virginia, eastern Tennessee, the District of Columbia, Hawaii, and Alaska. In 1984 the company added Kentucky, West Virginia, Ohio, Maryland, and Oregon. Although it was a logical part of Coors' early market territory, Oregon was not available until it repealed its law barring the sale of packaged unpasteurized beer. Illinois and the six New England states were added in 1985 and Michigan in 1986. New York and New Jersey were added in 1987 and Pennsylvania and Delaware in 1988. Despite this rather orderly spread, the distribution was extremely thin in many of the states added in the 1980s. Moreover, the Coors company had always had a distinctly western image among both business people and consumers.

The company had beer sales of $1,264,786 in 1988, compared to $1,133,339 in 1987, $1,084,836 in 1986, and $1,077,880 in 1985. (See Exhibit 3). The company's share of the U.S. market for beer was 8.9 percent in 1989, compared to 8.8 percent in 1988, 8.4 percent in 1987, 8.1 percent in 1986, 8.0 percent in 1985, and 7.8 percent in 1980. In 1989 the company sold 16.6 million barrels of beer, compared to 14,738,000 barrels in 1980.

Canada had looked attractive to Coors for several years for its first international expansion. Consumer awareness of Coors was already high in western Canada. Yet it was perplexing to think seriously about distributing in that country when there were still many states in the United States having only scattered availability of Coors products. Distribution in Quebec would require French-speaking salespersons and French language advertising. Montreal-based Molson Companies, Ltd., and Coors held extensive talks in 1985 about three possibilities: distribution of imported Coors products in Canada by Molson, licensing Molson to make Coors products, and a joint venture in Canada. The Coors executives

EXHIBIT 3 Income Statement of Adolph Coors Company and Subsidiaries

	For the years ended		
	December 25, 1988	December 27, 1987	December 28, 1986
	(In thousands, execept per share data)		
Sales......................	$1,680,968	$1,503,805	$1,464,881
Less–federal and state beer excise taxes...............	159,271	153,066	149,951
	1,521,697	1,350,739	1,314,930
Cost and expenses:			
Cost of goods sold..........	1,021,084	878,183	846,185
Marketing, general and administrative......	408,348	362,293	336,528
Research and project development............	22,723	21,682	23,443
	1,452,155	1,262,158	1,206,156
Operating income...........	69,542	88,581	108,774
Other (income) expense:			
Interest income...........	(8,894)	(10,582)	(13,214)
Interest expense..........	2,642	2,604	3,219
Miscellaneous–net........	(1,181)	10,511	8,376
	(7,433)	2,533	(1,619)
Income before income taxes	76,975	86,048	110,393
Income taxes...............	30,100	37,900	51,000
Net income.................	$ 46,875	$ 48,148	$ 59,393
Net income per share of common stock...........	$1.28	$1.32	$1.65

commented, "We have a product that is difficult to replicate and we want to protect the Coors mystique." Nevertheless, an agreement was reached with Molson for that company to make Coors products in Canada. They became available in Canada, except for the Maritime Provinces, by the end of 1985. For the first time not all Coors products were being made in the same plant and using the fabled "Pure Rocky Mountain Spring Water." A few independent financial analysts suggested a merger between the Coors and Molson corporations.

Coors Company operated only one brewery, but this facility in Golden was the largest brewing plant in the United States. For several years the company had had tentative plans to enlarge the facility, but there had

EXHIBIT 4 Production in 1989 as Percentage of Production Capacity

Company	Percentage
Anheuser-Busch	95
Miller	95
Stroh	76
Coors	90
Heileman	75
Pabst (excluding Pearl, Falstaff, General)	60

not been a need so far. (See Exhibit 4). No finished product was stored at the plant. Golden was reasonably centrally located for the company's geographical distribution area until the middle 1970s. Yet even by the early 1970s, in terms of the population density of the markets served, the plant could not be considered logistically well located. This was primarily because of the importance of the California demand for the product. Among the secondary reasons for geographical expansion of the marketing area, mainly eastward and southeastward, was to make logistics more rational. In particular, the cultivation of Texas, the nation's second most important beer market, was desirable for logistical balance. Another interesting point was that the average shipping distance for a unit of beer had been rising rapidly for several years, going up 20 percent between 1982 and 1984 alone, as the company pushed farther afield. Intensive cultivation of the upper East Coast would push this figure up drastically. Three-fourths of Coors output was sent by rail and one-fourth by truck.

This organization took an option in 1979 to buy a large parcel of rural land in the Shenandoah Valley near Elkton, Rockingham County, Virginia, in case it should actually expand nationwide and might need additional production capacity, storage space, or packaging operations on the East Coast or a combination of these. The tract consisted of 2,245 acres. At first there were aggressive, noisy demonstrations by temperance groups, but they stopped. In 1987 the company built a $70 million plant on this tract to package Coors beer in cans, bottles, and kegs. Considering the number of brands of beers, the types of container, sizes of containers, and variations by state on legal requirements for labeling, the plant had to work with 238 different containers. Beer arrived by refrigerated rail tank car from Golden. Annual packaging capacity was 2.4 million barrels and employment was about 240. An expansion plan for this facility costing $5.5 million was announced in early 1990.

Whether a brewery would be built on the tract remained undecided, but the economic evidence was favorable on balance if there was no purchase of Stroh or selected Stroh breweries and brands. Moreover, Peter Coors stated that the company had found an exceptional source of pure spring water there that matched the quality of Golden's pure Rocky Mountain spring water. If built, the brewery would be put up in phases as eastern demand warranted. If built in the early or middle 1990s, the cost of such a brewery would probably be about $550 to $600 million for an annual capacity of ten million barrels.

The Coors company was partially integrated up-channel in that it produced its own bottles and cans. In fact, it owned and operated the nation's largest aluminum can factory. Moreover, the company supplied itself with natural gas and coal from its own fields and mines and grew all its own barley. The company was slightly integrated down-channel in that it owned its own beer wholesale distribution firms in Tustin (California), Spokane, Omaha, Denver, and Boise. These distribution investments furnished profit as well as what management termed "better insight in working with the company's independent distributor network."

The Coors company was in excellent financial health. (See Exhibits 3 and 5). It did not have any significant debt, short- or long-term. In fact, the management was philosophically opposed to borrowing money and tried to finance its expansion and other needs through its stream of profits.

The U.S. beer industry exhibited a seasonal pattern in demand. Sales rose in the warm weather and fell in the cool weather. Coors Brewing experienced the same pattern as the industry. The third quarter, July–September, at Coors typically accounted for about 34 percent of sales, whereas the first quarter, January–March, accounted for only about 19 percent. The second quarter and fourth quarter accounted for about 27 percent and 20 percent, respectively.

Established in 1873, Adolph Coors Company was now managed by the founder's grandsons, William K. and Joseph Coors, and Joseph, Sr.'s five sons, Jeffrey, Peter, Joe, Jr., Grover, and John Coors. William Coors was chairperson of the board of directors. Joseph Coors had been vice-chairperson of the board and president until June 1985, when he yielded the presidency to Jeffrey Coors. The latter had been serving as divisional president of operations and technical affairs. At the same time, Peter Coors, who had been serving as divisional president for marketing, sales, and administration, was appointed president of the newly carved-out brewing division. Joe Coors, Jr. was made president of Coors Ceramics Company. The company's attempt at diversification of the business and the ages of William and Joseph Coors, both in their early seventies, made it advisable to make some changes. The five sons were in their thirties and forties. Early in their careers, Jeffrey and Peter had been what were essentially unspecialized vice-presidents. There were several other vice-presidents. The family owned 86 percent of the corporate stock, and the remaining 14 percent of the shares of stock carried no voting rights.

EXHIBIT 5 Balance Sheet of Adolph Coors Company and Subsidiaries

Assets	December 25, 1988	December 27, 1987
	(In thousands)	
Current assets:		
Cash and cash equivalents.................	$ 10,425	$ 31,074
Short-term interest bearing investments...	61,757	82,380
Accounts and notes receivable, less allowance for doubtful accounts of $1,092 in 1988 and $2,095 in 1987.......	152,102	109,208
Inventories:		
Finished....................................	24,118	17,254
In process.................................	40,159	32,881
Raw materials............................	62,835	64,357
Packaging materials......................	43,642	40,208
	170,754	154,700
Prepaid expenses and other assets.........	74,270	66,591
Accumulated income tax prepayments	11,544	7,703
Total current assets.....................	480,852	451,656
Properties, at cost, less accumulated depreciation, depletion and amortization of $854,639 in 1988 and $754,813 in 1987.....	1,033,012	975,781
Excess of cost over net assets of businesses acquired, less accumulated amortization of $1,569 in 1988 and $1,296 in 1987.........................	21,719	3,356
Other assets.................................	35,182	25,700
	$1,570,765	$1,456,493

The Coors family was close-knit, inward-looking, and conservative. This philosophical stance and personality characteristic had been reinforced by a family tragedy in 1960, when another son, Adolph Coors III, was kidnapped and murdered.

The company was rethinking its philosophies of marketing and general management. Some officials, including Peter Coors, described the corporation as arrogant about itself and its output. Ideas that did not originate within the family were not even considered. The firm was frequently referred to by outsiders, investment counselors, and workers as "baronial" and "feudal" and a "nineteenth-century industrial dynasty." Yet more potential changes were coming in the form of the younger

EXHIBIT 5 *(Continued)*

Liabilities and Shareholders' Equity	December 25, 1988	December 27, 1987
	(In thousands)	
Current liabilities:		
Short-term borrowings......................	$ 18,000	$
Accounts payable...........................	135,460	85,627
Accrued salaries and vacations............	43,772	39,132
Taxes, other than income taxes............	27,532	26,542
Federal and state income taxes............	9,771	9,418
Accrued expenses and other liabilities.................................	49,630	48,531
Total current liabilites..................	284,165	209,250
Accumulated deferred income taxes	205,169	189,056
Other long-term liabilities....................	19,367	26,376
Shareholders' equity		
Capital stock:		
Class A common stock, voting, $1 par value, authorized and issued 1,260,000 shares...............	1,260	1,260
Class B common stock, non-voting, no par value, authorized and issued 46,200,000 shares..............	11,000	11,000
	12,260	12,260
Paid-in capital.............................	30,299	28,773
Retained earnings.........................	1,042,429	1,013,865
	1,084,988	1,054,898
Less–treasury stock, at cost, Class B shares, 10,786,576 in 1988 and 10,863,376 in 1987............	22,924	23,087
Total shareholders' equity..............	1,062,064	1,031,811
Commitments and contingencies		
	$1,570,765	$1,456,493

Coors men and a new marketing officer. A new senior vice-president for marketing, Robert A. Rechholtz, then age forty-two, arrived in 1982 from Schlitz, where he had held the same title.

However, allegations of rigid inflexibility were exaggerated. It was worth noting that Coors was the first brewer to adopt aluminum cans, now widely used in the industry. Management admitted, on the other hand, that its improved Press-Tab II, a can that was environmentally appealing to the company's largely western market because it had no pop-top, was a mistake because the average consumer found it impossible to open.

Top management's old-fashioned views, provincialism, and egotism had been temporarily reinforced by a fad occurrence on college campuses during the mid-1970s. Coors beer was the "in" beer among millions of educated young adults, people who were likely to enjoy good incomes and community positions in the future. This voguish product was carried long distances outside the normal trade territory by students. An informal distribution network arose among enthusiasts, and few college parties were complete without Coors. The bubble burst by 1977.

Labor relations in recent years had been stormy and harmful to Coors. In 1977, Local 366 of the Brewery Workers Union struck the company's plant, and it was quickly joined in a boycott by several politically liberal groups that were strongly opposed to the Coors company because of the Coors family's conservative political stands. The effect of the boycott was particularly noteworthy in California, the company's largest market. Greatly increased advertising by Miller and Anheuser-Busch simultaneously affected Coors in California, so it was not known how much effect the unions and their political sympathizers really had on the sales. Coors' share of the important California market dropped from 40 percent to 20 percent. By the early 1980s, this figure had risen to only a little over 20 percent and essentially stabilized thereafter. Opponents of Coors claimed all the credit. To the consternation of the labor movement, about two-thirds of Coors employees returned to work soon after the strike began. The management hired replacements, necessarily, of course, non-union members, for the remaining jobs. Not only did the strike fail, but the workers even petitioned the U.S. Department of Labor to hold an election on the fate of the local union. In accordance with normal legal procedures, such an election was held under government supervision, and the workers overwhelmingly rejected Local 366 as their bargaining agent. The new hirees were allowed to vote in the election. It was not known how any individual voted, but it was likely that most of the new hirees voted to get rid of the union. Thus, the Carter administration decertified the local union. Embarrassed and ego-involved national union leaders, some local union leaders in the other states, plus some radical left political groups, however, kept the boycott alive, despite the wishes of the concerned workers. The Coors company became the object of great pressure and vilification, which still existed. The Coors fad on college campuses might have lasted longer if it had not been for the boycott call. Many students in particular embraced the boycott even though the Coors workers had overwhelmingly voted out their union. Many liberal students were also extremely angry that the members of the Coors family made generous donations to conservative political groups.

The younger generation of Coors executives, including members of the family, wanted to make peace with the U.S. labor movement. They also felt that full development of Coors products in the East and parts of the Middle West would be held back for many years without reaching that peace. Therefore, Coors younger management negotiated an arrangement with the national unions. In return for the lifting of the boycott, there would be an opportunity for the national unions to persuade the Coors workers to form another union and an election would be held under federal supervision. In this election in late 1988 73 percent of the workers defeated the proposed union. It remained to be seen if the former boycotters would respect the wishes of the workers. It was feared that they would do whatever was necessary to harm the Coors organization. The psychological principle involved was that the boycotters wanted others to do what the boycotters wanted, not to stand for the freedom of others to do as they decided.

Relations between Coors and minorities received much adverse publicity in the early and mid-1980s. A tiny number of people alleged ethnic discrimination. However, two large, respected national civil rights groups, one predominantly black and one predominantly Hispanic, conducted their own inquiries and concluded the allegations were without merit. A national television news program of respected investigative journalists made an inquiry and concluded the same. The television program questioned the true motivations of the complainants in this matter. Clearly, Coors was no community leader in ethnic relations, but it was not engaged in discrimination.

On the other hand, the company clearly made a major public relations blunder in 1984. William Coors, not known as an articulate, smooth public speaker who could build goodwill for the organization, nevertheless addressed a meeting of minority business owners in Denver. He aggressively criticized the political and economic leadership of the new black African republics, including their educational and technical preparation. He organized and phrased the speech so poorly that it was misinterpreted as a criticism of the black race and received international publicity. Despite Coors's explanations, clarification, and apologies for the lack of clarity, significant public relations harm had been done and would linger.

Another public relations problem surfaced only in 1990, but the facts went back to 1981. In early 1990 a Denver television station, after receiving a tip, reported that there had been contamination of the Coors water supply in 1981 and that the company had not reported the problem to public health officials. Coors reported the incident to such officials in 1988. Solvent leaked from the Coors can plant into two of its forty groundwater wells in 1981. The level of contaminants from trichloroethane, a noncarcinogen, in the water was only a fraction of what government standards permitted. Coors stopped using water from the affected wells. Moreover, the chemical involved was highly volatile and could not have survived the brewing process even if it had got into the production process. The purity of the water had always been a promotional feature of Coors' products.

The Coors organization had always been production-oriented rather than marketing-oriented. It had concentrated on perfect uniformity and turned out only one beer until 1978. It was a high-medium to premium-priced product made in an unusual process that avoided pasteurization because the family was convinced that heat caused deterioration. The lack of pasteurization meant that extra care was used in handling and storing inventories of Coors. The company used refrigerated rail cars and trucks and had a corporate policy in effect in the channel of distribution to avoid offering Coors products to the public if they were more than sixty day old, since all Coors beer brands were unpasteurized. However, many employees of retail shops had no understanding of this point. In 1978 the company belatedly introduced a second product, Coors Light. Some family members, especially Jeffrey Coors, admitted to being furious that chemists in the organization had been secretly conducting some experimental work leading to the development of a light beer for the company. Management had previously told them not to do so.

The primary competitor in the reduced calorie category was Miller Lite, a successful brand that came out in 1975 and started the entire category of products. Miller Lite was introduced in response to consumer consciousness about feelings of fullness and the high calorie count in beers. However, the new Coors Light had 105 calories per twelve-ounce serving versus ninety-six for Miller Lite. Coors's regular beer had 145 calories versus 150 for Miller High Life. (See Exhibit 6).

Whether Coors Light was going to succeed was extremely questionable for several years. Michelob Light and Natural Light, both made by Anheuser-Busch, were number two and number three in the reduced-calorie category in the mid-1980s. At least fifteen other brands of light beer were launched in the industry. Yet Miller Lite, the innovator, was still hanging on to 57 percent of the light market in 1981 and, in fact, had surpassed its owner's flagship brand, Miller High Life. In 1982, Anheuser-Busch introduced Budweiser Light nationally after an eleven-month period of meticulous test marketing and supported it with heavy advertising. Regular Budweiser was the number one selling brand in the country, and its name carried great commercial value for the light version. Bud Light outperformed Natural Light quickly, and it became questionable whether the latter should be retained. By 1982, Coors Light was judged a modest success. By 1984 it was a major success, second in the reduced-calorie category and tenth in the industry. It moved to eighth place in the industry in 1985 with 3.1 percent of the industry's sales. However, Bud Light was only an insignificant distance behind, with 3.0 percent of the industry's sales, third place in the light category, and ninth

EXHIBIT 6 Calories per 12-ounce Serving, Selected Brands of Beer

Brand	Number of Calories
Michelob	168
Budweiser	156
Miller High Life	150
Schlitz	148
Stroh	148
Coors	145
Pabst	140
Budweiser (low alcohol)	137
Pearl	136
Michelob Light	134
Heidelberg	133
Stroh Light	115
Budweiser Light	108
Coors Light	105
Miller Lite	96
Schlitz Light	96
Heidelberg Light	96
Pabst Extra Light	70
Pearl Light	68

in the industry. In 1987 Bud Light surpassed Coors Light. However, in 1989 Coors Light, with 5.5 percent of the market, went ahead of Bud Light, which had 5.2 percent.

Coors, the flagship brand of the Coors Company, suffered a declining share of the market for several consecutive years. Even temporary rises in Coors sales did not obscure the long-run trend line downward. Production of Coors brand dropped from 12.1 million barrels in 1977 to 8.7 million barrels in 1985 and 5.1 million barrels in 1989. (See Exhibit 7). The company was finding it difficult to position this brand in the industry. In 1989 it brought back for this product the name Coors Banquet, which it had used earlier.

After appropriate test marketing in the early 1980s, Coors brewing added a premium Irish beer called George Killian's. It was under license from a French brewer, Societe Brasserie Pelforth. However, Coors Brewing decided later to call it Killian's Irish Red. Offered in only twenty-four states, it was growing slowly in sales and popularity. Geographical expansion for it had not been decided.

A test market was conducted in early 1984 for a proposed new product called Golden Lager. It was to appeal to consumers who wanted a little heavier taste and was aimed directly at Budweiser. Taste tests with blind-

EXHIBIT 7 Largest-Selling Beer Brands in the United States in 1989 (by Percent of Market)

Brand	Company	Percent of Market
Budweiser	Anheuser-Busch	27.6
Miller Lite	Miller	10.7
Coors Light	Coors	5.5
Bud Light	Anheuser-Busch	5.2
Busch	Anheuser-Bush	5.0
Miller High Life	Miller	4.1
Milwaukee's Best	Miller	3.9
Old Milwaukee	Stroh	3.7
Coors	Coors	2.7
Miller Genuine Draft	Miller	2.4
Total of top ten brands		70.8

folded consumers showed that Coors brand was as full-bodied as Budweiser, but consumers had a strong nonrational perception that the Coors brand was lighter than Budweiser. Golden Lager was provided in the advertising with the theme "a rich, full-bodied beer that could remind you of Budweiser." It failed badly. The constant comparisons to Budweiser were later considered a mistake. Moreover, the executives suspected that many people falsely perceived Golden Lager as a superpremium-priced beer.

Therefore, a test market for a new premium beer, Coors Extra Gold, was begun in early 1985 in selected regions of California, Florida, Texas, Idaho, and Nevada. This product was positioned to appeal to consumers who desired a more full-bodied beer. It had a distinctly darker color. The advertising was placed in the hands of Tatham-Laird & Kudner of Chicago. This brand was presented as "the beer with a taste you can see." It was characterized as "bolder, golder, broad shouldered beer, the way beer oughta be." Advertisements featured power, muscles, sports prowess, and whimsical violence. There was a little humor, but the appeal was strongly to those who longed to be seen as extremely masculine. This product succeeded, reached national distribution by 1989, and had a 0.6 percent share of the market in 1989.

The company began a test market of Colorado Chiller in late 1985. It was to compete in the wine cooler segment of the beverage industry, but it was not wine-based. Instead, like White Mountain Cooler from Stroh, it was based on malt and citrus. Anheuser-Busch had failed with a similar type of product quite a few years earlier. Colorado Chiller was dropped.

The Coors organization test marketed for over five years a super-premium beer named Herman Joseph's 1868 to honor the founder of the company and the year he arrived in the United States as a young stowaway. If the tests were successful, it was planned to roll out the new product, introducing it in several cycles of a few states each until it was distributed everywhere the company offered Coors and Coors Light. The test area was expanded, but the sales data were distinctly mixed. The length of the test market was one of the longest ever recorded on any type of product in the United States. The emotional involvement with the name of the founder made it more difficult than normal to perform an evaluation in a completely rational manner. Eventually the company adopted the product, calling it Herman Joseph's Original Draft. In late 1987 the company began to offer a reduced calorie version called HJ Light. Both products reached national distribution in 1989 and were available in both twelve-ounce non-returnable bottles and half-barrel kegs. Herman Joseph's Original Draft was renamed Coors Original Draft in 1989. However, both were dropped at the end of 1989.

A joint venture was formed in 1985 by Coors Brewing, Molson Companies, Ltd., of Montreal, and Kaltenberg Castle Brewery of Neuschwanstein, West Germany. They created Masters Brewing Company "to investigate new products that might be marketable here in the United States." A new beer that had been under development since mid-1984 was on the market by the end of 1985 in four selected metropolitan areas, Miami, Boston, Columbus, and Washington, D.C. The product, made in the Coors plant, was named Masters Beer, and the launch was not considered a test market. Geographical expansion was to follow. Advertising for the new beer heavily emphasized the ages and experience of the three members of the joint venture. One of Canada's big three brewing firms, Molson was founded in 1786, and the venerable Kaltenberg Castle company was founded in 1260. There was some consideration of constructing brewery capacity for this product on the tract of land Coors owned near Elkton, in Rockingham County, Virginia.

Molson and Coors began their joint planning for Masters Beer in early 1982. The Bavarian firm was brought into the venture in September 1984 because the fundamental concept for the product and the joint company required a German presence. A German participant could provide technological knowledge and advice. Just as important, if not more so, was the consumer perception that Germany was the home of beer and the place where the finest beer in the world was made. As part of the $2.5 million spent on research and development by Molson and Coors for the joint venture, there was research on American consumer behavior. It showed clearly that the Americans who were studied perceived European-made beers as of finer quality than American beers and perceived Germany as the finest source of beer in Europe.

The Masters Brewing Company was a prominent part of an industry reaction to imports and the additional segmentation of consumers. This reaction dealt with "specialty beers," that is, those outside the U.S. and Canadian tradition but not foreign-made. It was especially important in view of a nongrowing demand for beer. There was the feeling or suspicion among some industry executives that, if some consumers were going to drink less beer at any given time, then those people might want the product to be "more advancing" or have "more bite" or both. Jeffrey Coors stated that if there were a trend toward specialty beers, Coors Brewing wanted to lead that trend. This posture was unlike the corporate tradition of Coors. The Masters venture was unsuccessful and the product was withdrawn from the market.

Coors had never had a popular-price beer until it rolled out Keystone and Keystone Light in September 1989. Among the reasons was that the population was aging and popular-price beers were known to be consumed mostly by older people. Also, a higher percentage of beer consumed was consumed off-premises. Price was much more meaningful in a purchase to take home than a purchase in a bar or restaurant. Moreover, Coors had nominally finished its geographical expansion, which had provided nearly all of its growth for years. This meant that to gain volume and share it had to do something more. As indicated earlier, the Keystone brand products might have to be considered for elimination in favor of one or more of the Stroh products. Also in late 1989 Coors began test markets of a non-alcoholic beer and a mineral water tentatively named Coors Pure Rocky Mountain Spring Water.

In the mid-1980s Coors authorized Asahi Breweries in Japan to make Coors brand in that country. The product quickly became the third best selling foreign beer in Japan. Then Coors Light was added in 1988.

Winterfest, a special holiday beer available only from mid-November to early January, was launched in 1986 solely in Colorado. In 1987 it was offered in most territories and the consumer response was moderately encouraging.

Coors supported proposed federal legislation in 1987 that would have required beer labels to include information on alcohol content. When this proposal failed, Coors submitted labels and advertising campaigns containing alcohol-content statements to the Bureau of Alcohol, Tobacco, and Firearms for approval. That office rejected the material on the grounds that the Federal Alcohol Administration Act prohibited such disclosures. Then Coors filed a lawsuit in late 1987 challenging the statute. The company stated that it believed that consumers had a right to know alcoholic content in order to make informed choices. Also, it said that disclosure would underscore to the consumer that beer was a beverage of moderation. The U.S. Justice Department agreed with Coors, stated that in its opinion the statute was unconstitutional and declined to defend it. However, the Justice Department said that it was up to Congress to amend the statute, that Congress needed time to do so, and that the status quo should be maintained until Congress could take action. Social critics and some competitors alleged that Coors merely wanted to be able to inform consumers that its products were stronger than what they assumed. In turn, critics said, this would encourage the introduction of even stronger beers by competitors.

Until recent years, Coors Brewing spent little on advertising. At the beginning of the 1970s, it budgeted $3 million to $4 million annually, but this figure grew rapidly. By the early 1980s, despite dramatic increases in its advertising expenditures, Coors Brewing was still underspending its major national competitors if advertising were expressed as a ratio to barrels of beer produced. The discrepancy ranged from about 10 percent to 50 percent depending on which firm one compared Coors to. The company continued to push the advertising budget upward.

By 1984, Coors Brewing's advertising reached $138,750,000, which was 14.8 percent of its beer sales, and in 1985 the corresponding figures were $165,050,000 and 15.3 percent. (See Exhibit 8). If advertising were expressed as spending per barrel, Coors Brewing apparently had become one of the largest spenders in the industry whereas it had been one of the smallest spenders fifteen years earlier. It was ordinarily to be expected that advertising per unit of product would have to rise in a period when extensive new geographical territories were being entered. Whether this percentage leadership in the industry would continue was very much a topic for internal discussion. The advertising budget rose to $180,000,000 in 1986, $208,713,000 in 1987, and $245,433,000 in 1988. Advertising expenditures totaled 19.4 percent of beer sales in that year. Coors augmented print and electronic media with sponsorship of concerts and some sporting events, such as rodeos, motor sports, and the Coors International Bicycle Classic.

In the early and mid-1980s, the advertising for Coors brand had been using a theme, "Coors is the One." The expression "the difference worth tasting" was repetitively used. Actor Mark Harmon was featured in many of the messages built around this theme. The objectives were two-fold: to gain consumer awareness of Coors and to position the brand as "a distinctive superlative product—the desired choice among premium beers." In the late 1980s the Coors brand switched its theme to "An American Original, the first draft beer in a can." Coors Light used the "Silver Bullet" theme for several years but turned to the theme "It's the right beer now" in the late 1980s. Herman Joseph's Original Draft and HJ Light had used the theme "The smoother, the better." Killian's Irish Red employed the tag line "Killian's Red, Instead" rather effectively and was associated with St. Patrick's Day whenever possible. Coors Extra Gold used the tag line "full tilt taste."

EXHIBIT 8 Advertising Expenditures of
Coors Brewing by Year

1988	$245,400,000
1987	208,700,000
1986	180,000,000
1985	165,050,000
1984	138,750,000
1983	118,742,000
1982	88,103,000
1981	85,817,000
1980	66,752,000
1977	9,831,000

Until recent years, Coors Brewing relied on a conservative, in-house advertising department to a greater extent than most other brewers. The company retained a large national advertising agency under contract for at least media relations but would not delegate much decision-making authority to the agency. For the light beer, Peter Coors was able in 1978 to switch the advertising to a large international agency based in New York. By the mid-1980s, each Coors product was in the hands of a large advertising agency.

Recognizing the importance of another type of promotion, Coors Company appointed a person in 1983 to be in charge of participation in exhibitions, conventions, trade shows, and similar events plus selected public entertainment events and gave her four full-time employees. The company took part in about 100 such occurrences each year. Only very rarely did participation include giving samples of the product. The Coors approach was different from the competitors in two ways. First, the list of events always included many events that were not designed for the trade but for the general public, such as state fairs and rodeos. Second, there was an emphasis on the use of games to gain the involvement of passers-by, whether in a trade or a public meeting. Every game participant won at least a token prize. One interesting activity judged highly successful was letting a person or small group of people make their own proposed television advertisement for Coors and then playing it back for these people plus all others who wanted to watch. This usually drew large crowds and created large amounts of good will.

Non-Brewing Divisions

The Coors company had made some effort to diversify. Coors Energy Company owned or had interests in several hundred oil and gas wells and coal deposits in four Western states and held oil and gas leases on several hundred thousand acres of land. Coors Packaging Corporation made cartons in Paoli, Pennsylvania, Lawrenceburg, Tennessee, and Franklin, Ohio. Coors BioTech Products Company was located in Johnstown, Colorado. Using the Coors knowledge of fermentation chemistry, this plant produced refined starch, fructose syrup, and animal nutrition supplements. Coors owned grain elevators in seven western and southern cities and paper converting plants in Boulder, Colorado, and Lawrenceburg, Tennessee. Suncoa Foods, Inc., of Greeley, Colorado, manufactured snack foods. In 1984, Suncoa test marketed the CocoMo candy bar made with brewer's yeast by a patented process. The product provided chocolate flavor without caffeine or other potentially objectionable ingredients. Coors owned an aluminum recycling plant that produced aluminum coil and sheet, but it was not yet profitable. Coors Porcelain Company was another subsidiary, and it itself had some related subsidiaries, including Royal Worcester Industrial Ceramics, Ltd., in Wales, which was bought in 1984. Other ceramics locations were in Norman, Oklahoma; Hillsboro, Oregon; Lakewood, Grand Junction, and Denver, Colorado; El Cajon, California; Benton, Arkansas; Glenrothes, Scotland; and Rio Claro, Brazil. In 1988 it acquired Alpha Optical Systems of Ocean Springs, Mississippi. The nonbeer subsidiaries rather consistently provided about 17 percent of the company's sales revenue in the middle and late 1980s. Taken as a whole, the non-porcelain subsidiaries were unprofitable in most years, but the porcelain subsidiaries earned acceptable profits in most years.

Advise the Coors organization.

SOURCE PERRIER

The highly successful French company, Source Perrier, S.A., realizing its increasing competition in the West European markets, had been thinking about its potential in North America for several years. It believed that a lag relationship (i.e., what happened in a given industry in one country would probably occur later in a second country), existed in the demand pattern. Perrier's management felt that U.S. demand for bottled mineral water was most likely about four decades behind French demand, and that U.S. awareness of this water and sales thereof had to rise. Such lags, however, are seldom of this duration.

Moreover, two arch rivals—BSN, the French company with its Evian and Badoit brands, and Nestle, the Swiss company with its Vittel brand—had decided to enter the U.S. market. In France Perrier's sparkling product competed with Badoit; its still, or non-sparkling product, called Contrexeville, competed with Evian and Vittel. Perrier was naturally carbonated to what most people Would call a heavy level, while Badoit was only slightly carbonated. Source Perrier also offered other brands, the Volvic and St. Yorre, in France. By the early 1990s Source Perrier controlled about half of the French market. Earlier, however, Perrier had had a much larger share of the French market. When on the verge of being abandoned by its owners in 1973, Badoit was successfully promoted and presented in France as superior to Perrier for use with meals, especially because it was less carbonated. To the growing concern and anxiety of Perrier's management, Badoit graciously acknowledged Perrier as good, and more suited as an aperitif. Bottled water was clearly an established part of the consumption pattern in France, whose population was not growing.

Convinced of the small risk involved, Source Perrier, using an insignificant amount of its capital, opened a two-person U.S. operation in New York City in 1976. Later it set up U.S. headquarters in Greenwich, Connecticut, and called the organization Great Waters of France, Inc.

For decades very small quantities of Perrier had been exported to the United States for sale in elite lounges and restaurants in certain metropolitan areas. Source Perrier, despite the advice of several management consulting firms who thought that not enough Americans would be attracted to the drink, seriously entered the U.S. market in 1976. Gustave Leven, the president and 20 percent owner, suspected there were enough Americans who would like something that had no alcohol and no sweetness to make the venture profitable. About three million bottles were sold in the United States in 1976, which the company considered a good start. From 1976 to 1978 Perrier delivered its product directly to retail accounts in selected metropolitan areas. To further enlarge its business, soft drink and beer companies began delivering Perrier's product to its accounts in 1978. In 1980 Perrier's U.S. sales reached $100 million; and, by the beginning of the 1990s Perrier brand imports constituted about three-fourths of all U.S. imports of mineral water.

Source Perrier was a very old company located in southern France, initially owned by British interests, when its management asked a French stockbroker to find a buyer in 1946. The stockbroker's son, Gustave Leven, quickly bought the little firm, with its primary asset—the bubbling spring in the town of Vergeze in Provence, a spring known and appreciated since Roman times. Bottling operations were inefficient, even primitive; workers filled each of the famous little green bottles individually by hand, dipping them into the spring, and then used their feet to help put the bottle caps on. Sales were small, but the product carried a special cachet and was distributed through the most expensive eating and drinking places in western Europe. Leven realized at that time the product's enormous potential in Europe.

In this era when distribution was limited to elite eating and drinking places in the United States, Perrier was, of course, offered only in the individual serving size, which contained six-and-a-half ounces. Maintaining this individual serving size, the organization began its large scale development in the United States, preparing these bottles in a six-pack. This famous little glass bottle, green and pear shaped, was visibly and strongly identified with the company name and brand. After considerable thought, Source Perrier added a twenty-three-ounce glass bottle—aimed chiefly for use at a meal for several people, and eleven ounce cans in a four-pack. The large bottle was green and pear shaped; the can, predominantly green. Since these distinctive bottles were frequently considered a "trade dress," the company had attempted to register the bottle design in jurisdictions with provision for such legal protection. The labels on the bottles were marked prominently on the front with the words, "Bottled in France," and displayed the sentence, "Since 1863, bottled only at Source Perrier, Vergeze, France." The word, "Imported," was imprinted clearly on the front of the cans; the location of the famous spring was given on a side panel. The words "Sodium free" were also displayed prominently on the front panel of both bottles and cans. While retail prices of Perrier were not perfectly uniform, the prevailing prices in grocery stores in 1990 were as given in Exhibit 1. The challenge was to keep prices low enough to appeal to middle-income people yet high enough to retain the traditional snob appeal. The prevailing retail price of Evian brand water was $1.59 for a 50.7 ounce bottle; this amounted to $1.00 per quart.

An interesting brand with which Americans had virtually no experience entered the market aggressively in 1990. Strathmore, imported and distributed by Bri-Al Trading Company of Chicago, was bottled at Forfal, Scotland. Both sparkling and still water were available under the brand name. The sparkling version was available in a 33.8 ounce bottle at $1.03, which was 98 cents per quart, and a 50.7 ounce bottle at $1.33, which was 84 cents per quart. This large bottle was being specially promoted at 93 cents, which was 59 cents per quart, to arouse consumer awareness of the brand. The large bottle was available in orange, lime, lemon, and unflavored versions. The non-sparkling water was available only in the 33.8 ounce bottle and was priced like the sparkling version. The labels emphasized pictures of the famous and picturesque Glamis Castle in Scotland and spoke of this building as the birthplace of Queen Mother Elizabeth and Princess Margaret. The company attempted ex-

EXHIBIT 1 Prevailing U.S. Retail Prices of Perrier Brand

	Item Price	Unit Price (Quart)
Six-pack of bottles	$3.31	$2.72
Twenty three-ounce bottle	1.13	1.57
Four-pack of cans	2.47	1.80

ploiting the generally quite favorable popular image of unspoiled rural Scotland. The label even urged the reader to visit the Glamis area and Vale of Strathmore. A careless or rapid reader would infer a connection between the castle and the water source, but no connection was claimed.

Four other foreign mineral water competitors had just entered the United States and threatened vigorous competition for Source Perrier. In 1989 Victoria Springs introduced its orange, grapefruit, and lemon-lime flavored water from Australia and in 1990 added an orange-mango formulation in 9.5 ounce bottles in four-packs. Canadian Shield Spring Water Company, Ltd. launched its brand, called Canadian Spring, in plain, berry, mint, and key lime in seven and twenty-five ounce bottles in late 1989 with plans for national distribution by 1991. Western Canadian Water of Vancouver introduced Canadian Glacier Natural Mountain Water in late 1989 in the important California market. Strongly using a theme of purity, this unflavored brand claimed to have less salt than a number of other brands because of fewer dissolved solids. Canadian Glacier started in the United States with 1.5 liter bottles and in 1990 added a six-pack of small bottles. Minalba Waters of America, a Brazilian organization, launched its water imported from the village of Campos do Jordao. The roll-out of Minalba started in late 1989 and the brand was to be national by 1991. Both the exotic origin and health were emphasized by promoters Tommie Agee and Art Shamsky, two members of the famed "Miracle Mets" baseball team that won the 1969 World Series. Minalba in particular was being supported by incentives to retailers to try the product. These companies joined several other foreign suppliers that had been in the United States just a short while longer, including Naya from the Province of Quebec in Canada and Gravenstein and Appollonaris, both from West Germany.

A few soft drink and other companies, both national and regional, attempted to compete with Perrier by presenting their club sodas and seltzer mixers as alternatives. The most aggressive of such competition came from Canada Dry, but Vantage, Seagram's, Schweppes, and White Rock were also important. Some seltzers contained relatively high levels of sodium, but the ones without sodium competed well against Perrier.

Through advertising to consumers, middlemen, and the restaurant-bar trade, Perrier brand had positioned itself in the United States as a high-prestige soft drink rather than as a fine, or the finest, mineral water. It was a fashionable product for the non-drinker and the health and/or diet conscious person who sometimes used alcohol. Perrier brand was indelibly linked with the word "Yuppie." Detractors and some users sometimes called it "designer water."

In connection with such positioning, the company had noted through the years that many consumers of Perrier water frequently added a twist of fruit to their serving. In the hope of making the product more interesting plus providing convenience and saving time, the company test marketed in the mid-1980s and then added versions with small amounts of natural lemon, lime, orange, or berry. These were offered in both the can and the large bottle and at the same price as the unflavored.

There were three traditional reasons in Europe for drinking mineral water. First, public water supplies were not dependably safe in most places until recently. In fact, there were still sanitation problems in much of southern Europe. Second, tap water in Europe often had an undesirable taste or smell, or both, which might be natural or the result of chemical treatment to purify the water. Also tap water was often cloudy or of an odd color. Third, in Europe various mineral water companies often made medical claims for their products, such as aiding digestion, alleviating the discomfort of hangovers, and even preventing heart attacks, which attracted consumer attention and built loyalty. Occasionally such a company merely promoted the mineral content of the water as a desirable dietary supplement. Although strict regulators on a few business matters, European governments tended to have very few regulations on medical claims and did a poor job of enforcing the regulations in place. Such claims had never been scientifically proved, and most probably could never be so proved. Relevant U.S. regulations at federal, state, and local levels were the most stringent in the world. Perrier formerly made medical claims for its product in Europe but had toned them down in recent years, primarily to a hint that the product aided digestion. The motivation to drink mineral water in order to be chic did not come about until long after the other three reasons.

In the United States virtually all public water supplies were perfectly safe all the time, but many consumers suspected that their community was always on the verge of finding something wrong. More important, there was a growing percentage of cities scattered throughout the country that had problems of taste, odor, and color. Very few sizeable regions had shown much demand for mineral water, with the exception of California, where per capita consumption almost equaled that of France. Also there had long been considerable use of mineral water along the coast of Louisiana and the northern half of the coast of Texas because of the local water's natural sulphur content, which most people found unpleasant. Several parts of Massachusetts, Connecticut, and New York State were considerable users. After a dozen years of full national distribution, Perrier brand found that its sales were predominantly along the East Coast, the West Coast, and Texas. A similar but not so sharp geographical pattern prevailed for Source Perrier as a whole. U.S. per capita consumption of mineral water was 28 quarts per year in 1989, compared to about 70 in France and 42 in all of Western Europe combined. Exhibit 2 presents trend line data on U.S. per capita consumption

EXHIBIT 2 U.S. Consumption of Selected Beverages in Gallons per Capita, Recent Years

	1975	1980	1983	1985	1987	1988	1989
Bottled water	1.2	2.7	3.4	4.5	5.7	6.4	7.0
Soft drinks	26.3	34.2	37.0	40.8	44.1	45.9	47.4
Juices	6.8	6.9	7.8	6.2	6.2	6.1	6.1
Coffee	33.0	27.4	26.6	25.8	25.3	25.0	24.6
Tea	7.3	7.3	7.3	7.3	7.3	7.3	7.3
Milk	22.5	20.8	20.1	20.2	20.7	20.9	21.0
Beer	21.6	24.3	24.3	23.8	23.9	23.6	23.2
Wine	1.7	2.1	2.2	2.4	2.4	2.3	2.1

of mineral water compared to several other beverages. Approximately 70 percent of American gallonage consumed was still (i.e., noncarbonated).

Acquisitions of North American firms began to interest Source Perrier in the early 1980s. In 1980 the company bought Calistoga in California and Poland Spring in Maine. At that time executives of Source Perrier were worried about the name "Poland Spring," because they thought the only word association in the consumer's mind would be the Polish reform leader Lech Walesa. However, they decided to retain the name and later found that it worked out all right. Later it bought Arrowhead in California, Great Bear in New Jersey, Ozarka in Arkansas, Oasis in Texas, and Zephyrhills in Florida. Still later Source Perrier bought Montclair of Canada, owned by Nestle, and Pepsico's Ice Mountain brand. The purchase of Montclair brought to an end a sharp competitive penetration of several East Coast metropolitan areas. However, it had not been clear if Nestle would have continued making the large investments of capital necessary to make Montclair a major brand. The acquisition of Arrowhead Drinking Water Company, the most important water company in southern California, almost doubled Source Perrier's share of the U.S. market. The water of each of the forementioned companies was sold in several adjoining states. The cost of transporting water was prohibitively high and kept each brand out of distant markets. Nevertheless, Poland Spring was distributed across thirteen northeastern and Atlantic seaboard states. It sold at retail for 73 cents for a twenty-eight-ounce bottle, which amounted to 83 cents per quart. Poland Spring was available in lemon, lime, orange, cherry, and cherry-berry, but the full line was handled by only very large stores in locations reasonably close to the spring.

The fact of retailers, even very large ones, not handling every size and flavor variation of the product was a characteristic of distribution that bothered all mineral water companies. Moreover, even if a retailer carried, say, six variations of a product, it was frequently out of stock on two or three of them.

These acquisitions put Source Perrier squarely into the low-price mass market where people were simply looking for a replacement for tap water. In that large market most large grocery store chains added very inexpensive house brands of mineral water in the late 1980s, most of which were priced 50 percent below the American brands Source Perrier had acquired. The mass market also included an important segment in which very large cooler jugs of mineral water were delivered on regular truck routes to offices and small jugs to a small percentage of homes. Water was very heavy and large containers awkward to carry home from the store. After making its acquisitions Source Perrier had about half of its U.S. sales in stores and about half by truck delivery route. In addition, the water market in the United States included a small segment of tap water that had been carefully filtered and then bottled for sale. Such water was usually grocery chain house brands and almost always priced 10 to 15 percent below the same chain's house brand of mineral water.

There were several major competitors in the U.S. popular-price market besides the supermarket house brands. McKesson Corporation, the number two mineral water company after Source Perrier, operated Sparkletts, Alhambra, Aqua-vend, and Crystal Bottled, while Anjou, the number three company, operated Sierra Spring, Silver Springs Ozone, and Hinckley-Schmitt. Clorox Corporation operated Aqua Pure, Deep Rock, Deer Park, and Emerald Coast, while the Japanese firm Suntory International operated Crystal Perfection, Kentwood, and Polar. Sammons operated Carolina Mountain, Mountain Valley, and Diamond Water. In 1989 Coors Company, whose principal business was brewing, put into test market a brand called Pure Rocky Mountain Spring Water. Price and container size had not been decided.

Source Perrier's group of companies now accounted for about 24 percent of the value of the mineral water industry's sales in the United States. McKesson Corporation held about 9 percent, Anjou about 5.3 percent, Suntory about 4 percent, Clorox about 2 percent, Culligan about 1.8 percent, Evian about 1.7 percent, and Sammons about 1.5 percent. Thus eight companies accounted for one-half of sales, while about 400 small companies accounted for the remainder.

The proximity and relatively high income of the United Kingdom attracted Source Perrier for many years, but it did not reach full national distribution there until 1977. The build-up in the United Kingdom ran just slightly ahead of that in the United States, the two simultaneous national efforts in 1976 and 1977 thus taking a large share of management's time. By the early 1990s Source Perrier held about 65 percent of the British market, but British per capita use of mineral water was very low.

For some years Source Perrier had had some diversified investments in European chocolate, hard candy, and cheese operations, but it sold these in 1989. In France Source Perrier had for many years also bottled several sweet soft drinks under franchise from the brand owners. In fact, Source Perrier had had for many years the exclusive rights to Pepsi-Cola in all of France. However, Pepsico, very unhappy with its stable four percent snare of the French market versus 31 percent held by Coca-Cola, unilaterally canceled the contract in 1990. Source Perrier then put up for sale all of its sweet soft drink operations.

Source Perrier now had worldwide sales of about $2.2 billion, about 25 percent of that in the United States. U.S. sales of the Perrier brand were about $160 million. Source Perrier's French and U.S. sales clearly were its most important, both in Perrier brand and its other brands. Source Perrier distributed in 125 countries, but in most the distribution was only nominal. What is more, the company considered that its distribution in the United States was only a fraction of its potential. It was eager to cultivate all national markets that were realistically promising and become truly global. Management was quite aware and troubled, however, by the fact that in the nations in which bottled water was needed the most the per capita income levels were very low.

The Water Contamination Incident

Source Perrier suffered a major blow to its Perrier brand operations in early 1990. In a routine check in North Carolina, employees of a county laboratory noticed excessive benzene and reported the findings to state authorities. It was about twice the level allowable under U.S. regulations. This level was judged not to be dangerous, but it constituted a technical violation of the standards of the U.S. Environmental Protection Agency for drinking water. Benzene is a chemical that in extremely high dosages has been linked to cancer in animals.

The North Carolina state health department did not believe that a recall was necessary because of the negligible concentration of the contaminant but did insist on issuing a health advisory, cautioning the public that the product should not be used until further testing could be done. Health authorities stated that people would have to drink larger amounts of the contaminated Perrier every day for many years to increase their risk of cancer by one in a million. Health authorities told Ronald V. Davis, the executive in charge of Source Perrier's U.S. branch, that they would be issuing the advisory. Later the same day Davis issued a recall of all Perrier water in the United States, which went beyond what the North Carolina and federal health officials were empowered to do in a case of such low level contamination. The action by the U.S. subsidiary of

Source Perrier was done to demonstrate its desire to behave with great prudence and, it hoped, to minimize damage to its product's valuable reputation. The U.S. recall involved 72 million bottles. The executive and the U.S. branch were praised widely in the news media and among consumer protection groups for doing more than was necessary and for swift action.

At first the French parent company announced that the error had apparently occurred somewhere in the bottling and packaging operations at Vergeze. It then elaborated by saying that the trouble came from benzene used by an employee in cleaning the equipment on the production line from which the U.S. supplies came. However, just to be safe, the parent company also closed down the spring in France for examination, even though it had up-to-date health certification from the French government. Source Perrier at first did not recall its product in Europe. However, four days later the same chemical problem showed up in Denmark and the Netherlands as governments there looked into the matter. The company then recalled its product worldwide, which involved over 160 million bottles.

Source Perrier found that engineers failed to change filters at the Vergeze plant. These filters were designed to clean tiny impurities from the gas that is mixed into the spring water to give Perrier its fizz. The gas, mainly carbon dioxide with minute quantities of benzene and other compounds, existed naturally in the spring water. According to company spokesmen, since the turn of the century Perrier had separated the gas from the water and piped it through the filters before mixing it back into the water for bottling. They stated that both the water and the gas were tapped independently from isolated wells at different depths, within the same geological formation, and then recombined. The water was in a carbonated state underground but not recovered that way. However, the perception of the public and the implications from promotional messages had always been that the water was extracted from the ground with the carbonation process having been completed in nature. In fact, Source Perrier often said that "Perrier's carbonation process takes place naturally underground." Moreover, the company had long used the promotional themes, "naturally sparkling from the center of the Earth" and "the Earth's first soft drink." Production resumed a short while later, after the French government pronounced the production pure and safe. Post-incident containers would be marked "Nouvelle Production" (New Production). The U.S. Food and Drug Administration planned a site visit to the water facilities at Vergeze and would have to give approval for importing the water into the United States again. That approval was considered almost certain, because the benzene could be easily removed. However, the F.D.A. prohibited Perrier from saying the product was naturally sparkling.

Perrier belatedly announced that the critical delay in installing new filters was caused by the fact that Perrier had never had a benzene contamination problem in the past and hence was not even monitoring for that chemical. Instead, the filters were for the purpose of screening out hydrogen sulfide, a natural chemical, and minute amounts of other things such as benzene. Without that screening the water would smell like rotten eggs. When, in 1988 the company began extracting the water from a different spot in the spring it found that the gas had lower concentrations of hydrogen sulfide and thus the filters did not need to be replaced so often. Short-run damage to brand share of the market was expected to be extremely severe, especially since there were now many attractive substitutes. Long-run damage was very unclear. The public might think well of the U.S. branch for its action but think poorly of the French parent for implying something that was not true, slow action, and avoidance of a clear explanation. The recall was probably going to cost about $75 million, and sales lost during the period necessary to restock customers would probably total a similar figure.

Advise Source Perrier.

CASES IN MARKETING

MACMILLAN SERIES IN COLLEGE MARKETING

Bagozzi   PRINCIPLES OF MARKETING MANAGEMENT

Beisel   CONTEMPORARY RETAILING

Berman and Evans
RETAIL MANAGEMENT, Fourth Edition

Bowersox, Closs, and Helferich
LOGISTICAL MANAGEMENT,
Third Edition

Chapman and Bradley
DYNAMIC RETAILING, Second Edition

Cohen   THE PRACTICE OF MARKETING MANAGEMENT, Second Edition

Douglas
WRITING FOR PUBLIC RELATIONS

Etzel and Woodside
CASES IN RETAILING STRATEGY

Evans and Berman   MARKETING,
Fourth Edition

Evans and Berman   PRINCIPLES OF MARKETING, Second Edition

Galloway, Evans, and Berman
PAINTCO III: A COMPUTERIZED
MARKETING SIMULATION

Greer   CASES IN MARKETING,
Fifth Edition

Hair, Anderson, and Tatham
MULTIVARIATE DATA ANALYSIS,
Second Edition

Hartley   SALES MANAGEMENT

Hise and McDaniel
CASES IN MARKETING STRATEGY

Hisrich and Peters
MARKETING DECISIONS FOR NEW AND
MATURE PRODUCTS, Second Edition

Johnson and Wood
CONTEMPORARY LOGISTICS,
Fourth Edition

Katzenstein and Sachs
DIRECT MARKETING

Kincaid   PROMOTION: PRODUCTS,
SERVICES, AND IDEAS, Second Edition

Lewison   RETAILING, Fourth Edition

Lewison   ESSENTIALS OF RETAILING

Lewison and Hawes
CASES IN RETAIL MANAGEMENT

Lill   SELLING: THE PROFESSION

Morris
INDUSTRIAL AND ORGANIZATIONAL
MARKETING

Mowen   CONSUMER BEHAVIOR,
Second Edition

O'Connor   PERSONAL SELLING

Onkvisit and Shaw
INTERNATIONAL MARKETING

Risch   RETAIL MERCHANDISING,
Second Edition

Runyon   ADVERTISING,
Second Edition

Runyon and Stewart
CONSUMER BEHAVIOR, Third Edition

Scheuing   NEW PRODUCT MANAGEMENT

Seitel   PRACTICE OF PUBLIC RELATIONS,
Third Edition

Soldow and Thomas
PROFESSIONAL SELLING:
AN INTERPERSONAL PERSPECTIVE

Tull and Hawkins
MARKETING RESEARCH, Fifth Edition

Tull and Kahle
MARKETING MANAGEMENT

Weeks, Perenchio, Miller, and Metcalf
MERCHANDISING MATHEMATICS

Weilbacher
ADVERTISING, Second Edition

Weilbacher   CASES IN ADVERTISING

Weilbacher
MARKETING MANAGEMENT CASES,
Fourth Edition

Wood and Johnson
CONTEMPORARY TRANSPORTATION,
Third Edition